Dominica

the Bradt Travel Guide

Paul Crask

edition
2

www.bradtguides.com

Bradt Travel Guides Ltd, UK
The Globe Pequot Press Inc, USA

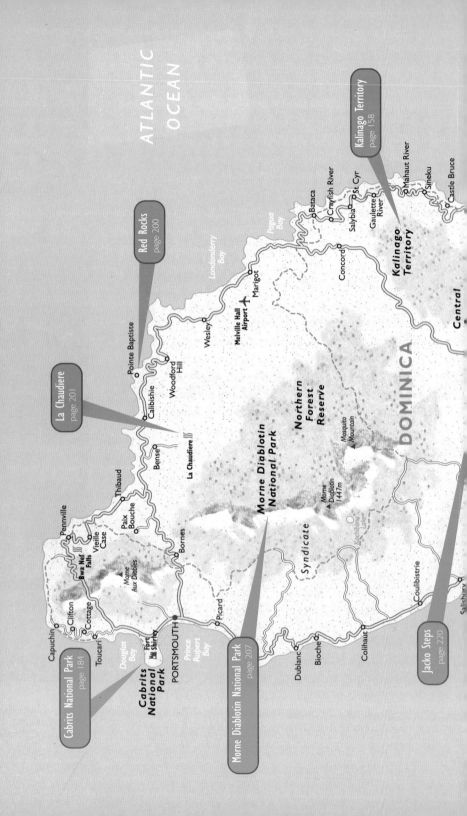

ATLANTIC OCEAN

Kalinago Territory
page 158

Red Rocks
page 200

La Chaudiere
page 201

Cabrits National Park
page 184

Morne Diablotin National Park
page 207

Jacko Steps
page 220

Mahaut River
Sineku
Castle Bruce
Crayfish River
St Cyr
Batac a
Salybia
Gaulette River
Kalinago Territory
Concord

Pagua Bay

Landonderry Bay

Pointe Baptiste

Wesley

Melville Hall Airport
Marigot

Calibishie
Woodford Hill

Bense
La Chaudiere

Thibaud
Pennville
Paix Bouche
Vieille Case
Bwa Nef Falls
Bornes
Morne Aux Diables
Clifton
Cottage
Capuchin
Toucari
Douglas Bay
Fort Shirley
Cabrits National Park
PORTSMOUTH
Prince Rupert Bay
Picard

Syndicate
Morne Diablotin 1447m
Morne Diablotin National Park
Northern Forest Reserve
Mosquito Mountain
Lachbona Lake

DOMINICA

Central

Dublanc
Bioche
Colihaut
Coulibistrie
Salisbury

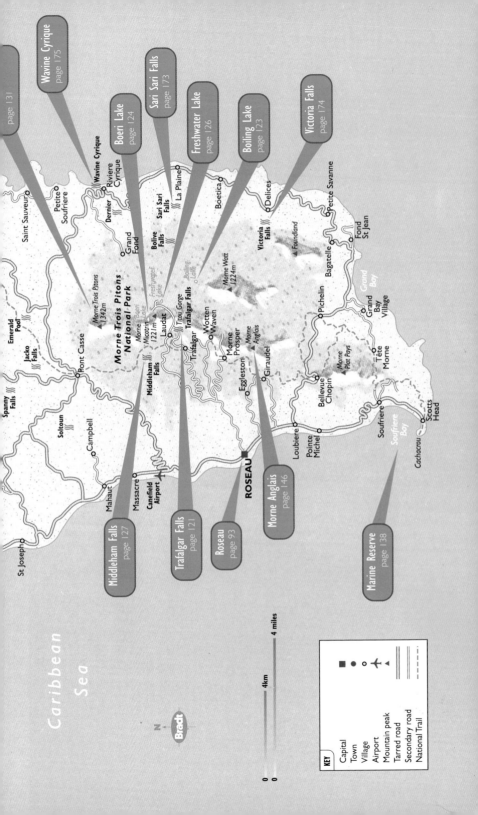

Dominica
Don't miss...

Music, dance and cultural festivals
Annual Carnival celebrations include costume parades, the Carnival Queen show and the Calypso Monarch competition
(CS) page 25

Mountains and rainforest
Dominica's interior is a breathtaking spectacle of imposing mountains and vast swathes of rainforest (CS) page 3

Rivers and waterfalls
The magnificent Victoria Falls on the White River
(PC) page 174

Volcanic landscapes
The Valley of Desolation on the Boiling Lake trail, a mystical domain of steaming fumaroles, hot rivers, bubbling mud and vivid colour
(PC) page 114

Wholesome food and wellness
Rejuvenate with a wealth of fresh fruits and vegetables, wellness therapies and natural hot spas
(CS) page 86

top Dominica's Boiling Lake is said to be the second largest of its kind in the world (PC) page 123

above La Chaudiere river cascade and pool near Bense (PC) page 201

left Morne Trois Pitons, the highest peak in Morne Trois Pitons National Park, which has been designated a UNESCO World Heritage Site

(PC) page 131

above   The unusual Red Rocks at Pointe Baptiste (PC) page 200

below left   The 'father' falls, with a drop of around 65m, and the 'mother' falls, with a drop of around 35m, make up the Trafalgar Falls (CS) page 121

below right   Woodford Hill Beach, as pretty as any in the Caribbean (PC) page 193

top	Downtown Roseau is best explored on foot (CS) page 95
left	Wall mural in Roseau, by local artist Hilroy Fingal (CS) page 26
below left	The area around King George V Street is referred to as the French Quarter, and retains the character of a more historic Roseau (CS) page 97
below right	Fresh fruits and vegetables at Roseau's New Market (CS) page 105

AUTHOR

Born in England, Paul Crask grew up in Yorkshire and graduated from Leeds University in 1988. He also spent time in former East Germany, studying at what was once the Karl Marx University of Leipzig. After graduating he travelled to Japan where he lived and worked as a teacher for two years before backpacking around the world from the Far East back to Europe via North America. He worked in London for ten years before dropping out and embarking on a radical lifestyle change with Dominica-born wife, Celia.

Though he has been visiting the island since the mid 1990s, Paul has been living in Dominica permanently since 2005. He is a regular feature writer for travel magazines, and is the author of two Bradt Travel Guides: *Dominica* and *Grenada, Carriacou and Petite Martinique*.

For more information go to www.paulcrask.com.

D1638438

PUBLISHER'S FOREWORD   *Hilary Bradt*

I'd had it in mind to publish a guide to Dominica since the 1980s when I recruited Royston Ellis to be a Bradt author. At that time Royston had a house on Dominica and showed me photos of this wonderful lush, mountainous landscape which seemed so different from my preconceived idea of a Caribbean Island. Then he moved away and Dominica went onto the backburner until Paul Crask offered to write the insider's guide we wanted. And what a wonderful job he's done! It's written with such love of his chosen home that you can almost smell the rainforest and ocean, and feel that you have met most of the islanders. Paul wrote in his introduction to the first edition: 'When I set out to write a guidebook to my adopted home it was my aim to be as inclusive and as representative as possible'. He ends up ' ... I don't know how well I have succeeded ... but ... I have given it my best shot'. He's succeeded.

Second edition published June 2011 First published 2007

Bradt Travel Guides Ltd
IDC House, The Vale, Chalfont St Peter, Bucks SL9 9RZ, England
www.bradtguides.com
Published in the USA by The Globe Pequot Press Inc,
PO Box 480, Guilford, Connecticut 06437-0480

Text copyright © 2011 Paul Crask
Maps copyright © 2011 Bradt Travel Guides Ltd
Photographs copyright © 2011 Individual photographers (see below)
Project Manager: Elspeth Beidas

ISBN: 978 1 84162 356 6

British Library Cataloguing in Publication Data
A catalogue record for this book is available from the British Library

Photographs Liz Chiz (LC), Paul Crask (PC), Pierre Deschamps (PD), R Dirscherl/FLPA (RD/FLPA), Gerry Ellis/Minden Pictures/FLPA (GE/MP/FLPA), George H H Huey/Corbis (GH/C), Arun Madisetti, *Images Dominica* (AM), 1333809 Ontario Ltd/Dreamstime. com (OL), Dennis Sabo/Shutterstock (DS/S), Celia Sorhaindo, Tropical Ties (CS), Stubblefieldphoto/Dreamstime.com (S/D)

Front cover Purple-throated carib (GE/MP/FLPA)
Back cover Carnival (CS), Emerald Pool (CS)
Title page Ixoras (CS), Calabash (CS), Dancing (CS)

Maps David McCutcheon

Typeset from the author's disc by Wakewing
Production managed by Jellyfish Print Solutions; printed in India

Acknowledgements

Special thanks to Wai'tukubuli National Trail project manager, Eddison Henry, and his team for their refreshing collegiality and great companionship.

CONTRIBUTORS

Irvince Auguiste is a former Kalinago chief and member of the Kalinago Council. He is the driving force behind the *Kalinago Touna Auté* concept near the village of Concord where he spends much of his time guiding visitors and developing this unique project.

Stewart Bell is an award-winning Canadian journalist and the author of three non-fiction books, *The Bayou of Pigs*, *The Martyr's Oath*, and *Cold Terror*. For more information go to www.stewartbell.net.

Terri Henry is a writer, health and wellness consultant, ecotherapy facilitator and mother of two beautiful eco-babies. For more information go to www.onelovelivity.com and www.childofnatureblog.com.

Rahel Joseph is a Rastafarian housewife and mother of two. Together with husband Octave, she owns and runs the *Hide-Out Cottage* in Geneva, Grand Bay. For more information go to www.hideout.ch.

Dr Lennox Honychurch is Dominica's most prominent historian. He is also a conservationist and responsible for the restoration of the Fort Shirley Garrison in the Cabrits National Park. For more information go to www.lennoxhonychurch.com.

Billy Lawrence is an experienced scuba diving professional who owns and manages a small dive centre called *ALDive* in Loubiere. He has been diving in Dominica for 20 years. For more information go to www.aldive.com.

Trudy Scott Prevost is a health and wellness consultant, master yoga teacher and holistic education expert. For more information go to www.rainbowyogaindominica.wordpress.com.

Nelly Stharre is a Dominican recording artist who has achieved international acclaim. She devotes much of her life to causes, helping to highlight inequality, AIDS and abuse, and has been the inspiration behind a number of high profile regional benefit concerts. For more information go to www.myspace.com/nellystharrenatureislandgirl.

DEDICATION

This edition is dedicated to Dominica's hard-working trail, tour and dive guides.
You all rock.

I would also like to mention the people behind the greens;
Dominica's abandoned and forgotten.
To the homeless, the addicts, the abused, the physically and mentally ill,
the poor and the hungry, I hope that the mantra
'*tourism is everybody's business*'
will one day benefit you.

Peace and love.

FEEDBACK REQUEST

Things change. Not that much, but they do. Usually it is restaurants and bars opening and closing, but occasionally there are other goings on that take place after my submission deadline. One thing that I know will definitely change over time is the Wai'tukubuli National Trail. The trail itself is an ongoing development but there are likely to be new places springing up along the route that offer hikers a place to drink, eat or rest. Also expect more campsites; something Dominica has long needed. Whenever I notice a significant change I will post it on my website updates.bradtguides.com/dominica and I encourage you to get in touch to tell me about anything you may spot when you are here (e *info@bradtguides.com*). Thanks and happy travels.

LIST OF MAPS

Cabrits National Park	185	Northern beaches	195
Castle Bruce to Petite Soufriere	165	Portsmouth and environs	187
Dominica	ii–iii	Rosalie to Delices	167
Douglas Bay to Capuchin	189	Roseau Botanical Gardens	111
Grand Bay	141	Roseau centre	96
Kalinago Barana Auté	161	Roseau city	92
Kalinago Territory	152	Roseau Valley	113
La Haut to Blenheim	191	Salisbury to St Joseph	215
Layou River	220	Southwest Dominica	134
Marigot to Wesley	193	St Joseph to Massacre	217
Morne Trois Pitons National		Syndicate and Morne Diablotin	208
Park	114	Wai'tukubuli National Trail	228–9

Contents

	Introduction	VII
PART ONE	**GENERAL INFORMATION**	**1**
Chapter 1	**Background Information**	**3**
	Geography 3, Climate 3, Natural history and conservation 4, A brief history of the island 12, Government and politics 15, Economy 16, People 20, Language 21, Religion 22, Education 22, Culture 23	
Chapter 2	**Practical Information**	**31**
	When to visit 31, Highlights 32, Suggested itineraries 33, Tour operators 34, Tourist offices 36, Red tape 36, Consulates and embassies 36, Getting there and away 37, Health 39, Safety 45, Women travellers 46, Disabled travellers 46, Travelling with children 47, Gay travellers 47, What to take 47, Money and budgeting 48, Getting around 49, Accommodation 54, Eating and drinking 55, Public holidays and events 60, Shopping 61, Arts and entertainment 62, Media and communications 63, Business 66, Cultural etiquette 67, Travelling positively 69	
Chapter 3	**Activities and Special Interests**	**71**
	Tour operators and private guides 71, Site fees and passes 71, Birdwatching 72, Boat tours 73, Bus and jeep tours 73, Canyoning 74, Cycling and mountain biking 74, Education and research 74, Fishing 75, Gardens, farms and food 75, Hiking 76, Horseriding 80, Kayaking 81, Off-roading 81, Photography tours 81, River tubing 82, Scuba diving 82, Snorkelling 86, Wellness 86, Whale watching 89, Zip-lining 90	
PART TWO	**THE GUIDE**	**91**
Chapter 4	**Roseau and Environs**	**93**
	A brief history of Roseau 93, Getting there and away 94, Orientation and getting around 95, Where to stay 100, Where to eat and drink 102, Bars and nightlife 104, Shopping 105, Other practicalities 106, What to see and do 109	

| Chapter 5 | **Roseau Valley and Morne Trois Pitons National Park** | **113** |
| | Getting there 115, Where to stay 116, Where to eat and drink 118, What to see and do 118 | |

| Chapter 6 | **The South** | **133** |
| | Getting there 133, Where to stay 135, Where to eat and drink 136, What to see and do 136 | |

| Chapter 7 | **The Kalinago Territory and the East** | **153** |
| | The Kalinago 153, Getting there 154, Where to stay 155, Where to eat and drink 157, What to see and do 158 | |

| Chapter 8 | **Portsmouth, Cabrits National Park and the North** | **177** |
| | Getting there and away 177, Where to stay 177, Where to eat and drink 181, Shopping 182, Other practicalities 183, What to see and do 184 | |

| Chapter 9 | **Northern and Central Interior, Morne Diablotin and the West** | **205** |
| | Getting there and away 205, Where to stay 205, Where to eat and drink 207, What to see and do 207 | |

| Chapter 10 | **The Wai'tukubuli National Trail** | **227** |
| | Segment 1: Scotts Head to Soufriere 227, Segment 2: Soufriere to Bellevue Chopin 230, Segment 3: Bellevue Chopin to Wotten Waven 232, Segment 4: Wotten Waven to Pont Cassé 235, Segment 5: Pont Cassé to Castle Bruce 236, Segment 6: Castle Bruce to Hatton Garden 237, Segment 7: Hatton Garden to First Camp 241, Segment 8: First Camp to Petite Macoucherie 242, Segment 9: Petite Macoucherie to Colihaut Heights 244, Segment 10: Colihaut Heights to Syndicate 246, Segment 11: Syndicate to Bornes 247, Segment 12: Bornes to Pennville 249, Segment 13: Pennville to Capuchin 250, Segment 14: Capuchin to Cabrits 251 | |

| Appendix 1 | **Accommodation at a Glance** | **253** |

| Appendix 2 | **Hikes at a Glance** | **255** |

| Appendix 3 | **Further Information** | **257** |

| Index | | **260** |

Introduction

Wai'tukubuli is the name the indigenous Amerindians, the Kalinago, gave to this island before Columbus turned up. It means 'tall is her body' and from the moment you land here you can understand why. Volcanic peaks dominate the landscape and vast swathes of rainforest cover the entire island in a blanket of greens. From high elevations, hundreds of streams and rivers make their way down to the sea, some tumbling from cliffs as waterfalls, others meandering slowly, creating crystal clear pools and fresh water lakes along the way. Volcanic activity is evident in the form of fumaroles, hot springs, black sand beaches, and a boiling lake. Endemic species of parrots, hummingbirds, and a mesmerising variety of tropical plants and flowers add further colour and interest, and the heritages of South America, Africa and Europe combine to create a fascinating bouillon of music, dance, food, language and cultural festivals.

Excluding those who turn up for the day on cruise ships, Dominica has relatively few visitors. With no international airport and a name many still confuse with the Dominican Republic, you can legitimately consider yourself to be on a Caribbean island that has, despite many efforts to the contrary, somehow managed to stay off the beaten track. It is branded the 'Nature Island' with good reason, for it is very different to the image of the Caribbean that most conjure up in their minds. Indeed people from this region often describe Dominica as 'how the Caribbean used to be', before the rest of the world moved in.

Dominica is a destination for nature lovers, for hikers, scuba divers, culture vultures, and those who are looking for peace, relaxation and a place to recharge. Hundreds of hiking trails criss-cross the island, and the 200km Wai'tukubuli National Trail is a mouthwatering prospect for serious trekkers. Dominica's scuba diving is some of the best in the eastern Caribbean, whales and dolphins are off the coast all year round, and the Kalinago Territory and cultural events such as Creole, Carnival and Independence make this a fascinating place for those interested in heritage and the arts.

Dominica is also an island with its share of problems, of course. For starters it is relatively poor in financial terms, relying heavily on donor countries, remittances and low-interest loans. Its banana industry was almost wiped out by changes to world trade rules, there are many abandoned and struggling farms, and its eco and agro tourism sectors are still in their infancy. Poverty is real here, there is no safety net for the homeless and the abandoned, and career opportunities for young people are limited.

Despite its challenges, Dominica remains a safe place and, once you break the ice, you will find its people are genuine and friendly. Get away from the population centres and you will also discover a natural environment that will take your breath away and give you a fresh perspective on life. Make an effort to engage with people, offer them encouragement, support cultural events, and buy locally made crafts and products if you can. Dominica offers you an unforgettable holiday as well as an opportunity to make a positive difference to people in a very direct way.

Dominica is interesting. It is raw and natural, it is still relatively undiscovered, and it is extremely beautiful. I hope you enjoy it.

Part One

GENERAL INFORMATION

DOMINICA AT A GLANCE

Location West Indies at 15°N and 61°W, between Guadeloupe and Martinique
Size Approximately 47km long, 26km wide and 750km² in area
Capital Roseau
Main airport Melville Hall (DOM)
Status Parliamentary democracy within the Commonwealth of Nations
Population 70,000
Languages English and French Creole
Economy Agriculture and tourism
Main religion Roman Catholic
Currency East Caribbean dollar (EC$)
Exchange rates US$1 = EC$2.67 fixed; £1 = EC$4.3 variable; €1 = EC$3.8 variable (March 2011)
Electricity supply 220–240V, 50Hz. Commonly UK-style 3-pronged outlets.
Time GMT –4 hours
International telephone code +1 767
Flag Cross of yellow, black and white stripes on a green background with a red circle at the centre. Within the circle are ten green stars and a sisserou parrot.
National bird Sisserou parrot (*Amazona imperialis*)
National flower Bwa kwaib (*Sabinea carinalis*)

Background Information

GEOGRAPHY

Dominica is an independent island nation located in the West Indies at 15°N and 61°W, between the French islands of Guadeloupe and Martinique. It is the most northerly of the Windward Islands and is approximately 47km long and 26km wide. The island is 750km² in area and faces the Atlantic Ocean to the east and the Caribbean Sea to the west. Located on the southwestern coast is the country's capital, Roseau, which is also its main sea port.

The interior of Dominica is one of the youngest and most mountainous landscapes in the eastern Caribbean. At the centre of the Lesser Antilles island chain, Dominica's creation is still very evident in its high concentration of dead and dormant volcanoes, sulphur deposits, hot water springs and gas vents that are found both above and below sea level. Running down the centre of the island is a series of volcanic peaks, deep valleys and river gorges, all cloaked in a dense blanket of rainforest, montane thicket and elfin woodland. Dominica's highest mountain is Morne Diablotin, which at 1,447m dominates the north of the island.

Rainforest is by far the most widespread vegetation type in the interior, followed by dry scrub woodland growing along the coastal margins. In the higher elevations there are several thousand hectares of montane forest and elfin woodland. Fumarole vegetation can be found in several places including the Morne Trois Pitons National Park, the Valley of Desolation, and the area around the Boiling Lake.

The coast of Dominica stretches for some 148km and is where most of the population lives. On the Atlantic coastline the inshore waters can be rough and unpredictable, particularly near the mouths of rivers. In stark contrast to this is the west coast, where the Caribbean Sea laps gently along the shore and rough waters are very rarely experienced. Dominica has a combination of black and white sand beaches though most of its coastline is rocky. In many places steep, rugged cliffs plunge dramatically into very deep seas.

CLIMATE

Dominica has a tropical climate with average daytime temperatures typically ranging from around 26°C in January to 32°C in June. Rainfall can be very heavy and sustained, especially on the Atlantic coast and in the mountainous interior of the island. Average annual rainfall is around 700cm in the interior and 100cm on the west coast. Most of the rain arrives with trade winds from the Atlantic, resulting in frequent showers on the east, or windward coast, heavy and persistent rainfall inland, and lighter showers on the west, or leeward coast. The period between July and December is when Dominica is usually at its wettest and is also the time when it becomes most vulnerable to tropical storms and hurricanes. The driest and sunniest months tend to be from December to June but showers should always be anticipated and some parts of Dominica are wet all year round. The combination of heat and water can also make the island very humid, though breezes from the trade winds often help to make humidity levels a little more bearable.

Hurricanes that have the potential to impact Dominica tend to develop from tropical depressions in the Atlantic Ocean to the southwest of the Cape Verde Islands. They are essentially the rains and storms of the African monsoon season that make it all the way across the continent to the west coast and then into the Atlantic. If sea surface temperatures are warm enough and atmospheric wind shear low, then these disturbances can develop into tropical storms and hurricanes that track westwards to trouble the Caribbean, Central and North America. Historically, the Atlantic hurricane season is usually at its peak, and most threatening to the Lesser Antilles, during the months of August and September. Hurricane David was the island's most destructive storm in recent times, causing widespread devastation in August 1979.

NATURAL HISTORY AND CONSERVATION

HABITATS Found at the highest elevations, along the mountain tops and the tall ridges of Dominica's interior, is **elfin woodland**, or **cloud forest**. Frequently cloaked in a veil of mist and cloud, the moisture and dampness of this environment provide ideal conditions for mosses, lichens and ferns to thrive. A low-growing regionally endemic tree, known locally as the *kaklen* or *kaklin* (*Clusia mangle*), dominates the terrain, growing in a dense, tangled blanket some 2–3m above the ground. *Kaklen* has thick, ovate leaves, dark red, hard-skinned fruit, and small white flowers. The *palmiste moutan*, or mountain palm (*Prestoea montana*), occasionally pushes its way through the *kaklen* and other low-growing trees and ferns to reach heights of up to 7m. Other small- to medium-sized palms include the *Geonoma dussiana* and the *Geonoma pinnatifrons*, known locally as the *yanga*. Also commonly found at these higher elevations is the *kwé kwé wouj* (*Charianthus alpinus*) which is a low-growing tree with small clusters of red flowers with yellow stamens. The flowers and shrubs of the elfin forest typically bear their fruit in these small clusters and include two endemic species of thoroughworts: *Chromolaena impetiolaris* and *Chromolaena macrodon*. Two other endemics are *Inga dominicensis* and *Bealeria peteolaris*; they are more usually found growing in the heights of the Morne Diablotin National Park (see page 11).

Located at a slightly lower elevation is a layer of **montane forest**, or montane thicket. This is a habitat of transition that includes mosses and lichens, such as the endemic *Parmelia cryptochlora*, that are also found in elfin woodland. Common trees of the montane forest include the infamous *bwa bandé* (*Richeria grandis*) of the Euphorbiaceae family (see page 59), and the *resinier montagne* (*Podocarpus coriacius*), a kind of yew. Both of these trees, along with others, can also be found at lower elevations.

Below the montane forest is Dominica's vast and impressive **rainforest**. In this area of more modest rainfall, with deeper, well-drained soil, you will see magnificent trees such as the *gommier* (*Dacryodes excelsa*), also known regionally as the *tabonuco* or *candlewood* because of the flammable gum-like sap that oozes from its bark. These trees tower upwards of 30 or 40m and provide food and shelter for Dominica's endemic parrots (see page 6). The rainforest is also the habitat of several species of *chatanier* (*Sloanea dentate*, *Sloanea caribaea* and *Sloanea berteriana*), both large and small leaf varieties, which have huge buttress roots that stretch far out across the forest floor. Other trees known locally as the *mang blanc* (*Symphonia globulifera*), *mang wouj*, *bwa kanno* (*Cecropia peltata*, or the trumpet tree) have prop roots and are also common in this habitat. The *karapit* (*Amanoa caribaea*) produces both buttress and prop roots and is one of the most abundant species of large tree growing in the rainforest. Together with the *balata* (*Manilkara bidentata*), also known as *bulletwood*, these two trees are often used in construction because of their durability.

Along the unsheltered east cost of Dominica you will see **littoral woodland**. The vegetation here tends to have thick leaves to withstand the wind and salt spray. Shaped by strong Atlantic trade winds, the trees and shrubs along this coast visibly reflect the effects of the weather. Common trees include white cedar, sea grape, almond and coconut.

On the west coast of Dominica, usually sheltered from the severest weather, you will see lots of dry **coastal woodland**. The west coast has less rainfall than the rest of the island and this is reflected in the type of vegetation found here. Many of the trees are semi-deciduous and they shed leaves during excessively dry periods to conserve moisture and nutrients. Common species such as the *kampech* (*Haematoxylum campechianum*, or logwood) also have sharp thorns.

Growing in the volcanically active areas of the island, such as the Valley of Desolation, the Boiling Lake, Wotten Waven, Galion, Cold Soufriere and the Soufriere Sulphur Springs, are examples of **fumarole vegetation**. The plants found here are able to withstand both steam and sulphur-laden gases. *Kaklen* can also be seen growing in this type of habitat.

PLANTS AND FLOWERS Close to 200 different species of fern have been officially recorded in Dominica, as well as around 20 species of bromeliads, 75 orchids, and a dozen other endemic plant species. The tree fern (*Cyathea arborea*), known locally as *fougère* or *fwigè*, is widespread and can be found both within the heart of the rainforest as well as on its more deciduous margins. On forest trails look out for the *pawasol agouti* (*Selaginella*), a low-growing fern that covers the forest floor and provides a hiding place for the elusive agouti (see page 8). The *zʼailes mouches* (*Caludovica insignis*) is a very common rainforest plant with palm-like leaves that split into two lobes. It is one of several plants that were traditionally used by the indigenous Kalinago for thatching shelters and also for waterproofing baskets. Bromeliads include both epiphytes (plants that grow on top of other plants in a non-parasitical manner, deriving nutrients from air and rainfall) as well as terrestrial varieties. *Ananas grand bois* (*Glomeropitcairnia pendulifera*) is the

ROUCOU

Roucou (*Bixa orellana*), also known as *annatto*, is a fruiting tree that grows to around 5m in height and produces prickly, heart-shaped pods each containing around 50 seeds. These seeds are coated in a reddish pigment that produces a vibrant dye. Dominica's Amerindian settlers used this dye as a body paint. For centuries it has also been used as a medicinal plant that is thought to be useful for treating skin problems, fevers, dysentery, liver disease and even hepatitis. The leaves are used to calm the stomach and also as an antiseptic. Today roucou is still used worldwide as a food colouring – often as an alternative to saffron – as well as a herbal remedy and an ingredient in skin and hair care products.

largest bromeliad found in Dominica and is often seen on the branches of trees in rainforest, montane thicket and elfin woodland habitats.

Dominica's **national flower** is the *bwa kwaib* (*Sabinea carinalis*). It is an arboreal blossom found growing in dry coastal areas and, when in bloom, displays bright red flowers. Good examples can be seen in the Botanical Gardens in Roseau (see page 109) and within the garrison at Fort Shirley in the Cabrits National Park (see page 184).

Throughout Dominica, both in the wild and in lovingly tended gardens, it is common to see many varieties of colourful flowers and plants such as allamanda (*Allamanda cathartica*), angel's trumpet (*Brugmansia candida*), anthurium (*Anthurium andraeanum*), bird of paradise flower (*Strelitzia reginae*), bougainvillea (*Bougainvillea*), ginger (*Alpinia purpurata*), hibiscus (*Hibiscus*), heliconia (*Heliconia*) and ixora (*Ixora*). Flowering trees such as the flamboyant (*Delonix regia*) are usually seen growing along the drier west coast and are very bright and colourful when in full bloom.

Dominica also has many interesting and delicious types of vegetables and fruits. Dominicans often tend a family garden of sorts where they grow vegetables and traditional crops such as yams, dasheen, sweet potatoes, or tannias. These *provisions* are staples of the Dominican diet (see page 55). The *calabash* is a large round gourd that is cultivated on vines and harvested for use both as a vegetable and, when mature, as a functional container, or eating bowl. It is also dried and ornately decorated by local artisans (see page 27) and makes for a unique and pretty souvenir. Coconut palms grow just about everywhere, as do several varieties of mango. Farmlands of oranges, grapefruit, limes, avocado pears, coffee and cocoa are in abundance throughout the island, as are the commercial smallholdings of banana plants which are primarily cultivated for export. Other seasonal fruits that can be seen almost everywhere around Dominica include pawpaw (papaya), guava, breadfruit, soursop, passionfruit, cherry, pineapple, watermelon and carambola. For further information, see box on page 58.

Medicinal plants play an important role in Dominican life despite the increased availability of over-the-counter and prescription drugs. Rastafarians, Kalinago and predominantly the older generation of Dominicans have succeeded in preserving the knowledge of their ancestors, and so a variety of bush teas and other herbal remedies are still in common use. What may seem like a weed to many may in fact be *verveine* (*Stachytarpheta jamaicensis*) or *tabac zombie* (*Pluchea symphytifolia*), plants that are often used to make tea infusions for colds, fevers and other such ailments. Take a walk in the forest with someone who knows about this subject and you will be amazed at the depth and variety of ordinary looking plants that contain extraordinary medicinal properties.

BIRDS Almost 200 species of bird have been recorded in Dominica including endemics and regional endemics. Most are migratory, of course, and it is thought that only around 60 of the recorded species are actually resident on the island. Dominica's endemic birds include the imperial Amazon parrot (*Amazona imperialis*), commonly known as the **sisserou**. The large and colourful yet extremely elusive sisserou is a highly endangered species and is seen mostly in the elevated mature rainforest of the island's highest mountain, Morne Diablotin (see page 207). Dominica's second endemic parrot is the **jaco** (*Amazona arausiaca*) which is smaller than the sisserou, greater in number, and usually found at slightly lower elevations throughout the island's rainforest interior. To date nine regionally endemic bird species have been recorded: the Lesser Antillean swift

(*Chaetura martinica*), the blue-headed hummingbird (*Cyanophaia bicolor*), the Lesser Antillean flycatcher (*Myiarchus oberi*), the Lesser Antillean peewee (*Contopus latirostris*), the forest thrush (*Cichlerminia lherminieri*), the scaly-breasted thrasher (*Margarops fuscus*), the trembler (*Cinclocerthia rufcauda*), the plumbeous warbler (*Dendroica plumbea*), and the Lesser Antillean bullfinch (*Loxigilla noctis*).

Dominica has four species of hummingbird: the purple-throated Carib (*Eulampis jugularis*), the green-throated Carib (*Sericotes holosericeus*), the Antillean crested hummingbird (*Orythorhyncus cristatus*) and the regionally endemic blue-headed hummingbird (*Cyanophaia bicolor*).

Along Dominica's inshore waters, especially in the Scotts Head and Soufriere Bay area (see page 137), you can see magnificent frigatebirds (*Fregata magnificens*) circling and occasionally fighting other seabirds for their catch. Other coastal birds include brown pelicans (*Pelecanus occidentalis*), brown boobies (*Sula leucogaster*), and occasionally the neotropic cormorant (*Phalacrocorax brasilianus*). The red-billed tropicbird (*Phaethon aethereus*), the white-tailed tropicbird (*Phaethon lepturus*) and several species of petrels and terns may also be observed.

Sandy shorelines, freshwater lakes and rivers provide a habitat for the belted kingfisher (*Ceryle alcyon*), the ringed kingfisher (*Ceryle torquatus*), the cattle egret (*Bubulcus ibis*), the green heron (*Butorides virescens*) and a variety of plovers and sandpipers. Along the swampy and brackish margins of the Indian River (see page 199) you are very likely to observe the common moorhen (*Gallinula chloropus*) and the Caribbean coot (*Fulica caribaea*). If you are lucky you may also catch sight of a white ibis (*Eudocimus albus*) and several species of teal and duck.

Dominica's forest habitats are home to a variety of bird species. The mangrove cuckoo (*Coccyzus minor*) and the rufous-throated solitaire (*Myadestes genibarbis*), commonly known as the **mountain whistler**, or *siffleur montagne*, are particularly vocal. The unmistakable call of the mountain whistler sounds rather like a squeaky bicycle wheel and accompanies hikers throughout Dominica's elevated rainforest interior. The ground dove (*Columbina passerina*), the bananaquit (*Coereba flaveola*), the Lesser Antillean saltator (*Saltator albicollis*), over 20 species of warbler and around five species of flycatcher can also be seen and heard in the island's vast tracts of forest and woodland.

Birds of prey observed in Dominica include the northern harrier (*Circus cyaneus*), the broad-winged hawk (*Buteo platypterus*), the merlin (*Falco columbarius*), the American kestrel (*Falco sparverius*), the barn owl (*Tyto alba*) and the peregrine falcon (*Falco peregrinus*).

MAMMALS The **agouti** (*Dasyprocta leporina*) is a wild land mammal that is thought to have been introduced by Amerindians and is still common in the forests of South America. Roughly the size of a rabbit, it is a ground-dwelling rodent that is related to the guinea pig. It has dark fur and pink ears and is built for running at speed. A herbivore, the agouti may be spotted scouring the forest floor looking for fallen fruit and nuts. During the hunting season (usually October to December) it is targeted by bush hunters and eaten for its meat.

The **manicou** (*Didelphys marsupialis insularis*) is a tree-dwelling opossum that is thought to have been introduced at the beginning of the 19th century. Though common, it is nocturnal and therefore rarely encountered. Wild pigs (*sus scrofa*) are common though very elusive. They live in the depths of Dominica's interior, particularly in the southern and eastern foothills of Morne Diablotin where local hunters have reportedly come across some very large and aggressive specimens. Unless you are hiking in the deep bush, it is extremely unlikely your paths will ever meet.

Twelve species of bat have been recorded on the island, of which four are endemic to the region: the Lesser Antillean long-tongued bat (*Monohyllus plethodon*), the Lesser Antillean tree bat (*Ardops nichollsi*), the Antillean cave bat (*Brachyphylla cavernarum*), and the mouse-eared bat (*Myotis dominicensis*). It is the Antillean cave bat that makes its home in Tou Santi (Stinking Hole) on the Middleham Falls hiking trail (see page 127) Dominica's largest bat is the fisherman bat (*Noctilio leporinus*) which is rufous-coloured and lives in sea caves. Bats are most common in the forest though many can be seen emerging from the corrugated gaps of galvanized steel roof tops at dusk.

REPTILES AND AMPHIBIANS The **zandoli** (*Anolis oculatus*), or tree lizard, is endemic to Dominica. Zandoli are small and very well camouflaged lizards. They live in woodlands and gardens throughout the island though they are more prominent on the west coast. The adult male has an orange and yellow throat fan which he extends to attract females. The **abòlò** (*Ameiva fuscata*), or ground lizard, is also endemic to Dominica. It is very common on the west coast and is much larger than the zandoli. It is often seen and heard in dry coastal woodland and gardens. The house gecko and tree gecko are lizards that usually appear at night on the prowl for moths. They are both known locally as the *mabouya*, the Kalinago name for an evil spirit. The Lesser Antillean iguana (*Iguana delicatissima*) is also quite commonly seen, particularly on the drier west coast (a good place to see them is in the gardens of the Sunset Bay Club at Batali, see page 206). A new arrival to the island is the Puerto Rican crested anole lizard (*Anolis cristatellus*) which appears to be increasing in numbers in the southwest. It is an invasive species which, it is feared, may threaten the native zandoli.

Of the four species of snake found on the island, none are venomous. The largest is the **boa constrictor** (*Constrictor nebulosa*), or *tête chien*, which can grow to 3.5m (8ft) and is particularly unusual because it does not lay eggs, but instead gives birth to live young. There are also two types of common grass snake which are regionally endemic and are known locally as the *kouwès nwé* (*Alsophis antillensis*), also known as the Antilles racer, and *kouwès sayga* (*Liophis juliae*). Both snakes are usually seen in drier coastal woodlands though they can also be found in semi deciduous woodland and rainforest margins.

The largest frog found on the island is known locally as the **mountain chicken** (*Leptodactyllus fallax*), or *crapaud*, which is endemic to both Dominica and Montserrat. Mountain chicken used to be considered the national dish, though the chytrid fungus disease that has plagued amphibians around the world also reached Dominica, sparing the *crapaud* from the restaurant menu but nevertheless seriously reducing its number to near extinction. Dominica responded to the threat of this disease by banning amphibian imports, protecting the *crapaud* from hunting and by establishing a molecular diagnostic laboratory at the Botanical Gardens under the Darwin Initiative Project and with assistance from the Zoological Society of London. Though working very closely with their colleagues on the island of Montserrat in an attempt to protect the mountain chicken, experts in Dominica fear the outlook remains bleak for this species which is now very rarely encountered.

In addition to the *crapaud*, there are also three tiny tree frogs found in Dominica, one of which is endemic to the island and found in higher elevations. The two others, including Johnstone's whistling frog, are endemic to the region.

BUTTERFLIES AND OTHER INSECTS Over 50 species of butterfly have been recorded in Dominica, two of which are endemic to the island. They are the Dominican Snout (*Libytheana fulvescens*) and the Dominican hairstreak (*Electrostrymon dominicana*). Both endemics are usually found in dry areas, particularly along the west coast of Dominica. To date, seven of the recorded species are considered regionally endemic. They are: the St Lucia mestra (*Mestra cana*), the lesser whirlabout (*Polites dictynna*), the sub-tailed skipper (*Urbanus obscurus*), Godman's leaf (*Memphis dominicana*), Godman's hairstreak (*Allosmaitia piplea*), the bronze hairstreak (*Electrostrymon angerona*), and the broken dash skipper (*Wallengrenia ophites*). Perhaps the most commonly observed butterfly in Dominica, however, is the monarch butterfly (*Danaus plexippus*) which is very widely distributed across the island.

Dominica is home to over 60 endemic beetle species, including one of the largest in the world, the Hercules beetle (*Dynastes Hercules*). Other notable insects include moths, fireflies, stick insects, grasshoppers, crickets, centipedes and millipedes. Several insect species are endemic to Dominica, others to the region.

FRESHWATER FISH AND CRUSTACEANS Dominica's many rivers are home to several species of fish, the most common of which is the mountain mullet (*Agonostomus monticola*). You may also come across over ten recorded species of freshwater shrimp, crayfish and edible shellfish. Within the Morne Trois Pitons National Park, the Freshwater Lake (see page 126) is home to a species of tilapia (*Tilapia mossambica*) that was introduced to this natural reservoir.

There are around 20 recorded species of river and land crab in Dominica. The cyrique (*Guinotia dentata*) is usually seen in wet places, around rivers and pools, and is cooked for food. The black crab (*Gegarcinus ruricola*) is usually found in dry forest areas along Dominica's west coast and is the primary ingredient of *crabback*, a delicacy that is eaten during the Creole and Independence season (see page 31).

Titiwi is the Kalinago name that is still used today for a type of goby (*Sicydium punctatum*) that hatches in fresh water, develops in the sea, and then returns to the rivers to spawn. Dominica's fishermen catch nets full of these small fish which are traditionally eaten as an *ackra*, a small fritter that is fried in oil (see page 56).

MARINE ENVIRONMENT The powerful deep seas of Dominica's rugged north, east and south coasts are beautiful in their strength. Fierce waves crash wildly against cliffs of volcanic rock generating tall plumes of white spray. A formidable undertow toys with large boulders and pebbles, causing them to rumble like thunder as they are dragged up and down this weather-beaten shoreline. Sheltered bays and inshore reefs along these coasts offer some respite from the mighty Atlantic. In the northeast, between Marigot and Hampstead, alluring beaches of light sand and shallow water lie undisturbed on the fringes of dense forests of coconut palms.

In the calmer Caribbean Sea along the west coast of Dominica it is possible to see whales and dolphins all year round, and the underwater environment is developing a reputation for some of the very best scuba diving in the world. Beneath the surface there are steep drop-offs descending into the abyss, sea pinnacles rising from the seabed, volcanic fumaroles and an exuberance of aquatic life. Reflecting the dramatic topography above the water, Dominica's pristine marine environment is a miracle of nature, a spectacular fusion of life, colour and depth.

Coral reefs Dominica's reefs have a foundation of granite cliffs and large boulders. Reef topography is varied, though many consist of steep walls and pinnacles.

Shallow reefs tend to run quickly away into deeper waters or lie on narrow ledges above precipitous drop-offs. The waters around the reefs are usually clear due to their depth and the fact that silt in water-borne run-off from the island's heavy deluges tends to dissipate very quickly. They are also very nutrient-rich, providing the essential ingredients for life and an extremely healthy marine environment. Hard and soft corals are found on Dominica's reefs. Common gorgonians include sea fans and sea whips. Stony coral varieties include finger coral, star coral, sheet coral and brain coral.

Fish Large numbers of fish live in and around the reefs and occasionally the shadows of migratory pelagics can be seen passing by in the deep blue of the ocean beyond. The abundance of fish life, and in particular the huge numbers of juveniles, is testament to the purity of the environment. The reefs are nursing grounds to many species including damselfish, butterflyfish, angelfish and surgeonfish. Large shoals of yellow and blue striped grunts hover along the margins of reef edges, groups of soldierfish may be found suspended beneath overhangs or in the shadows of arches or small caverns, and goby, blenny, jawfish and flounder find their home in patches of sand. Parrotfish, cowfish, trunkfish, trumpetfish and spotted drum are just some of the many common varieties decorating an already colourful reef system, where in every nook and cranny a moray or sharptail eel may also be making its home.

Sharks are rarely seen along the west coast. The most common is the nurse shark which can sometimes be found resting on the sand beneath plate coral. Whale sharks have been recorded, as have hammerheads and reef sharks. Rays are more regular sightings, including the stingray and the spotted eagle ray. Barracuda are also present, as are large schools of predatory jacks and mackerel.

It is perhaps the more unusual species of fish that are of greatest appeal to recreational divers, conservationists and marine photographers. The longlure frogfish (*Antennarius multiocellatus*) is one such example. Through the use of camouflage, the frogfish is able to make itself look like part of the sponge or coral it is inhabiting. The first spine of its dorsal fin is highly modified and acts as a lure to fish that swim by. The frogfish then makes a movement thought to be the fastest of all animals alive: in around one-sixth of a second it extends its mouth and sucks in prey which can be even larger than itself. The frogfish has a voracious appetite and is also cannibalistic. If fishing is bad in one area, it simply takes its rod and lure and moves to the next. In addition to the frogfish, Dominica's reefs are home to a variety of other interesting fish such as the seahorse, the scorpionfish, pipefish, batfish and flying gurnard.

Other marine creatures Along the east coast of Dominica endangered giant leatherbacks (*Dermochelys coriacea*), the largest of all living sea turtles, return to lay their clusters of eggs in the sand. The giant leatherback is one of four species of turtle observed in the waters around Dominica. The hawksbill turtle (*Eretmochelys imbriocota*) is by far the most common. The green turtle (*Chelonia mydas*) and the loggerhead turtle (*Caretta caretta*) may also be seen, though more rarely.

Dominica's waters are home to a number of echinoderms including the very aptly named donkey dung sea cucumber, long-spined urchins and a variety of colourful crinoids. Octopus and squid are also evident and there are several varieties of crab, lobster and shrimp. Fanworms, fireworms, feather duster worms and Christmas tree worms are widespread. There are lots of sponges inhabiting Dominica's reefs, including tube, vase, volcano and rope varieties. Perhaps the most impressive, however, is the giant barrel sponge, which can be found in large numbers all along the dramatic coral formations of the west coast.

Whales and dolphins Several species of whale routinely visit the deep coastal waters of Dominica. The most prevalent is the sperm whale (*Physeter macrocephallus*) which actually breeds here and is observed, often with calves, all year round. Other species of whale that may be sighted here include short-finned pilot whales (*Globicephala melaena*), humpback whales (*Megaptera novaeangliae*) and false killer whales (*Pseudorca crassidens*)

Pods of dolphin are often spotted along the west coast, even from the shore. The most common visitors are spinner dolphins (*Stenella longirostris*) though other frequently observed species include bottlenose dolphins (*Tursiops truncatus*), Atlantic spotted dolphins (*Stenella frontalis*) and Fraser's dolphins (*Lagenodelphis hosei*).

CONSERVATION Reflecting the need to protect and preserve its rich natural environment, both above and below sea level, Dominica has a number of national parks, forest and marine reserves.

National Parks The most well known national park is the 7,000ha **Morne Trois Pitons National Park**, a UNESCO World Heritage Site. The south of Dominica is dominated by a concentrated cluster of forest-covered dormant and dead volcanoes and many lie within the boundaries of this park. The highest is the three-peaked summit of Morne Trois Pitons itself at 1,342m.

Morne Micotrin, sometimes called Morne Macaque, is 1,221m tall and is located a short distance to the south of Morne Trois Pitons. Nestled within a circular crater between these two mountains is the 2ha Boeri Lake. At an elevation of 853m it is the highest mountain lake on the island. A short distance to the east of Morne Micotrin is the 4ha Freshwater Lake at an elevation of 762m.

A high ridge runs southwards from Morne Micotrin until it reaches the pointed and weather-beaten summit of Morne Watt at 1,224m. To the east of this imposing mountain is the Valley of Desolation, a barren volcanic landscape of steaming vents, geysers, hot rivers and cascades, boiling grey mud and a crust of colourful, sulphur-stained rock. Located at the northern end of the valley is the famous **Boiling Lake**, a flooded fumarole some 66m in diameter. It is one of the largest of its kind in the world, second only to Frying Pan Lake in Waimangu Volcanic Rift Valley, New Zealand. The lake's nebulous, boiling hot waters spill over a cleft on its eastern margins and create the White River which runs from this turbulent source down a deep valley beneath the Grand Soufriere Hills, passing over several waterfalls, including the Victoria Falls near Delices (see page 174), until it joins the Pointe Mulâtre River and finally the Atlantic Ocean. At the park's southern tip is Morne Anglais which rises to 1,123m above Dominica's western shore.

In January 2000 the 3,335ha **Morne Diablotin National Park** was established. The park contains rainforest, montane forest and elfin woodland habitats and has some of the most dense and least explored terrain in all of Dominica. At the heart of the park is Dominica's highest peak, Morne Diablotin, which rises to 1,447m, and dominates the landscape in the north. This park was created primarily to protect the habitat of Dominica's two endemic and endangered Amazon parrots, the sisserou and the jaco (see page 6), but is also home to many other bird species, as well as mammals such as the agouti and wild pigs (see page 7).

The 525ha **Cabrits National Park** was established in 1986. It is located to the north of Portsmouth on a peninsula formed by two volcanic peaks, East Cabrit at 140m and West Cabrit at 171m. Within the park, and its most prominent feature, are the semi-restored ruins of the 18th-century Fort Shirley Garrison (see page 184). The park contains dry coastal woodland and is connected to the mainland by the island's largest swamp and wetland area. Around the coastline is 421ha of marine environment that has been designated the Cabrits Marine Reserve.

Forest Reserves When it was formed in 1977 the **Northern Forest Reserve** covered 8,900ha, but it ceded land to the formation of the Morne Diablotin National Park in January 2000. Located in the north of Dominica, it is a vast tract of montane and rainforest habitats and contains some of the island's largest tree species.

Extending down from the Northern Forest Reserve to the valleys of the Layou and Pagua rivers are further high ridges and areas of dense forest. The Layou is Dominica's longest river, and the area to the north and east of the Layou River valley is the 410ha **Central Forest Reserve**, Dominica's oldest forest reserve, which was established in 1952.

Soufriere Scotts Head Marine Reserve (SSMR) The SSMR is located in the southwest of Dominica and contains some of the island's most visited and well-known dive sites. The aim of the reserve is to protect the marine environment at the same time as providing structure and balance to the demands of both tourism and the traditional fishing heritage of the villages in this region. The reserve runs from the isthmus of Cachacrou to the Champagne Reef system south of the coastal community of Pointe Michel, and is comprised of priority zones for fishing, scuba diving and marine nurseries. Within the reserve, dive sites such as L'Abym, La Sorciere, Danglebens Pinnacles and Scotts Head Drop-off provide visiting scuba divers with a spectacular combination of life, colour and dramatic reef formations. The waters here are extremely deep, and the reefs largely bereft of sand, so turbidity is rarely a problem and thus visibility is usually excellent all year round. Scuba diving and snorkelling in the SSMR draws a US$2 fee per snorkeller or scuba diver which goes towards its management, much in the same way as the site pass system is designed to work for designated 'eco' attractions on land.

Organisations A selection of government ministries and organisations that are involved in the management and preservation of Dominica's natural environment and cultural heritage:

Forestry, Wildlife & Parks Division Roseau; ☎ 767 266 3429. Government department responsible for the management & conservation of Dominica's forests, wildlife & national parks.
Dominica Organic Agriculture Movement (DOAM) www.doamdominica.org. Non government organisation (NGO) providing advice, news, classes, workshops & seminars on organic methods for Dominica's farmers.

Society for Heritage Architecture Preservation & Enhancement (SHAPE) ☎ 767 275 5031 or 767 440 3430; www.shape.dm. A non-profit group promoting awareness & appreciation of Dominica's buildings of architectural & historic interest.
Wai'tukubuli Ecological Foundation ☎ 767 440 1764; e bernardwiltshire@cwdom.dm. Environmental NGO promoting & lobbying for increased environmental awareness, preservation & development of Dominica with the environment in mind.

A BRIEF HISTORY OF THE ISLAND

Visitors interested in the detail of Dominica's history should pick up a copy of *The Dominica Story – A History of the Island* by local historian and anthropologist, **Lennox Honychurch**. For further information, see www.lennoxhonychurch.com.

EARLY SETTLERS Dominica's first arrivals are believed to have been Orinoco River tribes who made their way up the island chain from South America some 5,000 years ago. Archaeologists and historians describe these people as basic hunter-gatherers, living off wild plants and shellfish. Around 400BC these tribes are thought to have been displaced by an Arawak tribe called the **Igneri** who also migrated from the Amazon River Delta and occupied the Windward Islands, from Grenada to Guadeloupe, for many years. Like the Taino tribes who settled in the Greater Antilles, the Igneri worshipped nature spirits, often represented by three-cornered *zemi* stones or conch shells. They carved curious designs on rock faces, often close to water sources, which we now refer to as Amerindian petroglyphs, several examples of which have been discovered in the southeastern Caribbean. So far in Dominica only one very small and quite inaccessible petroglyph has been uncovered in the very north of the island.

The Igneri are thought to have engaged in inter-tribal trade; they farmed, built thatched houses, made pottery, wove cotton and crafted ocean-going canoes. They are believed to have lived on the island for around 1,000 years before the arrival of another Arawakan people called the **Kalinago**.

Considered by archaeologists and anthropologists to have been a more war-like Amerindian tribe, the Kalinago probably displaced the Igneri by around the end of the 14th century, just 100 years before the arrival of Columbus and the first Europeans to the region. Like their predecessors, the Kalinago also worshipped ancestors and nature spirits in the form of iconic *zemis*, and they also excelled at boat-building and fishing. Carved out of the trunks of *gommier* trees (see page 4), their larger boats, called *canoua*, were said to be up to 15m long and capable of travelling long distances across open seas. Smaller craft included the *couliana*, also carved out of whole tree trunks, and *pwi pwi*, a very simple raft that was probably used more for inshore fishing. These vessels would carry Kalinago men on hunting trips for fish, lobster, shellfish and conch, as well as on raiding parties to other islands. Kalinago women would probably have had a more domestic role, taking care of the children, cooking, running the farms, weaving hammocks and making baskets from the dried outer bark of the *larouma* reed.

NEW ARRIVALS On 3 November 1493 Columbus's fleet sighted the island the Kalinago had called **Wai'tukubuli**, meaning 'tall is her body'. He named it Dominica.

Through enslavement and disease, it is said to have taken just 30 years of Spanish occupation to eradicate the Taino people of the Greater Antilles and, as slave labour became a scarce commodity, the Spanish turned their attention to capturing the Amerindian people of the Lesser Antilles. Amazingly, the Kalinago steadfastly resisted these raids for two whole centuries and Dominica remained largely untouched by Europeans.

In 1635 France claimed Dominica as her own and in 1642 French missionaries arrived on the island for the first time. The Kalinago continued to hold the French and the British in check, however, and in 1686 both countries signed a treaty stating that Dominica would be a neutral island belonging to this indigenous tribe. In spite of this agreement, French incursions from Martinique and Guadeloupe increased and small lumber, cotton and tobacco settlements were eventually established. The French shipped in African slaves to work their estates but it was not until the 1760s, after Dominica was ceded to the British following the Seven Years War, and then again 18 years later following the Battle of the Saints, that these estates expanded and the population of African slaves became comparable with other Caribbean islands. African slaves were seen as a cheaper and more durable alternative to traditional white indentured labour. Unused to the tropical Caribbean climate, these indentured servants from England, Ireland and Scotland were soon replaced by large numbers of slaves from West Africa. In the meantime the Kalinago population was declining rapidly. Years of intense fighting, resistance, and disease had severely diminished their numbers, and in 1730 there were thought to be less than 500 on the island.

The British were brutal masters and the flogging of slaves was common. Many slaves managed to escape captivity by running away into the dense forest and forming small settlements in remote mountain locations. British plantation owners in the region called these bands of escaped slaves **Maroons**. Towards the end of the 18th century Dominica's Maroon population had grown significantly in number. They were fairly well-armed and launched many successful and violent raids on estates, plundering food, setting fire to buildings, and, on occasion, murdering plantation workers. A legion of 500 men was formed to deal with the Maroons, and those captured were often tortured and executed in public. One notorious chief, Balla, was gibbeted and, it is said, took a whole week to die. The Maroon Wars reached a bloody conclusion in 1814; ageing chief Jacko was shot on 12 July and by November the same year well over 500 Maroons had either been killed or recaptured. Several Maroons were publically hanged, their heads cut off and displayed on stakes around the island.

In 1795 the French attempted to recapture Dominica from the north but failed. Then again in 1805 they launched a fierce siege of Roseau. The British defences were outnumbered by ten to one and soon Roseau was ablaze. Retreating all the way to the Cabrits garrison near Portsmouth, the British regrouped and prepared for a final battle. However, it did not materialise. Instead, the French commander demanded a ransom for the return of members of the British legislature, looted the now completely destroyed town of Roseau of everything of value, including slaves, and then sailed back to the French colonies.

For the next hundred years Dominica became an island of isolated village communities and small plantation estates that grew sugar, coffee, limes and coconuts. Despite the fact that it was under British rule, Dominica's main influences came from the neighbouring French colonies of Martinique and Guadeloupe. When British land owners were forced to either abandon or sell off failing estates, it was often the increasing number of free coloured *mulattos* arriving from Martinique and Guadeloupe who took over and made them viable again. The African slaves that had been brought by French settlers began to absorb French language and culture, and so it was not long before **Creole**, a combination of French vocabulary and strong African dialect and syntax, was spoken as a first language. A new Creole culture was born which, in addition to language, was also reflected in dance, games, music, instruments and modes of dress.

INDEPENDENT PEOPLE In 1838, following the abolition of slavery, Dominica became the first and only British Caribbean colony to have a legislature that was not controlled by the white planter class. However, it was not to last. The planters began lobbying for greater British rule and in 1871 Dominica became part of the Leeward Island Federation. In 1896 Crown Colony government was re-established.

Dominica's first Crown Colony administrator was a man called Hesketh Bell. In a six-year period from 1899 to 1905 he constructed Dominica's first highway, the Imperial Road, which ran from Roseau to Bells, he connected Portsmouth to Roseau by telephone, he initiated the first electricity service, he designed the Public Library for which he had secured funding from the famous philanthropist, Andrew

Carnegie, he opened a new jetty at Roseau and he made proposals to set aside some 1,530ha for the island's indigenous Amerindians, the Kalinago. Over the next 60 years Dominica's population increased and its infrastructure and social institutions slowly developed to support it. In 1967 Dominica achieved Associated Statehood, giving the island total self-governance, and on 3 November 1978, exactly 485 years to the day after Columbus had first sighted the island, Dominica was granted full independence from Britain.

The birth of the new **Commonwealth of Dominica** was testing. On 29 August 1979 Hurricane David hit the island causing widespread devastation, and in 1981 a very odd incident took place. A group of North American mercenaries and former Dominica Defence Force officers attempted an overthrow of the government of Eugenia Charles. The mercenaries were made up of Canadian and US right-wing extremists, gangsters, former soldiers and even Ku Klux Klan Grand Wizard Don Black. This bizarre operation, code-named Red Dog, was meant to restore former Dominica premier Patrick John to power in a kind of puppet regime which would allow this group to exploit the island and turn it into a form of criminal paradise that would launder money and manufacture and export illicit drugs. For countless bizarre reasons, the coup attempt was a disaster and failed before it left the shores of the United States. In Dominica Patrick John faced trial and was found to have been a supporter of the attempted coup – a charge he has consistently rejected. Eugenia Charles, the Caribbean's first female prime minister, went on to lead Dominica for 15 years.

For a very interesting account of the Red Dog incident, pick up a copy of *Bayou of Pigs* by Canadian journalist Stewart Bell.

The powerful influences of nature, together with a turbulent history, are still evident in contemporary Dominica. Direct descendants of the Kalinago live in a semi-autonomous territory on the east coast. They weave *larouma* reed baskets for visitors and for export, and they hand-carve *gommier* canoes for both local and regional fishermen. Ruins of estate houses, fortifications and mills can be found across the island, many people have reconnected and have strong affiliations with their African roots, and the culture of French Creole is very much alive in language, food, dance and traditional costume. Village communities retain strong identities, and very many Dominicans continue to eke a living from land, river and sea.

GOVERNMENT AND POLITICS

Dominica is a parliamentary democracy within the Commonwealth of Nations. The head of state is the president who is appointed by parliament for a five-year term. The president and prime minister make up Dominica's executive branch. Dominica's legislative branch, or parliament, is the House of Assembly, where 21 are ministers elected by popular vote in single-seat constituencies, five senators are appointed by the president on the advice of the prime minister and four on the advice of the leader of the opposition.

Dominica has ten administrative divisions, or parishes. They are St Andrew, St David, St George, St John, St Joseph, St Luke, St Mark, St Patrick, St Paul and St Peter. The Ministry of Kalinago Affairs represents the interests of the Kalinago population and the affairs of the Kalinago Territory together with the Kalinago Council. Dominica's village councils are elected by popular vote and are responsible for local amenities, services and sanitation.

There are three main political parties in Dominica. The Dominica Labour Party (DLP), the Dominica Freedom Party (DFP), and the United Workers Party (UWP).

The mercenaries who decided to invade Dominica in 1981 were an unlikely alliance of misfits – Vietnam vets, Ku Klux Klansmen, militant Rastafarians, disgruntled Dominican soldiers, the ex-prime minister and a gun-loving mobster from Toronto. Dominica was having a tough time back then. Hurricanes had battered the island, the economy was struggling and the government had all but collapsed. The American and Canadian mercenaries who decided to take advantage of Dominica's troubles had a simple plan: invade Roseau by sea, overthrow Prime Minister Eugenia Charles and get rich. Financed by US investors, they were going to strip the island of its resources and open casinos, drug labs and arms depots. What could go wrong?

When I began investigating this little-known piece of Caribbean history for my book, *Bayou of Pigs*, I soon realised this was the strangest story I had ever come across in two decades of journalism. Nobody could make up a tale this bizarre. To find out what had happened, I tracked down the members of the conspiracy one by one. I soon found that some were dead. One had been murdered in Canada, another was executed by hanging, and a financier had killed himself with a shotgun. The leader of the coup, Mike Perdue of Houston, had died of AIDS in prison. Even those still alive weren't easy to find. One had changed his name and was living in a Colorado trailer park. Another was in a Canadian prison, serving time for gun trafficking. When I told him I wanted to put his mug shot in the book, he told me not to. He said he had better photos. A week later an envelope arrived in the mail. Inside were a half-dozen pictures showing him posing with machine guns and ammunition belts. One of the group had undergone a sex change. She suggested we meet in person so that, following the interview, we could 'have a little shag on the couch.' Let's stick to phone interviews, I said. A few people would not talk to me but most did. In fact, some of them still had papers from the plot – photographs taken during reconnaissance missions to Dominica, even plane tickets and hotel and car rental receipts. I was also able to get copies of the invasion plans, which diagramed how the mercenaries would land at Rockaway Beach and storm the police headquarters in Roseau.

When I began to read the US government's file on the coup, I was confused at first. The memos contained a lot of references to GOD, which isn't usually something you find in FBI correspondence. It puzzled me until I figured out

LAW Dominica's judiciary is independent of both executive and legislative branches and its legal system is based on English common law. Dominica's law upholds freedom of speech and freedom of religion, and it prohibits discrimination based on race, gender, place of origin, colour and creed. The island's only security force is the Dominica Police Force, which is overseen by the prime minister's office. Dominica's law prohibits arbitrary arrest and it does not detain political prisoners.

ECONOMY

Dominica's economy is for the most part dependent on a combination of tourism and agriculture. Its foreign relations are driven by the need for economic and social development and Dominica usually seeks financial assistance in the form of low interest loans and grants when it comes to major infrastructure projects. Key donors and economic partners are the European Union, China, Venezuela, Japan, that GOD was Washington shorthand for the Government of Dominica. So I guess you could say that Dominica is GOD's paradise. When I began visiting the island, hiking to waterfalls and walking the beaches, I quickly realized that was true, even if it almost became a crooks' paradise. In the weeks before the coup, the conspirators met in Toronto, Louisiana and Antigua. They plotted. They recruited. They raised money and bought guns. And they carefully mapped out how they would remove Prime Minister Charles from office and install Patrick John in her place. 'Imagine what you could do if you owned your own country,' said Wolfgang Droege, the Canadian KKK boss who was deputy-leader of the plot. The problem was, the conspirators were not only ambitious, they were also imbeciles. The ship they hired to transport them and their guns to Dominica was immediately infiltrated by US agents. The ship's captain, Mike Howell, had tipped off the Bureau of Alcohol, Tobacco and Firearms. Special Agents John Osburg and Wiley Lloyd Grafton posed as crewmen on the ship as they secretly tape-recorded the conspirators. The ATF called its investigation Bayou of Pigs – a Louisiana take on the infamous Bay of Pigs invasion of Cuba. Canadian police also found out. The mercenaries wanted to bring a news reporter along with them to document their invasion for posterity, so they 'embedded' a Toronto radio reporter named Gord Sivell. Once he found out that lives would be lost, Sivell went to the police. Police in Dominica got wind of the plot as well, through their own inquiries. The FBI knew, the US State Department knew. The Royal Canadian Mounted Police knew. The Dominica coup may have been one of the worst kept secrets in the history of mercenaries. On 27 April 1981, as the soldiers of fortune were about to set sail from New Orleans, police moved in and made the arrests. They seized guns, ammunition, inflatable rafts, Tennessee whiskey and Nazi flags. More than two dozen people were arrested and ultimately convicted in the US, Canada and Dominica. 'It was an exercise in stupidity,' Bob Prichard, an Army veteran who was convicted for his role in the plot, told me. 'The worst part was, I was stupid enough to go along with it.'

Stewart Bell is an award-winning Canadian journalist and the author of three non-fiction books, The Bayou of Pigs, The Martyr's Oath, *and* Cold Terror. *For more information go to www.stewartbell.net.*

Morocco, and the US via the Caribbean Development Bank (CDB), the IMF/World bank, and the US Agency for International Development (USAID).

Dominica is a member of the Organisation of Eastern Caribbean States (OECS) and is committed to an agreement to allow the free movement of goods and labour across OECS-participating countries. The OECS is in turn committed to the CARICOM (Caribbean Community) ambition to develop the Caribbean Single Market Economy (CSME). Dominica is also a member of ALBA (Alianza Bolivariana para los Pueblos de Nuestra América – the Bolivarian Alliance for the People of our Americas). The aim of ALBA is to attempt economic integration of member nations of South America and the Caribbean based on a premise of social welfare, bartering and mutual financial assistance.

Dominica's economic welfare is also underpinned by remittances from its diaspora – Dominicans living and working overseas. These remittances are significant and a major source of external funding and benefits in kind for individuals and families living here.

AGRICULTURE Historically, agriculture has been and still is the traditional mainstay of the Dominican economy. Growing produce for consumption and trade is a practice that has sustained the people of the island ever since they first arrived here. These days, in the face of world trade and overwhelming competition from large-scale food producers, Dominica's agriculture industry is in a state of decline and flux. The farming of bananas for export to Britain and other EU countries has been struck a severe blow by successive changes to trade rules, removing subsidy support for small island growers and pitting them against the economies of scale that are enjoyed by mass producers. Many Dominican farmers have not been able

A FAIR TRADE

Fairtrade labelling was set up in the late 1980s to increase market access for small-scale farmers (at the bottom of the supply chain) who were struggling to survive amid tumbling prices and economic uncertainties. The advent of the Single European Market caused a radical shift in banana supply as the various national trading arrangements were harmonised under a single import system. As the European market has become more open, retailers have started to source more directly from producers, inevitably choosing lower-cost suppliers, resulting in bananas from Latin American plantations and now west Africa replacing higher-cost ones from traditional Caribbean smallholders. Between 1992 and 2007, UK banana imports increased from 545,000 tonnes to 927,000 tonnes, a growth of 41%. In the same period, imports from Caribbean countries fell from 70% to less than 30% of imports. Cheaper Latin American 'dollar' bananas, almost insignificant in 1992, now make up around half of UK imports, with Costa Rica the UK's biggest banana supplier accounting for 25% of total imports in 2007.

Caribbean producers remain almost entirely dependent on UK sales and so their falling share of the UK market has had a devastating effect. Dominica, St Vincent and St Lucia have lost more than 20,000 of their 25,000 small-scale banana growers since 1992. There are now less than 4,000 small farmers remaining of which over 3,500 are Fairtrade certified.

After decades in which smallholders have been squeezed out of markets by larger plantations, the world is beginning to wake up to the damage this has caused socially and environmentally. The Fairtrade model demonstrates that small-scale farmers can achieve greater productivity while preserving the natural environment and the well being of people working on the land, as well as delivering high-quality products.

> We decided to convert all bananas to Fairtrade as it became clear what a massive difference it would make to the communities where they were grown. It was a relatively easy decision as a third of all our customers were already buying Fairtrade bananas. We have also committed to increase purchases from small producers while increasing the length of contracts to suppliers to three years.
>
> Matt North, Banana buyer, Sainsbury's

Extracts from Unpeeling the banana trade, *a Fairtrade Foundation briefing paper of 2009, and subsequent updates. For information on the Fairtrade Foundation contact: Room 204, 16 Baldwins Gardens, London EC1N 7RJ;* 020 7405 5942; f 020 7405 5943; e mail@fairtrade.org.uk; www.fairtrade.org.uk.

to survive these events and have left the industry altogether, sometimes preferring to sell their land to real estate developers and speculators. Those who remain in this troubled sector have had to change the way they manage and operate their businesses, producing and selling to specialist markets both at home and abroad. The damage inflicted by globalisation has also extended to the image and attraction of farming for the young people of Dominica, with many no longer considering it a viable or worthwhile occupation. Those who are interested often find it very difficult to get started if they have no assets with which to secure loans for the purchase of workable agricultural land.

Organic and sustainable farming is developing, however, and with the assistance and support of organisations such as The Fairtrade Foundation, Dominica Organic Agriculture Movement (DOAM), and NAYA, the Youth in Agriculture Movement, an agriculture industry with a different perspective and focus is slowly starting to take shape. In addition to bananas, grapefruit and pomelos, yams, oranges, plantains and coconuts are also major agricultural commodities. Other crops include mangoes, pineapples, watermelons, avocado pears, lemons and limes, sweet potatoes, ginger, seasoning and hot peppers, and cocoa beans.

Agrotourism is linking the infant organic farming movement with the growing ecotourism sector (see below). Some rural communities have enthusiastically embraced organic farming and they have established educational farm tours for visitors as a means to supplement income as well as promote their products.

Dominica's Wai'tukubuli National Trail (see *Chapter 10*) passes through or nearby several farmlands and the hope is that more farmers will embrace the presence of hikers and use the opportunity to develop agrotourism businesses of their own.

FISHERIES Fishing is a traditional occupation in Dominica and every coastal village has its community of fishermen. Colourful boats can be seen pulled up on the beach or moored close to the shore, and there is usually a regular spot where daily catches are sold. Many fishermen sell directly to hotels, restaurants and supermarkets, some sell at established fish markets in Roseau, Marigot and Portsmouth, and others simply meander around village communities either in a pick-up truck or pushing a barrow, blowing a conch shell to let people know there is fish for sale.

Migratory pelagics such as marlin, tuna and dorado are usually caught from small boats using long lines and artificial lures. This takes place several miles offshore using fish attracting devices (FADs) that are usually floats made from an assortment of tree branches or palm fronds. Small fish are drawn to these floating structures, creating a concentrated food source for larger predators.

Inshore fishermen use basketware or chicken-wire traps and seine nets to catch mackerel, ballyhoo, jacks and small tuna. Almost all lobsters that are caught are sold directly to hotels and restaurants and you will rarely see them for sale elsewhere. Unlike most of the Eastern Caribbean, conch is fairly uncommon as the sea around Dominica's coastline gets very deep very quickly.

TOURISM Because of its very dramatic and largely unspoiled natural environment, Dominica's tourism authorities promote the island as an ecotourism destination. In addition to hikers, scuba divers, researchers, botanists, birdwatchers and other nature enthusiasts, Dominica receives over 500,000 cruise ship passengers each year. These day-visitors are an important source of income for local people, in particular tour operators, bus drivers, and souvenir vendors, though income per visitor is in actual fact very low compared with stay-over travellers. Official statistics for 2009 show earnings of EC$159million from 75,000 stay-over visitors (that's EC$2,120 per head), and EC$35millon from 530,000 cruise ship visitors (just EC$62 per head). Despite this anomaly and the negative impact large cruise ships have on the natural environment, cruise lines and their passengers offer direct marketing and revenue opportunities and continue to be courted. There are indeed plans afoot to construct a brand new cruise ship terminal at Woodbridge Bay to the north of Roseau.

Community tourism is a strategy aimed at assisting local communities to develop and implement tourism related initiatives. Since the decline of the agriculture sector in the majority of Dominica's rural areas, the government has sought to arrest the slump by trying to get people involved in the tourism industry. 'Tourism is everybody's business' is a phrase you may well come across during your visit to the island. Look out for community projects and try to support them if you can.

COTTAGE INDUSTRIES Handmade soaps, wood and tree fern carvings, rum punches, Kalinago basketwork, essential oils, decorated calabash bowls, and exotic fruits are just some of the products developed or grown by small cottage industries scattered throughout the island. From roadside vendors selling *braf* or *souse* on a Saturday morning (see page 55) to seasoning peppers, bay rum and oil, tonics, herbal teas, coconut water, coffee, mineral water and beer, Dominica's home grown businesses are important for the development of the country's economy and in particular the local communities where these cottage industries are based. For a list of local products see page 107.

PEOPLE

For outsiders the Dominican psyche can be difficult to understand and first impressions are often somewhat misleading. Serious, sometimes stern outward countenances usually give way to broad smiles and friendly conversation however (though you may have to work hard for it sometimes), and what may look like a heated exchange is usually just a lively discussion or debate that ends in jokes and laughter. Of course there are exceptions, but visitors should have no reservations about engaging with a friendly and interesting people. Once the ice is broken, Dominicans are very keen to talk about their lives and their country and will indulge themselves by offering you, the visitor, plenty of information, help and advice. Politics and social commentary are always hot topics, though Dominicans will willingly offer you an opinion on absolutely any subject at all, from world affairs to how best to park your car.

POPULATION Dominica's population is estimated at around 70,000 with some 20% or so living in or around the capital, Roseau. The population has actually declined in recent years due to the migration of many young people abroad, particularly to the United States (often via the US Virgin Islands), the UK and Canada, where they go in search of opportunity and prosperity. Though the estimated size of the Dominica diaspora varies considerably, commonly quoted statistics are that around half of Dominica's households have at least one close family member currently living abroad and that 30% of households have experienced close family migration abroad over the last ten years.

ETHNICITY The majority of Dominicans are descendants of slaves brought to the island by the French and British from west Africa. Dominica is the only island in the eastern Caribbean that is still home to a people who were here before the

CUTLASS AND MACHETE

The weapon of choice for sailors and pirates in the 17th and 18th centuries was the cutlass. It is a short sabre with a broad curved blade and was useful for close combat on ship and shore, as well as for cutting through rope and wood. On land it was also used as an agricultural tool, particularly effective for cutting through rainforest and harvesting sugarcane.

Also used both as a weapon and an agricultural tool was the machete. Very similar in shape and length to a cutlass, the machete has a broad blade with a very thin, sharp cutting edge. It is, however, much less elegant in design than the naval cutlass, and is sometimes called the 'poor man's sword'. Variations of the machete exist in many countries across the world. The *parang*, *golok* and *bolo* are similar long knives used in Malaysia, Indonesia and the Philippines. In Nepal it is the *kukri* and in China the *dao*.

In Dominica today the machete continues to be used as an agricultural tool for cutting overgrown bushes, trees, weeds and for harvesting crops, and the household that does not possess at least one is very much in the minority. Commonly referred to as a cutlass, the tool is in fact a simple machete, rather than its upmarket relative. Visitors to Dominica may see both men and women walking along the roadside carrying one. This should not cause alarm, although it almost certainly will at first.

arrival of Columbus in 1493. The Kalinago are of Amerindian descent and number some 3,000, the majority of whom live on the east coast in or around the 1,530ha Kalinago Territory.

LANGUAGE

The official language of Dominica is English, which is spoken throughout the island. The unofficial language of Dominica, and very commonly used, is **French Creole**, also called Kwéyòl, Patwa or Patois.

The European settlers in Dominica and throughout the Caribbean brought with them many slaves from west Africa to work on plantations. These slaves developed an indigenous language that combined the syntax and vocabulary from their native African languages with those of their European oppressors. In Dominica, together with Martinique, Guadeloupe and St Lucia, a French Antillean Creole was born.

Often considered rudimentary, sometimes not even a real language, many Creoles have been in a state of decline and loss. When Dominica became a British Crown Colony, English was firmly established as the language of the ruling classes and for many years Creole was viewed as a dialect spoken only by servants, farmers and peasants. The influence of the French has remained strong, however, and in recent times Creole language and culture has undergone significant recognition and revival, ultimately resurfacing as a key part of the island's national heritage. These days Creole is very commonly used and you will often hear Dominicans using it to converse with each other.

In the northeast of the island, around the villages of Marigot and Wesley, it may still be possible to hear a dialect that combines African with English rather than French. This is because the British estate owners in this area brought African slave workers from English-speaking islands such as Antigua. This English Creole is known locally as **Kockoy**.

The English spoken by Dominicans reflects both the past and the present. Sentence structure frequently resonates with the syntax of African languages and the continued influence of Creole. A high English remains and reminds us that a Dominican class society, particularly in and around the capital Roseau, is still mirrored in the language spoken by its people. Inevitably, through the prevalence of cable TV and contact with an increasing number of tourists, a North American English is now also born on the island and you may well experience people '*Yanking it*' with you. Please ask them to be proud of their own heritage, rather than yours.

RELIGION

From the moment Columbus arrived in 1493, the *zemi* stones and ancestral spirit worship of the Amerindian tribes across the region were brutally replaced by the crucifix and the Roman Catholic Church. Vieille Case (or Itassi as it was known to the Kalinago) was the site of the first Roman Catholic Mass in 1646, and in the early 18th century French Jesuits erected the first Roman Catholic church in Roseau. Many more churches were built across the island as well as schools, health services and the Credit Union movement. Today, with around 80% of the population as followers, Roman Catholicism is by far the dominant religion. Faith is very strong and the Church's influences and principles find themselves deeply woven into the fabric of modern Dominican society.

A number of other Christian denominations are present on the island including Methodists, Pentecostals, Seventh Day Adventists, Baptists and Jehovah's Witnesses. Other minority religions include Islam, Baha'i and Rastafarianism. Dominica's constitution provides for religious freedom of all faiths. To date there is no humanist movement.

EDUCATION

Primary school education is mandatory in Dominica. It lasts for seven years and ends with the common entrance exam. Secondary education was made universal in 2005 and lasts for five years. It is completed by pupils sitting examinations for the Caribbean Examinations Council Secondary Education Certificate, or GCE O Levels. There are also a number of non-governmental primary and secondary schools operating on the island.

Dominica's State College opened its doors in September 2002. Its formation amalgamated a number of disparate tertiary education establishments under one roof with the aim of better organising standards, policies and opportunities. The college offers further education in traditional as well as vocational subjects such as hospitality and tourism, nursing, agriculture and teacher training.

The University of the West Indies (UWI) Open Campus offers Dominicans the opportunity to enrol in some degree programmes that may take place entirely within Dominica, or may be split between the Dominica school and the main UWI campus.

Dominica's tertiary education system receives small but welcome boosts through scholarships that are awarded by individuals, organisations or governments. It is through such scholarships that talented Dominicans of all backgrounds are able to pursue further education in institutions abroad that, under normal circumstances, would be well beyond the reach of most pockets.

CULTURE

Following the decline and subsequent retreat of the Kalinago population to the northeast of the island, it was left to the European colonists and their west African slaves to stamp a new cultural identity upon the rugged face of Dominica. Of the Europeans it was the French who made the greatest impression, due largely to the proximity of Guadeloupe and Martinique, and the movement of traders and free coloured *mulattos* – a term once used to describe people of both black and white parentage but which is now regarded by many as derogatory due to its association with slavery. African tribal traditions including dance, dress and belief systems merged with the culture of France, from the dances and festivals of its royal courts to the language, music and fashions of its Caribbean settlers. Whilst Kalinago place names fared better than those concocted by the British, it was without doubt the emergent **French Creole** that dominated the cultural landscape of Dominica from the 19th century onwards. Despite Dominica becoming a British Crown Colony, Creole culture not only survived, it continued to prevail in the villages and among the island's freed slaves.

Today Creole is one of the essential ingredients of Dominica's heritage and, together with a fresh perspective of Kalinago history and tradition, and the revival of a turbulent African legacy, a bewitching brew of the past merges with the present to leave us with a multi-cultural bouillon of sound, colour, word, and a little bit of magic.

TRADITIONAL COSTUME Commonly worn by women from the 1800s to the 1960s, the *wob dwiyet* is now only seen at national festivals such as the Creole and Independence celebrations that take place during October and November each year. Starting life as a dress worn on Sundays or feast days when slave women were able to discard their drab uniforms and dress up in the kind of colours to which they were more accustomed, the traditional Creole *wob dwiyet* dress was born. Over the years the style has been modified and accessories have been added to develop this attire, but the combination of bright skirt over white chemise, with lace adornments, coloured head scarf and kerchief is in essence the same as the national dress that is worn today.

The wearer of the *wob dwiyet* is known as the *matador* and for formal occasions she may choose to wear a headpiece, or *tête en l'air*, made of a square piece of **madras**. This square of Indian cotton, made by the Kalabari in the vicinity of Chennai (formerly Madras), was known as the *mouchoir madras* and became very popular with Creole women towards the end of the 18th century. French, English and Portuguese merchants were involved in the trade of madras, or *injiri*, as it is known in India, around 400 years ago. It is thought these merchants brought the material to west Africa where it was worn by the Igbo in southern Nigeria. Traditionally madras was made with vegetable dyes which ran, or 'bled', each time the material was washed, becoming blurred over time. Today most madras is still made in India but with chemical dyes.

MUSIC AND DANCE Traditional music and dance finds its roots in the island's history. From the slaves of west Africa and the influences of their British and French oppressors, songs, music and dance emerged that can still be enjoyed today. The drum, or *la peau cabwit*, provides a traditional beat that has echoes of Africa, whereas lyrics are often sung by women in an enchanting French Creole.

The *bélé* is a Creole dance of African origin. The *tambou twavail* or *tambou bélé* drum is the centrepiece and the dance moves, particularly in the *bélé rickety* variant, reflect a courtship between the man and the woman as they move in turn towards the drum and its resonating rhythm. By the time the dance reaches its conclusion, the drum is booming loudly and the man and woman are dancing together with quick steps and vigorous body movements, symbolising their union.

The **quadrille** is a more formal square dance that originates in the French courts of the 19th century. Four couples traditionally dance together. The ladies, known as the *dam*, dance in *wob dwiyet* costume, with the men, known as the *kavalyé*, leading. Often referred to as 'heel and toe', the quadrille's style is aristocratic, graceful and elegant and today it is a key part of Dominica's Independence celebrations. Its traditional accompaniment is a **jing ping** band. This is usually a four-instrument ensemble that comprises a tambourine (*tambal*), a long boom pipe (*boumboum*), a rattle or scraper (*shak-shak*, or *gwage*), and an accordion which replaced the original bamboo flute. Other traditional dances include the **lancer**, a British version of the quadrille, and the **mazook**, which has its origins in the polka.

Dominica's popular music scene really began in the 1960s with **calypso** and **steelpan** music. These genres are still very popular and the Swinging Stars calypso band that was formed in Roseau in 1959 still performs to packed houses today, though the line-up has changed somewhat. In the 1970s a new Dominican music style called **cadence-lypso** became fashionable across the Caribbean. This music combined calypso with *kompa*, a Creole music genre from Haiti. Popular Dominican exponents of cadence-lypso include Ophelia Marie and Gordon Henderson with his band Exile One. **Zouk** music from Martinique and **soca** from Trinidad arrived in Dominica in the 1980s and eclipsed the cadence-lypso scene. Zouk takes its influences from reggae and salsa, and soca is a fusion of calypso and Trinidad's Indian music, sometimes called *chutney* music. One of Dominica's most popular soca bands, Windward Caribbean Kulture (WCK), combined cadence-lypso with jing ping to produce **bouyon** music, which has also become a very popular genre in Dominica, Martinique and Guadeloupe.

Dominica today has a number of very talented musicians playing an assortment of traditional styles as well as jazz, reggae, soul and R&B. International recording artists from Dominica include Ophelia Marie, Nelly Stharre, Nasio Fontaine and Michele Henderson (see page 62 for more about Dominica's contemporary musicians).

CARNIVAL The festival of Carnival, or *Mas Domnik*, that takes place on the Monday and Tuesday before Ash Wednesday each year, is a time when Dominicans party hard, 'jump up', 'free up' and really let their hair down. Although today the music is a modern combination of calypso, steelpan and bouyon, often transported in electronic format with huge amplifiers and speakers crammed on to flat-bed trucks, the colourful costumes and the spirit of dancing are still tantalising reflections of the past. French settlers may have brought the festival of *masquerade* to Dominica, but it was the African slaves who added a raw rhythm, vibrancy and just a hint of rebellion. It is that colour, spirit and edge that is still in evidence in today's carnival.

The calypsos that are sung in competition prior to Carnival hark back to the *chante-mas*, a tradition of song and satire that evolved as part of the preparations for carnival. The female *chanteulles* would sing short, cutting ballads that ridiculed administrators or perpetrators of bad deeds. Today calypso songs are much longer, though the lyrics still contain a large dose of irony or political and social commentary.

Carnival costumes were originally little different from those worn in African tribal festivals. Today they are of modern materials and design, although one or two original themes survive. Most notable is the **sensay** costume, its fierce mask and horned headpiece with ruffles of cloth strips completely covering the wearer and cascading in layers from the head down to the ground.

ARCHITECTURE Many of the small wooden houses that can be seen in villages across Dominica are based on a simple design that goes back to the days of the earliest settlers. These small houses, called *ti kai* or *kai kwéyòl*, typically have a half-hip shingle roof designed for hurricanes, quick water run-off and to provide air circulation. They have a small veranda, jalousie-style windows with strong hurricane shutters and are sometimes raised on piles or pillars. Today the roofs are often made of modern galvanised steel which sound like thunder when it rains. Elements of the French Creole style are evident in some of the older buildings across Dominica, but especially in the French Quarter in Roseau. King George V Street provides an excellent example of beautiful verandas, jalousie windows, wooden shutters, ornate and intricately designed fretwork beneath the eaves of the upper floors.

Unfortunately due to fire, sackings and hurricanes, many of Dominica's original buildings are gone. Those that remain and are being preserved, however, offer a glimpse into the island's colonial past. There are some interesting military fortifications and ruins such as those at Cachacrou, Fort Young, Fort Shirley and Capuchin. Also there are a number of estate houses and ruins of estate buildings dotted across the island. Bois Cotlette, Clarke Hall and Morne Rouge estates are great examples. The Kalinago Barana Auté, or Kalinago model village by the sea, is an interesting representation of traditional Kalinago building design and construction.

Dominica is beginning to recognise the value of its architecture in terms of cultural heritage and as a visitor attraction. Unfortunately a number of historical buildings have either been neglected or torn down and replaced by something more modern and made of concrete. Obtaining sufficient support and funding for restoration projects is always a problem but hopefully an increasing number of visitors expressing an interest in the architectural heritage of Dominica will help to generate a greater concern for architectural preservation throughout the island.

ARTISTS One of Dominica's most famous historic painters is actually Italian. Born in Rome in 1730, **Agostino Brunias** was hired by Sir William Young, governor of Dominica in 1771, as his personal artist. Brunias fell in love with the island and stayed there until his death in 1796. During his life he painted many scenes of Dominica: detailed images of people working the fields, washing, cooking and dancing that offer an interesting insight into the Dominica of the day. Brunias's works were reproduced in prints, many of which left the country. You can see examples of his work in the Dominica Museum opposite the Roseau cruise ship berth.

Today Dominica has a number of very talented artisans including painters, illustrators and sculptors. Here is a selection.

Painters A young Dominican artist, **Shadrach Burton**'s scenic landscapes are inspired by the beauty of his island. For more information visit his website: www.shadrachburton.com.

Earl Etienne is perhaps the country's most established contemporary artist. Though his style changes, he is best known for his technique of *bouzzaille* which incorporates smoke and soot patterns from which images of Dominican folk life emerge. His paintings of traditional *bélé* are also excellent. Earl Etienne has a gallery called **the art asylum** located in the community of Jimmit on the west coast. For more information: www.earletienne.com.

Hilroy Fingal is an artist who is inspired by Dominica's natural environment and its African heritage. His colourful paintings and intricately decorated calabash bowls are on display at his home in Canefield (he hopes to establish a gallery here) and at Jungle Bay Resort & Spa (see page 155).

Marie Frederick was born in France and now lives and works in Dominica. Her inspiration is the daily life of the island and she paints in acrylic, ink, watercolour and oil. Her unique Indigo studio and gallery is located in the northern village of Borne. For more information: www.indigo.wetpaint.com.

Glenford John was born in Dominica and now lives in New Jersey. His colourful paintings are heavily influenced by the natural environment and culture of his island home. For more information: www.glenford-john.artistwebsites.com.

Pauline Marcelle is a modern artist who has received international acclaim at exhibitions in New York and Vienna, where she now lives. Her artworks use the media of paintings, objects, film and text. For more information: www.paulinemarcelle.com.

Petros Meaza was born in Ethiopa and now lives and works in Dominica. His colourful paintings are inspired by his new home and the spirit of his native Africa. For more information: www.petrosart.com.

Ellingworth Moses is a Dominican artist who paints scenery and very colourful abstracts that incorporate the use of thread. He has a gallery at 27 King George V St, Roseau, and a website: www.emosesart.com.

Lowell Royer is an up-and-coming Dominican artist whose works in acrylics are colourful, eye-catching and beautiful depictions of people and life on the island. For more information http://lowell-royer.fineartamerica.com.

Arnold Toulon was born in Dominica and now lives in St Lucia. In 1994 he gave up using 'contrived' paint brushes and replaced them with used phone cards and an ice pick. His thought-provoking work is exhibited in St Lucia and around the Caribbean.

David G Wilson is a self-taught painter whose anthropomorphic works are captivating. Born in Dominica and now living in New York, Wilson also works with sculpture. For more information: www.davidgwilson.com.

Other artists really worth looking out for include: Carla Armour, Lennon Jno Baptiste, Alwin Bully, Tiffany Burnette-Biscombe, Gharan Burton, Tam Joseph, Bernard Richards, Kelo Royer, Carol Sorhaindo and Paul Toulon.

A special mention should also be made for **Ronald Moreau** who, despite having cerebral palsy, has a great ability to draw. He specialises in the buildings of Roseau and has a talent for straight lines, dimensions and symmetry. Ronald is a big fan of Carnival and usually leads the costume parade, so look out for him. For more information about Ronald, and all of Dominica's other talented painters, please enquire at the Old Mill Cultural Centre in Canefield. You will also find paintings on display and for sale at a number of hotels and restaurants around the island.

Sculptors

Sculptors Born in England and now living in Dominica, **Roger Burnett** is a figurative sculptor, watercolour painter and illustrator. His studio is located in Antrim Valley, between Roseau and Pont Cassé. For more information: www.sculpturestudiodominica.com.

Louis Desire is a Haitian-born sculptor who lives and works in Dominica. His wood carvings are quite exquisite and much sought-after. His studio is next to the Old Mill Cultural Centre.

Peter Giraud is a self-taught, philosophic sculptor from Dominica who now lives in Canada. His fine art works have been exhibited throughout the Caribbean. For more information: www.gallerygiraud.com.

Other artisans

Other artisans Dominica is home to some very imaginative and talented craftspeople who create ornaments, batiks, calabash bowls and bags, jewellery, masks and so on. Here are just a few. Please look out for them and others when you are out shopping for mementos.

Bongo Moon, aka Peter Thomas, who makes drums and a variety of imaginative craft works from coconuts. He sells his wares around Roseau.

Albert Casimir has been hand-carving wooden wall decorations and jewellery for many years. He has a small shop over the Roseau River in Pottersville, Roseau. For more information: www.dominicanwoodcarver.com.

Ezekiel Jno Baptiste is a calabash carver from La Plaine. He makes wall hangings, bags, bowls, cups and lamps. You can usually find his work in Cocorico Boutique, Roseau.

JP Bumby creates batik and shibori fabrics, and produces table cloths, wraps, and sarongs in her textile studio in the village of Trafalgar.

Patricia Charpentier is a very talented ceramic mosaic artist and calabash carver who is based at Citrus Creek Plantation near La Plaine. Patricia also makes essential oils.

Jannice De Gallerie makes batik and tie-dye design wraps, bags and shirts. She has a shop on Fields Lane, Roseau.

Julien James of Natural Mystic Creation is from the west coast village of Tarou. He makes jewellery and other trinkets from coconut shells and calabash. The boutiques in Roseau sometimes have his pieces.

Israel Joseph (*Nom Fwigè film; www.paulcrask.com*) carves masks from tree ferns. He has a shop by the side of the road in Mahaut River in the Kalinago Territory. His wife, Victoria, makes traditional *larouma* basketware.

Julie Joseph of Green Eye Productions creates very original carvings in wood and *fougère* (tree fern). He has a small shop and gallery located on the west coast highway near the bridge in Loubiere.

Andy Manly of Caribbean Creative makes wooden furniture, lighting and hand-blown glassware. He is also an interior designer. For more information: www.caribbeancreative.com.

Virginia Peter has a small company called Art Natur-El. She creates very original artwork and bookmarks from natural materials.

Beatrice Pfister from the village of Mero makes jewellery from seeds and patchwork bags from a variety of materials. Check the boutiques in Roseau.

Carol Sorhaindo makes very original cards using banana leaves. She is also a talented artist, painting Dominica scenery on canvass and stone.

You are sure to come across many more skilled craftspeople on your travels, especially as you pass through the Kalinago Territory where many basket weavers and calabash bowl carvers have roadside stalls. Patronise them if you can. A little goes a long way in Dominica.

WRITERS, POETS AND STORYTELLERS Dominica's two most famous literary icons, Jean Rhys and Phyllis Shand Allfrey, lived around the same time and were daughters of British settlers. In more recent times a number of home-grown writers have achieved success and today, thanks to the Nature Island Literary Festival and Book Fair (see page 63), the Dominica Writers Guild, and a growing movement of talented young poets, there continues to be a healthy interest in the written and spoken word.

Jean Rhys was born in Cork Street, Roseau in 1890. Her father was a Welsh doctor and her mother a member of the Lockhart family who owned the Geneva Estate at Grand Bay. Rhys left Dominica at the age of 16 for schooling in England, during which time the Geneva Estate house was razed to the ground by arsonists. In 1936 she made a last trip to Dominica which included a visit to the remains of Geneva, and it was the attacks on this family estate that were reflected in the burning of 'Coulibri' in her acclaimed 1966 novel, *Wide Sargasso Sea*. Jean Rhys died in 1979.

Phyllis Shand Allfrey was born in 1908, a year after Jean Rhys left Dominica for England. In 1954 her only novel, *The Orchid House*, was published. It is a largely biographical story of the three daughters of a once wealthy but now impoverished white family, told through the eyes of Lally, a black nurse. The book received praise and was even made into a film for British television. A grass roots activist and Fabian socialist, Allfrey returned to Dominica in 1954 and founded the Dominica Labour Party, the country's first political party. Phyllis Shand Allfrey died in 1986.

Elma Napier was born in Scotland in 1892 but settled in Dominica in 1932 where she spent the remainder of her life. She lived with her husband at Pointe Baptiste (see page 194) and became the first woman to be elected to a Caribbean legislature. She loved exploring the island and wrote an autobiography of her life in Dominica called *Black And White Sands*. Napier died in 1973 was was buried next to her husband 'in a quiet place under trees' at the Pointe Baptiste Estate.

Lennox Honychurch is the author of a number of educational books including *The Dominica Story – A History of the Island*, first published in 1975, and still Dominica's definitive historical reference. A Doctor of Philosophy and an anthropologist, Dominica-born Honychurch is also an artist, poet and conservationist. He is actively involved in the preservation of historical sites, including Fort Shirley in the Cabrits National Park (see page 184).

Irving André is a novelist. His work *A Passage to Anywhere* is the poignant story of a young man's journey into adulthood and the decision to stay in Dominica or seek his fortune abroad. Other works by André include *Distant Voices* and *The Island Within*.

Gabriel Christian is a novelist whose work includes *Rain on a Tin Roof* which is a collection of short stories portraying life in Dominica.

Giftus John is a storyteller and poet. His book *Mesyé Kwik! Kwak!* is a collection of short stories set against the backdrop of the west coast village of St Joseph where he grew up. He has also written a collection of poems called *The Island Man Sings His Song*.

Alick Lazare is a writer and poet. His popular novel *Pharcel* tells the story of a Maroon, a runaway slave, in colonial Dominica.

For more about Dominica's writers and further reading please see *Appendix 3* on page 257.

Kont is a form of traditional storytelling that draws upon history, superstition and legend. **Lawrence Brumant** of the northern village of Paix Bouche (see page 191) is one of Dominica's most well-known tellers of *kont* with stories such as *How Dominica Got its Name*, *The Wise Lawyer* and *Désirée*.

FOLKLORE Dominican culture is embellished with a number of colourful myths and legends that have their origins in the spirit tales, practices and beliefs of west African tribes as well as in later Creole folkloric influences. For some Dominicans this lore extends beyond simple superstition and is still to be found lurking in the shadows of the island's more contemporary practices and belief systems.

Obeah, a kind of magic or witchcraft, is still practised by traditional shamans or herbalists. Based on a belief in supernatural forces that can forge or quell evil spirits, Obeah men or Obeah women may be engaged to cast spells or create potions.

There are two night spirits the unassuming visitor may wish to look out for. The *soucouyan* of west African origin sheds her skin and flies through the forest in a ball of flames on the lookout for the blood of people and animals. If her skin happens to be found it can be rubbed with salt to make it difficult and painful for her to put back on, or alternatively a calabash of peas can be placed next to it which she must count before she is able to transform herself back into a human. Successful escape from a *soucouyan* may just place you in the hands of **La Diablesse**, however, which is altogether bad news. This beautiful woman walking through the forest by the light of the moon lures men deeper and deeper into the woods, where she transforms herself into a wild old crone who causes her victims to either go mad or die. Avoiding the *soucouyan* and La Diablesse does not mean you are out of those deep woods just yet, however. Go for a swim in a river and you may come across **Mama Glo**, a female spirit of lakes and rivers who also takes on the appearance of a beautiful woman or even a mermaid. She may command you to undertake a series of menial tasks with a promise of reward, but if you choose to disobey she may turn very nasty indeed. Take a nap on the forest floor and you may be visited by a *jombie*, or evil spirit. If it finds you sleeping, the *jombie* could destroy your health or bring you a lifetime of bad luck. Fortunately there is a remedy for its curse. Unfortunately it requires the help of Obeah....

2

Practical Information

WHEN TO VISIT

The busiest time of year is the annual cruise ship season which starts in November and runs for six months until the end of April. During this period there can be two, three, sometimes even four ships calling at the same time. Lots of buses and taxis taking these day-visitors on tours means that certain roads can become a little congested, some of the more accessible sites rather crowded, and Roseau gets a little steamier and noisier than usual. It is also more difficult to catch a public bus as many drivers drop their village routes in favour of the more lucrative tour business. Whatever the pros and cons of cruise ships, it is certainly a lively time of year, and full of vibrancy as Dominica experiences a temporary population explosion with visitors from the US, Canada and Europe escaping cold winter climates back home. Dominica's weather at this time of the year is usually good. November and December can be a little unpredictable as the seasons change from wet to dry, but from January onwards the clouds on the west coast become fewer and the air and sea temperatures begin to rise again. Visitors should note, however, that Dominica's topography makes it rather a wet island, especially in the elevated forests of the interior, and you should always be prepared for showers or even the occasional short but heavy downpour.

Late October and early November is the time for Independence celebrations, Creole Week, and Dominica's World Creole Music Festival. This is one of the best times for culture vultures and music lovers to visit Dominica, though accommodation, flights to the island and the inter-island ferry do get full very quickly and should therefore be booked well in advance. The music festival attracts people from around the world but especially those from the French-speaking islands of Guadeloupe and Martinique. Access routes from those countries in particular can become very congested.

Carnival preparations and events start in January and reach their peak on the Monday and Tuesday before Ash Wednesday. This is a real party period in Dominica with around-the-clock festivities. Dominica's diaspora, living in the UK and North America, often choose to come home to visit family at this time of year and, combined with the efforts to promote Carnival as a tourist attraction, it is becoming a busy occasion. Many Dominicans love and look forward to absolutely any reason to party and Carnival is the biggest excuse of them all. You can enjoy the street parades, the 'jump-up' dancing and drinking, and the Carnival Queen and Calypso Monarch competitions. Though it is certainly not on a par with anything that Rio produces, Dominica's own, unique version of Carnival is an extremely colourful and lively time to be on the island, and definitely worth the experience.

The weather from January to June is hot and, on the west coast, usually quite dry. April, May and June are great months for hiking the interior and climbing the high peaks as cloud cover is usually minimal and views across the island are often unrestricted. Trails, though in places wet all year round, become a little less so at this time of the year and rivers and waterfalls are far more predictable. As the cruise ship season has wound down by now, the more popular and accessible sites are also less crowded.

The Atlantic hurricane season starts in July and ends in November, though it usually peaks in the Caribbean region in the months of August and September. Hurricanes form on the west coast of Africa or mid-Atlantic and make their way westwards towards the Caribbean and the Gulf of Mexico. Whether tropical depressions become tropical storms and then develop into hurricanes is down to sea temperatures, high and low pressure areas and wind shear. Due to the island's vulnerability during this period, August and September tend to be very quiet months and many hotels and tour operators choose to close and take a holiday themselves.

HIGHLIGHTS

The **Boiling Lake** (see page 123) is perhaps Dominica's best-known natural attraction. In actual fact it is probably the hike there that is the highlight rather than the destination itself. It takes the best part of a day, but if you have the time and energy you definitely should take on the challenge. After a hike, consider a long hot soak in one of the **hot sulphur spas of Wotten Waven** (see page 89). Try out the very popular Screw's or one of the more intimate alternatives such as Ti Kwen Glo Cho or Tia's.

Dominica has countless waterfalls. Unmissable are the **Trafalgar Falls** (see page 121). The viewing platform is very accessible but if possible you should try to make it to the pools. The 'father' falls is particularly special. A short though tricky hike along the White River brings you to the spectacular **Victoria Falls** (see page 174). Also on the east coast, a similar river and forest hike takes you to the equally impressive **Sari Sari Falls** (see page 173). Though they should never be attempted during periods of heavy rains, these two waterfalls are definitely worth seeing. In the heart of the interior, the twin **Spanny Falls** (see page 224) are good fun and their pools are nice for bathing. Children and adventurous adults will love the rope climb to the second waterfall. One of Dominica's more unusual falls, but also worth the rather toe-curling trip is **Wavine Cyrique** (see page 175). It is not for the faint-hearted.

If your schedule allows and you have the energy, you should try to get to the top of at least one of Dominica's peaks. **Morne Anglais** (see page 146) probably has the best all round views though **Morne Micotrin** (see page 128) is also very rewarding. Of Dominica's two highest peaks, you have the best chance of good views on **Morne Trois Pitons** (see page 131) and the challenging climb is great fun.

Notable hikes with a difference include **Jacko Steps** (see page 224) which has a fascinating history as well as an unforgettable wade along a gorgeous stretch of the Layou River. **Horseback Ridge** (see page 172) in the Kalinago Territory, though driveable, is a lovely walk. It has panoramic interior and coastal views and also offers an opportunity to interact with Kalinago people. The **Red Rocks** (see page 200) at Pointe Baptiste should certainly be on your agenda. A short and very easy trail brings you to this unusual coastal formation. Combine it with a walk to and a swim in the lovely **La Chaudiere** pool near Bense or a bathe in the sea at **Woodford Hill Beach**, a beautiful stretch of sand that is comparable to any in the Caribbean.

In addition to the Boiling Lake, Dominica has several other lakes that are worth seeing. The **Freshwater Lake** can be eerie and cloud covered, but a hike along the circular trail is an interesting way to experience the diversity of Dominica's natural history and, if the mist does clear, there are good views of Dominica's volcanoes as well as down to the coast at Rosalie. **Lake Mathieu** (see page 219), or 'Miracle Lake', was formed in 1997 by a massive landslide. It is now Dominica's largest lake and worth a visit.

Hiking enthusiasts will enjoy all 14 segments of the 200km **Wai'tukubuli National Trail**. Whether you take on their entire challenge or just part of it, you will discover that walking Dominica is absolutely the best way to experience the essence and diversity of the island.

The adventurous should also go **scuba diving** (see page 82) and if you have not done it before, take a try-dive or a certification course. It is worth it. Imagine everything you see above water reflected below it; to experience Dominica fully you really have to get wet. Easy conditions along the west coast also make it a good place to learn. And on the subject of adventure, try **canyoning** (see page 74). If hiking takes you on and across Dominica and scuba diving plunges you beneath it, then canyoning brings you right into the heart of the island.

Don't miss the **Kalinago Territory**. The **Kalinago Barana Auté** (see page 160) at Crayfish River is an interesting experience; a model village showing how Dominica's indigenous people used to live. **Kalinago Touna Auté** (see page 162) at Concord is a living village, giving you the opportunity to meet and interact with Kalinago people and see how they live today. This is an adventurous project that is different, interesting and worth supporting. Take home some Kalinago craft, especially *larouma* basketware (see page 159).

Creole Week (see page 62) is a nice time to come to Dominica. Traditional costume, dancing, Creole in the Park and the World Creole Music Festival all take place during this period. There are a variety of heritage events throughout October and they end in the first week of November with Independence celebrations. If you enjoy culture, tradition, music and food, then this will be for you.

SUGGESTED ITINERARIES

Instead of suggesting itineraries for a week, two weeks and so on, I thought it would be more useful to create 14 different days that you could then use to plan your ideal holiday schedule. I have also named some places to eat which are good at the time of writing but may obviously change over time. Check updates.bradtguides.com/dominica for updates.

- The Boiling Lake hike followed by a swim up Ti Tou Gorge and then a hot sulphur bath at Wotten Waven to work on those tired muscles. Dinner in or around Roseau; try Sea Lounge, Talipot, Ancient Capital or Le Bistro.
- Cabrits National Park, Fort Shirley, a swim at Purple Turtle Beach, and then a late afternoon trip up the Indian River. Purple Turtle is handy for lunch and there are several nice restaurants in this area for dinner. Try Iguana Café at Glanvillea for something a little different.
- Papillote Gardens, Trafalgar Falls, a massage, some yoga, and/or a hot sulphur bath at Wotten Waven. Papillote Wilderness Retreat and River Rock Cafe are good places for lunch in Trafalgar.
- La Chaudiere, Red Rocks, Woodford Hill Beach. Escape Bar & Grill at Pointe Baptiste, Coral Reef or Calabash in Calibishie, or perhaps Pagua Bay near Marigot for something to eat.
- Victoria Falls and Sari Sari Falls (but only when it isn't raining). Citrus Creek at Taberi is a nice place for a late lunch and a bathe in the river. The restaurant at Jungle Bay is also handy.

2

- Wavine Cyrique followed by Twa Basens to cool and clean off. Again, Citrus Creek or perhaps a trip down to the restaurant at Jungle Bay are good dining options. If you are heading back towards Roseau, Emerald Pool is on the way.
- Horseback Ridge followed by a stroll around Kalinago Barana Auté. Have lunch there or head down towards Castle Bruce and call in at Islet View Restaurant or Domcan's. Again, if you are heading back to Roseau, consider taking in Emerald Pool.
- Snorkelling at Champagne then down to Scotts Head for a climb up to the top of Cachacrou and then a swim to cool off. Late lunch and a cold beer in Scotts Head. Chez Wen and Rogers are both good choices.
- Climb Morne Trois Pitons and follow it with a cool down in the Layou River. Afterwards, head to the beach at Mero where there are several nice places for drinks and eats.
- Hike to Middleham Falls from the Laudat end, or walk the circular trail around the Freshwater Lake. Go for a swim up Ti Tou Gorge and then head down to Trafalgar. Grab a bite to eat at Papillote or River Rock, then take in the Trafalgar Falls. End your day with a late afternoon hot sulphur bath at Wotten Waven.
- Have breakfast in Roseau (try Cocorico) and then take a look around the town. Walk through the French Quarter and then up to the Botanical Gardens. Take the Jack's Walk trail to the top of Morne Bruce. Head south to Scotts Head or north to Mero for a swim.
- Drive up to Bells and do the Jacko Steps hike. Afterwards, if you still have the energy, take in the Spanny Falls. Finish up at a beach bar in Mero.
- Spend a day canyoning and follow it up with a hot sulphur bath at Wotten Waven.
- Spend a morning scuba diving, zip-lining at Wacky Rollers Adventure park or enjoying a ride on the Rainforest Aerial Tram. After lunch, chill out in the Botanical Gardens, and maybe watch a game of cricket.

TOUR OPERATORS

There are some international tour operators who offer flight and accommodation packages to Dominica, but not that many. They tend to offer accommodation in the larger and better known hotels only or they specialise in activity packages such as scuba diving. By far the most flexible way to arrange a holiday to Dominica

MY TOP TEN HIKES

If your hiking time is limited, here is my top ten.

The Boiling Lake (from either Ti Tou Gorge or Freshwater Lake; see pages 123 and 212)
Wai'tukubuli National Trail segment 12 (see page 249)
Wai'tukubuli National Trail segment 4 (see page 235)
Wai'tukubuli National Trail segment 8 (see page 242)
The Freshwater Lake circular trail (see page 126)
Jacko Steps (see page 224)
Morne Trois Pitons (see page 131)
Morne Anglais (see page 146)
Perdu Temps (see page 150)
Sari Sari Falls (see page 173)

is to work out your own itinerary (see above for ideas) and then book flights, accommodation and transport via the internet or over the phone.

INTERNATIONAL OPERATORS Here are some international operators offering flights, accommodation and specialist activity packages to Dominica:

AdventureFinder US; www.adventurefinder.com
Caradonna Dive Adventures US: ↘ 1 800 328 2288; Canada: ↘ 1 800 803 1383; www.caradonna.com
Newmont Travel UK; ↘ 020 8920 1155; www.newmont.co.uk

Responsible Travel UK; ↘ 01273 600030; www.responsibletravel.com
Spafari US; ↘ 1 800 488 8747; www.globalfitnessadventures.com

LOCAL AGENTS Here are some local agents offering both accommodation and/or activity packages:

Decide On Dominica ↘ 767 255 1104; e pamela.richards@whitchurch.com; www.decideondominica.com. This operator will organise everything for you – from international & connecting flights to accommodation, tours, even weddings.

Travel Barefoot ↘ 767 449 3372; toll free US & Canada: ↘ 71 800 252 1993; e info@travelbarefoot.com; www.travelbarefoot.com. This tour operator offers a wide range of packages & can also organise accommodation, island tours, car rentals, scuba diving & more.

WEDDING SERVICES The tourism authorities of Dominica are very actively promoting the island as a wedding destination with a difference. Instead of blue seas and white sand beaches, they suggest you choose to have your wedding and honeymoon set against a backdrop of rainforest, waterfalls and so on instead. Several hoteliers offer honeymoon packages; check their websites. The following also offer all inclusive bespoke wedding packages.

Fort Young Hotel ↘ 767 448 5000; e fortyoung@cwdom.dm; www.fortyounghotel.com. For more information see page 100.

Jungle Bay Resort & Spa ↘ 767 446 1789; e info@junglebaydominica.com; www.junglebaydominica.com. For more information see page 155.

Marriage requirements At the time of writing, amendments to the Marriage Act were afoot. These changes proposed to eliminate a minimum period of time that you must be on island prior to the ceremony (the current version of the Act states you must be on island for two days). The reason for this is to attract extra wedding business from cruise ship passengers. Other changes would also make the process easier: an online application form which you could print and have signed by a magistrate, Justice of the Peace or Notary Public in your own country; and Dominica's religious ministers may be allowed to conduct marriage ceremonies in places other than the church. The following are the proposed licence fees: EC$300 or US$110 if you are resident on island for two days; EC$500 or US$185 if you are not resident on island; EC$500 or US$185 for a weekend or public holiday ceremony and marriage licence.

If you do not complete the proposed online application then both parties must be able to produce proof of citizenship (passport and birth certificate), proof of divorce if applicable, and a copy of a death certificate if you are a widow or widower. Please check www.dominica.dm for updates on weddings and marriage requirements.

TOURIST OFFICES

Dominica Discover Dominica Authority, 1st Flr Financial Centre, Roseau; ✎ 767 448 2045; e tourism@dominica.dm; www.dominica.dm
UK The Saltmarsh Partnership, The Copperfields, 25d Copperfield St, London SE1 0EN; ✎ 020 7928 1600; e dominica@saltmarshpr.co.uk

US Dominica Tourist Office, 110–64 Queens Bd, PO Box 427, Forest Hills, NY, 1137–6347; ✎ 718 261 9615; e dominicany@discoverdominica.com

RED TAPE

ENTRY REQUIREMENTS All visitors require a valid passport. You may also be asked to show either a return or an onward ticket. Arriving passengers must complete an immigration form which, if you have not been given one prior to landing in Dominica, you can pick up in the arrivals area. You must be able to provide details of your hotel or the address of family, friends etc so be sure to have this written down somewhere. Complete your form before standing in line or you may be sent to the back. There is no hurry; relax, you are on island time now.

CUSTOMS It is common practice for customs officers to ask you to open your luggage at ports of entry in Dominica, so do not think you are being singled out in any way. Arriving passengers must complete a customs declaration form and hand it to a customs officer prior to inspection. Usually the customs officer will ask you where you are staying, whether you are here on business or vacation, whether you are bringing any food items and so on. Just answer honestly, be polite and smile – even though you may be very hot, tired and ready for a rum punch and a shower by now! Among other things, you must be sure to declare fruits, plants, cut flowers, vegetables, meat, pharmaceuticals, toy guns, commercial merchandise and currency above US$10,000 or equivalent. If you are a smoker and like to roll your own, you should know that cigarette papers are very likely to be confiscated by customs officers.

DEPARTURE TAXES When you leave Dominica you have to pay departure tax of EC$59 (US$22) after check-in. Children under 12 are exempt.

CONSULATES AND EMBASSIES

Visitors from the United States and Canada should note that there is no representative consulate in Dominica. Instead you will be referred to your consulates in Barbados. For the other consulates listed, do not be surprised if you are put through to a Dominican business or law firm as that is where the consular representative may be located.

Belgium ✎ 767 448 2168
Canada (Barbados) ✎ 246 429 3550
Cuba ✎ 767 449 0727
France ✎ 767 448 0508
Germany ✎ 767 449 7395
Netherlands ✎ 767 448 3841
Norway ✎ 767 449 8300

People's Republic of China ✎ 767 449 0088
Spain ✎ 767 445 5355
Sweden ✎ 767 448 2181
UK ✎ 767 448 7655
US (Barbados) ✎ 246 436 4950
Venezuela ✎ 767 448 3348

BY AIR Dominica has two airports, both too small for commercial passenger jets. This means that for long-haul journeys you have to fly to another Caribbean island and then transfer to an inter-island air service. The most popular hubs are Puerto Rico, Antigua and Barbados.

Canefield Airport is in the southwest, just a few kilometres north of the capital Roseau. This airport is very small with a short runway and is predominantly used by small island hoppers, charter aircraft and courier services. Dominica's main airport is **Melville Hall Airport (DOM)** in the northeast. American Eagle and Liat both have scheduled flights to and from this airport.

Flights from the US and Canada
Most of the major North American airlines have flights to Antigua (ANU), Barbados (BGI) or St Martin/St Maarten (SXM) where there are regular connecting Liat, BVI Airways and Winair services to Dominica (see below). Please check their websites for latest prices and special offers.

American Airlines ☎ 1 800 433 7300; AA reservations desk at Melville Hall Airport ☎ 767 445 7204; www.aa.com. American Eagle flights are daily between San Juan, Puerto Rico (SJU) & Melville Hall, Dominica (DOM). Flight time is just under 2hrs. Please check for schedule variations.

Flights from the UK
Flights from the UK to Dominica are usually via Antigua, though it is also possible to fly via Barbados and St. Lucia. Prices are usually very similar. Flying to Antigua from the UK usually means a same-day connection to Dominica is possible. Please check tour operator or airline websites for latest prices, schedules and any special offers..

British Airways ☎ 0870 850 9850; www.britishairways.com. Flights are daily from London Gatwick (LGW) to Antigua (ANU), Barbados (BGI) & St Lucia (SLU).

Virgin Atlantic ☎ 0870 380 2007; www.virgin-atlantic.com. Flights are daily from London Gatwick (LGW) to Antigua (ANU), Barbados (BGI) & St Lucia (SLU).

Flights from France
Air France www.airfrance.com. Flights are daily from Paris Orly (ORY) to Guadeloupe (PTP) & Martinique (FDF) where inter-island flights or high-speed ferry services connect to Dominica.

Inter-island flight services and connections
BVI Airways www.gobvi.com. Operates scheduled inter-island flights between Dominica, St Maarten/St Martin & Tortola.

Liat ☎ 1 888 844 5428; Liat desk at Melville Hall Airport ☎ 767 445 7242; e reservations@liat.com; www.liat.com. Liat serves 22 destinations in the Eastern Caribbean & has its main hubs in Antigua & Barbados. Liat flights to & from Dominica arrive & depart from Melville Hall Airport.

Winair ☎ 1 866 466 0410; e reservations@fly-winair.com; www.fly-winair.com. Scheduled inter-island flights between Dominica, St Lucia & St Maartin/St Martin.

Melville Hall Airport
Though there is constant talk of an international airport one day, Dominica's Melville Hall Airport is currently the island's primary air terminus and will probably continue to be so for some time to come. It is located on the Atlantic Ocean shoreline of Londonderry Bay in the northeast of Dominica, between the villages of Marigot and Wesley. It has a very simple layout of departure and arrivals halls with a small bar and restaurant in between. Major airline check-

in desks (Liat and American Airlines) are clearly marked. You will also see a desk for the payment of your departure tax which you must do after checking in and before departing. The airport has an information office and an ATM located near the arrivals hall.

Once you have cleared immigration and customs you will exit the arrivals hall and be greeted by official Airport Taxi Association drivers asking if you need a ride. All prices and drivers are regulated and there is information posted on the wall outside the arrivals door. If you are unsure about anything, check at the tourist information booth. Confirm the price of the trip with the driver before leaving. If you are collecting a hire car, make your way past the restaurant and departure hall to the wooden buildings up the steps. Car hire firms have their desks here. Be sure to bring your domestic licence with you.

Baggage The **Liat** allowance for checked baggage is one piece at a maximum of 23kg (50lbs). The allowance for cabin baggage is one piece weighing no more than 7kg (15lbs).

The **American Eagle** allowance for checked baggage is two pieces totalling no more than 23kg each. The allowance for cabin baggage is one piece at a maximum of 7kg.

Please note that scuba gear is considered part of your checked bag allowance and so baggage charges may be applied if you are over the maximum weight.

Please check with airline websites for updates on baggage allowances and restrictions. Also make sure your checked bags are properly tagged with your name and address. Should your bags not turn up at the airport with you (sadly this does happen), make your way to the Liat or American Airlines check-in desk in the departure hall and complete the requisite forms. Usually baggage delays are short and you can expect your luggage to arrive the following day. There are exceptions to this rule, of course, especially during busy periods such as Carnival. Your hotel knows the score and will help you out.

BY FERRY A ferry service is operated between Dominica, Guadeloupe and Marie-Galante by **Caribbean Spirit** (✆ 767 445 5013; *www.caribbean-spirit.fr*). This service runs to and from the cruise ship berth at the Cabrits, Portsmouth. For schedules, prices and advance bookings check the website.

L'Express des Îles (*www.express-des-iles.com*) operates a high-speed ferry service between the islands of Guadeloupe (including Les Saintes), Dominica, Martinique and St Lucia. The ferry arrives at and departs from the terminal on Roseau's Bay Front regularly throughout the week, although the schedule does change at certain times of the year. For timetables, pricing and bookings see their website. Tickets and updated schedule information may also be obtained in Dominica from H H V Whitchurch Travel Agency (*Old St, Roseau;* ✆ 767 448 2181; f 767 448 5787; e *hhvwhitchurch@cwdom.dm; www.whitchurch.com*).

BY PRIVATE YACHT Visitors to Dominica arriving by private or charter vessel should contact the Dominica Port Authority on VHF channel 16. Customs clearance is mandatory before anchoring. Two copies of the crew and passenger list are required and you must pay an environmental levy. Ports of entry are in Portsmouth on the northwest coast, Roseau on the west coast, and Anse Du Mai on the east coast. While there is no properly established marina in Dominica, popular anchorages are Prince Rupert Bay on the northwest coast, Mero and Batali Bay on the mid-west coast, and Castle Comfort and Loubiere in the southwest. The

Soufriere Scotts Head Marine Reserve on the southern tip of Dominica is out of bounds as an anchorage.

Dominica's marina and provisioning services are fledgling but they are also very personal.

ALDive Loubiere; ☏ 767 440 3483; m 767 275 3483; e aldive@aldive.com; VHF CH16
Cobra Tours & Yacht Services Ltd Portsmouth; ☏ 767 245 6332 or 767 445 3333; e info@ cobratours.dm; VHF CH16
Dominica Marine Center Newtown, Roseau; ☏ 767 448 2705; m 767 275 2851; e info@ dominicamarinecenter.com; VHF CH16 or 19

Dominica Yacht Services Dive Dominica, Castle Comfort; ☏ 767 448 2188; e dive@ cwdom.dm
Pancho Services Castle Comfort; ☏ 767 448 1698; m 767 235 3698 or 767 295 0525; e panchoservices@yahoo.com

 HEALTH *Dr Felicity Nicholson*

BEFORE YOU GO There are no immunisation requirements for visitors to Dominica except proof of vaccination against **yellow fever** for those over one year of age if coming from a yellow fever endemic zone (eg: certain countries in sub-Saharan Africa and South America). If the vaccine has been deemed unsuitable for you, travellers should obtain an exemption certificate from a registered yellow fever centre (eg: some GPs and most travel clinics). If you are unsure whether this applies to you, then check with a doctor ideally before you leave home and at least ten days before entering Dominica. There is no endemic malaria but there are other mosquito borne diseases to avoid. Dominica's water is safe to drink though travellers who have particularly sensitive stomachs may wish to consider bottled water as an alternative. Even if the water is clean the different mineral content can lead to an upset stomach. It is recommended that standard vaccinations such as tetanus are up to date. These days **tetanus** is combined with **diphtheria** and **polio** in an all-in-one vaccine (Revaxis), which lasts for ten years. Travellers should also consider protecting themselves from **hepatitis A** and possibly **typhoid** for longer stays and more rural visits. Visitors requiring health care in Dominica are required to pay up front for treatment. Medical insurance is strongly recommended, particularly if participating in activities such as hiking or scuba diving. Ensure that your policy covers you for the activities you wish to enjoy. Vaccination against **hepatitis B** is recommended for long stays, for those working with children, or in a medical setting. Carriage of the virus in the local population is estimated at 2–10%. The course comprises three doses of vaccine given over a minimum of 21 days if time is short for those aged 16 or over. For those under 16 the minimum time to complete three doses is two months. Both these schedules require a booster dose in one year to give longer-lasting protection. Wherever possible the longer course of 0, 1, and 6 months is preferred for more sustained protection.

TRAVEL CLINICS AND HEALTH INFORMATION A full list of current travel clinic websites worldwide is available on www.istm.org/. For other journey preparation information, consult www.nathnac.org/ds/map_world.aspx. Information about various medications may be found on www.netdoctor.co.uk/travel.

UK
Berkeley Travel Clinic 32 Berkeley St, London W1J 8EL (near Green Park tube station); ☏ 020 7629 6233; ⏰ 10.00–18.00 Mon–Fri; 10.00–15.00 Sat

The Travel Clinic Ltd, Cambridge 41 Hills Rd, Cambridge CB2 1NT; ✆ 01223 367362; e enquiries@travelclinic.ltd.uk; www.travelcliniccambridge.co.uk; ⏰ 10.00–16.00 Mon, Tue & Sat, 12.00–19.00 Wed & Thu, 11.00–18.00 Fri

The Travel Clinic Ltd, Ipswich Gilmour Piper, 10 Fonnereau Rd, Ipswich IP1 3JP; ✆ 01223 367362; ⏰ 09.00–19.00 Wed, 09.00–13.00 Sat

Edinburgh Travel Health Clinic 14 East Preston St, Newington, Edinburgh EH8 9QA; ✆ 0131 667 1030; www.edinburghtravelhealthclinic.co.uk; ⏰ 09.00–19.00 Mon–Wed, 09.00–18.00 Thu & Fri. Travel vaccinations & advice on all aspects of malaria prevention. All current UK prescribed anti-malaria tablets in stock.

Fleet Street Travel Clinic 29 Fleet St, London EC4Y 1AA; ✆ 020 7353 5678; e info@fleetstreetclinic.com; www.fleetstreetclinic.com; ⏰ 08.45–17.30 Mon–Fri. Injections, travel products & latest advice.

Hospital for Tropical Diseases Travel Clinic Mortimer Market Centre, Capper St (off Tottenham Ct Rd), London WC1E 6JB; ✆ 020 7388 9600; www.thehtd.org; ⏰ Wed 13.00–17.00 & Fri 09.00–13.00. Consultations are by appointment only and are only offered to those with more complex problems. Check the website for inclusions. Runs a Travellers' Healthline Advisory Service (✆ 020 7950 7799) for country-specific information & health hazards. Also stocks nets, water purification equipment & personal protection measures. Travellers who have returned from the tropics & are unwell, with fever or bloody diarrhoea, can attend the walk-in emergency clinic at the hospital without an appointment.

InterHealth Travel Clinic 111 Westminster Bridge Rd, London SE1 7HR, ✆ 020 7902 9000; e info@interhealth.org.uk; www.interhealth.org.uk; ⏰ 08.30–17.30 Mon–Fri. Competitively priced, one-stop travel health service by appointment only.

MASTA (Medical Advisory Service for Travellers Abroad) At the London School of Hygiene & Tropical Medicine, Keppel St, London WC1E 7HT; ✆ 09068 224100 (this is a premium-line number, charged at 60p per minute); e enquiries@masta.org; www.masta-travel-health.com. For a fee, they will provide an individually tailored health brief, with up-to-date information on how to stay healthy, inoculations & what to take.

MASTA pre-travel clinics ✆ 01276 685040; www.masta-travel-health.com/travel-clinic.aspx. Call or check the website for the nearest; there are currently 50 in Britain. They also sell malaria prophylaxis, memory cards, treatment kits, bednets, net treatment kits, etc.

NHS travel websites www.fitfortravel.nhs.uk or www.fitfortravel.scot.nhs.uk. Provide country-by-country advice on immunisation & malaria prevention, plus details of recent developments, & a list of relevant health organisations.

Nomad Travel Clinics Flagship store: 3–4 Wellington Terrace, Turnpike Lane, London N8 0PX; ✆ 020 8889 7014; e turnpike@nomadtravel.co.uk; www.nomadtravel.co.uk; walk in or appointments ⏰ 09.15–17.00 every day with late night Thu. Also has clinics in west & central London, Bristol, Southampton & Manchester – see website for further information. As well as dispensing health advice, Nomad stocks mosquito nets & other anti-bug devices, & an excellent range of adventure travel gear. Runs a Travel Health Advice line on ✆ 0906 863 3414.

Trailfinders Immunisation Centre 194 Kensington High St, London W8 7RG; ✆ 020 7938 3999; www.trailfinders.com/travelessentials/travelclinic.htm; ⏰ 09.00–17.00 Mon, Tue, Wed & Fri, 09.00–18.00 Thu, 10.00–17.15 Sat. No appointment necessary.

Travelpharm www.travelpharm.com. The Travelpharm website offers up-to-date guidance on travel-related health & has a range of medications available through their online mini-pharmacy.

Irish Republic

Tropical Medical Bureau 54 Grafton St, Dublin 2; ✆ +353 1 2715200; e graftonstreet@tmb.ie; www.tmb.ie; ⏰ until 20.00 Mon–Fri & Sat mornings. For other clinic locations, & useful information specific to tropical destinations, check their website.

USA

Centers for Disease Control 1600 Clifton Rd, Atlanta, GA 30333; ↘ (800) 232 4636 or (800) 232 6348; e cdcinfo@cdc.gov; www.cdc.gov/travel. The central source of travel information in the USA. Each summer they publish the invaluable Health Information for International Travel.

Canada

IAMAT (International Association for Medical Assistance to Travellers) Suite 10, 1287 St Clair Street West, Toronto, Ontario M6E 1B8; ↘ 416 652 0137; www.iamat.org

Australia and New Zealand

TMVC (Travel Doctors Group) ↘ 1300 65 88 44; www.tmvc.com.au. 30 clinics in Australia & New Zealand, including: *Auckland* Canterbury Arcade, 174 Queen St, Auckland 1010, New Zealand; ↘ (64) 9 373 3531; e auckland@traveldoctor.co.nz; *Brisbane* 75a Astor Terrace, Spring Hill, Brisbane, QLD 4000, Australia; ↘ (07) 3815 6900; e brisbane@traveldoctor.com.au; *Melbourne* 393 Little Bourke St, Melbourne, Vic

South Africa

SAA-Netcare Travel Clinics ↘ 011 802 0059; e travelinfo@netcare.co.za; www.travelclinic.co.za. 11 clinics throughout South Africa.

IAMAT (International Association for Medical Assistance to Travelers) 1623 Military Rd, #279 Niagara Falls, NY 14304-1745; ↘ 716 754 4883; e info@iamat.org; www.iamat.org. A non-profit organisation with free membership that provides lists of English-speaking doctors abroad.

TMVC Suite 314, 1030 W Georgia St, Vancouver, BC V6E 2Y3; ↘ (604) 681 5656; e vancouver@tmvc.com; www.tmvc.com. One-stop medical clinic for all your international travel health & vaccination needs.

3000, Australia; ↘ (03) 9935 8100; e melbourne@traveldoctor.com.au; *Sydney* 428 George St, Sydney, NSW 2000, Australia; ↘ (2) 9221 7133; e sydney@traveldoctor.com.au **IAMAT (International Association for Medical Assistance to Travellers)** 206 Papanui Rd, Christchurch 5, New Zealand; www.iamat.org

TMVC NHC Health Centre, Cnr Beyers Naude & Waugh Northcliff; ↘ 0861 300 911; e info@traveldoctor.co.za; www.traveldoctor.co.za. Consult the website for clinic locations.

INSECT BITES

Mosquitoes and sand flies Although there is no risk of malaria in Dominica, mosquito bites can still spoil your trip. It is worth bringing insect repellent containing DEET (50–55% for preference) and ensuring you apply it both day and night when you are out and about. Scratching bites can result in open wounds and infections so try to resist. Most hotels in Dominica will either have mosquito screens or bed nets though you could consider taking your own to ensure that they are freshly impregnated with permethrin and do not have holes. Failing this, electric standing or ceiling fans usually work well as a night-time deterrent.

Dengue fever occurs throughout the Caribbean. This virus is transmitted by a day-biting mosquito (*Aedes aegypti*) which is why it is important to use insect repellents during the day. Use your sun screen first and the insect repellent second. If you are in forested areas then you would be advised to also wear long sleeved cotton clothing and trousers for added protection. There are four types of dengue fever for which there is currently no cure. Dengue is rarely fatal if you have not had it before. However, even a primary infection can be unpleasant and causes a fever, with a headache, joint and muscle pains and sometimes a rash. It can be likened to a prolonged attack of influenza. Repeated infections with different strains can lead to a more serious haemorrhagic form of the disease, which can result in death. It is important, therefore, to avoid mosquito bites whenever possible by applying a good insect repellent (see above) during the day as well as in the evening to avoid other biting insects.

Sand flies are members of the subfamily *phlebotominac* and are tiny blood-sucking insects. They are attracted to warm-blooded animals, such as you, and can sometimes be a nuisance on beaches and in areas of mangrove. As with the mosquito, the small bites of the female can irritate and become inflamed if you rub or scratch them. Insect repellent containing DEET will help.

Chiggers (*Trombicula alfreddugesi*) Chiggers are known locally as *bête wouj*, and are the parasitic larvae of the harvest mite that move to the tips of leaves and grasses. When you brush against them, they migrate to your body and then spend a time rummaging around, trying to find a nice protected warm spot (often beneath the waistband of underwear or in other places you would really rather they not venture) where they pierce your skin and suck up the tissue. An extremely irritating rash appears which is caused by an allergic reaction to the salivary secretions of the larvae which drop off the skin once they have had their fill of you. They leave you with the rash as a memento of their visit, however, which can develop into severe welts if you scratch them a lot or if you are particularly sensitive to having insects partying in your nether regions. Insect repellents containing DEET help to prevent them hopping aboard your body in the first place.

Biting ants These little chaps can catch the unaware by unpleasant surprise. Bites are usually the result of either standing and pausing on a nest or by brushing against or holding on to branches or foliage where ants are going about their business. They are all over you in seconds and their bites are like needles. Take care where you put your feet and hands and, if you have rested clothes or shoes anywhere, give them a good shake before putting them on again.

TRAVELLERS' DIARRHOEA Around 50% of travellers will get a bout of diarrhoea which can spoil a good holiday so it is always wise to take basic precautions. Try to be sure water is safe to drink. Even though the tap water may be fine in Dominica it is always wise to drink bottled water instead. You should clean your teeth in bottled water too. Avoid food that has been left around or looks like it has been reheated – buffet meals are often the worst culprits. Food should be thoroughly cooked and served piping hot. Remember to wash your hands before eating. If you do get diarrhoea, in most cases it will settle down after 24 hours with rest, drinking plenty of fluids and taking rehydration salts (eg: Electrolade). Many people these days prefer to stop the diarrhoea at the first sign. Using a single dose of the antibiotic ciprofloxacin (500mg) taken together with two Imodium or other stopping agent will do the trick in most cases. If the diarrhoea persists then a second tablet of ciprofloxacin can be taken 10–12 hours later with a single stopping agent. The ciprofloxacin should always be taken with plenty of fluids and alcohol must be avoided. If the diarrhoea comes with a fever and/or blood and/or slime then you should seek medical help immediately as it is important to get the correct diagnosis and if necessary the appropriate antibiotics. That said, by taking sensible precautions you can minimise your chances of getting diarrhoea while still being able to eat and enjoy local foods.

PRICKLY HEAT A very itchy red skin rash known as *miliaria*, or prickly heat, is caused by sweating a lot in humid weather conditions. This can be a common problem for visitors who are not used to tropical climates. Dead skin cells and bacteria block sweat glands and the skin becomes inflamed. Air conditioning, cold showers, calamine lotion or, in severe cases, steroid creams can bring relief. Aloe vera may also help. If you find you are suffering from heat rash, try to avoid exerting yourself for a couple of days to reduce sweating and give your skin a chance to recover. Cool shaded rivers and easily accessible waterfall pools are alternative outings, as is a nice shady bar with a fresh juice or a cold beer, of course.

DEHYDRATION, HEAT EXHAUSTION AND HEATSTROKE High temperatures, humidity, exertion and a lack of adequate fluids will inevitably result in dehydration, heat exhaustion and possibly heatstroke. It is incredibly easy to become dehydrated in a tropical climate. Most people do not even realise that their irritability, weariness and dizziness is actually due to a lack of water, and travellers frequently underestimate the volume of water they should consume to remain healthy. Exertion in the tropics can require up to three litres a day, which is quite a rehydration challenge. When out walking take as much water as you can carry – at least one to two litres per person. Drink plenty of water before hiking and drink at regular intervals during your outing. Do not wait until you are thirsty. Carbonated soft drinks or beer are no substitute for water.

Heat exhaustion occurs when the body's cooling system hits overdrive. Profuse sweating, pale clammy skin, fast shallow breathing, nausea, headaches, rapid weak pulse and stomach cramps are all signs of heat exhaustion. It is important to counter this quickly by trying to cool the body down. Sit in the shade, take a dip in a river or pool, drink plenty of water and relax.

Heatstroke can be fatal. This occurs when the body's cooling system has collapsed completely. Skin becomes hot and red, breathing slows and confusion and dizziness lead to unconsciousness. Cooling the body down is paramount and immediate medical assistance is essential.

SUN DAMAGE In a very short period of time the hot Caribbean sun will redden and burn your skin. Try to stay in the shade as much as you can, wear a hat, protect your skin with a sunscreen (at least SPF 20) and wear good-quality sunglasses to protect your eyes. Sun reflecting on the water can be especially damaging if you are exposed to it for too long without adequate protection. If your skin is not used to the sun, limit direct exposure as much as possible. Wearing a T-shirt to protect your back when snorkelling is also a good idea. If you absolutely must sunbathe, try to limit direct exposure to 20–30 minutes and stay out of the sun during the hottest part of the day. That will easily be enough. Sunburn is not only harmful to your skin, it is very painful and can ruin your holiday. Wearing light-coloured, loose shirts, skirts and trousers made from cotton is the best solution.

SCUBA DIVING INJURIES Certified scuba divers should always dive conservatively and within recreational dive limits. If you do not know what they are, or have forgotten, check with your certifying organisation. Do not dive beyond your training and avoid alcohol and strenuous activities before and immediately after dives. Diving in Dominica is mostly easy, though wall diving means you are exposed to very deep waters. Maintain good buoyancy and always check your depth and no decompression limits. Dive with a buddy but do not share a dive computer.

Decompression sickness can be avoided by diving conservative profiles, ascending slowly and making safety stops at 5m. Signs and symptoms of decompression sickness include tingling or numbness in extremities, aching joints, rashes, headaches, dizziness and nausea. If affected, request 100% pure oxygen and seek medical assistance. Decompression sickness can be fatal and whilst the most severe symptoms become apparent within the first two hours of surfacing, problems can emerge up to 24 hours after diving. Allow dive crew to help and advise you. They are trained in managing dive emergencies.

Dominica has a recompression chamber located at the Princess Margaret Hospital, Roseau. It is always a sensible precaution to take out dive insurance to cover the cost of any evacuation and emergency recompression treatments that may be required.

Emergencies ✆ 999
Princess Margaret Hospital Federation Drive, Roseau; ✆ 767 448 2231

Divers Alert Network (DAN) Americas ✆ 1 919 684 2948 for information; ✆ 1 919 684 4326 for diving emergencies

AQUATIC LIFE INJURIES Whether scuba diving, snorkelling or just having fun in the sea, it is always possible to pick up an injury from aquatic life. Dominica's seas are very safe, there are no dangerous sharks patrolling the shore, and aquatic life injuries tend to come from contact with sea urchins or small jellyfish. Sea urchins are bottom dwellers, usually found around rocks. They have sharp spines that can pierce the skin of your feet if you stand on them. Typically the tips of the spines break off and embed themselves under the skin. This can be very painful and if not treated may cause an infection. It is prudent to seek medical assistance. A local remedy for the removal of sea urchin spines is to heat up some soft wax (a special soft wax that can be bought at a pharmacy), place the hot wax over the affected area and cover with a bandage. Leave it on overnight and the spines disappear. Incredibly, it works.

Contact with small jellyfish can result in a small but painful sting. Rubbing makes it worse. If possible remove any visible traces of tentacles with tweezers (not with your fingers, as the tentacles still retain their sting) and douse the affected area with white vinegar. Most dive boats and operators will carry a bottle of white vinegar in their first aid kit especially for this type of injury.

You should also avoid contact with fire worms. They look a little like hairy caterpillars and you may see them crawling over rocks or reef formations in both deep and shallow water. Touching them causes the bristles to embed into your skin, resulting in irritation and a rash.

SEXUALLY TRANSMITTED DISEASES Unprotected sex is risky in any part of the world and Dominica is no exception. The official incidence of HIV infection is relatively low, however discrimination and the stigma attached to the disease may mean that reported cases do not reflect the true picture. Common sense and caution is the best advice. If you must indulge, use condoms or femidoms, which help reduce the risk of transmission – these are best bought from home to ensure their quality. If you notice any genital ulcers or discharge, get treatment promptly since these increase the risk of acquiring HIV. If you do have unprotected sex, visit a clinic as soon as possible; this should be within 24 hours, or no later than 72 hours, for post-exposure prophylaxis.

SAFETY

Dominica is a safe country for visitors. Precautions you should take here are no different from those you would take anywhere else in the world. It is usually very safe to walk around, both by day and by night. Most Dominicans are sensitive to issues concerning tourists and recognise that unpleasant experiences will inevitably affect everyone. There are extremely few incidents of visitors experiencing crime and when it does occur it is usually dealt with expediently by the authorities and penalties for the perpetrators are severe. As the population is small and anonymity almost impossible, offenders are quickly identified and prosecuted. Take common-sense precautions such as dressing conservatively, avoiding conflict and not flaunting wealth openly. If approached by people asking for money, either give them a dollar or two, or politely decline and walk on. Do not lose your temper or decide to give someone a lecture. It is simply not worth it and it will ruin your day. It is not uncommon for Dominicans themselves to admonish people they see asking visitors for money. If you do find yourself in a threatening situation your focus should be on getting through it as peacefully as possible and not fighting back.

Perhaps the riskiest part of any visit to Dominica is when driving. Some of the roads are challenging, often narrow with pot-holes, deep drainage gutters and sharp corners. Dominican driving practices also present you with a potential hazard. There appears to be no happy medium when it comes to the way local people drive and you should simply expect the unexpected. See page 52 for more information about both car hire and the challenges of driving in Dominica.

WOMEN TRAVELLERS

Inevitably as a visitor you will attract attention – whatever your gender or age. This attention should not, however, be misinterpreted as a threat. Dominica is a safe place and most people are either just curious, perhaps looking for a conversation or friendship, or interested in trying to make a few dollars. Try to relax and always be polite, even if you are not really in the mood for it.

Women travellers are likely to be more vulnerable to unwanted attention than men, but you should not let this spoil your experience nor prevent you from exploring and enjoying the island. The best advice, as always, is to use common sense. If you can, try to avoid going to remote places alone, both by day and by night, try to dress as conservatively as your taste in fashion will allow, and do not bathe topless. Consider carrying a flashlight at night and trying to blend in as much as you can. Wearing similar clothing to local people is one way of doing this, as is not wearing nor flaunting ostentatious jewellery. If you do attract unwanted attention from amorous men, be as polite and good humoured as possible in the way you express your wish to be left alone. Try to extract yourself as quickly from the situation as you can – the longer you converse, the harder it is to leave. Avoid conflict, resist becoming angry and do not try to humiliate or belittle those you feel are harassing you. Some recommend wearing dark sunglasses as this helps you avoid eye contact and may also enhance your confidence.

DISABLED TRAVELLERS

Dominica is not very disabled-traveller friendly. There are few provisions at hotels though some have ground floor rooms and a couple (Garraway and Fort Young, see page 100) also have elevators. Cottage style accommodation is also an option worth considering as many are fairly obstacle free.

Roseau, however, is a nightmare if you are in a wheelchair. Most footpaths are narrow and very uneven, often with drops, steps, gratings, potholes, vendors or parked cars to negotiate your way around. The road is your only option and then you have vehicular traffic to deal with. Most banks and ATMs are accessible.

Private minibus or taxi tours may be the most comfortable way for you to experience Dominica. Your hotel may also be able to arrange something specific to your needs. Accessible sights include: the Botanical Gardens (see page 109), some areas of the Kalinago Barana Auté (see page 160), Touna Auté (see page 162), beaches such as Purple Turtle (see page 198), Mero (see page 216), Woodford Hill (see page 193), and if you are interested in a hot sulphur bath, Tia's (see page 89) has a very accessible and private pool, close to the entrance. The Rainforest Aerial Tram (see page 120) may also be an enjoyable option. A good time to visit may be during Creole and Independence festivities in October when you can enjoy traditional dancing, steel pan, music and food at reasonably accessible village, town and park venues.

For help, information and advice contact the Dominica Hotel and Tourism Association (*PO Box 384, 17 Castle St, Roseau;* ✏ *767 440 3430;* e *dhta@cwdom.dm*).

TRAVELLING WITH CHILDREN

Dominica is a great place to explore with children – they can enjoy a sense of freedom and adventure in a natural environment that may simply not be possible at home. There are lots of good hotels, cottages and self-catering options to choose from. All of the west coast beaches are safe for bathing (Purple Turtle is perhaps the best, see page 198) as are many in the northeast, such as Hodges Bay (see page 198) which is particularly good. There are plenty of outdoor activities that are fun for families: some of the shorter, less demanding hikes such as Syndicate Nature Trail (see page 218), Cabrits trails (see page 202) and Glassy (see page 172); rivers and waterfalls such as Trafalgar Falls (see page 121), Emerald Pool, Spanny Falls (see page 224), and La Chaudiere (see page 201); and other activities such as river tubing (see page 82), kayaking (see page 81), snorkelling (see page 86), Wacky Rollers Adventure Park (see page 90), Rainforest Aerial Tram (see page 120), Indian River boat ride (see page 199), Kalinago Barana Auté (see page 160), Kalinago Touna Auté (see page 162), and whale watching (see page 89). If you decide to take on any of the more challenging hikes, please take a good guide with you (see page 79). It will enhance your experience as well as your safety.

If you are travelling with very young children you will find baby products in most of the better known supermarkets as well as the pharmacies in Roseau (see page 108). As they are imported, they can be quite expensive, however, so you will need to balance cost with convenience when planning your trip and deciding what to bring with you from home.

GAY TRAVELLERS

The Roman Catholic Church is by far the predominant religion on the island and so majority views on homosexuality are in accord with church doctrine. Dominica's homosexuals are essentially a silent community, forced to maintain a low profile and unable to express their sexuality openly without prejudice.

However you choose to deal with this is your choice, of course. But you should be aware that overt displays of your sexuality will certainly draw attention, and it will always be unpredictable in nature.

WHAT TO TAKE

Dominica has a hot and humid climate. It can also get very wet. You will need to bring shorts, light skirts and tops, and at least one swimming costume. Bring a hat to protect your head and sunglasses to shield your eyes from the sun. For hiking a pair of training shoes is fine, but if you prefer proper hiking footwear then try to find something that has a good grip in the wet. Hard plastic soles are not very good for this. Some hikes require river crossings or scrambles over rocks, so your choice of footwear is quite important. Bring a light rain jacket. If you are staying in the interior, on the east coast or at a high elevation, take a sweater too, as it can become cool in the evenings. Lightweight trousers are also good for the evenings when mosquitoes are on the prowl.

You will need a small backpack for day trips – a waterproof one is best. Take a small first-aid kit, sunscreen, after-sun and mosquito repellent.

If you are a photographer, it is always worth bringing sufficient digital storage media with you as well as a supply of extra batteries. A waterproof bag, to protect your gear in the rainforest, at waterfalls, when you are crossing rivers and on dive or whale watching boats, is also a prudent addition.

Roseau's supermarkets and pharmacies (see page 108) have a good selection of toiletries and medicines, but if you are taking prescription drugs please ensure you bring them with you.

You should not have too many difficulties with electrical appliances. The supply is 220V, 50Hz with UK-style three-pin plugs and sockets, but many hotels and self-catering accommodations have duel voltage systems, and so 110V with two-pin sockets is quite common these days. It is certainly worth checking in advance whether your choice of accommodation offers the supply you need. With regards to electrical appliances themselves, please remember that you are travelling to a tropical climate where heat, exposure to direct sunlight, and high levels of humidity may have a detrimental effect on sensitive equipment if it is not adequately protected. Moisture absorbing sachets are quite inexpensive and can be placed in camera bags, backpacks and so on during your trip.

$ MONEY AND BUDGETING

CURRENCY Dominica's currency is the Eastern Caribbean dollar (commonly written EC$ though officially XCD) and it has been fixed to the US dollar at a rate of US$1 = EC$2.7 since 1979. Notes come in denominations of EC$100, EC$50, EC$20, EC$10 and EC$5. Coins come in denominations of EC$1, and then 50, 25, 10, 5, 2 and 1 cents. The Eastern Caribbean dollar is also the official currency of Anguilla, Antigua and Barbuda, Grenada, St Kitts and Nevis, St Lucia, Montserrat and St Vincent. It is issued by the Eastern Caribbean Central Bank which is based in St Kitts and Nevis.

US dollars are widely accepted across the island and you will usually be quoted prices in both EC and US dollars. You will also find that euros are accepted though not as commonly as the US dollar. Please be aware that the euro to EC dollar rate is not fixed.

Travellers' cheques can be exchanged at the main banks and in some of the larger hotels. ATMs can be found at the main banks in Roseau, at both airports, at some of the large supermarkets, and at the National Bank of Dominica in Portsmouth near the Indian River. Most stores and hotels accept all major **credit cards** though many do not accept American Express.

BANKS Banking hours are usually Monday–Thursday 08.00–14.00 and Friday 08.00–16.00, but some banks and branches have a slight variation on this.

First Caribbean International Bank
Roseau branch Old St, Roseau; ☎ 767 448 2571; ◷ 08.00–15.00 Mon–Thu, 08.00–17.00 Fri

Portsmouth branch Grandby St, Portsmouth; ☎ 767 445 5271; ◷ 08.00–14.00 Mon–Thu, 08.00–17.00 Fri

National Bank of Dominica
Head office Hillsborough St, Roseau; ☎ 767 255 2300; ◷ 08.00–14.00 Mon–Thu, 08.00–16.00 Fri

Roseau branch Independence St, Roseau; ☎ 767 255 2624; ◷ 08.00–14.00 Mon–Thu, 08.00–16.00 Fri

Canefield branch Imperial Rd, Canefield; ☎ 767 449 2140; ◷ 09.00–16.00 Mon–Thu, 09.00–17.00 Fri

Portsmouth branch Bay St, Portsmouth; ☎ 767 445 5430; ◷ 08.00–14.00 Mon–Thu, 08.00–16.00 Fri

Royal Bank of Canada
Dame Eugenia Charles Bd, Roseau; ☎ 767 448 2771; ◷ 08.00–14.00 Mon–Thu & 08.00–16.00 Fri

Scotiabank International

Hillsborough St, Roseau; ↘ 767 448 5800;
⏰ 08.00–14.00 Mon–Thu, 08.00–16.00 Fri

MONEY TRANSFERS There are **Western Union** and **Moneygram** agents in Roseau, Portsmouth and several village locations around the island. You will also find one at the Roseau Ferry Terminal on the Bay Front.

BUDGETING Though you can find very reasonably priced hotel and self-catering accommodation, Dominica is not a cheap destination. In fact some restaurant prices are not too far off those you would expect to see in New York or London. Unfortunately, the standard is not always comparable. The same goes for the price of goods in supermarkets, with imported products especially high. This can really take you by surprise if you are not prepared for it. Nevertheless, with a bit of planning, you should be able to find a combination of accommodation, dining and daytime activities that suit both your taste and your wallet. Here are some basic tips on how you can do it. This is a very broad guide for two people.

Low budget You can find good guesthouse and self-catering apartment accommodation for as little as US$30–50 per night (see listings) and, if you arrive in the low season, you can probably find or negotiate good rates at some of the smaller hotels and lodges. There are also a few campsites emerging and more should develop over time. If you confine your dining to local eateries you can enjoy a traditional lunch (see page 55) for around US$5–7. *Rotis* (see page 57) are good value at around US$3–4. Roadside barbeques are also fairly cheap options. Ask at your hotel for suggestions. Buy a weekly site pass for US$12 per person (see page 71), which works out at less than US$4 per day in total for the two of you. Walk, hitch rides, or take public buses everywhere. The highest one-way bus fare is only around US$4 per person (see page 50).

Medium budget The choice of mid-priced accommodation is wide and varied with rates falling somewhere between US$75 and US$125 per night. It is a nice idea to stay in at least two different places if you can. This cuts down travelling time to sites and gives you a little more variety and local colour. Car rental rates work out at about US$50 per day for a standard 4x4 jeep. It costs in the region of US$40 to fill up with fuel. Consider renting a car for half your stay and using public buses to more accessible places on other days. Buy a weekly site pass and try to eat locally (see above). Give yourself an occasional dining treat at one of the fancier restaurants where a main course costs around US$20–30. Ask at your hotel for suggestions and recommendations.

High budget You can stay at a really nice hotel for US$125–175 per night (or more) and either rent a car for the whole week or go on organised, guided excursions with a tour operator. Whatever your preference, a weekly site pass is still a good option. Treat yourself to some wellness therapies, a relaxing massage or yoga classes, for example, and dine out at a combination of local eateries and international restaurants.

GETTING AROUND

The best way to get around Dominica is by car but you may well find the roads and local driving practices more than a little challenging. Some visitors find

2

driving around Dominica quite a stressful experience. Having said that, a bus ride can also be a seat of your pants affair that may leave you with a renewed lust for life, not to mention a case of motion sickness, by the time you get off. Organised tours and private taxis usually go at a more sedate pace, though they can be a more expensive option.

BUSES Roseau is the main hub for bus transport though there is no central terminus. Local people have become accustomed to knowing where all the different bus stops are in the capital, but as a visitor you may find it very confusing. Buses to different parts of the island depart from bus stops located on different streets and at no fixed times. They tend to leave when the driver is happy he has enough passengers, or when he has finished eating his lunch, chatting with his friends and so on. During rush hour times in the early mornings and late afternoons, and also when children leave school, buses are at their busiest and run more frequently. They are usually crammed full and their drivers apply a very heavy foot to the accelerator in order to return and collect more fares as soon as possible. From time to time you may also come across a somewhat bizarre situation where there is a bus in a village waiting to depart for Roseau, and there are people standing there also wishing to travel to the capital, but they would rather try to hitch free rides with passing vehicles than pay a bus fare. This can be frustrating as the driver will rarely leave with a near empty bus. Nevertheless, despite its peculiarities, hair-raising speeds, questionable overtaking practices, no timetable, no organised central terminus and no bus or route numbers, if you do ever manage to get to grips with it in your short stay in Dominica, the bus network can actually be quite a fun and very inexpensive way to get around. You will meet local people and you will get a glimpse of the real life that goes on beyond the tourist attractions. So give it a try.

Dominica's buses are small minivans and can be identified by the letters 'H', 'HA' or 'HB' on the licence plate. Many bus drivers also decorate the front windscreen of their vehicles with a name or a slogan so that they become recognisable along the routes they drive. In addition to designated bus stops, simply flagging down a bus along the roadside is perhaps the most common method of reaching your destination. If travelling to remote areas or across the island, expect to use a number of different buses to get from one place to another; and be prepared to wait. Some bus drivers may simply not go beyond a certain point and walking the final stretch may be your only option. You should also note that most buses stop running in the evening and there are reduced numbers on Sundays.

TAXIS Dominica's taxi drivers are licensed by the government and should display official credentials. There are no standard rates for private taxi hire and so it is down to the individual driver and a little negotiation on your part. Most taxi drivers offer island tours but they must have additional credentials as tour guides to show you around sites or take you hiking. Some taxi drivers have this dual licensing, and others work in partnership with tour guides. Here is a small selection of taxi companies offering island tours. It is also worth asking at your hotel for a recommendation.

Alwin's Taxi Service Roseau; ☏ 767 448 4260 or 767 235 4260

Colt's Taxis & Tours Pointe Michel; ☏ 767 235 2878

Daniel's Tours & Taxi Service Pointe Michel; ☏ 767 440 3640

Fredo's Taxi & Tours Loubiere; ☏ 767 448 5874 or 767 615 5200

Island Tours & Taxi Service Roseau; ☏ 767 440 0944

Levi Baron Pichelin; ☏ 767 265 9128

Linton's Taxi & Tours Roseau; ☏ 767 235 2709

Here are the locations of bus stops in Roseau and Portsmouth, together with routes and a selection of fares.

ROSEAU BUS STOPS

Kennedy Avenue (*near the Arawak House of Culture*) Buses to Rosalie, Riviere Cyrique, La Plaine, Morne Jaune and Boetica.

King George V Street (*opposite Jolly's Pharmacy*) Buses to Newtown, Castle Comfort, Loubiere and Pointe Michel.

Old Street (*near the Old Market*) Buses to Soufriere and Scotts Head.

Old Street (*next to Whitchurch supermarket*) Buses to Eggleston and Giraudel.

Corner of Castle Street and Cross Street Buses to Stowe, Bagatelle, Fond St Jean and Petite Savanne.

River Bank, along from the New Market (*outbound traffic bridge*) Buses to Portsmouth and villages along the west coast highway, Castle Bruce, Kalinago Territory, Marigot, Wesley, Calibishie (via Portsmouth) and Vieille Case (via Portsmouth).

River Bank, between Independence Street and Great George Street (*inbound traffic bridge*) Buses to Goodwill, Canefield, St Aroment, Massacre, Mahaut and St Joseph.

Cross Street Buses to Morne Bruce and Kings Hill.

Hanover Street (*Old Market end*) Buses to Bellevue Chopin, Pichelin, Grand Bay and Tete Morne.

Hanover Street (*New Market end*) Buses that go all the way to Delices and Boetica.

King George V Street (*near Astaphans*) **and Valley Road** (*just over the junction with King George V St – look for 'Keep Clear' markings on the road*) Buses to Trafalgar, Wotten Waven, Shawford, Morne Prosper and Laudat.

PORTSMOUTH BUS STOPS

By the mini roundabout on the southern end of Bay Street Buses to Roseau and villages along the west coast.

Along the south side of Benjamin's Park (*right at the mini roundabout above*) Buses to Calibishie, Vielle Case, Pennville, Wesley and Marigot.

Bay Street (*near the market*) Buses to Toucari, Cottage, Clifton and Capuchin.

BUS FARES Here is a sample of one-way bus fares from Roseau.

Calibishie (via Portsmouth) EC$11	Portsmouth EC$9
Canefield EC$2.50	Rosalie EC$7
Castle Comfort EC$1.75	Scotts Head EC$4
Grand Bay EC$5	Soufriere EC$4
Kalinago Territory EC$11	Trafalgar EC$3.50
Laudat EC$4	Wotten Waven EC$3

Ask the driver to let you know when you get to your destination and pay when you get off. Try to have change or small notes. Public bus fares are regulated by parliament and you are not expected to tip. Some bus drivers may try to offer you private taxi tours. Let them know you are not interested and that you simply want to make use of the public bus service.

Practical Information **GETTING AROUND**

2

Mally's Taxi & Tours Roseau; ☏ 767 448 3114 or 767 235 2105

New Horizons Taxi & Tours Roseau; ☏ 767 277 5497

CAR HIRE A number of car hire companies operate in Dominica, some large and some small. The difference between the two is usually price and selection, with the smaller companies being a little cheaper but with a limited choice of vehicle models. The most common rental cars are small 4x4 vehicles. Prices vary but you should expect to pay between US$30–60 per day depending on the vehicle, with discounted rates usually offered for longer rental periods. Collision damage waiver is usually an additional cost. Some rental companies offer free drop-off and pick-up at airports and hotels. Be sure to check.

The government requires the purchase of a visitor's temporary driving licence. This costs US$12 for a one-month licence (this is the minimum) and is usually obtained from the car hire company itself. Visitor licences can also be purchased at either Canefield or Melville Hall airports (ask customs officers), or in Roseau from the Inland Revenue building which is located on the street to the side of the House of Assembly. In order to rent a car and purchase a visitor licence, you must be able to present either your domestic or international driving licence, so make sure you bring it. If you are renting a car it is a good idea to also carry a mobile phone with you in case you break down, have an accident, lose your keys or lock them in the vehicle.

It is definitely worth contacting car hire companies for quotes and bookings prior to arrival, especially at busy periods such as Carnival and Creole. Also check to see if it is possible to collect the car and drop it off at the airport. Here is a selection of car hire companies.

Best Deal Rent A Car ☏ 767 449 9204; e bestdeal@cwdom.dm; www.bestdealrentacar.com
Bonus Car Rentals ☏ 767 448 2650 or 767 445 8042 (Melville Hall Airport); e cphillip@cwdom.dm
Budget Rent A Car ☏ 767 449 2080 or 767 445 7687 (Melville Hall Airport); e budgetdominica@cwdom.dm
Courtesy Car Rental ☏ 767 448 7763 or 767 445 7677 (Melville Hall Airport); e courtesyrental@cwdom.dm
Discount Car Rental ☏ 767 445 8291 or 767 445 8291 (Melville Hall Airport); e discountrental@cwdom.dm

Garraway Rent A Car ☏ 767 448 2891; e garrawaye@cwdom.dm
Island Car Rentals ☏ 767 255 6844; e reservations@islandcar.dm; www.islandcar.dm
Lindo Park Car Rental ☏ 767 448 2599; e lindopark@cwdom.dm; www.lindoparkrental.com
Road Runner Rental ☏ 767 440 2952; e roadrunnerrental@cwdom.dm; www.roadrunnercarrental.com
Valley Rent A Car ☏ 767 448 3233; e valley@cwdom.dm; www.valleyrentacar.com

Check the car over very carefully prior to signing any documentation. Look for scratches and bumps, test lights and brakes, and examine tyre tread. Make sure any bodywork defects are properly recorded on the rental agreement. If the vehicle has poor tyre tread, request a replacement. If the car handles poorly when you first take it out, return it and request a replacement straight away. Do not settle. Dominica has some unforgiving, tricky and remote roads.

All rental cars will either run on unleaded petrol or diesel. It will cost between EC$100–120 to fill up your car. There are petrol stations all around the island, but it is always prudent to ensure you have a full tank before setting off. You will find petrol stations in the following locations: Anse Du Mai, Calibishie, Castle Bruce, Coulibistrie, Delices, Jimmit, La Plaine, Marigot, Picard, Pichelin, Portsmouth,

Riviere Cyrique, St Joseph and Wesley. In Roseau and environs you will be able to fill up in the following locations: Castle Street, High Street, Goodwill (Federation Drive), Pottersville, Canefield, Newtown and Castle Comfort.

DRIVING IN DOMINICA Many visitors find driving in Dominica quite a stressful experience. It is, however, the most convenient way of getting around, especially if your stay is a short one and you want to see and do as much as possible.

Driving in Dominica is on the left, though it may not seem like it sometimes. Roads are slowly being improved, but this is a long, ongoing process and you may come across roadworks and diversions during your stay. Most roads are narrow with many sharp, blind corners and very steep precipices on one side or another, so you need to exercise caution and always keep your speed low. Whenever you approach a blind corner, hit your horn several times to let anyone coming the other way know you are there. Do not be shy about this. Beeping horns is like a language in Dominica and it may prevent a very nasty surprise. Look out for pot-holes. Dominica's heavy rains erode surfaces and wash away makeshift repairs very quickly. Though they are definitely improving, some roads are very bad and pot-holes can be deep and wide. Drive around them when the roads are clear but be really careful on bends.

Unfortunately driving practices in Dominica also present a risk to you. Many people drive far too fast for the roads, they overtake on corners, they pull out without either looking or giving any warning, or they may suddenly stop in the middle of the road for a conversation with a friend. Driving safety and etiquette is a real problem and sadly it seems to be getting worse rather than better.

Inevitably there will be a vehicle right up against your rear bumper and the driver will probably hit his horn to indicate he wishes to pass. Let him pass every time, even if it means slowing down and pulling over. Do not race, nor be stubborn; it is not worth getting angry about. Though you may find it hard to relax, do try to remember you are on holiday and smile about it. Wherever you are, always watch for vehicles pulling out from the side of the road without any warning, and look out for very deep drainage ditches, especially on bends and when parking. When passing parked cars that you suspect may be about to pull out or are indicating, blow your horn to tell them you are coming. Try to encourage etiquette if someone stops for you or lets you pass by thanking them or giving them a couple of quick bursts of the horn. Keep your speed slow at all times and do try to enjoy the ride!

HITCHING Hitching or *riding* is very common in Dominica. It is often possible to wave down a pick-up truck and jump on the back for a free ride. Conversely, when driving, expect to see people asking for a ride along the main highways or on the outskirts of villages. Hitching a ride is quite an effective way to get around, though it may involve long waits, sometimes in heavy downpours. It is also a nice way to meet Dominicans and experience a side to the island that is not possible in other circumstances.

SCOOTER HIRE Whatever you do, be careful. A scooter is a handy way to get around Roseau and environs but it is not without its fair share of hazards. Look out for vehicles pulling out or stopping in front of you without warning and take care in the rain.

C & S Scooter Rentals Newtown, Roseau;
℡ 767 277 7460, 767 315 3675

ACCOMMODATION

The pick of Dominica's accommodation reflects a congruity of design with the natural environment and cultural heritage in mind. Sometimes this design is simple and traditional, other times it is luxurious and modern. Whether money is no object or you are travelling on a tighter budget, whether you want to get back to basics or you prefer to keep the jungle at arm's length, there should be something for you here.

Accommodation is spread around the island. This means that staying in more than one place is a good idea as it gives you the opportunity to explore different regions without having to travel too far each day. Take time to plan what you would like to do and then look for your preferred type and price of accommodation in those places. Some hotels have free airport shuttle buses which is useful for getting back to Melville Hall Airport. You may also want to think about staying in the northeast, not too far from the airport, towards the end of your stay, so you do not have too far to go when it is time to leave.

CHARGES AND RATINGS Hotel accommodation charges are subject to a 10% government tax (VAT). Some hotels will also add an additional 10% service charge. Be sure to check prior to booking whether the rates quoted include or exclude these charges, especially the latter. If a service charge is added, ask what it is for and whether it is distributed among staff.

There is no official hotel grading or ratings system in place in Dominica though the Discover Dominica Authority together with the Dominica Hotel and Tourism Association are in the process of implementing standard requirements that may well lead to some kind of ratings system in the future. If you have any questions about accommodation standards, please get in touch with the Dominica Hotel and Tourism Association (✆ 767 440 3430; e dhta@cwdom.dm).

Note The accommodation listed in this guide is deliberately selective and by no means comprehensive. Price codes quoted are current at the time of writing and are based on double occupancy per room per night during the peak season, or roughly the equivalent for self-catering accommodation with weekly rates, unless stated otherwise. Please be aware that price codes are meant as guides only and are subject to change.

CAMPING Opportunities to camp are still quite limited in Dominica though more and more are beginning to appear. It is illegal to camp on beaches or in any other public places, but it is fine to camp on private land so long as you have the owner's permission. If you are arriving with camping gear you should be prepared to tell customs and immigration officials what your plans are upon arrival.

✖ EATING AND DRINKING

When the Amerindians arrived in Dominica it was a combination of seafood and cassava that formed the basis of their diet. As agricultural practices developed on the island, root crops such as yams, sweet potatoes and tannias were cultivated for food. Among other things, the European settlers introduced bananas, breadfruit, mangoes, plantain, cocoa, coffee and sugar. West African slaves working the coffee and sugar plantations tended to have a staple diet of root crops, or *provisions*, which they spiced up with seasonings such as peppers, bay leaves, parsley and thyme, adopting the influences of the French. Following the abolition of slavery, these Caribbean Creole culinary practices continued to develop, particularly with the arrival of freed slaves from the French islands, and are the foundation for the local traditional dishes served in many of Dominica's snackettes and Creole restaurants today.

LUNCH Sometimes it seems that Dominicans would not be able to survive the day without having their lunch. Despite busy lifestyles and the influence of fast foods, almost everything comes to a standstill for what many Dominicans continue to regard as the main meal of the day. In local eateries a menu board may simply say 'fish lunch' or 'chicken lunch' and typically it will consist of a main ingredient, such as fish or chicken, with a fairly standard selection of rice, red beans and boiled *ground provisions*.

LOCAL DISHES There are many traditional dishes for you to try. Perhaps one of the oldest and most basic is the one-pot dish, or *braf*. One-pot cooking simply means placing all the ingredients you have, whatever they may be, in one large pot, cooking them up in water and seasoning to create a nutritious broth. This dish tends to be eaten in homes rather than in restaurants, though some local eateries do serve it, especially on Friday nights (fish *braf*) and Saturday mornings (pig and cow's foot *braf*). Try Miranda's on the Imperial Road in Springfield.

Most local dishes are rich in vegetables and seasonings. You may find meat and seafood dishes in some local eateries a little overcooked. This is a legacy of the past, and a lack of proper refrigeration. The Dominican palate has become accustomed

PROVISIONS

When eating out or shopping for food, you will come across *provisions*, also known as *ground provisions*. This term refers to any one or a collection of root crops such as varieties of yam, eddoe, dasheen, sweet potato or tannia. The term is occasionally stretched to include breadfruit, plantain, and green bananas (rather confusingly known as *figs*) though purists will contest this inclusion. *Provisions* are usually boiled and served with a main meat dish. They also appear prominently in traditional soups or one-pot *brafs* (broths). *Provisions* are very filling and are high in carbohydrates. Grown and eaten by slaves working plantations and estates, they remain a staple food across the Caribbean, especially for those whose work involves a lot of physical activity.

to eating meat dishes in this way. Larger restaurants are more likely to cook meat and seafood in a more international manner, though you should always check when ordering. **Hot pepper sauce**, made from scotch bonnet peppers, is used to spice up dishes. Be very careful with it though: just a few drops can completely transform a dish, and maybe not in the way you want!

Calalou **soup** is a very traditional dish made from young *dasheen* leaves (a *ground provision*), and occasionally spinach. It is a thick green soup that is often served with crab. It is delicious and usually a speciality on restaurant menus during the Creole season (see page 31). Other popular soup dishes are pumpkin soup, **goat water**, which is a goat meat stew, and *chatou* **water**, a soup made with octopus. *Sancoche* is a traditional dish made from coconut milk, *provisions* and usually codfish. *Ackra* is a kind of seasoned and fried fritter, often made from codfish, breadfruit, tannia and, from September to November, in the days after the moon's last quarter, *titiwi*, which is a juvenile goby caught in fine nets at the mouths of rivers. In September each year the west coast village of Layou hosts the Titiwi Fest where, along with music, river and beach activities, you can sample a wide variety of *titiwi* dishes. **Crab backs** are a delicious savoury dish and are also available during the Creole season. The land crab's flesh is mixed with a secret combination of spices and seasonings and then stuffed back into the shell, sprinkled with breadcrumbs and baked in a hot oven. **Curried goat** is a popular spicy meat dish (and yes, it is goat), usually served with rice, and, when in season, **stewed agouti** is another local delicacy. A common staple is a heavily seasoned rice dish called *pelau*, usually a lunch dish served as chicken *pelau*.

Vegetarians should have few problems finding good food in Dominica. With a preponderance of fresh fruit and vegetables, the choice is varied. *Tannia ackra*, rice and peas, fried plantain, breadfruit puffs, *provisions*, vegetable *sancoche* and macaroni cheese are all staple foods and very common dishes.

If you happen to hear the distinctive sound of a **conch shell** being blown then it means a fisherman is selling his catch. The fish caught locally and used in Dominican cooking will typically include tuna, marlin, flying fish, jacks, snapper and dorado (*mahi mahi*), also known locally as *dowad* or *dolphin*.

Popular roadside snacks include **bakes**, a fried flour and water dough that is usually stuffed with seasoned saltfish, tuna or cheese. You will also see people

RESTAURANT PRICE CODES

The following codes are used in this guide to indicate the average price for a main course in a restaurant or local eatery. Typically the most expensive thing you can eat in a restaurant is usually lobster which may run to EC$80 or so. One of the cheapest dishes is probably *roti* which costs around EC$10. Excluded are prices for roadside snacks such as barbecue chicken, plantain and so on, which cost less than EC$10.

$$$	EC$50+
$$	EC$20–50
$	<EC$20

Please remember that some menu prices, especially in hotel restaurants, may exclude local tax (VAT = 15%) and service charge (usually 10%). This can make quite a difference to your bill so please check.

Rahel Joseph, The Hide-Out Cottage, Geneva (www.hideout.ch)

There are many interpretations of **ital** food within the **Rastafarian** movement, but generally speaking it is the name given to food which is wholesome, natural, pure and from the earth. Usually most people following an *ital* diet will avoid all red meat and many are strict vegetarians. Vegetables and fruits should avoid chemicals and additives so most will be organically grown. Because of the purity of *ital* food, it is considered a form of natural medicine and is thought to be absorbed by the body more easily than meat. According to Rastas, eating *ital* makes you vital!

BREADFRUIT WITH *ITAL* SAUCE

1 breadfruit	1 onion
250g lentils	salt, garlic and fresh herbs
1 papaya or christophene	vegetable bouillon cube
¼ pumpkin	thyme, rosemary or celery
1 tin coconut milk	

Peel, slice and remove seeds from the breadfruit. Place in a pot, cover with water and add a teaspoon of salt. Boil until the breadfruit becomes soft. Place lentils in a pot, cover with water and boil. Add peeled and sliced pumpkin, papaya or *christophene* when the lentils begin to soften. Add salt, bouillon cube, onion, garlic and other fresh vegetables if desired. Add the coconut milk and, when boiling, fresh herbs such as thyme, rosemary and celery. Steam for a minute and then serve with the breadfruit decorated with marigold. Coconut water is a nice drink to accompany this dish.

selling fried or barbecue chicken, corn and plantain. A filling snack is **roti**, a flat bread most commonly stuffed with either curried vegetables or chicken. It is a very inexpensive dish that is very filling and great if you are on a tight budget.

LOCAL DRINKS

Non-alcoholic Freshly made juices are always available, the selection being determined by season and what is ripening. Lime squash and freshly made ginger beer are particularly refreshing drinks on hot days. Passionfruit, pineapple, orange and grapefruit juices are also commonly served. Less familiar drinks may include cherry juice, barbadine punch, soursop and carambola. All of them are worth trying if available. **Sorrel**, known in some parts of the Caribbean as hibiscus tea, is a delicious drink, usually available around the festive season. It is made from the sepals of the sorrel flower (*Hibiscus Sabdariffa*) and is fruity and fragrant. It is also served as a warm, spiced tea or as a wine, and tastes rather like a European Christmas mulled wine. **Coconut water** extracted from unripe *jelly* coconuts is an acquired taste, though it is very refreshing, especially direct from a coconut. Always drink coconut water and/or fresh fruit juice in moderation. Too much may have the effect of a laxative.

When thirsty, drink water. Tap water is usually clean and safe to drink, though after heavy rains it may become dirty for a short period and so should be avoided. Usually the water supply is temporarily suspended if it has been contaminated with

Seamoss is the name given to a red algal genus called *Gracilaria* which is cultivated in many parts of the world for its *agar*, a gelatinous polymer which is used as a preservative jelly, a culture medium, a laxative, a clarifying agent in brewing, a thickening agent in baking and cooking, and in the Caribbean as the basis for a thickened milk drink or dessert. In Dominica, Seamoss comes in several flavours including ginseng, peanut, linseed and *bois bandé*. The drink is said to be vitamin-rich and a useful tonic for a variety of medical conditions.

dirt. Following reconnection, always run the tap until the water runs clear again. If in doubt, boil it first. Local bottled water is also available from most food stores, restaurants, bars and petrol stations.

Arabica coffee beans are cultivated in the heights of Dominica's interior, and ground and sold as **Café Dominique** by local firm Parry W Bellot & Co Ltd. Some villagers will also cultivate their own. You can buy it in supermarkets and also in souvenir shops. There are also several blends of **cocoa tea** available which are made from locally grown cocoa and mixed with a variety of spices to make a delicious hot beverage. You should also try local **bush tea**. These teas are made from an assortment of plants and are believed to have medicinal properties for many

FRUITS AND VEGETABLES

Some of the less familiar fresh fruits and vegetables you may come across in Dominica are:

ACKEE Related to the lychee, toxic when immature or overripe, commonly grown and eaten in Jamaica, usually fried with salt fish.

BARBADINE Large fruit grown on a vine, eaten as a fruit or cooked and served as a vegetable when unripe. Sometimes combined with lemon and sugar as a juice.

BREADFRUIT Large round fruit with white flesh that is sometimes fried in butter or served in a salad.

CANEP Small round fruit with thin green skin and soft, tart flesh. Often sold in bunches by the roadside.

CARAMBOLA Also called star fruit, eaten as a fruit or blended as a juice.

CHRISTOPHENE A pear-like green-skinned squash, usually eaten boiled or fried as a vegetable.

CUSTARD APPLE Heart-shaped fruit with sweet, custard-like flesh. Usually eaten as a dessert.

DASHEEN A small, starchy tuber, usually eaten like a potato.

GREEN BANANA Confusingly referred to as *figs*, actually unripe bananas, usually boiled and eaten as a *provision*.

GUAVA Original Arawakan name for this scented fruit which is eaten raw, turned into jam or blended as a juice.

MANGOSTEEN A reddish purple fruit when ripe with sweet and creamy white flesh.

NONI Fruit with a pungent odour when ripe (hence the name *vomit fruit* in some countries). Considered medicinal, it is either eaten as a fruit or blended as a drink.

conditions from colds, headaches and fevers to stomach aches and even insomnia. They can be drunk as hot teas or cooling teas and whether they work or not, they are certainly very refreshing. Ma Pampo, who is claimed by many Dominicans to have been the world's oldest person, put her longevity down to 'dumplings and bush tea'. She died in 2003 and is said to have been 128 years old. Ask for bush tea at local snackettes, bars and eateries.

Alcoholic drinks Dominica has two main rum distilleries. The Belfast Estate produces Soca rum, Red Cap rum and Bois Bandé rum, and the Macoucheri Estate produces dark and light Macoucheri rum which is distilled from sugarcane grown on its own grounds. Dominicans will decant rums from these distilleries into bottles as a basis for their own individual blends of **rum punch** and **bush rum**, the latter being white cask rum with an infusion of herbs, spices or tree bark. One of the island's most famous blends of bush rum is ***bois bandé*** which is said to have a tumescent effect upon male drinkers. Locals will often refer to it as a 'natural Viagra'. Stripping pieces of the bois bandé tree's much sought-after bark is common practice, though illegal in the national parks where it is mostly found. Other popular bush rum blends are *spice* which has cinnamon added, *pueve* with pepper, *nannie* with rosemary, and *l'absent* with aniseed. Bush rums are usually sold in local rum shops and bars though you may also find them in regular bars and restaurants. Try Rudy's Islet View Restaurant near Castle Bruce for just about the widest selection of bush rums on the island (see page 158).

OKRA Long, crisp green pods, often used as a flavouring for stews and soups. Also eaten parboiled and fried.

PASSIONFRUIT Round yellow fruit with soft sweet pulp. Usually blended for juice.

PAWPAW Also called papaya, with an elongated shape, yellow when ripe and eaten as a fruit. Green, unripe pawpaw is often used in salads or pickles.

PLANTAIN A type of banana that is either fried or boiled and eaten as a *provision*. Also seen as fried plantain chips, a popular snack.

POMMERAC Large fruit with bright red skin, often used to make jam.

SAPODILLA Round fruit with reddish brown skin. Fleshy pulp is often used to make custard or ice cream.

SORREL Member of the hibiscus family, a plant with edible flowers, fruits and leaves. Usually brewed as a tea or blended for juice. Also used as a natural medication and traditionally consumed at Christmas.

SOURSOP Large green ovoid fruit with soft spines. Tart white flesh is sweetened to make a delicious juice or ice cream. A sweet version is also found (called sweetsop) and can be eaten as a fruit.

SUGAR APPLE Similar to a custard apple but with sweet white flesh. Usually eaten as a dessert.

SWEET POTATO Not a yam, and not a potato. Actually belonging to the bindweed family, this elongated vegetable has a sweet flavour. It is often boiled, roasted or mashed.

TAMARIND Segmented pod with a reddish-brown shell. The inner pulp is mixed with sugar to make tamarind balls, a popular confectionary.

TANNIA A small, starchy tuber, usually eaten like a potato.

TARO Also called eddoe, a small potato-like tuber. Usually eaten like a potato.

YAM Large tuber which is boiled, fried or roasted as a staple *provision*.

Rum punch is usually a little smoother than bush rum blends. Popular varieties are those made from lime and from passionfruit. Take care when drinking rum punches as their mild flavour masks what is often a very high alcohol content.

Dominica's national beer is **Kubuli** which is brewed using natural spring water by the Dominica Brewery at Snug Corner near the southern village of Loubiere. In 2002 this lager beer won a gold prize at the Brussels Monde Selection Awards.

PUBLIC HOLIDAYS AND EVENTS

JANUARY Public holidays for New Year's Day and New Year's Holiday (Merchants' Day) are on 1 and 2 January. Calypso 'tents' or heats take place at various venues during January in the build up to the Calypso Monarch Final that is held at Carnival time in February/March.

FEBRUARY/MARCH Dominica's Carnival, or *Mas Domnik*, takes place on the Monday and Tuesday before Ash Wednesday. These two days are also public holidays. The Carnival season runs throughout the month and includes: the Carnival Queen Show, the Calypso Monarch competition, Pan By The Bay (steel pan drumming on Roseau's Bay Front), costume parades, T-shirt band parades, street jams and 'jump-ups', and traditional *la peau cabwit* drumming. Tewé Vaval is the symbolic burial, or sacrificial burning, of the spirit of Carnival that takes place on Ash Wednesday. Formerly a fairly sombre ceremony where people dressed in funeral attire and carried a coffin with an effigy of Carnival to a funeral pyre, this traditional event, like several others in Dominica, seems to have transitioned into a fête or 'jump up' and an excuse to extend the partying by an extra day. Visitors can experience Tewé Vaval at Bataca in the Kalinago Territory and in the west coast village of Dublanc. For more information about the heritage of Carnival see page 25.

APRIL Good Friday and Easter Monday are public holidays.

MAY Labour Day on 1 May is a public holiday. The Dominica Festival of Arts (**DOMFESTA**) takes place throughout the month of May. DOMFESTA is designed to promote and celebrate the arts in Dominica. Look out for a schedule of events and entertainment. May is the month for Dominica's **Hike Fest** where a series of hikes are organised by the Dominica Hotel and Tourism Association. The Giraudel and Eggleston village **flower shows** also usually take place in May.

JUNE Whit Monday is a public holiday.

JULY Dominica's annual **Dive Fest** takes place over one week in July. This event is organised by the Dominica Watersports Association and includes introductory pool and ocean scuba diving experiences, children's events, Kalinago canoe racing, evening cruises and parties. The aim of Dive Fest is to promote diving and watersports in Dominica, particularly to local people.

AUGUST Dominica celebrates Emancipation Day in August, which is also a public holiday. It is often accompanied by the annual Emancipation Hike. The annual **Nature Island Literary Festival & Book Fair** is held over one weekend in August. Writers, poets and performance artists from Dominica and the Caribbean converge to celebrate the literary word and encourage everyone to discover the artistic side in themselves. The village of Cochrane usually hosts its annual **Rabbit Festival** during the month of August.

SEPTEMBER Look out for Kalinago cultural celebrations taking place during September and don't miss the annual **Titiwi Fest** at Layou village. Enjoy a wide variety of fish dishes, music, river and beach activities at this very popular family day out.

OCTOBER October is the month for Creole and Independence celebrations. Look out for published events such as traditional dancing, music and singing. It is also a great time to eat; be sure to try a crab back at the very least.

Creole Week takes place during the last week of October and includes **Creole in the Park** (at Roseau's Botanical Gardens), **Creole Bod La Mer** (on Roseau's Bay Front), and the three-night **World Creole Music Festival** which is held at the Windsor Park Sports Stadium. Often there will be a number of other Creole events taking place, such as **Creole in the North** and **Creole in the East**. This is a great time to visit Dominica. The island is full of colour, music, dance and good food.

NOVEMBER 3 November is **Independence Day**, and the following day is **National Day of Community Service**, both of which are public holidays.

DECEMBER Christmas Day and Boxing Day, 25 and 26 December, are public holidays.

SHOPPING

Shopping for food, drink and toiletry items is rarely a problem in Dominica though you will usually have to visit a number of different places to get everything you need. In Roseau the larger supermarkets, Astaphans, Whitchurch, Save A Lot and Brizee's Mart (near Canefield) are usually well stocked and throughout the island there are numerous small general stores that hold basic essential items. The major shops also carry a good stock of baby foods, nappies, cleaning and sanitary products. If you are visiting from the US, you will recognise many brands. There are also plenty of pharmacies selling medicines, toiletries and prescription drugs. Generally speaking you will find prices on a par with those back home and in the case of some imported goods, a little more expensive. Do not expect to find shopping cheap in Dominica, it isn't.

Markets and roadside vendors sell fresh locally grown fruit and vegetables. The best times to go to the Roseau New Market are late on Friday evenings or early Saturday mornings. Expect the market to have wound down by Saturday lunch time. Most villages will have some form of Saturday market though they are much smaller affairs. There is also a good Saturday morning market in Portsmouth. If you pass through interior farming villages such as Bells, for example, look out for people selling fresh produce along the roadside. If you see people selling jelly coconuts, do stop and treat yourself to a refreshing drink.

You can buy fresh fish from the fish markets at Roseau, Marigot and Portsmouth, from fishing villages such as Fond St Jean, San Sauveur, and Scotts Head to name just a few, and also from wherever you hear the distinctive sound of a conch shell blowing.

Most shops open from around 08.30 and close between 16.00 and 17.30. Some stay open longer. The majority close from around 14.00 on Saturdays and are closed all day on Sundays.

Imported goods, particularly luxury items, are quite expensive, though there are a few duty free shops in Roseau where you can buy jewellery, watches, clothing, leather goods, souvenirs and so on. Bring your passport and onward ticket. In addition to the somewhat unimaginative, mass-produced souvenirs, there are some excellent original crafts sold in small stores, galleries and on some stalls. Try to buy local if you can (see page 27).

ARTS AND ENTERTAINMENT

CONTEMPORARY MUSIC Dominica's premier international music event is the **World Creole Music Festival** which takes place during the last week of October each year. This three-night event falls within Creole Week, which is part of Dominica's Independence celebrations. **Creole in the Park** is a four-day live music and Creole cultural event that is held in the Botanical Gardens, Roseau. It is an excellent family event that runs from lunchtime to early evening. There are stalls selling traditional Creole food and crafts, activities for children, and lots of good music. National and international musicians arrive on the island to perform during the Creole festival period. Although the week is a celebration of Creole culture and tradition, the music festival does not limit itself to a particular genre.

Concerts are staged throughout the year, some in aid of good causes. There are several popular venues such as Krazy Kokonutz in Castle Comfort, Harlem Plaza in Newtown, Fort Shirley at the Cabrits National Park, Azile Valley near Bornes, the Roseau Bay Front, Macoucherie Beach, Purple Turtle beach, and the State House Gardens in Roseau. Many live music concerts take place on village *savannahs*, which are local playing fields, while others may be completely impromptu street

MUSICIANS AND BANDS

Definitely worth seeing and supporting if you get a chance during your stay, here is a small selection of some of Dominica's talented musicians and bands.

Atunyah Up-and-coming reggae and dancehall singer.
Caribbean Vybez Popular reggae band.
Dr Silk Reggae singer and solo musician.
Fanatic Band Talented contemporary music band with excellent vocals.
Grammacks Popular cadence band.
Michele Henderson Internationally acclaimed and versatile female vocalist.
Marie-Claire Giraud Female vocalist who sings jazz, opera, hip hop and songs from musicals.
Midnight Groovers Almost a national treasure, still performing soca and cadence.
Nasio Fontaine Internationally acclaimed reggae singer.
Nelly Stharre 'Revolutionary Baby' and Dominica's queen of reggae.
Ophelia Marie Known as Dominica's 'Lady of Song', a very popular singer of cadence-lypso.
Suburban Reggae band.
Swinging Stars Very popular, long running calypso dance band.
Triple Kay Dominica's first buoyon band, with a cult following.
WCK Buoyon band, very popular with Dominica's youth.

jams. Look in the local press, listen to the radio (see *Media*, below) and ask your hotel for information about anything that may be happening during your stay. There is sure to be something going on.

Dominica has many talented contemporary musicians performing in a number of genres. Popular today is the *bouyon* style of music though reggae, soca, cadence and jazz are also performed. Musicians that have achieved success internationally include Nelly Stharre, Michele Henderson, Nasio Fontaine, and Ophelia Marie. Dominica's two main *bouyon* bands, WCK and Triple Kay, have achieved regional success, particularly among teenagers.

PERFORMING ARTS The Dominica Festival of Arts (DOMFESTA) takes place each May. The festival is designed to promote and celebrate the arts in Dominica and is a good time to catch a play, a choral performance or some traditional dancing. Your hotel should be able to help you find out about scheduled events.

Theatre performances usually take place at the Arawak House of Culture in Roseau, and the Old Mill Cultural Centre in Canefield. Sadly there is no regular schedule of events and performances are very ad hoc and often poorly publicised.

The **Alliance Francaise** (✆ 767 448 4557) hosts music, dance and films fairly regularly and it is always worth passing by or calling to see what may be on during your stay. It is located outside the eastern boundary of the Botanical Gardens, just next to the Bath Estate bridge on the Roseau Valley road (see map on page 92).

Choral performances and traditional dancing take place from time to time at the Arawak House of Culture and the Old Mill Cultural Centre. Ask at your hotel, listen to the radio, call in at the Old Mill Cultural Centre, or look out for billboards advertising forthcoming events.

The **Nature Island Literary Festival and Book Fair** is held every August in the grounds of the University of West Indies campus, next to the Alliance Francaise. The event attracts writers, poets and performance artists from around the region and is also meant to support and promote home grown talents. There are readings, workshops, open mic sessions, book stalls, and more. Previous guests have included Kwame Dawes, Colin Channer, Earl Lovelace and Derek Walcott. Both Dominica and the wider Caribbean have a number of talented performers and there is a growing subculture of young poets who are definitely worth seeing if you get the chance. For more information: www.facebook.com/natureislandliteraryfestival.

Many of the villages of Dominica have their own cultural groups. Some specialise in traditional *bélé* and quadrille dancing (see page 24), others have very talented steelpan, drum or jing ping players (see page 24). These groups are invited to perform at cultural events throughout the year though you are most likely to see them during the month of October when it is Creole and Independence time. Dominica's Kalinago also have a couple of excellent cultural groups. One of Dominica's most celebrated choral companies is the **Sisserou Singers**. If they are performing, go and see them.

2

❧ MEDIA AND COMMUNICATIONS

MEDIA Dominica has two independent national newspapers, *The Chronicle* and *The Sun*, each published once a week in English. There are two cable television companies, **Marpin 2K4** and **SAT Telecommunications**, each broadcasting a range of US television stations as well as local news and government information programmes. The three main radio stations broadcasting in Dominica are DBS

Radio (88.1FM), **Q95FM** (95FM), and **Kairi FM** (107.9FM, 93.1FM and 88.7FM). There is also a religious station called **Voice of Life** (102.1FM and 106.1FM).

POSTAL SERVICE The main branch of Dominica's post office (🕐 *08.00–16.00 Mon–Fri*) is located on Dame Eugenia Charles Boulevard opposite the Roseau ferry terminal. Postal delivery times between Dominica and the US and Europe fluctuate. Allow *at least* two weeks. Postal prices also vary according to content, though a regular letter to the US and Europe is around EC$1 and a postcard 55 cents. A second post office in Roseau is located within the grounds of the Government Headquarters building on Kennedy Avenue (🕐 *08.00–17.00 Mon, 08.00–16.00 Tue–Fri*).

If you receive packages from abroad you must collect them from the parcels office on the ground floor of the main post office and open them in the presence of a customs official, who will determine the level of duty that you must pay. Import duty varies according to the nature of the goods, but for those that may be considered luxury items, it can be as much as 60% of the value. Proof of identification is required when collecting packages. The parcels office closes for lunch during 13.00–14.00.

TELEPHONE
International calls The international dialling code for Dominica is +1 767 followed by a number consisting of seven digits. International dialling codes from Dominica are as follows:

PHOTOGRAPHIC TIPS   *Ariadne Van Zandbergen*

EQUIPMENT An SLR camera with one or more lenses is recommended for serious photography. The most important component in a digital SLR is the sensor; either DX or FX. The FX is a full size sensor identical to the old film size (35mm). The DX sensor is half size and produces less quality. The type of sensor will determine your choice of lenses as the DX sensor introduces a 0.5x multiplication to the focal length. FX ('full frame') sensors are the future, so I will further refer to focal lengths appropriate to the FX sensor.

Always buy the best lens you can afford. Fixed fast lenses are ideal, but very costly. Zoom lenses offer good flexibility with composition. If you carry only one lens a 24–70mm or similar zoom should be ideal. For a second lens, a lightweight 80–200mm or 70–300mm or similar will be excellent for candid shots and varying your composition. Wildlife photography requires at least a 300mm lens. For a small loss of quality, teleconverters are a cheap and compact way to increase magnification: a 300 lens with a 1.4x converter becomes 420mm, and with a 2x it becomes 600mm. NB 1.4x and 2x teleconverters reduce the speed of your lens by 1.4 and 2 stops respectively.

For ordinary prints a 6-megapixel camera is fine. For better results, the possibility to enlarge images and for professional reproduction, higher resolution is available up to 21 megapixels.

It is important to have enough memory space. You should calculate how many pictures you can fit on a card and either take enough cards or take a storage drive onto which you can download the cards' content.

Remember that digital camera batteries, computers and other storage devices need charging. Make sure you have all the chargers, cables, converters with you.

DUST AND HEAT Keep your equipment in a sealed bag, and avoid exposing equipment to the sun when possible. Digital cameras are prone to collecting dust

---

Belgium ℡ 011 +32 + number
Canada ℡ 1 + area code + number
Caribbean ℡ 1 + area code + number
China ℡ 011 +86 + number
Cuba ℡ 011 +53 + number
France ℡ 011 +33 + number
Germany ℡ 011 +49 + number
Guyana ℡ 011 +592 + number

Netherlands ℡ 011 +31 + number
Norway ℡ 011 +47 + number
Spain ℡ 011 +34 + number
Sweden ℡ 011 +46 + number
UK ℡ 011 +44 + number
US ℡ 1 + area code + number
Venezuela ℡ 011 +58 + number

Mobile phones Mobile-phone operators with outlets in Dominica include LIME, Digicel and Orange. If you do not have your own mobile phone or other handheld device with roaming services, it is possible to purchase a pay-as-you-go phone from one of these suppliers for as little as EC$100. All you need is identification. Some hotels lease prepaid mobile phones to their guests. If you are planning on hiking in Dominica, doing some exploring, or renting a car, you should think about having some kind of device with you, just in case. Save your hotel and car rental company as a contact and call them if you find yourself in difficulties. You will also find pay phones around the island; just keep a few dollar coins handy.

INTERNET Dominica has excellent high-speed internet services and many hotels offer both hard-wired and wireless connections to their guests. You will also find

2

particles on the sensor which results in spots on the image. The dirt mostly enters the camera when changing lenses, so be careful when doing this. You can have your camera sensor professionally cleaned, or you can do this yourself with special brushes and swabs, but note that touching the sensor might cause damage and should only be done with the greatest care.

LIGHT The most striking outdoor photographs are often taken during the hour or two of 'golden light' after dawn and before sunset. Shooting in low light may enforce the use of very low shutter speeds, in which case a tripod/beanbag will be required to avoid camera shake. The most advanced digital SLRs have very little loss of quality on higher ISO settings, which allows you to shoot at lower light conditions. It is still recommended not to increase the ISO unless necessary.

Generally, it is best to shoot with the sun behind you. When photographing animals or people in the harsh midday sun, images taken in light but even shade are likely to look nicer than those taken in direct sunlight or patchy shade.

PROTOCOL In some countries, it is unacceptable to photograph local people without permission, and many will refuse to pose or will ask for a donation. Don't try to sneak photographs. Even the most willing subject will often pose stiffly when a camera is pointed at them; relax them by making a joke, and take a few shots in quick succession to improve the odds of capturing a natural pose.

Ariadne Van Zandbergen is a professional travel and wildlife photographer specialised in Africa. She runs 'The Africa Image Library'. For photo requests, visit the website www.africaimagelibrary.co.za or contact her direct ariadne@hixnet.co.za.

wireless connectivity at a number of coffee shops and bars as well as at Melville Hall Airport. As more and more people have their own computer or handheld device these days, internet cafés seem to be fading away, being replaced by wireless hot-spots.

Calibishie Tourist Information Calibishie. Internet café

CATS Independence St, Roseau. Internet café.

Cocorico Café Dame Eugenia Charles Blvd (Bay Front), Roseau. Internet café (in the boutique) & wireless (in the café).

Cyberland Woodstone Shopping Mall, Great George St, Roseau. Internet café.

Rituals Coffee House Dame Eugenia Charles Blvd (Bay Front), Roseau. Wireless.

Tomato Café Picard, Portsmouth. Wireless.

Zam Zams Citronniere, Roseau. Wireless.

COURIERS Private international courier services offer a quick, reliable alternative to the postal system.

DHL Agents: HHV Whitchurch Travel Agency Ltd, located on the corner of Hanover St & Kennedy Av, Roseau; ☎ 767 448 5887; e dhldominica@ whitchurch.com

Fedex Agents: Express Courier, located on the corner of Cork St & Old St, Roseau; ☎ 767 448 0992; e expresscourier@cwdom.dm

UPS Agents: LIAT Ltd, 64 King George V St, Roseau; ☎ 767 448 3185

BUSINESS

Business hours vary although most will start at 08.00–08.30. In the morning expect traffic to be heavy entering the capital from 07.45 onwards. Many workers will take their lunch at home or in the Botanical Gardens, which usually means a traffic exodus from Roseau at 13.00 with work starting again at 14.00. Most businesses will end their working day between 16.00 and 17.30 and so it is also busy at that time. A five-day week is standard though more and more businesses also open on Saturday mornings.

Working practices in some organisations, particularly those associated with government departments, can appear somewhat dated by modern standards. Completing one task may require several trips back and forth between different people with different roles and in different buildings. If you are lucky, the people you must deal with will all be available and located in the same place, but don't count on it. If you are in a hurry or if you tend to be an impatient person, you may well become frustrated by what are often very time-consuming processes, especially in the unforgiving heat of downtown Roseau. On the flip side, some things are surprisingly quick. If you have all the right documentation with you, it is entirely possible to open a bank account, get a cheque book and an ATM card all in the same day.

Service standards are not especially good in Dominica, in fact they are often far from it. Of course there are always exceptions and you may well find your holiday is replete with pleasant, happy smiling faces and attentive people. But the chances of this happening, unfortunately, are quite slim. People who serve you may not smile, they may not say anything, they may not look at you, and they may well deal with you while having a conversation with someone else. If you are used to standing in line and waiting your turn, you may also be in for a few surprises. People may simply push in front of you, shout over your head, or even demand service from the person who is actually in the process of serving you – as if you were not there at all. If you are used to a very fast, high standard service culture, then you will find all of this quite a challenge.

How to deal with it? Meet it head-on with a flourish of smiles, a hearty 'good morning' or 'good afternoon', a broad grin, a 'please' and a 'thank you' at absolutely every opportunity, and a warm and meaningful 'have a nice day' when you leave. It is the only way to get through it. Frustration, anger and shouting may be a release, but they get you absolutely nowhere and in the end it just spoils your day. Being a little overboard with courtesy will make you smile inside (really, it will) and you never know, some of it just may rub off if everyone makes a point of doing it.

CULTURAL ETIQUETTE

DRESS When walking around Roseau or any other town or village for that matter, please wear a top. You should also dress appropriately when entering churches and people's homes; bikinis, swimming costumes or no shirt will certainly offend and embarrass, though it is unlikely anyone will actually challenge you about it.

Sunbathing topless is not a good idea and you will almost certainly draw unwanted attention or cause offence.

DRUGS AND ALCOHOL Please confine your consumption to bars and do not walk around the streets drinking alcohol, unless it is Carnival, of course! Although you may well encounter someone smoking marijuana somewhere, and may even be offered some, please remember it is actually illegal and penalties are severe.

DEALING WITH BEGGARS At some point in time you are likely to be asked by a beggar for money, especially in Roseau, where the situation for the destitute hardly ever seems to improve. Many are drug addicts or alcoholics and you should know that if you give, this may well be where your money goes. You could buy some bread or a food item, but this is often sold by the beggar to a street vendor and the cash used to satisfy a habit. The decision whether to give or not has to be yours alone. Please resist lecturing and being rude, however.

TAKING PHOTOGRAPHS OF PEOPLE In recent times Dominicans have become very sensitive about photography. The reasons are not clear but it may well have something to do with hoards of cruise ship visitors pointing cameras everywhere when they come ashore. Some visitors can be very rude, sticking cameras in people's faces (especially when it comes to particularly photogenic subjects such as the elderly, the young, Rastas, Kalinago and so on). It therefore seems fairly understandable that Dominicans have become a little fed up with it.

Please do not assume it is okay to take photographs of people. If you do wish to take a photograph of someone, try the following:

- Ask for permission first.
- Offer to share by email the photograph you wish to take, and then actually email that photograph to the person as soon as possible (if you do not email it, eventually people will simply consider this type of offer a ruse).
- Offer a 'contribution'. Some people will accept a few dollars in return for allowing you to take their photograph.
- If your request is declined, please respect that decision and, however tempting, do not try to take the photograph candidly.

If you are genuinely taking photographs of scenery that just happens to have people in it, there is not much you can do; take the photograph. If anyone ever challenges you (some people can be a little too sensitive, or are perhaps even seeking conflict or an argument), simply tell them you are photographing Dominica's beautiful scenery (it is always a good idea to emphasise how beautiful you think Dominica is), and perhaps offer to show them the photographs you have taken.

THE LAST WORD No matter how ridiculous or irritating the situation, do not get into arguments and always resist conflict. One thing is certain: it will spoil your mood, your day, perhaps even your entire holiday. Some Dominicans seem to love an argument or a debate. Sometimes everything seems so serious you are certain things must end badly, but then someone makes a joke or laughs and you realise it was either not serious in the first place or the situation has been deliberately defused. People will often see how hard they can push each other.

With this in mind, swallow your pride and back down with a laugh, a smile or a joke; the louder and more exaggerated the better. Keep laughing and smiling, massage your opponent's ego (do not belittle them) and let him or her enjoy the satisfaction of having the last word. If you succeed in defusing the situation, then that makes you the real winner, right?

ARTISTS UNITE TO END VIOLENCE AGAINST WOMEN

Nelly Stharre

In May 2010 I was invited to join a campaign to end violence against women. Being an ambassador for youth affairs and a passionate advocate for peace and an end to injustices of all kinds, I was very excited to participate. It is easy to write and perform songs about these kinds of things, but much harder to stand up and try to make a difference.

Under the umbrella of the United Nations Development Fund for Women, regional artists were invited to a meeting in Barbados to see if we could come up with ways to help bring about change in our societies. As musicians, we do not always realise the responsibility we have; our voices and songs stick in the minds of people and, in the case of the younger generation, perhaps even more so than teachers, parents or politicians. Music influences mind sets and cultural expression, so we can play an important role, and should do so positively.

'Music is the weapon of the people with no guns and ammunition.'

Domestic violence has been on the increase in the Caribbean region; indeed we have higher rates of sexual violence than the world average. The UNiTE movement, together with UNIFEM, is trying to deal with issues of this sort. In Barbados, we musicians met with regional judiciary, UN members and other representatives from society across the region to work out how to help. I felt extremely privileged to be part of this dedicated group of men and women.

I believe the universe is open to goodness; all we have to do is let it in. And when we get a chance to make a difference, we have to give it all we've got. Please support us so that victims are no longer afraid to speak out.

'We must unite. Violence against women cannot be tolerated.' UN Secretary General, Ban Ki-moon.

For more information go to www.un.org/en/women/endviolence.

Nelly Stharre is a Dominican recording artist who has achieved international acclaim. She devotes much of her life to causes, helping to highlight inequality, AIDS and abuse, and has been the inspiration behind a number of high profile regional benefit concerts. For more information go to www.myspace.com/ nellystharrenatureislandgirl.

www.stuffyourrucksack.com is a website set up by TV's Kate Humble which enables travellers to give direct help to small charities, schools or other organisations in the country they are visiting. Maybe a local school needs books, a map or pencils, or an orphanage needs children's clothes or toys – all things that can easily be 'stuffed in a rucksack' before departure. The charities get exactly what they need and travellers have the chance to meet local people and see how and where their gifts will be used.

The website describes organisations that need your help and lists the items they most need. Check what's needed in Dominica, contact the organisation to say you're coming and bring not only the much-needed goods but an extra dimension to your travels and the knowledge that in a small way you have made a difference.

TRAVELLING POSITIVELY

Throughout this guide you will be encouraged to look out for and to try to support local businesses, farmers, artists and so on. Dominica also has many practical problems that a number of NGOs and local groups of volunteers try to resolve or improve upon. Dominicans living abroad are continually a great source of assistance to these organisations by sending materials and helping with fundraising. Visitors to Dominica can also make a big difference. Think about contacting one of these organisations before or during your visit and asking how you might be able to help.

Abilities Unlimited Federation Drive, Roseau; ☎ 767 448 2203. Craft workshop for the blind & disabled.

Alpha Centre Goodwill, Roseau; ☎ 767 448 6509. A voluntary school for people with mental deficiencies, sensory, physical & communication disorders. The centre provides education, parental skills training & support for children.

Child Rights Information Network (CRIN)/ Christian Childrens Fund 16 Bath Rd, Roseau; ☎ 767 448 8817; e ccf@cwdom.dm. Helps poor families provide for their children, establishes pre-schools, trains pre-school teachers, provides educational materials, & pays for bus fares, specialist medical fees, spectacles, basic building materials for homes.

Dominica Infirmary Home for the Aged
Independence St, Roseau; ☎ 767 448 2636. Provides institutional care for the destitute, aged & infirm. Also provides a day care centre for the elderly.

House of Hope Delices; ☎ 767 446 2208. A home providing 24hr care for severely disabled & neglected children & young persons.

Operation Youth Quake Roseau; ☎ 767 448 4174. Provides a rehabilitation service for deprived, abused, delinquent, disadvantaged & neglected children.

REACH Roseau; ☎ 767 448 8096; e reach@cwdom.dm. Dedicated to relieving the plight of the elderly in Dominica, especially those abandoned by their families. REACH also supports many of the other charitable organisations in Dominica & is a good portal for your donations.

3

Activities and Special Interests

There are many ways to enjoy Dominica, with a wide variety of activities suitable for all budgets, interests, ages and abilities. A healthy interest in the great outdoors, natural history and cultural heritage, plus a positive attitude towards a bit of exercise, adventure and excitement, will all certainly help you to get the most out of your stay on this very beautiful island.

TOUR OPERATORS AND PRIVATE GUIDES

Dominica has a good selection of established tour operators and professional guides. Licensed tour guides are trained and certified by the Discover Dominica Authority and should be able to present an official photo identification card upon request. Bus and taxi drivers are usually licensed to provide vehicle transportation tours only. Those drivers who extend transportation to include guided tours of sites should also have been trained under the tour guide training programme. Such drivers should be able to present two forms of certification: one as a certified bus or taxi driver, and a second as a licensed tour guide.

You are very likely to be approached by people offering you tours during your stay in Dominica, particularly in Roseau when cruise ships are in, or at popular hiking trailheads. The best advice is to do as much forward planning as you can so you are not forced to make spur-of-the-moment decisions that you may feel uncomfortable with or even regret later on. Depending on what you are doing, first of all decide whether you require a guide or not, and then try to engage one in advance. You will find guide and operator listings with activities and hikes in this book. Be sure to agree the cost of the activity before you begin. Do not engage a guide who seems to avoid giving you a price or who asks you to say how much you think you should pay. The larger tour operators usually publish their tours and prices which makes it much easier for you. Alternatively, you could ask your hotel to either recommend or organise a guide or a tour. Prices quoted will usually be in US dollars, but do check.

SITE FEES AND PASSES

The Ecotourist Site User Fee Programme was established in 1997 to generate revenues from non-residents for the maintenance and upkeep of some of the island's most popular natural attractions. The user fee programme currently covers 12 designated ecotourism sites: Emerald Pool, Boiling Lake, Freshwater Lake, Boeri Lake, Middleham Falls, Cabrits National Park, Syndicate Nature Trail, Indian River, Trafalgar Falls, Morne Trois Pitons, Morne Diablotin, and Soufriere Sulphur Springs. The Botanical Gardens are also a designated ecotourism site though the fee is currently not collected.

Permits can be purchased directly at the Emerald Pool, the Cabrits National Park, the Indian River, Trafalgar Falls, the Syndicate Nature Trail and Soufriere Sulphur Springs. Permits for the other sites can be purchased from independent vendors usually located close by – look for signs. A forestry officer can help you. Permits can also be purchased from tour operators and some hotels, such as Fort Young.

There are two types of permit currently available. A **site pass** costs US$5 and is valid for one site for one day only. A **week pass** costs US$12 and is valid for all sites for one week. A week pass is not only much better value, it is also the most convenient option. The user fee system is operated by the Ministry of Agriculture's National Parks section.

At the time of writing no fee has been determined for hiking all or segments of the Wai'tukubuli National Trail (see page 227), though you can certainly expect something to be introduced, and it may well affect the existing site pass system. Check updates.bradtguides.com/dominica for updates.

Scuba divers and snorkelers wishing to enjoy the sights of the Soufriere Scotts Head Marine Reserve (see page 12) must pay a **marine reserve fee** of US$2 per person. This fee is usually collected by dive and snorkelling operators. If you choose to go snorkelling independently at Champagne Reef (see pages 83 and 145) then Irie Safari, located at the entrance, will usually collect this fee from you.

BIRDWATCHING

Most organised birdwatching tours will incorporate the Syndicate Nature Trail in the Morne Diablotin National Park. This region is the primary habitat of the endangered sisserou parrot and also the jaco parrot (see page 6). The relatively even trail passes through an incredibly beautiful rainforest habitat with magnificent specimens of *chatanier* and *gommier* trees to name just two. The lookout points across the Dublanc River valley offer good opportunities to see parrots in flight. The best time to go there is very early in the morning or late in the afternoon. Also in this region is the short trail to the Milton Falls (also known as the Syndicate Falls, see page 200). This is also a good place to see and hear parrots, especially at the beginning of the farm track before you reach the river.

The hiking trails throughout the Morne Trois Pitons National Park also provide lots of opportunities to get close to Dominica's bird life. From the viewpoint at the summit of Morne Nicholls *en route* to the Boiling Lake, it is often possible to see jaco parrots in flight against a background of dense forest canopy. The Middleham Falls trail is also a good place to hear jacos, though they are much harder to see. The Layou River and the Indian River are especially good for observing water birds, including the ringed kingfisher (*Ceryle torquata*), the green heron (*Butorides striatus*) and the snowy egret (*Egretta thula*). Near the mouth of the Layou River there are often brown pelicans (*Pelicanus occidentalis*), cattle egrets (*Bubulcus ibis*) and royal terns (*Sterna sandvicensis*).

Further information on the birds of Dominica may be obtained from the Forestry, Parks and Wildlife Division just off Valley Road near the Botanical Gardens (see Roseau map on page 92).

Bertrand Jno Baptiste ☎ 767 446 6358; m 767 245 4768; e drbirdy2@cwdom.dm. Nicknamed 'Dr Birdy', Bertrand Jno Baptiste is one of Dominica's best known birdwatching experts. He offers tours for birders of all levels of interest & will also help you find the specific birds you are interested in observing & photographing.

KHATTS (Ken's Hinterland Adventure Tours) ↘ 767 448 1660; toll free: ↘ 866 880 0508; e info@khatts.com; www.khattstours. com. Established & popular tour operator offering a wide variety of general & specialist tours, including birdwatching.

BOAT TOURS

Some operators offer boat trips along the west coast, including sunset or party tours. You can also charter local river boat operators in the Portsmouth area, notably from Purple Turtle Beach and the Indian River visitor centre (see page 199). Scuba dive operators also offer coastal tours from time to time. See listings on page 82.

Wai'tukubuli Eco Tours (WET) ↘ 767 275 7001, 767 275 3150; e info@wetdominica.com; www.wetdominica.com. Exciting coastal rides in custom rigid inflatable boats. Excursions include coastal tours, snorkelling & whale watching, & also day trips to the French islands of Marie-Galante & the Saints. Bring swimwear, sunscreen & towels.

BUS AND JEEP TOURS

If driving Dominica's roads yourself presents too much of a challenge then bus and jeep tours are good alternatives. In addition to the operators listed below, you should check with your hotel to see if they run tours themselves or whether they recommend anyone. Please note that during the peak season (November to April) many of these operators may be booked up with cruise ship tours. Please consult with them before coming to Dominica and then confirm any booking you have made shortly before you arrive.

Alwin's Taxi Service ↘ 767 446 4699; m 767 225 2112; e alwinhilltaxi@hotmail.com; www.alwinhilltaxi.com. Offering sightseeing tours all around the island.

Antours ↘ 767 440 5390; m 767 245 0886; e antours@yahoo.com; www.dominicacruise.com, www.antours.dm. Offers a variety of sightseeing day tours in an open air 4x4 'safari truck' around the island. Minimum 6 people per tour.

Bumpiing Tours ↘ 767 315 0493; m 767 265 9128; www.bumpiingtours.com. Specialising in hiking tours, Levi & his colleagues also offer day trips to a number of the more accessible attractions.

Cool Breeze Tours ↘ 767 245 1776; e coolbreezetours9@yahoo.com. English, Spanish & French speaking tour operator with a variety of tours to island-wide attractions.

Eddie Tours & Taxi Services m 767 245 2242, 767 614 8555; e eddietours2001@yahoo.com. Family business offering sightseeing tours, guided tours & a range of other visitor services.

Eddison Tours & Yacht Services ↘ 767 225 3626; e info@eddisontours.dm; www.eddisontours.dm. Portsmouth based operator offering a selection of island-wide sightseeing trips & Indian River tours.

Fredo's Taxi & Tours ↘ 767 448 5874; m 767 615 5200; e fredos40@hotmail.com; www.fredostours.com. Offering scenic tours to & around the island's main attractions.

Jenner Robinson ↘ 767 276 4659; e jenna23dm@yahoo.com. Specialising in the north & northeast, experienced guide Jenna offers a range of tours including hiking.

Jon Vee Tours ↘ 767 449 6463; m 767 235 2375; e jonvee_11@live.com. Offering custom tours throughout the island for individuals, families & groups.

KAHETO (Kalinago Heritage Tours) ↘ 767 614 0418; e kalinagotours@gmail.com. Bus tours & heritage excursions around the Kalinago Territory with Kalinago guides.

KHATTS (Ken's Hinterland Adventure Tours) ↘ 767 448 1660; toll free: ↘ 866 880 0508; e info@khatts.com; www.khattstours.com. Offering wide range of bus tours to all the island's major attractions.

Off The Beaten Trail ⟍ 767 275 1317;
e adquatics@yahoo.com; www.woodydominica.
shutterfly.com. Personalised island tours by Land
Rover with Woody. Nature walks, sightseeing,
secluded beaches & waterfalls.

Wacky Rollers ⟍ 767 440 4386; e wackyrollers@
yahoo.com; www.wackyrollers.com. Full & half-
day tours in open air 4x4 vehicles to waterfalls,
rivers & more. Advance bookings & a minimum of
4 people required.

CANYONING

If you are adventurous and want to see and experience something very different in Dominica then you should certainly take a canyoning trip. No experience is necessary as training, along with equipment, is provided before you set off. Most canyoning takes place within the river canyon below Ti Tou Gorge, though there are a number of other exciting and challenging routes for the more experienced. The trip involves rappelling down waterfalls, jumping into pools, and hiking the river – usually for about four hours – until you reach your exit point. The waterfalls, pools and rock formations in the canyons are quite breathtaking and Cathedral Canyon, one of the last you come to, is perhaps one of the most naturally beautiful places on the island. Highly recommended.

Escape Tours Ltd ⟍ 767 616 7118; e escape@
canyonspeleo.com; www.canyonspeleo.com.
French & English speaking experienced
canyoneers & cavers offering Dominica
canyoning trips in the autumn & winter.
Canyoning excursions are customised to your
level of experience & ability. All technical
equipment is included.
Extreme Dominica Adventure Tours
⟍ 767 448 0500; e extremedominica@
gmail.com; www.extremedominica.com.

Located in the village of Shawford on the road
to Trafalgar. Trained by TI Mountaineering in
the US, Extreme Dominica's expert local guides
offer a range of canyoning trips depending
on your experience. All equipment, training &
transportation to & from the canyon is included.
Advanced training courses are available.
Helmet-mounted mini camera's are a great way
to remember your adventure. Easy to operate,
simply purchase a memory card & take it home
with you.

CYCLING AND MOUNTAIN BIKING

Surprisingly, mountain biking has not really taken off yet in Dominica though it must surely only be a matter of time before it does. Whether road cycling or mountain biking along farm feeder roads or mountain tracks, Dominica has interesting and varied terrain, making this an extremely enjoyable year-round activity.

Nature Island Dive Soufriere; ⟍ 767 449 8181;
e natureidive@cwdom.dm;
www.natureislanddive.com. Independent hire
or accompanied tours. Local bike trails take you
inland above Soufriere to the village of Galion &

along old lime plantation footpaths. Alternatively
simply bike along the coast to Scotts Head & do
some snorkelling. Biking tours to the Layou Valley
& Cuba Road above Mero are also available.

EDUCATION AND RESEARCH

Dominica is home to several higher education and research institutions.

All Saints University Roseau;
www.allsaintsuniversity.org. Offers 4 & 5 year MD
& Medical Sciences BSc programmes.

**Archbold Tropical Research & Education
Centre** Springfield; www.clemson.edu/
public/rec/archbold. Extension of Clemson

University located in 80ha grounds, welcoming scientists, research & environmental groups. Accommodation in historic plantation house. **Ross University School of Medicine** Picard; www.rossu.edu. US medical school's Basic Science Campus located in Picard. Students typically spend 16 months in Dominica completing the basic science curriculum. **University of the West Indies** Roseau; www.uwi.edu Open campus of the University of the West Indies offering a range of undergraduate & postgraduate study options.

FISHING

While the seas have provided the people of Dominica with food and nutrition since the earliest settlers arrived, the recreational aspect of fishing is so far rather underdeveloped. Doubtless as Dominica's tourism industry grows, more sport fishing operators will emerge to offer visitors a chance to catch some of the marlin, bonito, skipjack, dorado (*mahi-mahi*), tarpon and mackerel that can be found in the island's offshore waters.

Shore fishing is definitely possible and if lucky, you may be able to catch snapper, jacks or kingfish. You do not need a permit for this. River fishing is restricted to residents, and only at certain times of the year. It is always worth checking with your hotel to see if they know any fishermen who could take you out with them on an inshore trip, perhaps followed by a barbeque on the shore – if you catch anything, that is.

Cabrits Dive Picard, Portsmouth; ☎ 767 445 3010; e cabritsdive@yahoo.com; www.cabritsdive.com. Half-day fishing charters by reservation on Mama's Money II. Fully equipped (tackle, outriggers, fishfinder).

Dive Dominica Castle Comfort Dive Lodge, Castle Comfort, Roseau; ☎ 767 448 2188; e dive@ cwdom.dm; www.castlecomfortdivelodge. com. Fully outfitted 10m Island Hopper (full tackle, outriggers, fishfinder, GPS, marine head & fighting seat), captain & crew. Full & half-day charters.

Island Style Fishing Fortune, Roseau; ☎ 767 265 0518 or ☎ 767 613 1773; e islandstylefishing@gmail.com; www.islandstylefishing.com. Experienced Captain Jerry Daway offers deep-sea sport fishing aboard his fully equipped boat, *Proud Mary*, a 37ft Searay (tackle, fighting chair, marine head). Full & half-day charters.

JC Ocean Adventures Mero; ☎ 767 449 6957; m 767 295 0757; e jorgama@msn.com; www.jcoceanadventures.com. Full & half-day charters on 22ft fishing boat (tackle, marine head). English & Spanish speaking.

GARDENS, FARMS AND FOOD

If you are interested in horticulture and organic farming then you have a number of options. Perhaps one of the best is simply to visit ordinary gardens where people grow flowers, herbs, fruit and produce for their own consumption and for sharing with their family and neighbours. Of course this is not always practical or possible for visitors but if you do come across an opportunity, take it. The care and attention people pay to their small pieces of land is extraordinary and the variety of plants and vegetables they grow, equally so. An alternative is to contact community tourism groups such as those in Giraudel, Eggleston and Bellevue Chopin. These community groups have been established in an effort to extend the tourism sector to rural and coastal villages and they could really do with your support. This is positive tourism in action, and a great way to meet ordinary Dominicans, as well as have fun and maybe learn something new. The third option is to visit some of the island's wonderful historic public and private gardens.

Taking Dominica's deliciously fresh produce to its natural conclusion is a Creole cooking lesson. If you are a dab hand in the kitchen and would like to be able to show off some Creole culinary skills back home, then this is definitely for you.

Antrim Valley Sculpture Studio & Gardens Antrim; ⟍ 767 449 2550; e sculptor@ cwdom.dm; www.sculpturestudiodominica.com. Visit the studio & tropical gardens of artist Roger Burnett. Advance booking required. Refreshments included.

Bellevue Chopin Organic Farmers Group Bellevue Chopin; ⟍ 767 316 2710 or 767 315 1175; e bellevue@communitytourism.dm, bcofmi@hotmail.com; www.bellevueorganicfarmers. communitytourism.dm. Community tourism group offering tours of a diverse & interesting selection of working organic farms against a gorgeous backdrop of mountains & forests. (For more information see box on page 139.)

Botanical Gardens Roseau. Dominica's historical public gardens are located on the outskirts of Roseau & are home to a number of domestic & exotic species. (For more information see page 109.)

Cocoa Cottages Shawford, Trafalgar; ⟍ 767 448 0412; e cocoacottage@gmail.com; www.cocoacottages.com. A cocoa & chocolate-making experience, from tree to organic product. Learn how chocolate is made, try & buy some in very relaxing surroundings.

Exotica Cottages Gommier, Giraudel; ⟍ 767 448 8839; e exotica@cwdom.dm; www.exotica-cottages.com. Caribbean haute cuisine classes for everyone with owner, Mrs Fae Martin.

Giraudel Eggleston Flower Growers Group Giraudel & Eggleston; e giraudeleggleston@communitytourism.dm. The communities of Giraudel & Eggleston are nestled on the slopes of Morne Anglais, overlooking Roseau & the Caribbean Sea. They are famous for flower growing. This community group organises tours of local gardens, flower arranging & Creole culinary lessons. (For more information on the Giraudel & Eggleston area see page 136.)

JTAS Giraudel; ⟍ 767 440 5827; e jtas@ cwdom.dm; www.experiencescaribbean.com. An integral part of the Giraudel Community Group, Daria & Michael welcome you to their home where you are invited to learn about local foods, try a bit of cooking for yourself, & enjoy the lovely gardens & views.

Papillote Tropical Gardens Trafalgar; ⟍ 767 448 2287; e papillote@cwdom.dm; www.papillote.dm. Perhaps Dominica's most celebrated private garden, Papillote has been the destination for horticulturalists for many years. Take a self-guided or an accompanied walk through the 2ha of beautiful tropical gardens where you may also enjoy natural hot springs & waterfalls. (For more information about the gardens see page 120.)

Rainforest Mushrooms Pont Cassé; ⟍ 767 449 1836. Guided organic mushroom farm tour, art & craft shop.

HIKING

The origin of Dominica's vast network of trails was one of necessity; escaping enslavement, hunting for food, travelling between communities, going to see a doctor, visiting family, getting to school, and so on. Before there were roads, everyone had to travel from one place to another on foot, on horseback, or by boat. Despite an increasing number of cars and motorcycles on the roads these days, Dominicans who live in rural communities still tend to walk a great deal; along tracks to isolated farms in the bush, to hunt agouti, wild pig, crabs and crayfish, and to travel between villages when buses or other forms of transport are scarce or unavailable. Perhaps because walking has traditionally been a necessity rather than a choice, it seems few Dominicans tend to walk for pleasure nowadays, however, and sadly hiking is an activity that seems to have become the domain of visitors rather than local people. There are exceptions, of course, and a number of local hiking clubs do run regular outings, but it is generally true that few Dominicans explore and know their island as well as you may do by the time you leave.

Dominica has hiking trails that suit all interests and levels of ability. Most are cleared forest, river or mountain paths with wooden steps or *fougère* (tree fern) logs for those places where the trail ascends, descends or passes over sodden ground. Official hiking trails are periodically maintained, have adequate signage, and are usually in good condition. Trails that come to an end at waterfalls often require a rather slippery scramble over boulders to reach the foot of the falls and the bathing pools. Safe routes over these boulders are not always obvious and local guides who know the terrain are worth their weight in gold in those circumstances.

Unofficial trails are less developed and are only maintained by the people who use them. Very few of these trails have any kind of signage along the route, save perhaps for a ribbon or a piece of cloth tied to a tree. Where there is a clear path this is not really a problem but when paths fork, cross rivers or pass through open clearings and scrubland, it is very easy to become lost. In subsequent chapters this book will describe trails in some detail, though it will also usually recommend a guide, particularly if the trail is difficult, hard to follow or simply disappears in places. Do not forget that things change. A *gommier* tree that marks a trailhead or a turning today might well be a Kalinago canoe tomorrow.

DIFFICULTY RATINGS For each of the hikes described in this guide there is an associated difficulty rating. This rating is based on a model devised by me. It does not relate to any grading standards used by the Ministry of Tourism, the Discover Dominica Authority, or any other source relating to Dominica. Instead it is based on personal experience of these hikes, made many times over several years, and it takes account of feedback from hikers who used the first edition of this guide. It is simply intended to be a basic indication of difficulty that may assist you with your selection and planning. Naturally, what may be tough for one person may be less so for another. There will always be variation, it can't be helped, and no system will ever be perfect, so please bear this in mind. Nevertheless, the ratings are relative so once you have completed one hike, you will hopefully have a better understanding of the numbers when selecting a hike for your next outing.

(TRED) Hike Ratings

Terrain	Unchallenging	Easy	Moderate	Challenging	Severe	Hazard!
Score	0	1	2	3	4	H

River X	No crossings	Easy	Moderate	Challenging	Severe	Hazard!
Score	0	1	2	3	4	H

Elevation	Flat	Easy	Moderate	Challenging	Severe	Hazard!
Score	0	1	2	3	4	H

Duration	< 1 hour	1–2 hours	2–4 hours	4–6 hours	> 6 hours
Score	0	1	2	3	4

Each hike is rated against four categories: terrain, river crossings, elevation (the severity of the ups and the downs), and duration (the time it takes to complete the hike). A score is given for each category with 0 being the lowest and 4 being the highest. The total is added up and then divided by the maximum possible score (16) and multiplied by ten to give a final rating out of a maximum score of ten.

HIKING GEAR

Here are some tips about the kind of hiking gear that is good for Dominica.

FOOTWEAR Footwear has to be rugged, able to stand up to tough terrain, get muddy and wet, keep you upright, and then be able to do it all over again the next day, without fail, and without falling apart. Dominica is very tough on footwear and this should be an important part of your preparation. Try to avoid heavy boots, and especially hard plastic soles. Heavy footwear will weigh you down and hard plastic soles are treacherous on wet rocks and wooden steps. Something with a little give is better, or look for shoes with Vibram soles which are designed to maximise grip. Closed toes are also important. Hiking sandals are fine but avoid anything with an open toe design. You need to protect your feet. I like to wear Merrell all terrain hiking shoes and occasionally Keen hiking sandals, depending on where I am going. A pair of sneakers can work well, but be prepared to dispose of them at the end of your trip. They may be a little soggy and have a rather unpleasant smell!

CLOTHING Clothing should be lightweight. T-shirts are just fine, though don't wear your best ones, and purpose-made hiking shirts with UV and mosquito protection are great, though expensive, options. Lightweight shorts that you can swim in and which dry out quickly are good. If you plan on climbing some of Dominica's peaks then you should also bring long hiking trousers to protect you from areas of razor grass. Long sleeve shirts are also good for this and have the added benefit of affording you more protection from mosquitoes, chiggers and so on (see page 41). A hat to protect you from both rain and the hot sun is advisable, as is a pair of sunglasses. And bring a rain jacket, you will need it.

The hazard (H) symbol is added to the score and final rating if the hike involves a particularly difficult section such as rock or tree root climbing.

Here is an example:

Morne Anglais: Terrain: 3H; River X: 0; Elevation: 4; Duration: 3. TRED rating: (10/16) x 10 = 6.3H. The hazard symbol is added because of the tree root climbing towards the summit. The duration relates to the whole hike – up and then back down again. By breaking the rating up into these four factors, I hope it makes things a little more meaningful than a simple 'easy', 'moderate', or 'difficult' description.

The most difficult hike possible would incur a rating of 10H. Fortunately none of the hikes in this guide are that tough! *Appendix 2* on page 255 lists all the hikes included in this guide together with details of their TRED ratings.

SETTING OUT The degree of preparedness required for your hiking trip will naturally depend on the difficulty and duration of the trail itself. It is essential to make sure your departure time is early enough to make it back before nightfall. Always plan to return to the trailhead by 17.00 at the latest, and inform someone of your plans and when you expect to return.

Take plenty of water with you; at least one or two litres each. It is very easy to dehydrate in the humidity of the rainforest and the heat of the tropical sun. Rivers and streams may provide handy refills if supplies run low, but only when you

ACCESSORIES A waterproof rucksack is a good idea but failing that bring along a waterproof bag that you can carry inside a regular rucksack to protect valuables and sensitive items such as cameras, phones and other handheld devices. Your rucksack should be comfortable to wear, have padded straps and some degree of protection for your back. Keep the size small but functional. Outer webbing to carry water bottles and clips for walking poles are very useful.

A water bottle or a wearable hydration system is a must-have. Some products have built-in filters that enable you to use tap water (which is usually safe to drink in Dominica) rather than buy bottled spring water each time you go out. If you are trying to minimise your environmental impact, and keep your costs down, then a reusable solution such as this is ideal. Camelbak has a number of good products.

Walking poles do help. Telescopic poles also allow you to stash them when they are not needed. They are a great aid to your legs on long forest trails, they provide support and stabilisation on steep descents, and they are also really useful on river crossings, especially if you are not quite sure how deep the water is! I take my Leki walking pole everywhere.

You should take a small medical kit with you that includes antiseptic solution or swabs, gauze, bandage, tape, and painkillers. Bring mosquito repellent that contains DEET and also sunscreen. A combination knife may also come in handy.

GPS and compass are not really needed in Dominica. Trails are usually well marked and orientation is fairly straightforward. The forest canopy is fairly dense in some places meaning it is difficult to get a continuous GPS signal unless you have a more expensive device. A situation that requires a GPS unit or a compass is also one where you probably ought to forget about the gadgets and just hire a local guide.

are sure there are no farmlands or houses upstream. If you are not sure, ask your guide. Wear sensible footwear such as walking shoes, trainers or strong sandals (see *Hiking Gear* box above). Flip-flops are really not a very good idea, and neither is walking barefoot.

Walking in Dominica's rainforest can often mean getting wet and dirty. A towel and a change of clothes either to take along or to leave in your car at the trailhead is a very sensible idea. If you take a change of clothes on the hike with you, be sure to put them in a waterproof or plastic bag. It is also a nice idea to have drinks and food waiting in a cooler on your return. As trails can become muddy and slippery and some of them require climbing through tree roots, you should take along a small first aid kit for any cuts, knocks or scratches you may pick up as souvenirs along the way.

Generally speaking, it is not a good idea to go to waterfalls or cross rivers if there has been heavy rain, or if heavy rain is expected. Flash flooding is not theoretical, it happens, and people have been killed by it in Dominica. Notable places to avoid hiking during periods of high rainfall are the Sari Sari Falls, the Victoria Falls, the Jacko Steps, and any other hike that involves significant river crossings. Use common sense and a reasonable degree of caution when deciding where to go in inclement weather. If local people advise against a hike due to heavy rainfall or swollen rivers, listen to them and do not go.

HIKING GUIDES First of all, I make no apologies for promoting the use of local guides. Good hiking guides know which way to go when routes become unclear, they are usually trained in first aid, and they can provide interesting information about the history of the trail, and the flora and fauna that may be seen along the way. Hiring guides also provides a source of income to local people and, by extension, their families and communities. There is absolutely no substitute for local knowledge and, by increasing the demand for trained guides, you are creating development opportunities for Dominicans. The reassurance a good guide can provide when a trail is new to you is also invaluable.

Most hotels and guesthouses will be happy to arrange hiking tours for their guests using local tour operators or independent guides. It is always worth asking. Some may even employ their own certified guides. Here is a list of some others you may wish to try.

Aaron Rolle ↘ 767 2767863. Hiking guide specialising in Morne Trois Pitons National Park hikes but with knowledge of many others.

Bumpiing Tours ↘ 767 315 0493; m 767 265 9128; www.bumpiingtours.com. Transportation to & guided hiking on most of Dominica's main trails & mountains.

David Victorin ↘ 767 449 3449; m 767 225 0006. Hiking guide with transport, specialising in the Boiling Lake, Middleham Falls, Fond England Falls, Wavine Cyrique & others.

Elvis Stedman ↘ 767 225 1971. Hiking guide & plant enthusiast with experience of many of Dominica's hiking trails, especially in the Morne Trois Pitons National Park which is his speciality. Good choice for the Boiling Lake.

Eric Hypolite ↘ 767 276 4252; www.naturelink.dm. A conservation biologist, Eric knows many of Dominica's hiking routes and is an expert on the Wai'tukubuli National Trail.

KAHETO (Kalinago Heritage Tours) ↘ 767 614 0418; e kalinagotours@gmail.com. Hike the trails of the Kalinago Territory & learn about nature & heritage with an experienced Kalinago guide.

Kello Tours ↘ 767 225 6276. Licensed guide, Kelvin Noel, specialises in the Boiling Lake trail & others in & around the Morne Trois Pitons National Park.

KHATTS (Ken's Hinterland Adventure Tours) ↘ 767 448 1660; toll free: ↘ 866 880 0508; e info@khatts.com; www.khattstours.com. Very respected tour operator offering both transportation to & guided hiking on the majority of Dominica's hiking trails.

Jenna Robinson ↘ 767 276 4659; e jenna23dm@yahoo.com. Specialising in the north & northeast, experienced guide Jenna offers a range of tours including hiking.

Mike Rabess (Hiker's Retreat, see page 157) ↘ 767 446 1076. A dedicated hiker, Mike knows & walks many of Dominica's hiking trails. Experienced hikers only.

Octave Joseph ↘ 767 446 4642; e seedatriva@ yahoo.com; www.hideout.ch. Experienced guide specialising in trails in the Morne Trois Pitons National Park & the south. A good choice for Perdu Temps & Victoria Falls.

Peter Green (Bushman Tours) e gbushmantours@hotmail.com. Peter is a very popular guide on the Boiling Lake trail as well as others in the Morne Trois Pitons National Park.

Wacky Rollers (WRAVE) Ltd ↘ 767 440 4386; e wackyrollers@yahoo.com; www.wackyrollers. com. Certified guides available for 'hikafaris' to popular hiking destinations around the island.

HORSERIDING

Horseriding tours usually begin with a short training session for beginners and include all equipment. They are fully guided and last around one hour. There is normally a maximum weight for each rider and tours may be cancelled in very wet weather.

Brandy Manor Equestrian Brandy, Bornes; ↘ 767 235 4871, 767 612 0978. Whether you are a novice or a seasoned rider, enjoy the trails through semi-deciduous woodland & rainforest, climb Sugarloaf Mountain & enjoy superb views of Prince Rupert Bay & the Morne Diablotin

National Park. Excursions can be combined with outdoor picnic & BBQ.

Cool Runnings Farm Rosalie; ☎ 767 285 6987; www.mermaidssecret.com (follow link to Cool Runnings Farm). Small livestock & organic farm offers horseriding for both beginners &

the experienced. Practice sessions & guided excursions on forest trails are followed by fun on the farm & lunch over a wood fire.

Rainforest Riding Portsmouth; ☎ 767 3619 & 767 265 7386. Accompanied horseriding in the Indian River area.

KAYAKING

In addition to the operators listed below, it is always worth checking out popular beaches such as Mero where local bars have been continually extending their beachside offerings. If you are staying in waterfront accommodation, you may also find that kayaks are available for rent. Be sure to wear a lifejacket and protect yourself with sunscreen, a hat and a shirt. It is very easy to get sunburned when out on the water.

Nature Island Dive Soufriere; ☎ 767 449 8181; f 767 449 8182; e natureidive@cwdom.dm; www.natureislanddive.com. Offers accompanied & unaccompanied ocean kayaking in SSMR.

Wacky Rollers (WRAVE) Ltd ☎ 767 449 8276440 4386; e wackyrollers@yahoo.com; www.wackyrollers.com. Accompanied kayak trips down the Layou River to the Caribbean Sea.

OFF-ROADING

Dominica has an immense network of remote farm access roads, tracks and forest trails, all of them great fun to explore either on foot, by 4x4 or all-terrain vehicles (ATVs).

Highride Nature Adventures ☎ 767 448 6296; e highriders@cwdom.dm; www.avirtualdominica.com/highrideadventures. A guided tour through tropical rainforest on ATVs. Taking place on a private estate with an organic farm, visitors drive along mountain trails that snake through the beautiful rainforest. Located close to Morne Anglais on the southern edge of the Morne Trois Pitons National Park, the trails

incorporate panoramic views of the Caribbean & Atlantic coasts.

Off The Beaten Trail ☎ 767 275 1317; e adquatics@yahoo.com. Off-roading, forest trails & tracks with Woody in his Land Rover Defender. Woody is often busy during the cruise ship season so you will need to contact him in advance.

PHOTOGRAPHY TOURS

Dominica offers so much to photographers; stunning land- and seascapes, impressive waterfalls, macro images of plants and flowers, colourful aquatic life and curious marine creatures. If your preference is for an organised excursion, perhaps including professional advice and tuition, there are a couple of options to choose from.

Images Dominica ☎ 767 245 6505, 767 614 1102; e info@imagesdominica.com; www.imagesdominica.com. Photography specialists offer tailor-made land & underwater tours. Scuba diving photographers must be certified. Tips & advice offered.

KHATTS (Ken's Hinterland Adventure Tours) ☎ 767 448 1660; toll free: ☎ 866 880 0508; e info@khatts.com; www.khattstours.com. Offers a land-based photo safari incorporating coastal, forest, volcanic & waterfall scenery.

RIVER TUBING

River tubing has become a very popular activity, particularly as a shore excursion for people visiting Dominica by cruise ship. Sit yourself in a large inflatable tube, shoot gentle rapids, and drift sedately along a river through Dominica's beautiful forest. Suitable for all ages, life jackets are provided and trained guides are on hand to tell you about the area and to assist in case of difficulties. Operators have vehicles to take you to the entry point and collect you at the exit.

Antours ⟍ 767 440 5390; m 767 245 0886; e antours@yahoo.com; www.dominicacruise.com, www.antours.dm. River tubing on the Layou River.
Hibiscus Valley Tours Concord, Marigot; ⟍ 767 445 8195; e hibiscusvalley@hotmail.com; www.hibiscusvalley.com. Tubing on the Pagua River.

Wacky Rollers (WRAVE) Ltd Roseau; ⟍ 767 449 8276; e wackyrollers@yahoo.com; www.wackyrollers.com. Popular operator offering river tubing along the Layou River.

SCUBA DIVING

Dominica has gained an international reputation for excellent scuba diving and it is a popular destination for marine biologists, oceanographers and photographers. Conditions are usually quite easy, with little or no current and rarely any surface chop, visibility is normally excellent, and there are lots of small marine creatures, fish, hard and soft corals, as well as spectacular underwater topography to see.

These conditions also make it a great place to learn to scuba dive or to do an accompanied try-dive. Most dive centres have in-house professional instructors offering a range of recreational and speciality dive courses. All scuba diving in Dominica must be undertaken via one of the island's dive centres and is usually from a boat.

Certified divers must remember to bring their certification card. Few operators will ask to see log books given the relatively easy conditions of diving here. If it has been a while since your last dive trip, do the sensible thing and take a short refresher and local orientation dive with an instructor before jumping off a boat. It will make your diving both safer and, with renewed confidence, much more enjoyable.

Typically a two-tank boat dive will cost around US$80–90 plus 10% VAT and marine reserve fees, if applicable, which are US$2 per diver.

DIVE SITES

Southern dive sites On the south coast of Dominica there are several dive sites that require either intermediate or advanced diving skills or experience. This is because conditions in the Atlantic can sometimes be a little rough and strong currents occasionally pick up during the dive. Interesting sites along this coast include **Suburbs**, a wall dive that drops to a shelf at around 40m before dropping again into the abyss, **Village**, another very dramatic wall dive, and **Condo**, which is a huge volcanic boulder at a depth of 18m. These sites tend to attract larger fish and the occasional migratory pelagic. Visibility is usually excellent here. **Des Fous**, **Mountain Top** and **Lost Horizons** are advanced sites that are only visited by special request due to both location and degree of difficulty.

At the tip of Scotts Head there are some excellent dive sites. **Swiss Cheese** and **Scotts Head Pinnacle** are particular favourites with a spectacular swim-through archway at 14m where you will come across lots of blackbar soldierfish. These two sites are part of the same formation and can be combined to make a great first or second dive. They should definitely be on your list. At the heart of the Soufriere Scotts Head Marine Reserve is a vast underwater volcanic crater. On the western edge of this crater is a wonderful wall dive called **Cachacrou**, the Kalinago name for the isthmus off Scotts Head village, and just beyond this site is a beautiful wall dive called **Scotts Head Point**. This site starts fairly shallow above a large patch of sand and reef before dropping spectacularly into the crater. A myriad of fish, in particular Creole wrasse, can fill your entire field of vision. On the northern edge of Scotts Head, within the shelter of Soufriere Bay, is the very popular **Scotts Head Drop-Off**. This site stretches to the east and west of the mooring and so can be experienced in two different ways. It is a nice sheltered site that combines the spectacular topography of Dominica's reefs with a wide variety of corals, sponges, fish and many other sea creatures. The three sea mounts of **Soufriere Pinnacles** on the north of the crater within sight of the beautiful Soufriere Church is a nice pinnacle dive and you will often encounter juvenile hawksbill turtles here.

La Sorciere, or Witches Point, lies directly below a tall cliff to the north of Soufriere and is a great wall dive. Turtle sightings are almost guaranteed, both along the wall as well as on the shallow reef above. A short distance to the north of La Sorciere is **L'Abym**, or the abyss, a dramatic wall dive located very close to the steep cliffs of the shoreline and dropping into the depths of the volcano. Another one for your list of must-do dives is **Danglebens Pinnacles**, a series of beautiful sea mounts on the northern edge of the Soufriere crater. There are two moorings for this site, both hooked to the tops of tall pinnacles at a depth of around 10m. The site drops to around 40m and is alive with a variety of corals and fish. Hawksbill turtle sightings are also common here. **Danglebens North** is a broad expanse of reef that runs from the shore until it ends in a steep wall. It is a very nice site with plenty to see in both the shallow areas close to the shore and along the deeper formation to the west.

Coral Gardens is a large flat reef system at a depth of around 15m that connects both Danglebens sites. It has seen some deterioration in recent years due to hurricanes and sea temperature rises but is now recovering well. Nurse sharks are commonly seen resting on the sand beneath coral shelves around the western edge of this reef formation. **Pointe Guignard** is a small site that runs around a rocky headland. It has some caves and a fun swim-through on the way back to the mooring. To the north of Pointe Guignard is **Champagne Reef**, a large flat formation that extends from the shore until it reaches a drop-off. Because of its popularity, this dive site has three moorings. Champagne has become best known for the submerged fumaroles located very close to the shoreline, that blow a constant stream of bubbles from the sea floor. To the southwest of the bubbles lie some encrusted cannons and chains, and to the east of the reef system are two small shipwrecks. The *Debbie Flo* is a wooden boat that was sunk in 1994 and the *Dowess* is the scattered remains of a steel vessel. Both wrecks lie at a depth of around 30m, have no fixed mooring and are rarely visited by dive operators. An interesting dive, however, is to drop down to the wrecks, explore them for a while, and then make your way up the Champagne Reef system to the bubbles, off-gassing naturally as you reach the shallows. **Solomon Reef** is an unusual and rarely visited site located rather incongruously beneath the very ugly quarry face between Loubiere and Pointe Michel. Despite its location, this reef formation is interesting and teeming with a rich variety of marine life.

Southern dive centres

ALDive Loubiere, Roseau; ☏ 767 440 3483; e aldive@aldive.com; www.aldive.com.

Experienced dive professionals offering boat diving, PADI & NAUI dive training. Equipment rental. Happy to accommodate requests for advanced dive sites such as Mountain Top. Small boat & personalised service. Nitrox available.

Anchorage Dive Centre Anchorage Hotel, Castle Comfort, Roseau; ✆ 767 448 2638; e reservations@anchoragehotel.dm; www.anchoragehotel.dm. Anchorage offers daily 2-tank boat diving & PADI dive instruction. Equipment rental.

Dive Dominica Castle Comfort Dive Lodge, Castle Comfort, Roseau; ✆ 767 448 2188; e dive@cwdom.dm; www.castlecomfortdivelodge.com, www.divedominica.com. Offers daily boat diving, enriched air (Nitrox), equipment rental, & PADI dive training. Established dive centre with 5 fully equipped boats.

Fort Young Hotel Dive Centre Roseau; ✆ 767 448 5000; e fortyoung@cwdom.dm; www.fortyounghotel.com. Uses the services of Dive Dominica (see above). Dive boats pick you up from & drop you back at the Fort Young boat jetty. Equipment rental.

Irie Safari Pointe Michel; ✆ 767 440 5085; e underwater@iriesafari.com; www.iriesafari.com. Located next to Champagne Reef, offering accompanied shore diving, PADI dive training & snorkelling equipment rental.

Nature Island Dive Soufriere; ✆ 767 449 8181; e natureidive@cwdom.dm; www.natureislanddive.com. Offers daily boat diving & PADI training. Located on the shores of the Soufriere Scotts Head Marine Reserve. Equipment rental & personalised service.

Central dive sites
To the north of Roseau, near Canefield Airport, lies the wreck of the Canefield Tug. The 20m tugboat that sank in 1979 following Hurricane David is rarely visited by divers these days due to high turbidity and poor visibility. Unfortunately run-off from the Boeri River has been supplemented by the heavy silting from a nearby cement factory, resulting in the decline of marine life on, and accessibility to, this dive site.

Central dive site topography is perhaps a little less dramatic than in the south, though the sites have excellent coral reefs, steep vertical walls and interesting marine life. Long shore currents do occasionally come into play, but more often than not these dives will suit beginner and intermediate divers. Just south of the coastal village of Tarou is **Rodney's Rock**, a volcanic outcrop with a shallow reef at a depth of about 15m. Off the beach at Castaways and Mero are two sites, **Maggie's Point**, a series of thin coral formations and sand patches, and **Castaways Reef**, a flat expanse of reef formations and sand that go down to 24m. Both sites are suitable for novices. A little further out is **Barry's Dream**, a nice wall dive that descends to around 35m. Close to the village of Salisbury, off the coast of Grand Savanne, are six dive sites, including four wall dives. **Lauro Reef** is a wall dive that drops quickly to 35m close to the shore, **Brain Coral Reef**, **Nose Reef** and **Whale Shark Reef** are stunning walls that are adorned with many barrel sponges, hard and soft corals and a variety of marine life. North of Grand Savanne is **Coral Gardens North**, a flat reef that starts shallow close to the shore and descends gradually to around 35m.

Central dive centres
East Carib Dive Salisbury; ✆ 767 449 6575; e eastcaribdive@yahoo.de; www.east-carib-dive.com. Small, independent dive centre, speaking English, German & French, offering boat & shore diving, & dive training.

Sunset Bay Club Dive Centre Coulibistrie; ✆ 767 446 6522; e sunset@cwdom.dm; www.sunsetbayclub.com. Hotel & dive centre offering boat diving & PADI dive training.

Northern dive sites
The beauty of diving in the north of Dominica is that not so many people do it, and so it can really feel like you have the place to yourself. The dive sites are good, in places quite challenging, and there is also the possibility of doing a bit of wreck diving. Just north of Pointe Ronde is **Ffutsatola Reef**, a rarely

visited site on the southern edge of Prince Rupert Bay near Portsmouth. **Sulphur Springs and Bubbles** is an unmarked region of diving that encompasses different diving options above submerged fumaroles. Much of the drama of this region lies below recreational diving limits, though some areas are as shallow as 6m. There are four main dive sites around the Cabrits peninsula. **Shark's Mouth** on the southern

SOLOMON REEF, A FAVOURITE DIVE

Billy Lawrence, ALDive (www.aldive.com)

When people ask me to take them on a favourite dive I often head for Solomon Reef. This rather obscure site is named after a judge who, in the 1940s, was killed in a landslide while travelling along the coastal road from Pointe Michel to Loubiere. Apparently he was a very unpopular figure and a folk song was penned about him which is still sung at festivals.

Located a short distance to the south of our dive centre in Loubiere is a quarry where *tarish* is excavated. *Tarish* is compressed ash and debris that results from the pyroclastic eruptions of Dominica's volcanoes and this area has always been mined for building materials. When I discovered that the quarry manager was a keen snorkeler, I invited him to come diving with me so that I could show him the lovely little marine eco-system that was lying so precariously on his doorstep.

Solomon Reef is a fantastic site that starts shallow and drops down to around 28m. It is ideal for both snorkelling and scuba diving. The quarry manager was so impressed by his experience that he agreed to help ensure the reef is preserved and protected from quarrying activities. The company has since taken measures to try to ensure the survival and prosperity of the reef including proper waste disposal, regular monitoring by the local 'Reef Check' team (*www.reefcheck.org*), community awareness programmes and coastal clean-ups.

From the moment you descend, the first volcanic rocks soon gave way to impressive coral reef formations and an impressive array of colourful basket, barrel and yellow tube sponges that are the hallmark of diving in Dominica. Some may argue that there are more beautiful reefs, of course, and this one has certainly had its fair share of storm damage, but I love it because it is so rich in interesting and colourful marine life. On a recent dive there we discovered a large pink seahorse. It was hanging on to a giant red basket sponge that seemed to be a housing estate for more varieties of shrimp (cleaner, scarlet, banded and spotted) than I have ever seen all in one go. We also saw several electric-blue Pederson's shrimps. It was great for the photographers among us.

We also see lots of moray eels hiding within the reef formation and, last time out, we discovered a hawksbill turtle nestled very contentedly in a crevice. I have also seen eagle rays, electric rays and the very elusive bat fish on this reef. It would have been tragic if Solomon's Reef had been lost to the quarry, but now I am very optimistic about its future. Confrontation rarely works. I strongly believe the best way to engage Dominicans and get them more interested in protecting their natural heritage is to keep talking to them about it and, if possible, show them the beauty of their island first-hand.

Time will tell if our intervention has succeeded. In the meantime, I'd like to invite you to come and see for yourselves.

Activities and Special Interests   SCUBA DIVING

3

edge is a series of large boulders encrusted with corals and sponges. The site extends from the shoreline to a depth of 40m. **Anchor Point** is also made up of boulders and extends from the shore. On the western tip of the peninsula is the boulder reef of **One Finger Rock** and to the north of this site, **Five Finger Rock**. The *Nadine L* was sunk in 2003 for divers and makes for an interesting dive – especially as a wreck dive for beginners. On the northern edge of the very pretty Douglas Bay is the steeply sloping reef of **Douglas Bay Point**. Around the corner in Toucari Bay are the twin sites of **Toucari Bay Point** and **Toucari Caves**, which are often combined into a single dive. Toucari Caves is a series of small, shallow caverns at a depth of around 12m. This is a very pretty site with an abundance of coral and fish life. At the tip of the island is **Point Break**, a spectacular though rarely visited wall dive with very strong currents, and only for advanced, experienced divers.

Northern dive centres
Cabrits Dive Centre Picard Estate, Portsmouth; ↘ 767 445 3010; e cabritsdive@yahoo.com; www.cabritsdive.com. PADI 5-star centre offering boat diving & a range of courses.

SNORKELLING

There are some nice sites around the coast for snorkelling. Shallow reefs are alive with hard and soft corals and an abundance of colourful fish. Conditions along the west coast are usually very calm making snorkelling a fun activity for both those who have done it before and those trying it for the first time. Snorkelling can be undertaken from the shore or from a boat with all of the island's scuba diving operators. Popular sites accessible from the shore include the sheltered drop-off at **Scotts Head** and the shallow fumaroles at **Champagne** just to the south of the village of Pointe Michel. Along the west coast near **Salisbury** and Sunset Bay Resort there are shallow reefs for snorkelling, and in the north snorkelling is good around the **Cabrits** and in the sheltered **Toucari Bay**.

If you are snorkelling at Champagne, after you have paid your marine reserve fee and perhaps rented equipment at Irie Safari, follow the boardwalk and then keep going all the way to the end of the beach. When you reach the rock formation at the far side, look for a white pole sticking out of the sea close to the shore line. It is in this area that you will find the bubbles. The encrusted cannons are much harder to find. They are located in a sandy patch between two rock formations a short swim to the southwest from the bubble site. Most people cannot make them out as they are so encrusted, but they are there, along with chain and also wooden boards just below the sand.

Champagne is a very popular site and is visited by many snorkellers both independently from the shore as well as on boat excursions from cruise ships during the high season. It is important therefore to protect this site as much as possible, so please do not stand on the reef, be very careful with your fins, do not litter the shoreline or the sea, and take only photographs and memories.

Please refer to the scuba diving operators listings for boat excursions, guided snorkelling tours and lessons (see page 82). Expect to pay around US$25 for guided snorkelling from a boat. The price usually includes equipment rental.

WELLNESS *with Terri Henry*

Imagine being surrounded by a lush rainforest environment, sinking into a deliciously warm sulphur spring bath and enriching your body with vital minerals emerging from the core of the earth. Alternate this luxurious hot soak with daring plunges into adjacent cold pools or bracing rivers for a powerfully healing hydrotherapy treatment. Then enjoy a mud scrub with rich volcanic earth and experience a complete sense of rejuvenation. If this sounds like your idea of a healing vacation, then Dominica offers a special retreat for optimal wellness in harmony with nature.

An eclectic array of holistic therapists live in Dominica and for such a small island the range of complementary therapies is vast. It is possible to find qualified practitioners in ayurveda, aqua mouvance, chiropractic, dance, gene keys, massage, osteopathy, physiotherapy, reflexology, Thai yoga massage and yoga to name but a few. Local herbalists with knowledge passed down from generations offer natural herbal remedies for preventative healthcare and curative measures.

Dominica's health and wellness offerings usually merge therapeutic treatments with the natural environment. Yoga classes are available in the rainforest, on the beach, in tropical gardens and under the moonlight. Massage can be enjoyed in a cabana overlooking a river, a covered veranda nestled in botanical gardens, a secluded country studio or tree-top therapy room with views and sounds of the crashing ocean waves below. Ecotherapy sessions draw participants into the midst of the rainforest to enjoy a sensory connection with nature and an exploration of personal development in unity with the natural world. Facials can be taken with locally sourced ingredients and feet soothed with pedicures using coffee and cocoa blends that smell good enough to eat.

Locally grown foods are also crammed with nutrients and taste that come from the hot sun, abundant rain and their just-picked freshness. Superfoods naturally available on the island include cacao, acerola cherries, coconut water, and coconut oil alongside many tropical fruits and vegetables bursting with flavour.

Unwind, relax and energise with any of the above and you will wish you could capture the ethereal essence of these experiences in a bottle to take home and relive when everyday stress takes over! The closest thing to doing so is to purchase some of the local natural products made with plant extracts and essential oils. Skin care soaps, creams and oils are widely available and are sure to delight with their aromatic fragrances and healing properties. There is also a wide range of packaged herbs and spices for both culinary and health purposes.

A feeling of vitality and exuberance often accompanies a visit to Dominica because, even if a wellness vacation is not the main intention of a visit here, you are sure to feel the positive healing effects that flow naturally from being on the island. Breathing in the rainforest air, taking a meditative moment next to gurgling rivers, feeling the exhilarating pounding of a gushing waterfall or simply being in awe at the verdant landscape can all rejuvenate mind, body and spirit. And of course just walking up and down a few hills in Dominica's rugged terrain is comparable to an hour on a Stairmaster in a gym – just a lot more sweaty and vastly more enjoyable.

Dominica has an emerging Health and Wellness Association which plans to be fully operational in 2011. A natural Health and Wellness Expo is held in May each year which offers samples of the natural therapies available, interaction with therapists and free workshops and displays.

Dominica may not be your typical destination for health and wellness, but specialised treatments, infused with joy and a touch of wildness offer a refreshing change from the norm. If you indulge in the adventure of a more outdoors, down-to-earth and sometimes do-it-yourself style spa activity, your body and soul will certainly thank-you for the experience.

Terri Henry is a writer, health and wellness consultant, ecotherapy facilitator and mother of two beautiful eco-babies. For further information: www.onelovelivity.com and www.childofnatureblog.com.

Studies have demonstrated a life-giving connection between nature and man; they found that simply looking at nature can actually be healing. More recently it has been shown that immersing ourselves in nature can help us to manage stress, ease anxiety, control depression, improve mental and physical fitness and release good hormones.

Yoga is recognised as a therapeutic treatment proven to work for carpal tunnel syndrome and other repetitive stress injuries; lower backache; incontinence; headaches; depression and more. It has also been proven that heart disease and prostate cancer can be prevented and even reversed with a yoga lifestyle programme in combination with a low fat diet, cardio exercise, stress management, and community support. The fact that such programmes are now covered by Blue Cross and Medicare insurance programs is a reflection of how seriously they are being taken.

Yoga has grown in popularity over the last ten years and these days you will find it to be a popular component of most holistic holidays. Practising yoga helps to make the body become fitter and less prone to injury, the immune system is strengthened, the mind is calmed, spatial and verbal memory are enhanced, virility is improved, blood sugar levels are lowered, and stress levels plummet – after just one yoga class! Yoga can be practised by all ages and abilities; from those in wheelchairs to the very fittest. There is no need for special clothing or equipment and a well trained teacher can help you experience yoga to the fullest.

Dominica helps you combine the benefits of nature and yoga. Close your eyes and visualise practising yoga as you sense the very essence of nature: imagine twinkling stars and moon against a night sky, a waterfall tumbling down a nearby cliff, birdsong ringing out across the rainforest, the sound of surf crashing on to a reef, and soft sands against the gold, orange, and yellow of a Caribbean sunset. Dominica offers yoga in nature; a way to take your health and wellness experience further and deepen your connection to the natural environment.

Trudy Scott Prevost of Rainforest Yoga is a health and wellness consultant, master yoga teacher and holistic education expert. For further information: www.rainbowyogaindominica.wordpress.com.

WELLNESS PRACTITIONERS

Amethyst Holistic Therapy with Cindi John; ☎ 767 225 0557; e amethyst@cwdom.dm. Massage, reflexology, seated acupressure massage, Indian head massage, hot stone massage.

Ariane Magloire ☎ 767 616 8687. Massage & physiotherapy island-wide.

Harmony Massage at Zen Gardens with Rita Bruce, Glo Gommier; ☎ 767 449 3737; e zengardens37@gmail.com. Aromatherapy, massage & reflexology. See page 206 for accommodation information.

Jungle Bay Resort & Spa Delices; ☎ 767 446 1789; e info@junglebaydominica.com.

Wide range of wellness services including yoga & massage. See page 155 for accommodation information.

Nature Isle Wellness with Martha Cuffy; ☎ 767 276 9455, 295 9323; e martha@ marthacuffy.com. Gene key therapy, lifestyle & wellness coaching, yoga, massage.

Onelove Livity with Terri Henry; ☎ 767 440 6549, 767 295 1655; e onelove@ onelovelivity.com. Ecotherapy, holistic wellness retreats, health & wellness consultancy, learn massage workshops.

Papillote Wilderness Retreat Trafalgar;
🕻 767 448 2287; e papillote@cwdom.dm.
Massage services & hot pools. See page 116 for
accommodation information.
Quantum Leap with Dr Janet Taylor Wotten
Waven; 🕻 767 440 3118, 767 616 0173;
e quantumleap@cwdom.dm. Holistic
chiropractic care.

Rainbow Yoga with Trudy Scott Prevost;
🕻 767 245 2474; e rainbowyoga@yahoo.com.
Full range of yoga services, classes & retreats,
health & wellness consulting. Island-wide.
Rasta Yoga Rosalie (Grand Fond Rd); 🕻 767 446
2247. Yoga & meditation ashram. See page 157
for yoga retreat packages.
Transcendental Meditation Centre Goodwill,
Roseau; 🕻 767 449 8154; e tmcentre@cwdom.dm.
Transcendental meditation.

HOT SULPHUR SPAS

Papillote Wilderness Retreat Trafalgar;
🕻 767 448 2287; e papillote@cwdom.dm;
www.papillote.dm. Long-established eco-resort
set in 2ha of stunning, landscaped private
gardens with natural hot springs, 4 hot pools,
1 cold pool & 2 waterfalls. Massage therapies also
available. Access to pools via steps.
Rainforest Shangri-La Wotten Waven; 🕻 767
440 5093; e shangrila@cwdom.dm. Wellness
resort located along the volcanically active River
Blanc offering hot & cold mineral rich pools,
natural steam sauna, river bathing & wellness
therapies. Restaurant & cottage accommodation
available. Access to hot pools via long track.

Screw's Sulphur Spa Wotten Waven; 🕻 767
440 4478. Very popular spa, beautifully designed
with large pools & bar. Access is via steps.
Ti Kwen Glo Cho Wotten Waven 🕻 767 440
3162. Hot & cold pools, 'hot bathtubs', mud
bath & waterfall. Natural surroundings, private
& peaceful. Rustic bar with local cooking by
request. Access to pool via garden track.
Tia's Bamboo Cottages Wotten Waven; 🕻 767
448 1998; e tiabamboocottages@hotmail.com.
Pretty gardens & cottages with 4 hot pools –
2 by the river & 2 enclosed in thatched huts for
privacy. Enclosed spa has easy access for people
with disabilities. Accommodation & restaurant.

WHALE WATCHING

Sperm whales breed in the waters around Dominica and therefore sightings of
these magnificent creatures are common. Pilot and humpback whales are also
frequently encountered as are large playful pods of spinner, Atlantic spotted and
bottlenose dolphins. Though dolphins can sometimes be seen from the shore, a
boat excursion increases the likelihood of sightings, and close encounters with
dolphins and whales are experiences treasured by many. Nevertheless before
opting for a whale-watching trip, you should be aware that there are absolutely no
guarantees when it comes to sightings. Operators reasonably claim success rates
of above 80% but it is possible for a whale-watching excursion to become simply a
rather expensive boat ride. Be ready for this. Your boat captain and his crew will do
their best, but if whales are not around or are travelling fast, it may just be one of
those days. Excursions usually take three to four hours and include refreshments.
Sea conditions along the west coast are usually calm though if you are prone to
seasickness, please take some medication ahead of your trip. Whilst prices vary,
adults should expect to pay up to US$50. There is usually a reduction for children.

ALDive Loubiere, Roseau; 🕻 767 440 3483;
e aldive@aldive.com; www.aldive.com.
Personal & friendly service on ALDive's 'deep sea
expedition'.
Anchorage Dive Centre Anchorage Hotel, Castle
Comfort, Roseau; 🕻 767 448 2638;

e reservations@anchoragehotel.dm;
www.anchoragehotel.dm. Operates 2 large whale-
watching catamarans, 1 of them sail-powered.
Dive Dominica Castle Comfort, Roseau;
🕻 767 448 2188; e dive@cwdom.dm;
www.castlecomfortdivelodge.com,

www.divedominica.com. Regular whale-watching trips aboard 2 fully equipped boats.
Fort Young Hotel Dive Centre Roseau; ☏ 767 448 5000; e fortyoung@cwdom.dm; www.fortyounghotel.com. Uses the services of Dive Dominica. Fort Young jetty pick-up & drop-off.

Island Style Fishing Fortune, Roseau; ☏ 767 265 0518, 767 613 1773; e islandstylefishing@gmail.com; www.islandstylefishing.com. Captain Jerry offers whale-watching trips aboard his fully equipped 10m twin-engine Sea Ray.

ZIP-LINING

The Wacky Rollers Adventure Park is located along the Layou River, very close to the west coast highway. It has a zip-lining and tree-top adventure course for adults and another for young children. It is great fun. River tubing and kayaking are also available (see pages 81 and 82).

Wacky Rollers (WRAVE) Ltd Roseau; ☏ 767 449 8276; e wackyrollers@yahoo.com; www.wackyrollers.com

Part Two

THE GUIDE

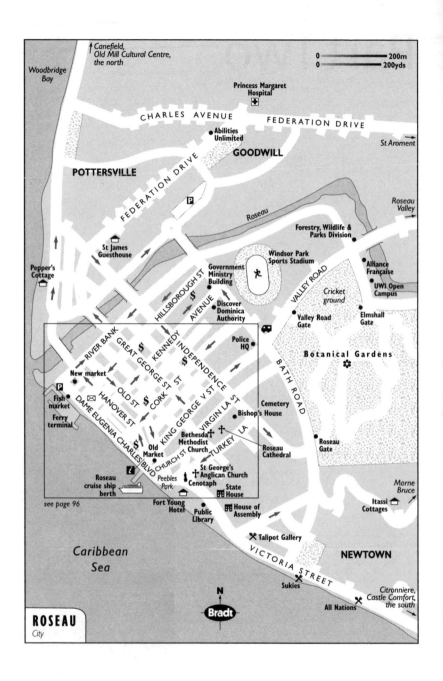

Caribbean
Sea

see page 96

ROSEAU
City

N

Bradt

4

Roseau and Environs

Roseau is Dominica's capital and its major seaport. It is located on the southwest coast of the island at the foot of a broad river valley. From the heights of Dominica's lush interior, the Roseau River runs through the town and eventually out to sea. The central shopping, administrative and business district of Roseau is to the south of the river, and the residential neighbourhoods of Pottersville, Goodwill and St Aroment are situated to the north. At the southern edge of the central district is the old French Quarter, where the original settlement was built. To its south is the coastal road and the neighbourhoods of Newtown, Citronniere and Castle Comfort.

First impressions of Roseau are generally mixed. For a capital, the town is very small and busy, habitually jammed with cars, people and buses. It is usually noisy and always hot. A lack of proper footpaths and a network of open gutters frequently force pedestrians out into the road amongst the traffic. This can make both driving and walking around town quite a precarious business. The buildings of Roseau are a blend of the old, the new and the downright ramshackle. Walk with your head down, dodging vehicles and getting steamy under the collar and the town can feel ugly and oppressive. Take your time, look up at the jalousie windows, the ornate fretwork verandas and the mountainous backdrop and it can be quite a different place altogether.

Ambitious plans are afoot to beautify Roseau and make it more visitor friendly. This may include boardwalks along the Bay Front, river paths, water taxis, pedestrian zones and more green spaces. To relieve traffic congestion, a new road bridge has been built to the east of the town, linking it with Goodwill and, at the time of writing, a fourth is under construction on the western edge of town that will help vehicles exit the capital for the west coast highway.

Love it or hate it, Roseau is inescapably the engine room of the island, the hub and the hubbub, where government, financial institutions, communications and transport services find their nucleus, where merchants trade and where farmers turn up from the countryside to sell their produce. It is also the location of the island's main port and where the majority of visiting cruise ships put in.

A BRIEF HISTORY OF ROSEAU

Chief Ukale's Kalinago settlement on the flat lands around the river mouth was called Sairi. During the French occupation of Dominica in the early 1700s the settlement was renamed Roseau after the preponderance of tall river reeds (*Arundo saccharoides*) that still grow wild in the Roseau Valley, particularly in the area between Wotten Waven and Trafalgar. The town almost had to endure a third name change during the British occupation when King George III decided to call it Charlotteville after his wife, but unfortunately for the royal couple the name did not stick and the town reverted to Roseau.

Foresters from Martinique arriving on Dominica's south coast began building houses in the area alongside the Kalinago in the early 18th century, and a French settlement in Sairi was soon established. A church and small wooden fort were erected, and, when the British arrived in 1761, the town of Roseau was developed still further and the Kalinago retreated to the east. In 1805, during a French attempt to recapture the island, the entire town was engulfed and destroyed by fire. Everything had to be rebuilt. Roseau has subsequently endured damage from a number of hurricanes and so a large part of the original settlement has either disappeared or has been reconstructed.

GETTING THERE AND AWAY

BY BUS Buses to and from Roseau run throughout the day. Depending on your location you may either have to wait a while or change to another bus at Portsmouth. Most buses do not run in the evenings though it is still possible to catch one up to around 21.00 on the west coast highway. Do not depend on it however. See box on page 50 for a directory of Roseau bus stops and sample fares.

BY CAR Roseau has a one-way system that can be a little confusing at first, but you will get used to it. The town is not large and looking at the direction of parked cars will help you in places where signage is poor. There are no traffic lights, but during the morning rush hour to work there are sometimes traffic police on duty, often compounding the mayhem.

If you are entering Roseau from the west coast highway you will cross a single lane bridge over the Roseau River and land on Independence Street which is one-way and goes in a straight line all the way through the capital to the Botanical Gardens and Bath Road. The Botanical Gardens can take you on to Valley Road which goes up the Roseau Valley, and turning right onto Bath Road will take you to the south via Newtown.

If you are entering Roseau from the south, you will usually pass along Victoria Street, and at the small traffic island near the Fort Young Hotel and the cenotaph, the left-hand lane brings you on to Dame Eugenia Charles Boulevard, commonly known as the Bay Front. Please note you cannot turn right onto Turkey Lane at this traffic island. If you are entering Roseau from the south and wish to bypass the heart of it, especially during busy periods, take a right turn just before the House of Assembly (the big pink building opposite DBS Radio) and then take a left at the end on to Bath Road. If you wish to go up the Roseau Valley, head into the Botanical Gardens at the Roseau Gate. Exit the gardens to the left at the Elmshall Gate and turn right at the next road junction near the Alliance Francaise. If you wish to head north, continue along Bath Road, cross over the bridge, take a right at the traffic island and go up into Goodwill. In Goodwill, a left turn at the traffic island in front of the Princess Margaret Hospital will bring you down to the west coast highway.

If you are approaching Roseau from the Roseau Valley you will come to a junction just over the Roseau River bridge. Left will take you past the Alliance Francaise and UWI Campus into the Botanical Gardens via the Elmshall Gate where you can bypass Roseau for the south (this is also a good way of getting back to Fort Young – just take a right when you see the DBS Radio station on Victoria Street). A right turn will take you past the Forestry & Wildlife Division office and around the back of the Windsor Park Stadium to the bridge that leads up to Goodwill. This is a good way of bypassing the heart of the capital if you are heading north along the west coast highway. Straight on at the initial Valley Road junction brings you to the top of King George V Street (you should see the Police Headquarters) where you must turn right on to Bath Road.

Great George Street is one-way and runs northwest out of town over the Roseau River. Once across the bridge, a left turn will get you on to the west coast highway and straight on will take you to Federation Drive, Goodwill and St Aroment. At the time of writing, a new bridge is being built at the northern end of Hanover Street by the new market, crossing the Roseau River, and taking traffic straight on to the west coast highway through Pottersville.

ORIENTATION AND GETTING AROUND

DOWNTOWN ROSEAU The best and most practical way to get around Roseau is on foot. The town is small and nowhere is very far. A lack of proper footpaths, extended porticoes and open gutters make walking quite troublesome, however, and it is important to keep a sharp lookout for traffic when you are inevitably forced on to the roads. Finding your way round the central area is fairly straightforward, as the layout is a grid system with all roads running in a straight line north to south or east to west. In the old French Quarter, the road layout is a little more interesting. Look out for small street signs on corners to help you find your way round and refer to the maps on pages 92 and 96.

Central Roseau Along the riverbank, at the northern tip of the Bay Front, is the **New Market**. Here fresh fruit and vegetables, flowers, seasonings, red meats and poultry are sold. The market is open every day except Sunday, but the majority of farmers and hucksters arrive to sell their goods on Friday evening and Saturday morning. From early in the morning, the Saturday market in Roseau is a very lively affair, in fact almost a social occasion, where people buy and sell, meet up and chat with their friends.

It is the largest market in Dominica and you should certainly pay it a visit. Please note that market vendors have become particularly sensitive about having their photograph taken. Please ask for permission and be prepared to receive a curt brush-off. Do not take it personally. If you would like to take photographs of their produce only, this is usually fine, but be sure to ask first to avoid any kind of unpleasantness. Resist trying candid shots; someone will spot you and a fuss may ensue. The reasons for this sensitivity are unclear but it may be a reaction to having too many lenses pointed in their faces over time, especially during the height of the cruise ship season. (See also *Photography* on page 64.) For information on the types of fruits and vegetables you may find here see page 58.

Located on the western edge of the new market along the bay front is the Roseau **fish market**, where it is possible to buy fresh fish daily except on Sundays. The fish market is quite basic but also quite lively on Saturdays; and it is always interesting to see fish steaks being chopped up with a wooden mallet and large machete! A little further along the Bay Front is the Roseau **ferry terminal** where you can catch the Express Des Îles high speed catamaran service that operates between Guadeloupe, Dominica, Martinique and St Lucia.

The Roseau City Council buildings, located opposite the fisheries complex and the ferry terminal, are some of the oldest still standing in the town. This was once the location of the town's **barracoon**, where slaves were temporarily barracked before being auctioned in the small courtyard beyond the archway on the south side of the building. The style of the barracoon is very similar to those constructed on the west African coast to house slaves prior to boarding ships for the West Indies.

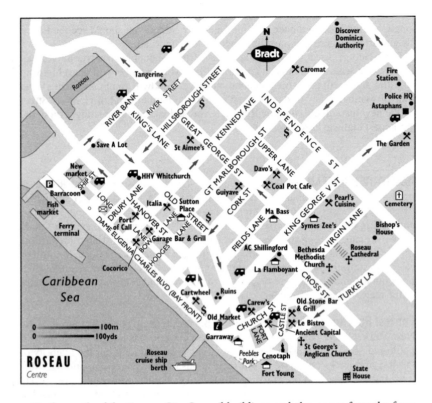

To the south of the Roseau City Council buildings and also across from the ferry terminal is the main **post office**. From here the Bay Front (Dame Eugenia Charles Boulevard) runs along the shore to the Fort Young Hotel at its southern tip. Along the Bay Front are a couple of bars and cafés, boutiques, souvenir and duty free shops, the tourist information building, the Dominica Museum (see page 98), the Royal Bank of Canada and the Garraway Hotel. In the centre of the Bay Front is the registry and court house. The Bay Front is also the current location of the Roseau **cruise ship jetty** though there are plans to construct a new jetty further to the south at Woodbridge Bay.

From the Bay Front, Roseau moves inland in blocks of shops, eateries, banks and other businesses. Most shops are quite small and functional with little to attract visitors who are accustomed to large shopping malls and a plentiful supply of just about everything. There are one or two interesting places in this part of town if you look for them, however. **Fields Lane** is a rather quaint, narrow street with some traditional old and colourful buildings. It is quite often rather peaceful here too, which is a welcome surprise in the ruckus of the town centre. On Cork Street you may come across a rather dilapidated old building with a small sign saying 'Cottage Industries Shoe Repairs', and along the pavement local cobblers mend shoes quite expertly for just a few dollars. On Hillsborough Street look out for the liberation colours of The Organic Shop, where you can buy a selection of organically grown fruit and vegetables.

The **Windsor Park Sports Stadium** is located on Bath Street at the end of Kennedy Avenue. It was funded by China and constructed by Chinese workers in 2008. With a capacity of around 12,000 spectators, the stadium hosts football and cricket matches as well as other large cultural and music events. The annual World

Creole Music Festival takes place here, and there have also been a number on one-day international cricket matches as well as World Cup qualifying football.

King George V Street and the French Quarter King George V Street runs from the Bay Front right across the town to the east and the entrance to the Roseau Valley. South of King George V Street is the area where French settlers developed a small village in the early 18th century. Referred to these days as the French Quarter, this area retains the character of a more historic Roseau which, despite the impact of hurricanes and conflagration, is still palpable when walking its meandering streets.

THE ROSEAU CATHEDRAL

In all likelihood the first Catholic church in Roseau was an open-sided wooden hut with a roof made of river reeds, and it would have been in such an inauspicious setting that Bishop Dom Gervaise administered the sacrament of confirmation to French foresters in 1727. French settlers arriving from Martinique established themselves along the south coast and began to concentrate in the Kalinago village of Sairi. In 1730 Father Guillaume Martel arrived and began work on a solid timber church for his growing congregation. The new church had a stone floor and was approximately 12m long by 5m wide. Located in the same area as the present cathedral, this timber structure survived for almost a hundred years until it was destroyed by a hurricane in 1816. It was not until 24 years later that a replacement was completed, only for everyone to decide it was far too small. Emancipation meant that former slaves were now also free to worship in Roseau's church, and so a programme of enlargement began that did not reach its conclusion until around a hundred years later.

In 1855 the main steeple was erected and in 1865 the Kalinago offered a hand by cutting and transporting timber from the *simaruba* tree from the northeast down to Roseau. For around three months, the Kalinago camped on the edge of town at night and installed a wooden ceiling in the cathedral by day. Around that time a huge stone pulpit carved by prisoners on the notorious Devil's Island penal colony arrived in Roseau from Cayenne in French Guiana. In 1873 the Chapel of St Joseph was constructed on the southeast corner with a crypt beneath it for deceased bishops and priests, and in 1878 Father Auguste Fort extended the aisles and had the east steeple built. Another hurricane inflicted considerable damage in 1883, but in its aftermath funds were collected to repair it along with other damaged churches around the island. It was during this period that the stained-glass windows were added. In 1902 new stone pillars were installed and new pews carved and in 1916 the west steeple was added, the stones for which came from the old church at Pointe Michel. This balanced the external appearance of the cathedral. In 1925 the cathedral was consecrated by Bishop James Morris.

There have been few changes since 1925, though one or two small, modern additions such as electric lighting, a clock and an address system have been installed. Originally named L'Eglise de Notre Dame du Bon Port du Mouillage de Roseau, the cathedral has developed its presence and stands majestically overlooking the town today as Our Lady of Fair Haven. Its size is deceptive. From the outside it seems quite small, but once inside it feels very spacious, light and airy thanks to the lovely stained-glass windows and the open windows that run along both east and west walls from the main entrance to the altar.

King George V Street is a thoroughfare of hustle and bustle. At varying times of the day it is busy with either traffic, shoppers, street vendors or schoolchildren, and at lunchtimes all of them at once. The eastern end is dominated by the Astaphans department store and Police Headquarters building. To the west of the junction with Independence Street there are a number of small shops, restaurants, snackettes and bars located in old buildings of stone and wood, and displaying some fine examples of traditional architecture. Upper floor jalousie-style windows are framed by heavy wooden shutters and iron and wooden verandas are decorated with ornate fretwork. To appreciate this street properly you must walk it looking up, rather than down, for that is where you will see the interesting architecture and get a better feel for the history of the place.

At the western end of King George V Street is the **Old Market Square**. This used to be a place where food produce was bought and sold, where slaves were auctioned and where public executions were carried out. Today it hosts a craft and souvenir market, though this is also scheduled to change. It is interesting to note how the old streets laid by the French settlers radiate out from this central point. King George V Street goes straight up to the Roseau Valley, Hanover Street goes in a straight line to the Roseau River, and Church Street leads to the Roseau Cathedral (see page 97). Located within the Old Market Square is a cast iron fountain where a well was once located, and the Dawbiney hucksters shelter which is still used today. Between the Old Market and the Bay Front is the town's former post office building, constructed in 1810. Today it houses the **tourist information** office (⊕ *08.00–17.00 Mon, 08.00–16.00 Tue–Fri, on w/ends for cruise ships*) on the ground floor and the **Dominica Museum** above (⊕ *09.00–16.00 Mon–Fri, 09.00–12.00 Sat; entrance fee EC$3 adults, EC$1 students*). The entrance to the museum is up a flight of steps on the Bay Front side of the building.

At the southern tip of Dame Eugenia Charles Boulevard is **Fort Young Hotel**. On a slightly elevated position above the original French settlement, a small wooden fort was constructed in 1720 to protect Roseau's inhabitants from attack. A sturdier stone structure was built in 1770 by Sir William Young, the first British governor of Dominica. Between 1778 and 1805 the French attempted to recapture the island and the fort was the scene of much fighting. It was as a direct result of this warfare that in 1805 the settlement of Roseau caught fire and was razed to the ground. From the 1850s the fort was used as a police station and a hundred years later in 1964 it was converted into a hotel. The hotel had to be rebuilt following Hurricane David 15 years later. The original battlements and ramparts of the fort can still be seen beneath its more modern additions.

Next to the Fort Young Hotel is **Peebles Park** which, even when cruise ships are in port, somehow seems to retain a peaceful serenity away from the excitement of the Bay Front and the Old Market. With its beautiful flamboyant trees, wide benches, lawn and bandstand, it is an oasis of calm. Take a seat and relax before heading back into the ballyhoo of town. On the small enclosed triangular lawn opposite the park is the **cenotaph**, a memorial to Dominicans who lost their lives fighting in World War I and II. The smaller memorial next to the cenotaph is in honour of the Free French who came to Dominica in 1940 from Martinique and Guadeloupe following the fall of France to Germany. These islands supported the Vichy regime until US naval blockades forced them to switch their allegiance to the Free French.

On the other side of Fort Young is the **Public Library**. Designed by Dominica's first Crown Colony administrator, Hesketh Bell, and funded by philanthropist Andrew Carnegie, the library was constructed in 1906. It is a beautiful building

This route will take between two and three hours at a leisurely pace. Take plenty of water.

Start in front of the Roseau cruise ship berth facing the old post office building, now home to the tourist information centre and Dominica Museum. Take the road between the museum and the Royal Bank of Canada and head eastwards away from the sea up King George V Street. To your right is the Old Market. Continue straight on up King George V Street, taking note of the traditional architecture of the upper floors. At the junction with Great George Street, on your left, is Norwood House, one of the last surviving 19th-century town houses built almost entirely of wood. Continue along King George V Street right up to the junction with Bath Road. The Police Headquarters building will be on your left.

Straight ahead is Valley Road, gateway to the Roseau Valley. A short distance up this road on the right is an entrance to the Botanical Gardens (Valley Road Gate). Enter the gardens and walk alongside the cricket ground, which should be on your left. At the intersection, go left and then follow the signs for Jack's Walk. Climb the steep footpath to the top of Morne Bruce and look out across the town from the viewpoint. Return back down Jack's Walk. At the bottom, take a left and then a right down the steps. The path emerges by the parrot sanctuary where it is possible to see sisserou parrots. A jaco parrot aviary is located nearby.

From the sanctuary head left at the junction and follow the path past the fallen giant baobab tree and the crushed school bus, and then exit the gardens through the Roseau Gate. Walk straight ahead at the road junction. Be careful because there is no footpath here. The Catholic cemetery is on your left. Take the second road on the left. This is Virgin Lane and runs past the Bishop's House and main entrance of Roseau Cathedral. Come out of the cathedral and walk around to the west side where there are steps leading down. The Bethesda Methodist Church is to your right. At the bottom of the steps turn left and follow the road to the first junction. Turn right along Turkey Lane and walk to the end. At the junction with the small traffic island, turn left. St George's Anglican Church is on your left-hand side followed by the grounds of the State House and then the House of Assembly. Cross the road and turn full circle, heading back towards town. The Public Library is on your left followed by the Fort Young Hotel. On the north side of Fort Young is Peebles Park with its flamboyant trees and bandstand. Cross the road to the cenotaph. On the far side of the cenotaph to the right of the Wacky Rollers (WRAVE) office is the pretty Fort Lane. Walk down this old cobbled street. At the bottom of Fort Lane turn left on Church Street and head back to the Old Market and the Bay Front where your walk began. Enjoy a refreshing drink from the Juice Man who usually stands by the market, or at the Cartwheel Cafe opposite the cruise ship jetty.

4

with a Georgian-style veranda around the south side overlooking a small garden and the sea. The library contains a good selection of reference books, particularly on Dominica.

Across Victoria Street, opposite the library, is the gated entrance to the grounds of the **State House**. Official residence of Dominica's governors and presidents since 1840, for the last 30 years it has been used primarily for official functions and state receptions. Next to the State House is the **House of Assembly**, Dominica's parliament building. It was originally constructed in 1811, but in 1979 it was destroyed by arsonists and had to be rebuilt.

On the corner of Victoria Street opposite the cenotaph and Fort Young is the **St George's Anglican Church** of the Diocese of the North Eastern Caribbean and Aruba. Built in the 1820s, the church was yet another victim of Hurricane David in 1979 and had to be reconstructed.

The roads and meandering lanes between King George V Street and Turkey Lane is a peaceful area to walk around and has some interesting architecture. The quaint Fort Lane between the cenotaph and Church Street is just one example of how Roseau perhaps once appeared. The cream and red painted house on the corner is a lovely example of the town's vernacular architecture. On the corner of Cross Street and Virgin Lane is the **Bethesda Methodist Church** which is situated in close proximity to the **Roseau Cathedral**. To the east of the cathedral is the **Bishop's House**, which was constructed in the late 1800s.

NORTH OF DOWNTOWN ROSEAU On the northern outskirts of Roseau are the districts of **Pottersville**, **Goodwill**, and a little further along the coast, beyond the port and the cliffs, **Canefield**. Above Goodwill, at the end of Federation Drive, is **St Aroment**. These areas are mostly residential, interspersed with small businesses and the occasional guesthouse. Dominica's Princess Margaret Hospital is located on Federation Drive in Goodwill.

Canefield used to be one of the largest sugar-and-lime producing estates on the island. Some of the original works buildings were restored and in 1988 the **Old Mill Cultural Centre** was opened, housing the offices of Dominica's Cultural Division. The centre hosts a sculpture workshop, theatre, art gallery and dance studio. It is a good place to call in and find out about events that may be taking place during your stay.

SOUTH OF DOWNTOWN ROSEAU To the south of Roseau along the coastal road are the residential communities of **Newtown**, **Citronniere** and **Castle Comfort**. Life in Newtown seems to revolve around the main thoroughfare, Victoria Street, which can be a lively place, especially in the evenings when locals can be seen sitting out on their stoops, discussing local affairs, listening to music, braiding hair, or just watching the world pass by. The playing field on the northern edge of the two joined-up communities is Newtown Savannah, where football matches are played and live music events are occasionally hosted. Castle Comfort is a community to the south of Citronniere. Aside from some hotels on the waterfront, most of Castle Comfort is residential and located on the hillside beneath the heights of Giraudel village and Morne Anglais.

 WHERE TO STAY

HIGH END

Fort Young Hotel (71 rooms) Victoria St, Roseau; 767 448 5000; e fortyoung@ cwdom.dm; www.fortyounghotel.com. Dominica's best-known resort & business hotel. Ocean-front rooms & suites, all with AC, en-suite bathrooms, telephone, TV & internet access. The hotel has a bar, 2 restaurants & a boardwalk café. There is a spa, gym, duty free shopping, a private jetty, a pool, sun terrace & jacuzzi. The hotel offers a wide range of tours, scuba diving, wedding, honeymoon & family packages. Very popular choice in a convenient location. **$$$–$$$$**

🏠 **Sisserou Villa & Sisserou Lodge**
(3-bed villa, 1-bed lodge) Reigate; 📞 767 277
8714; e fsawers@gmail.com;
www.dominicaaccommodation.com. Modern
SC lodge with bedroom, lounge, kitchen, TV,
internet, veranda & great views. Fully-equipped
& spacious villa, large dining terrace with views

MODERATE

🏠 **Anchorage Hotel Whale Watch & Dive
Centre** (32 rooms) Castle Comfort; 📞 767 448
2638; e reservations@anchoragehotel.dm;
www.anchoragehotel.dm. This resort-style
hotel offers 12 standard & 20 ocean front rooms
with en-suite bathrooms, AC, TV, telephone &
internet access. There is a terrace restaurant, bar
& swimming pool. The hotel has its own jetty, 2
large whale-watching catamarans, dive shop &
dive boat. PADI dive courses offered. **$$$**

🏠 **Evergreen Hotel** (16 rooms,
1 'Honeymoon Hut') Castle Comfort; 📞 767 448
3288; e evergreen@cwdom.dm;
www.evergreenhoteldominica.com. Very pleasant
hotel on the seafront south of Roseau. All rooms
have AC, en-suite bathrooms, TV, telephone.
Some have a balcony & sea view. There is also a
'Honeymoon Hut' for the romantics. The hotel has an
open lounge, restaurant, bar, sun deck & swimming
pool. Friendly with good service & well located for
hiking & scuba diving excursions. **$$$**, inc b/fast

🏠 **Garraway Hotel** (31 rooms) 1 Dame
Eugenia Charles Blvd, Roseau; 📞 767 449 8800;
e garraway@cwdom.dm; www.garrawayhotel.
com. Business-style hotel located on the Roseau
Bay Front close to the Old Market & historic
French Quarter. Combination of dbls & suites,
all with en-suite bathroom, internet access,
AC, TV, fridge & telephone. Executive suites
also available with business facilities. Ocean or
mountain views. Conference centre & business
services. Terrace bar overlooking the Roseau Bay
Front. Restaurant serves continental b/fasts &
international cuisine. Full packages including
tours, honeymoon & dive are available. **$$$**

🏠 **Castle Comfort Dive Lodge** (14 rooms)
Castle Comfort; 📞 767 448 2188; toll free:
📞 1 888 414 7276; e dive@cwdom.dm;
www.castlecomfortdivelodge.com,
www.divedominica.com. Well-established lodge
& dive centre with pretty gardens, private jetty
& 5 fully equipped boats offering scuba diving,

of Roseau & Caribbean. Both lodge & villa have
use of swimming pool, deck & gardens. Regular
housekeeping service, welcome packages & very
friendly hosts. Excellent, modern & clean SC
accommodation, ideal for exploring the south.
Lodge **$$$**, villa **$$$$$**

snorkelling, whale watching & sports fishing.
Each room has en-suite bathroom, AC & fans,
telephone, TV & wireless internet access. Waterfront
bar, balcony restaurant, sun deck, & small pool.
PADI scuba instruction. Wide range of dive &
accommodation packages available. Gift shop stocks
equipment & local crafts & souvenirs. Check website
or call for details & special offers. **$$–$$$**

🏠 **Hummingbird Inn** (9 rooms, 1 suite)
Morne Daniel Cliffs, Canefield; 📞 767 449 1042;
e hummingbirddominica@gmail.com.
www.thehummingbirdinn.com. Wooden chalet-
style accommodation in elevated woodland
location above the main highway between
Roseau & Canefield in the area of Rockaway
Beach. Rooms have en-suite bathrooms, fans,
veranda & garden views. Suite has large 4-poster
bed, small kitchen & living area. Kitchen
restaurant provides local cuisine by request.
Rooms **$$**, suite **$$$**

🏠 **Titiwi Inn** (1 apt with 3 rooms) Citronniere;
📞 767 448 0553; e info@titiwi.com;
www.titiwi.com. Spacious 3-bedroom apt with
dbl beds, en-suite bathrooms, AC, TV, lounge,
& fully-equipped kitchen. Master bedroom has
balcony with sea view. Wireless internet, terrace
bar & swimming pool with access to beach. Good
choice for families & friends exploring the south
or scuba diving. **$$–$$$**

🏠 **Sutton Place Hotel** (8 rooms) 25 Old St,
Roseau; 📞 767 449 8700; e sutton2@cwdom.dm;
www.suttonplacehoteldominica.com. Historic
hotel in the heart of the capital with 5 standard
rooms & 3 suites. All rooms have en-suite
bathrooms, AC, TV, telephone, hairdryer & wireless
internet. Rooms are traditionally decorated,
some with 4-poster beds. Suites have living
area, dining table & kitchenette. Pleasant Sutton
Grille restaurant with open patio area serving
continental b/fasts & international cuisine. Check
out the *roti* days on Sat & Wed. Popular Cellars Bar
downstairs. **$$–$$$**, inc b/fast

🏠 **La Flamboyant Hotel** (15 rooms) 22 King George V St, Roseau; ☎ 767 440 7190; e reservation@laflamboyanthotel.dm; www.laflamboyanthotel.dm. Chic & colourful business-style hotel located in downtown Roseau. Standard rooms have en-suite bathroom, AC, TV & internet access. Executive rooms also have fridge & business facilities. Creole restaurant & bar, conference facilities & laundry service. **$$**

🏠 **Itassi Cottages** (1 2-bed cottage, 1 1-bed cottage, 1 1-bed studio apt) Morne Bruce; ☎ 767 448 4313; e sutton2@cwdom.dm; www.avirtualdominica.com/itassi. Located on the slopes of Morne Bruce, near the Botanical Gardens, 2 SC cottages in the grounds of the owner. Lower cottage sleeps 4 & is a traditional wooden building that was once the maid's quarters. Upper cottage with studio room below sleeps 2 & is more modern with veranda, hammocks, louvre shutters & wooden floors. Cottages have SC facilities. All accommodation has en-suite bathroom, TV & fans. **$$**

BUDGET

🏠 **Ma Bass Central Guesthouse** (12 rooms) 44 Fields La, Roseau; ☎ 767 448 2999. A basic but very clean & well-run guesthouse down a quiet lane just off Independence St. The lovely Ma Bass has 12 rooms with shared bathroom & kitchen facilities. Top 3 rooms have private bathrooms. All rooms have fans. Verandas overlook the rooftops of the town with nice views of mountains & sea. An authentic, good value Dominica experience. **$**

🏠 **Peppers Cottage** (1 room) 21 Eliott Av, Pottersville, Roseau; ☎ 767 440 4321; e askpepper@pepperscottage.com; www.pepperscottage.com. Simple accommodation in a small urban cottage along seafront, close to town centre. AC, TV, kitchenette, & en-suite bathroom, rear patio & plunge pool. Owner operates a taxi & tour service. **$**

🏠 **St James Guesthouse 1 & 2** (11 rooms) Federation Dr & Church La, Goodwill; ☎ 767 448 7170; e stjamesguesthouse@hotmail.com; www.avirtualdominica.com/st-jamesguesthouse. Pleasant guesthouses located very close to each other & just a few mins' walk from downtown Roseau. Sgl, dbl & trpl rooms with ceiling fans, TVs, wireless internet access, mosquito nets. Most rooms have en-suite bathrooms, some are shared, 5 have AC. Very clean & tidy. Small restaurant & bar. Very welcoming owners Carol & Phil do the cooking. Complementary pick-up & drop-off to Roseau ferry terminal. Very good value, well-run accommodation. B/fast inc. **$**

🏠 **Sea World Guesthouse** (14 rooms) ☎ 767 448 5068; e seaworlddominica@yahoo.com; www.avirtualdominica.com/seaworld. Budget accommodation in seafront guesthouse on the coastal road in Citronniere between Newtown & Castle Comfort. All rooms have en-suite bathrooms, TV & fans. 12 rooms have AC. Roadside bar & grill, yacht servicing & private jetty. Popular with visitors from the French islands. **$**

🏠 **Symes Zee Guesthouse** (15 rooms) 34 King George V St, Roseau; ☎ 767 448 2494. Rooms for rent above a bar & restaurant on a lively street near French Quarter. All have private en-suite bathrooms & fans, AC also available. Some rooms can sleep up to 4 people. Handy location, especially for Carnival & Creole. **$**

✖ WHERE TO EAT AND DRINK

CREOLE AND INTERNATIONAL RESTAURANTS

✖ **Evergreen Hotel** Castle Comfort; ☎ 767 448 3288. Hotel restaurant & terrace bar overlooking the sea, serving a selection of local & international cuisine. **$$$**

✖ **Le Bistro** 5 Castle St, Roseau; ☎ 767 440 8117. Talented chef Vincent Binet serves French & Creole at this popular downtown eatery. **$$$**

✖ **Fort Young Hotel Waterfront Restaurant** Victoria St, Roseau; ☎ 767 448 5000. Classy hotel-restaurant serving a range of Creole & international dishes. Also look out for the Boardwalk Café & Balas Bar offering a selection of bar food. Happy hour on Fri. **$$–$$$**

✖ **Talipot Gallery** Cnr Victoria St & High St, Newtown, Roseau; ☎ 767 276 3747. A fusion of eclectic architecture, local artworks & haute Creole & international lunches & dinners on the veranda of the historic Palm Cottage. Reservations preferred. **$$–$$$**

✘ **Anchorage Hotel, Ocean Terrace Restaurant** Castle Comfort, Roseau; ☏ 767 448 2638. Hotel restaurant overlooking the sea, serving a selection of local & international dishes. $$–$$$.

✘ **Garraway Hotel** Dame Eugenia Charles Blvd, Roseau; ☏ 767 449 8800. Balisier Restaurant serves local & international cuisine. $$–$$$

✘ **Sutton Place Hotel** Old St, Roseau; ☏ 767 449 8700. Sutton Grille Restaurant serving local & international cuisine. Try the *rotis* on Wed & Sat. $$–$$$

✘ **Barana Breeze Restaurant & Bar** Castle Comfort Lodge, Castle Comfort, Roseau; ☏ 767 448 2188. Pleasant balcony & deck restaurant

CREOLE EATERIES

✘ **Guiyave** Cork St, Roseau; ☏ 767 448 2930. Creole restaurant located above patisserie. $$

✘ **Pearl's Cuisine** 50 King George V St, Roseau; ☏ 767 448 8707. Local cuisine, b/fast & lunches. Snacks downstairs, small restaurant upstairs with veranda. Daytime only. $–$$

✘ **Cartwheel** Dame Eugenia Charles Blvd, Roseau; ☏ 767 448 5353. Pleasant café located in an old building on the Bay Front near Roseau cruise ship jetty, serving coffee, juices & Creole lunches. Daytime only. $

✘ **All Nations** Victoria St, Newtown. Popular late-night bar & eatery serving good local food & takeaway. $

✘ **The Anchor Restaurant & Bar** Woodbridge Bay. Lively bar & local eatery located near the port. $

✘ **Carew's Limelight Bar** Old Market, Roseau. Cosy bar located in a beautiful old building opposite the Old Market. Serves local lunches, BBQ & snacks. $

ASIAN

✘ **Ancient Capital** Church St, Roseau; ☏ 767 448 6628. Serves very good Asian fusion cuisine. Located in the historic French Quarter. $$

✘ **Dynasty** King George V St, Roseau; ☏ 767 440 3021. Chinese restaurant. $$

✘ **The Garden** King George V St, Roseau; ☏ 767 448 3389. Chinese restaurant. $$

VEGETARIAN

✘ **Coal Pot Café** Woodstone Shopping Mall, Cork St, Roseau. Vegan, vegetarian & fish lunches, wholewheat bakes. $

with lovely sea views. Open for lunches & dinners. BBQ on Fri. $$

✘ **Port of Call** Kennedy Av, Roseau; ☏ 767 448 2910. Located near the Bay Front serving Creole & international dishes. $$

✘ **Cocorico** Dame Eugenia Charles Blvd, Roseau; ☏ 767 449 8686. Local & international lunches & refreshments. Popular with visitors. Daytime only. $$

✘ **Tiffany's** Shed No 15, Canefield Industrial Estate; ☏ 767 245 4793. Coffee, sandwiches, bagels, salads, wraps, *rotis*, beverages & great desserts in gallery surroundings. Original artwork & authentic Dominican crafts. Look for NAPP sign on west coast highway. Daytime only. $

✘ **Caromat Old Stone Snackette & Bar** Kennedy Av, Roseau. Nice little local bar & eatery. $

✘ **Fish N Tings** Kennedy Av, Roseau. Local dishes & takeaway. $

✘ **Italia** Kennedy Av, Roseau; ☏ 767 440 4837. No, not Italian, only by special order. But their local food is popular. $

✘ **Kato's Kubuli Bar** Woodbridge Bay, Roseau. Roadside bar & eatery located by the port. $

✘ **Mange Domnik** King George V St, Roseau. Tasty local snacks located next to The Art Gallery. $

✘ **Miranda's Corner** Springfield. Located on the Imperial Rd at Springfield. Very popular highway bar & eatery. Traditional offerings include bull's foot soup. $

✘ **St Aimie's Diner** Great George St, Roseau; ☏ 767 440 4464. Local lunches, dinners & snacks. $

✘ **New Century** Cnr Cork St & Old St, Roseau; ☏ 767 448 8808. Chinese restaurant. $$

✘ **Yacht Inn** Citronniere; ☏ 767 448 3497. Taiwanese restaurant located on the shoreline. $$

ROADSIDE BARBECUES There are scores of roadside barbecues, all selling a variety of chicken, ribs, fish, plantain, corn and so on. Here are a few popular ones.

✗ **Annette's** Old Market, Roseau. Located right outside Carew's Limelight Bar on a Fri night, Annette serves up BBQ chicken & steamed fish.
✗ **Icho** Canefield. Located on the west coast highway between Canefield & Massacre, right near the speed bumps & the mill ruins. Jamaican jerk a speciality. Bar.

✗ **Lester's** Federation Dr, Goodwill. Located just above the traffic island, serving BBQ chicken, ribs, kebabs & fish with a variety of vegetables & rice. Bar.
✗ **Rhona's** Canefield. Located in a courtyard on the west coast highway near the Canefield branch of the National Bank of Dominica. Good selection of BBQ food. Bar.

FAST FOOD
✗ **KFC** Riverbank, Roseau. The name says it all.
✗ **Perky's Pizza** Independence St, Roseau; ☎767 448 1628. Pizza & subs.
✗ **Pizza Hut Delivery** Cork St, Roseau; ☎767 617 7777. Pizza & pasta.

✗ **Pizza Palace** Riverbank, Roseau; ☎767 448 4598. Vegetarian pizza on wholewheat base.
✗ **Subway** Independence St, Roseau. Sandwiches & subs.

COFFEE, JUICE AND ICE CREAM
⊐ **Backyard Coffee Bar** Fields Lane, Roseau. A cosy little café. The challenge is to find it.
⊐ **Fadelle's Coffee Shop** Kennedy Av, Roseau. Indoor coffee shop.
Island Ice Cream Kennedy Av, Roseau. Local ice cream shop.
JB, The Juice Man Old Market, Roseau. Look out for The Juice Man & his stall outside the Ruins, near the Old Market. Great fresh juices made to order.

⊐ **Le Cafe Desiderata** Old St, Roseau. Outdoor coffee shop located in a cosy stone quarter at the back of the Desiderata boutique. Wireless internet.
Piwi Ice Cream Kings La, Roseau. Very good local ice cream.
⊐ **Rituals** Dame Eugenia Charles Blvd (Bay Front), Roseau. Coffee shop chain serving a selection of coffee, soft drinks, cheesecake & more. Wireless internet.

BARS AND NIGHTLIFE

☆ **The Cove** Canefield. Music venue & waterside bar located on the west coast highway. Serves bar food & occasionally hosts live events.
☆ **Davo's** Upper La, Roseau. Local bar & shop, lively on Fri nights.
☆ **Drop Anchor** Victoria St, Newtown. Pleasant waterfront bar with private dock. A great spot for visiting yachties. Occasional live music.
☆ **Fort Young Hotel** Victoria St, Roseau. Balas Bar located in hotel. Happy Hour with live music on Fri. Serves bar food.
☆ **Garage Bar & Grill** Hanover St, Roseau. Themed bar open daytime & evening. Also serves bar food.
☆ **Garraway Hotel** Dame Eugenia Charles Blvd, Roseau. Live music & DJs on Wed, live jazz on Tue; live music, happy hour & karaoke on Fri.
☆ **Harlem Plaza** Newtown. Very popular live music venue located in a restored 200-year-old building behind Newtown Savannah.

☆ **JR's Bar & Grill** King George V St, Roseau. Lively day & night-time venue for drinks & bar food.
☆ **Krazy Kokonut** Castle Comfort, Roseau. Popular night-time venue, often hosting live music events.
☆ **Old Stone Bar & Grill** Castle St, Roseau. Nice local bar with very good food in a quiet part of town.
☆ **Ruins Rock Café** Old Market, Roseau. Colourful bar located in the ruins of an old building.
☆ **Sukie's on the Bayfront** Newtown, Roseau. Small bar overlooking the sea opposite Newtown Savannah.
☆ **Sutton Hotel Cellars Bar** Old St, Roseau. Bar located beneath Sutton Hotel. Live music on Wed & Fri.
☆ **Symes Zee's** King George V St, Roseau. Bar with live jazz on Thu.

☆ **Tangerine Restaurant & Bar**   Great George St, Roseau. Located near the bridge, watch the world go by.

☆ **Zam Zam**   Citronniere, Roseau. Small & very pleasant, laid back waterside bar serving light Mexican bites. Occasional live music.

SHOPPING

SUPERMARKETS   Roseau has many small convenience stores selling household essentials as well as food and drink. There are also a few larger supermarkets that are usually fairly well stocked. Shopping is quite expensive in Dominica; at least comparable to the US and UK. For fresh produce, the **New Market** along the Roseau River is the best place to shop, especially on Friday nights and Saturday mornings, when most vendors set up their stalls and hucksters arrive selling from the back of pick-up trucks. Some market traders set up stalls on the streets of Roseau on Sunday mornings. This is also a good time to buy jelly coconuts and coconut water.

AC Shillingford   King George V St, Roseau. Supermarket & general store.

Astaphans   King George V St, Roseau. Supermarket downstairs, department store upstairs. Astaphans has a dedicated car park to the side which is free if you shop in the store. Just show your parking voucher to the cashier. The entrance to the car park is via the last left-hand turn off Independence St before you reach King George V St. It is a short narrow road & the car park entrance is at the end on the right.

Brizee's Mart   Canefield. Well-stocked supermarket with dedicated car park located just off the west coast highway on the way to Canefield. Look for it near the Autotrade garage; it is well signposted.

Green's Supermarket   Wallhouse. Small, modern supermarket with a good selection of items. Located just off the main west coast highway between Castle Comfort & Loubiere. Parking.

Save A Lot   River St, Roseau. Small department store. Supermarket on ground floor, toiletries & household goods on upper floor. Open Sun.

Whitchurch IGA   Old St, Roseau. Popular & well-stocked supermarket with deli counter. There is parking at the front & to the side of the store though it is not restricted to Whitchurch shoppers.

ORGANIC & SPECIALITY FOOD & DRINK

Fruits Plus   Cork St, Roseau. An Aladdin's cave of deli products imported from the French islands.

The Organic Shop   Hillsborough St, Roseau. Just look for the liberation colours. Small shop selling organic fruit & vegetable products.

Pirates   Long Lane, Roseau. A duty free shop with a 24x7 cooled 'wine cellar' with a good selection from France. You may also find ham, salami, cheese & chocolate.

ART, CRAFTS AND SOUVENIR SHOPS   Most craft and souvenir stalls are located in or around the main tourist areas such as the Bay Front and the Old Market. The Old Market hosts the highest concentration of souvenir stalls though there are plans to relocate them to a purpose built vendors' market nearby. If you take a tour bus up to Morne Bruce, to Trafalgar Falls or the Emerald Pool, you can expect to see the same type of souvenir stalls in those places too – especially during the cruise ship season. If you can, try to buy authentic Dominican art and crafts (see page 27). Here is a small selection of shops selling crafts and souvenirs.

Abilities Unlimited   (Workshop for the Blind) Federation Dr, Goodwill; ✆ 767 448 2203. Craft workshop for the blind & disabled. All sales income from this high-quality work goes to fund the workshop. Mats, basketwork & other souvenir items.

Albert Casimir   St John's Av, Pottersville. Original wood carvings.

4

The Art Gallery King George V St, Roseau. Located next to Norwood House, this small art gallery has works by local artists Ellingworth Moses & Earl Etienne.

Bionic Leather Craft Kennedy Av, Roseau. Handmade leather shoes & sandals.

Cocorico Dame Eugenia Charles Blvd (Bay Front), Roseau. A selection of authentic local crafts, jewellery, cards, Kalinago crafts & souvenirs.

Everybody's Gallery Hillsborough St, Roseau. Located near the Windsor Park National Stadium, a small private gallery containing paintings for sale by local artists.

Forever Young Dame Eugenia Charles Blvd (Bay Front), Roseau. Assorted crafts & souvenirs.

Green Eye Production Loubiere; ✆ 767 225 2002. Original carvings in wood & *fougère* (tree fern) by talented craftsman & musician Julie Joseph. Located on the highway near the bridge.

The Ruins Old Market, Roseau. Local herbs & spices, rum punches.

Shanise's Craft Centre Corner Hanover St & Hillsborough St, Roseau. Local art & crafts, carvings, masks, jewellery, T-shirts & souvenirs.

Shalom 40 Hillsborough St, Roseau. Upstairs shop selling a range of local crafts including jewellery, pottery, woodcarvings & clothing.

Tiffany's Shed No 15, Canefield Industrial Estate; ✆ 767 245 4793. Spacious gallery with original paintings, wood carvings, etchings & other local crafts. Art classes with Tiffany Burnette-Hiscombe, plus a good selection of food & drinks. Daytimes. Closed Sun.

LIFESTYLE BOUTIQUES AND DUTY FREE

Archipelago Wine & Spirits Long La, Roseau. Located behind Land Duty Free, selling wines, spirits, tobacco etc.

Baroon Kennedy Av, Roseau. Jewellery, watches, clothing & souvenirs.

Bijoux Terner Hanover St, Roseau. Located near the Ruins & the Old Market. Bags, accessories etc.

Cocorico Boutique & CocoChic! Cnr Dame Eugenia Charles Bvd (Bay Front) & Kennedy Av. Local crafts, souvenirs, spirits, tobacco, bags, sunglasses & more.

Desiderata Old St, Roseau. Quality clothing, furnishings & other lifestyle accessories.

Ego Boutique & Duty Free Cnr Hillsborough St & Old St, Roseau. Clothing, gifts & accessories.

Land Duty Free Emporium Dame Eugenia Charles Blvd (Bay Front), Roseau. Leather goods, alcohol, tobacco, sunglasses, local crafts & souvenirs.

Jewellers International Waterfront, Fort Young Roseau. Jewellery.

Kai K Dame Eugenia Charles Blvd (Bay Front), Roseau. Located next to the Cartwheel Café, selling high quality clothing & accessories. Duty free.

Pirates Long Lane, Roseau. Sunglasses, spirits, wines, cigars, chocolates, cheeses.

Whitchurch Duty Free Waterfront, Fort Young, Roseau. Cosmetics, perfumes, watches, pens, spirits, cigars.

MUSIC Dominica has some exceptionally talented musicians (see page 62). If you would like to purchase some of their music, ensure you insist on an original CD and not a copy. This way you can be satisfied your money is going to the artist and not to the pirates of the Caribbean.

Acoustic Video Cork St, Roseau. Located above a clothes boutique. Local & international artists on CD.

Graphix Great Marlborough St, Roseau. Graffiti artwork on frontage. Local & international artists on CD.

Muzik Land Great George St, Roseau. CDs & DVDs.

OTHER PRACTICALITIES

MONEY AND BANKS Most shops and vendors in Roseau will accept US dollars. Few will accept UK pounds or euros, the main reason being that the exchange rate

Try to support Dominica's cottage industries and buy local products rather than imported ones if you can. By no means a comprehensive list, here are some that are worth looking out for when you go shopping.

Aunty's Agro Processing Hot pepper sauce & seasoning pepper sauce.

Bannis Farm Products Fried breadfruit, banana & plantain chips from the village of Castle Bruce.

Belfast Estate Dominica rum including Soca, Bois Bandé & Red Cap.

Bello & Co Ltd Jams, Café Dominique (local coffee), cocoa tea, pepper sauce, bay rum tonic.

Benjo's Sea Moss Flavoured health drinks made from seaweed.

Blows Agro Products Teas, spices & gifts made from natural local ingredients.

Busy's Pure Honey Honey made near the village of Colihaut.

Caribbean Creative Paintings, hand-blown glass & unique hand-crafted furniture.

Coal Pot Products Handmade soaps & massage oils made from natural ingredients in the village of Grand Bay.

Dominica Brewery and Beverages Ltd Beverages such as Loubiere Spring Water, Kubuli beer & Kairi Malt.

Karl's Hot Sauce Hot pepper sauce.

Kennedy's Punches Try their peanut, passionfruit & lime punches.

Macoucheri Rum Locally distilled rum from the Macoucheri Estate on the west coast between Mero & Salisbury.

Natural Botanicals Soaps & shampoo made from natural products.

Nature Fresh Herbal teas, iced teas, noni, coconut water, & coconut oil from Wesley.

Nature Isle Volcanic Noni Medicinal noni (Morinda citrifolia) syrup from the northeast.

Rejuvananda Oil of Ojas Herbal oils from Toulon Agencies of Roseau.

Rootz Herbal Remedies Garlic syrup.

Sico's Herbal remedies for colds & fevers from the west coast village of St Joseph.

SureLifeSava Creole seasonings.

Tony's Punches Coconut, peanut, pineapple & lime punches.

fluctuates with these two currencies whereas there is a fixed rate with the US dollar (US$1=EC$2.67). The number of shops and restaurants that accept credit cards is increasing but do not make any assumptions. Check first. There may also be a transaction charge.

The price of goods from most shops and vendors will include local (VAT) tax. The exceptions to this rule are duty free shops, of course, and some hotels and restaurants. Again, check first by asking if the price quoted is tax inclusive.

Banks usually open between 08.00 and 14.00 Monday–Thursday and 08.00–16.00 Friday. All have ATMs that you can use to get local currency only (Eastern Caribbean dollars). Banks will also exchange currency and travellers' cheques. In addition to the banks listed below you can also find an ATM at HHW Whitchurch supermarket on Old Street, Breezee's Mart and Canefield Airport.

First Caribbean International Bank

$ **Roseau branch** Old St, Roseau; ☎ 767 448 2571

4

National Bank of Dominica

$ **Head office** Hillsborough St, Roseau; ↘ 767 255 2300

$ **Roseau branch** Independent St, Roseau; ↘ 767 255 2624

Royal Bank of Canada

$ Dame Eugenia Charles Blvd, Roseau; ↘ 767 448 2771

Scotiabank International

$ Hillsborough Street, Roseau; ↘ 767 448 5800

MEDICAL The **Princess Margaret Hospital** is the island's main medical facility and is located on Federation Drive in Goodwill. The hospital has a 24-hour casualty unit. For assistance: ↘ 767 448 2231.

Roseau's **pharmacies** are usually fairly well stocked and are open six days a week from 08.00–17.00 Monday–Friday and 08.00–14.30 Saturday. For assistance on Sundays, you should contact the Princess Margaret Hospital. If you are taking medication, please remember to bring it with you.

✚ **Bulls Eye Pharmacy** Federation Drive, Goodwill, Roseau; ↘ 767 449 8600; ◷ until 23.00 Mon–Sat

✚ **Garden of Eden Pharmacy** Hillsborough St, Roseau; ↘ 767 440 6651

✚ **Jolly's Pharmacy** 36 Great George St, Roseau & 8 King George V St, Roseau; ↘ 767 448 3388, 767 448 2788

✚ **New Charles Pharmacy** 20 Cork St, Roseau; ↘ 767 448 3198; e charlesp@cwdom.dm

✚ **Today's Pharmacy** Hillsborough St, Roseau; ↘ 767 277 2950

SAFETY Roseau is a safe town for visitors and you should not fear it. People are usually friendly and helpful. You will come across Roseau's beggars, who most people know by name, and who have been on the capital's streets for far too many years. Some beggars are addicted to drugs or alcohol, others are genuinely destitute or may suffer from mental illnesses. Aside from family and friends, there are no safety nets in Dominica and once you fall it is very difficult to rise again. The usual remedy is a few weeks in prison which, of course, is no remedy at all.

Beggars (known locally as *pawo*) will ask you for help, either in the form of a few dollars or some food. If you choose to decline they will rarely bother you again. If you choose to help you must accept that your money may be used to support a habit (even if you buy food, which some actually sell to turn into cash). The choice has to be yours. No-one can tell you what to do. Whatever you decide to do when you are approached, please just be calm and polite. Beggars mean you no harm, they are simply opportunists. I have yet to come across any 'professional' begging in Roseau so you may consider everyone you encounter a genuine cause.

There have been one or two robberies perpetrated by young people in the past, though they are very rare and take place in secluded areas. If you do find yourself in this situation, try to remain calm. Cash and cameras will be the target, so think about offering them up and then simply turning and walking away. They want the situation to end as quickly as you do. Credit cards and passports are of little use to opportunist thieves, who are always caught. This island is a small place and a difficult one in which to hide or keep a secret.

The emergency number is ☎ 999 and the Police Headquarters is located at the eastern end of King George V Street.

POST OFFICE There are two post offices in Roseau. The main one is located towards the southern end of Dame Eugenia Charles Boulevard (Bay Front) opposite the Roseau ferry terminal and is open 08.00–17.00 Monday, 08.00–16.00 Tuesday–Friday. The second post office is located within the grounds of the Government Headquarters building on Kennedy Avenue and is open 08.00–17.00 Monday, 08.00–16.00 Tuesday–Friday.

INTERNET Access to email and the world wide web is rarely a problem in Dominica. There are a couple of small internet cafés in Roseau, some wireless hotspots, and most hotels have fixed line or wireless high-speed internet access. Here are a few nice places to go.

🄴 **Cocorico** Dame Eugenia Charles Blvd (Bay Front), Roseau. Bay front café with wireless internet connectivity. Cocorico boutique has a PC hooked up to the internet.
🄴 **Cyberland** Woodstone Shopping Mall, cnr Great George St & Cork St, Roseau. Well-equipped, busy internet café.

🄴 **Le Café Desiderata** Old St, Roseau. Quaint coffee shop with wireless internet access located in a small courtyard at the back of this lifestyle boutique.
🄴 **Rituals** Dame Eugenia Charles Blvd (Bay Front), Roseau. Coffee shop on the Bay Front with wireless internet access.
🄴 **Roseau Public Library** Victoria St, Roseau. The library has wireless internet connectivity.

PUBLIC TOILETS There are two public toilets in Roseau. One is located at the side of the Tourist Information building on the Bay Front, just near the Old Market. The other is located next to the Roseau gate of the Botanical Gardens. You will need a dollar.

TRAVEL SERVICES
Going Places Old St, Roseau; ☎ 767 448 2550. For flights & holidays.
Liat King George V St, Roseau; ☎ 767 448 3980. For Liat flight bookings & hotels.

Whitchurch Travel Old St, Roseau; ☎ 767 448 2181. Located up the stairs next to the Whitchurch supermarket. For flights, holiday packages & L'Express des Îles inter-island ferry tickets.

WHAT TO SEE AND DO

THE BOTANICAL GARDENS On the east of the town are the beautiful Botanical Gardens (also called the Botanic Gardens). Planting of the 16ha land, formerly a sugar plantation, began in 1890. The original idea for the gardens was an economic one, propagating crop seedlings for the island's farmers. The ornamental gardens of today are the result of the lifelong work of Joseph Jones, who managed their development from 1892. Botanists from Kew Gardens in England supplied a profusion of tropical species that they had collected from all over the world, thereby transforming the gardens from a purely functional nursery to an attractive landscape of exotic trees and shrubs. Ornately decorated iron gates were put up, ponds were created and over 80 species of palm were also added. Part of the gardens was later lawned and set aside for a cricket ground and small pavilion.

Hurricane David wrought havoc on the gardens in 1979 and much was lost. With a strong resolve, however, the gardens were cleared of debris and replanted. Today Roseau's Botanical Gardens are a tropical haven of colour and tranquillity.

The gardens are still divided into an economic section and an ornamental section. The ornamental section on the western side is the most visible; the economic section is on the eastern side. Division of Agriculture, veterinary and laboratory buildings are located between the two sections in the southeast corner. The northernmost buildings are home to the two parrot aviaries where it is possible to see Dominica's endemic Amazonian parrots, the sisserou and the jaco. In 2010 members of the Forestry and Wildlife Division succeeded in breeding a sisserou after many years of trying.

In front of the Agricultural Division buildings are the crushed remains of a school bus. A giant African baobab tree fell on the empty bus during Hurricane David and it was left there, exactly as it fell, in memory of this great, destructive storm. The tree was cut, but lateral off-shoots grew and produced the tree you see today.

A walk through the gardens is a nice way to spend a couple of hours. The Forestry, Wildlife & Parks Division located just off Valley Road, opposite the Alliance Francaise, sells *An Illustrated Guide to Dominica's Botanic Gardens* which is a great source of information if you are interested in the local and exotic plants and trees that grow here. Just enter the old stone building, turn right and ask for the book at the reception desk. It costs about EC$15.

Highlights of the gardens include: the *bwa kwaib* (*Sabinea carinalis*), Dominica's national flower (look for it between the Roseau Gate and the crushed bus); the canon ball tree (*Couropita guianensis*), a South American species with unusual round fruits; Colville's glory (*Colvillea racemosa*), a really beautiful tree when in bloom; a gorgeous saman tree (*Samanea samaan*) that grows on the margins of the cricket ground; the golden shower (*Cassia fistula*), with fragrant golden flowers when in bloom; the velvet tamarind (*Dialium indum*), an evergreen with a tangy edible fruit; balsam (*Copaifera officinalis*), of which there is a huge specimen growing by the sisserou aviary; and the roucou (*Bixa orellana*) whose seeds were used as a food colouring and a dye for Kalinago body painting (see box on page 5).

There are also several species of palm including: the royal palm (*Roystonea oleracea*), the sago palm (*Cycadaceae*), the bottle palm (*Mascarena lagenicaulis*), the gouglou palm (*Acrocomia aculeate*), the century palm (*Corypha umbraculifera*), and the scheelea palm (*Attalea butyracea*).

In addition to cricket matches, the gardens are used for a range of activities including steelpan competitions, parades, independence celebrations and Creole in the Park, forerunner to the annual World Creole Music Festival.

The Botanical Gardens are within easy walking distance of downtown Roseau. Simply walk up King George V Street from the Bay Front and at the junction with Valley Road and Bath Road (by the Police Headquarters), go straight on. The Valley Road Gate is just a couple of hundred metres on the right.

MORNE BRUCE AND JACK'S WALK Situated on the eastern side of the Botanical Gardens is the steep pinnacle of Morne Bruce. From the summit of this low peak there are expansive views of the town and the sea beyond. Named after James Bruce, a captain of the Royal Engineers who designed many of the island's original fortifications in the 18th century, the site was selected by the British as the location for a military garrison. Today there is still a cannon overlooking the town as well as the original barracks and officers' quarters. The buildings on the summit are now used by the government and the police. The giant cross was erected in the 1920s.

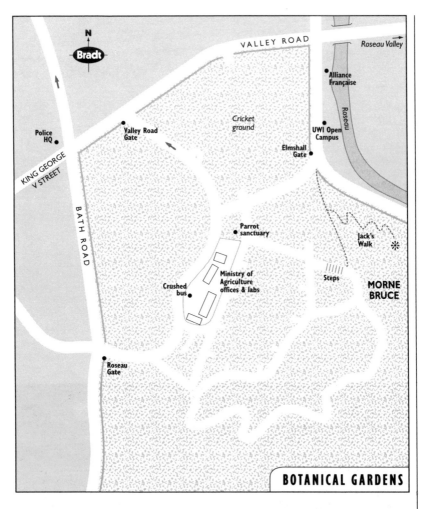

There are two ways to reach the summit of Morne Bruce. One is by road, taking the first turning on the left after the Anglican cemetery on Bath Road – simply follow the road up to the top. The more adventurous may wish to take a 20-minute walk to the top up a footpath called **Jack's Walk**, located on the northeastern side of the Botanical Gardens near the Elmshall Gate. The footpath is quite steep so take good care as well as plenty of water. The views of Roseau from the top are really worth the climb.

During the height of the cruise ship season it can get quite crowded at the viewing point on Morne Bruce as it is a popular stop-off for bus tours. There are also a number of souvenir vendors here at this time of the year. A nice time to go is later on in the afternoon, say around 17.00, when the heat of the day is waning and the sun is thinking about setting over the Caribbean. If you go by road rather than via Jack's Walk, look out for Mountain View Snackette and Bar; a very small, colourful place set back from the apex of a bend (you may only see it on the way up). It is a nice place to have a drink, enjoy the view, and watch the sun go down on a lovely Dominica day.

5

Roseau Valley and Morne Trois Pitons National Park

Roseau lies on a plain of flat land where a broad river valley meets the sea. **The Roseau Valley** stretches eastwards until its steep sides converge in the heights of Trafalgar and, above it, Laudat. From the crowded residential suburb of Bath Estate just beyond the Botanical Gardens, the Roseau Valley incorporates several small hamlets and villages. On the southern ridge at a height of 460m is the village of Morne Prosper which has developed a reputation for high quality farmed produce. On the northeastern ridge at a height of 600m is the hamlet of Laudat, gateway to several of the natural attractions of the Morne Trois Pitons National Park. In the valley below Laudat are the very popular twin waterfalls of Trafalgar and the village of the same name. Below Trafalgar are the residential settlements of Shawford and Fond Cani. On the southern edge of the valley is the village of Wotten Waven with its hot sulphur springs and volcanic fumaroles.

The **Morne Trois Pitons National Park** was established in 1975 and in 1997 it was designated a UNESCO World Heritage Site. It is approximately 7,000ha in size and contains a high concentration of dormant and dead volcanoes. The park's vegetation zones include deciduous and semi-deciduous forest, secondary

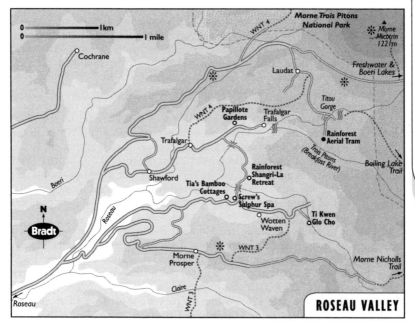

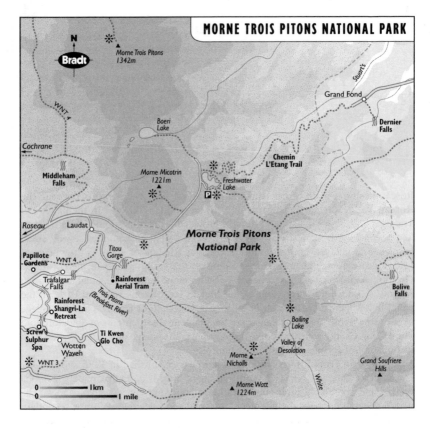

N

Bradt

Morne Trois Pitons
1342m

Stuart's

Grand Fond

WNT 4

Boeri
Lake

Dernier
Falls

Cochrane

Chemin
L'Etang Trail

Middleham
Falls

Morne Micotrin
1221m

Freshwater
Lake

P

Roseau   Laudat

**Morne Trois Pitons
National Park**

Papillote
Gardens

Titou
Gorge

WNT 4

Trafalgar
Falls

Rainforest
Aerial Tram

Bolive
Falls

Rainforest
Shangri-La
Retreat

Trois Pitons
(Breakfast River)

Screw's
Sulphur
Spa

Ti Kwen
Glo Cho

Boiling
Lake

Wotten
Waven

Valley of
Desolation

Grand Soufriere
Hills

WNT 3

Morne
Nicholls

White

0   1km

Morne Watt
1224m

0   1 mile

and mature rainforest, montane forest, and elfin woodland at the volcano summits. Volcanic activity can be seen within the park. The **Valley of Desolation** is a fascinating landscape of steaming vents, geysers, hot-water rivers and cascades, boiling grey mud and a crust of sulphur-stained rock. The **Boiling Lake** (see page 122) is a flooded fumarole with both a diameter and a depth of around 60m, reputedly making it the second-largest of its kind in the world (the largest is Frying Pan Lake in New Zealand).

Of the volcanoes within the park boundary it is the dominant three-peaked **Morne Trois Pitons** itself at 1,342m that is the highest (see page 131). From the summit there are spectacular views of lush and dense rainforest all around. To the south are the peaks of **Morne Micotrin** (1,221m, see page 128), **Morne Watt** (1,224m) and **Morne Anglais** (1,123m, see page 146). To the north is a vast blanket of green covering the area from the Central and Northern Forest Reserves to the distant summit of Morne Diablotin (1,447m) and the Morne Diablotin National Park (see page 207).

In addition to the Boiling Lake, the Morne Trois Pitons National Park has two other large freshwater lakes. The 2ha **Boeri Lake** (see page 124) is the highest mountain lake on the island at an elevation of 853m. A little beyond the Boeri Lake, though very difficult to get to, are two much smaller lakes. Located very close to the Boeri Lake, though at a slightly lower altitude of 762m, is the 4ha **Freshwater Lake** (see page 126). Within the park are several waterfalls that are worth visiting. The tallest is the **Middleham Falls** (see page 127), which can be found to the west of Morne Micotrin. Located quite close to, though less accessible than, the Middleham Falls are the **Fond England Falls** (see page 212). To the north of Morne Trois Pitons is the very popular **Emerald Pool** waterfall (see page 119) which has become a firm favourite for day visitors. Perhaps the least accessible, especially for the non-swimmer, is the waterfall located at the end of the water-filled **Ti Tou Gorge** (see page 120) near the village of Laudat. There are many other waterfalls located above and below Ti Tou Gorge which can only be accessed via a canyoning trip (see page 119).

The Morne Trois Pitons National Park's main habitat is rainforest. Common vegetation includes trees such as *chatanier* (*Sloanea dentata, Sloanea caribaea* and *Sloanea berteriana*), *gommier* (*Dacryodes excelsa*), *mang blanc* (*Symphonia globulifera*), *karapit* (*Amanoa caribaea*), *maho cochon* (*Sterculia caribaea*) and *bwa bandé* (*Richeria grandis*). There is an abundance of tree ferns and epiphytes such as bird's nest anthuriums, orchids and bromeliads. In the montane forest the vegetation becomes shorter and the trees have a noticeably smaller girth. *Palmiste moutan* (mountain palm), hibiscus and a wide variety of ferns are common. At the summit, mossy covered, low growing elfin woodland is dominated by plants such as the *kaklen* (*Clusia mangle*), *z'ailes mouch* (*Asplundia rigida*) and *kwé-kwé* (*Miconia mirablis*). Fumarole vegetation is found in the Valley of Desolation. Plants able to withstand hot and sulphurous gases include *kaklen*, bromeliads and grasses.

Birds that can be seen and heard throughout the park are numerous and include the bananaquit, all four species of hummingbird, thrashers, tremblers, warblers, vireos, and the unmistakable mountain whistler (rufous-throated solitaire). You will also come across the jaco, one of Dominica's two endemic species of Amazonian parrot. (For more information on Dominica's birds see page 6.) In the wet montane forests, particularly where the ground is very sodden, you may be lucky enough to hear the grunts of feral pigs, though they are extremely elusive and more commonly found within the Northern Forest Reserve. Other mammals that are found here include the agouti and several species of bat. Lizards include the endemic zandoli, and amphibians such as the Antillean tree frog are common throughout the park. You may also encounter the boa constrictor.

GETTING THERE

Given their proximity to the capital, the natural attractions of the Roseau Valley are very accessible and certainly worth seeing. A trip to the twin falls at Trafalgar, a visit to the volcanic fumaroles along the River Blanc and a soak in a hot sulphur spring at Wotten Waven make for a fun day out. However, as it is a narrow winding road with many blind corners, especially along the stretch to Laudat, please be careful and use your horn regularly if driving. These roads become very busy with tour bus traffic when cruise ships are visiting the island.

BY BUS See page 50 for information on where to catch buses from Roseau. As the Trafalgar Falls are a little way up from Trafalgar village itself, bus drivers may request a little extra to go all the way. Alternatively just get out and walk, though be prepared; the approach road is very steep. Buses will not go beyond Laudat village to the Freshwater Lake, Ti Tou Gorge and so on. You must walk there or hitch a ride.

BY CAR By car, head east along King George V Street and at the junction with Bath Road (with the Police Headquarters to your left), go straight across on to Valley

Road. The route passes the Botanical Gardens and then crosses a bridge over the Roseau River. Beyond the small residential suburb of Bath Estate, the road continues eastwards into the Roseau Valley. The Valley Road forks just beyond Bath Estate near the settlement of Fond Cani. The road to the right goes to Wotten Waven with a further right-hand fork a little further on that goes up to Morne Prosper. The road to the left heads towards Trafalgar and Laudat. The junction is clearly signposted.

After taking a left at this junction, you follow a winding road until you come to a second fork. The road to the left goes up to Laudat, the Rainforest Aerial Tram, Ti Tou Gorge, the Freshwater Lake, the Boeri Lake trail, the Boiling Lake trail, Morne Micotrin, and the Chemin L'Etang trail. The fork to the right goes to Trafalgar. Again this junction is well signposted.

Pass through the village of Trafalgar to get to the waterfalls. A junction to the right goes across the valley to Wotten Waven, straight on goes up to Papillote Wilderness Retreat, and the Trafalgar Falls visitor centre and car park.

If heading up to Laudat, stick to the main road all the way and be sure to use your horn on blind corners. You will pass a sign on your left and a narrow road that goes down to the Middleham Falls trailhead. A little further on is a junction where you may meet a park warden checking site passes. The concrete road straight ahead goes to the Freshwater Lake, the Boeri Lake trail, Morne Micotrin, and the Chemin L'Etang trail. The road to the right goes to Laudat village and, before it, a left-hand turn-off to the Rainforest Aerial Tram (which is signposted), Ti Tou Gorge and the Boiling Lake trailhead. If you are heading for one of these, keep going to the left of the hydro plant and balancing tank until you come to the Aerial Tram entrance. If your destination is the Boiling Lake trail or Ti Tou Gorge, park up around here and walk.

If you are heading for Morne Micotrin, the Freshwater Lake, Chemin L'Etang and the Boeri Lake, follow the concrete road at the Laudat junction all the way into the Morne Trois Pitons National Park. This road eventually splits with a left-hand fork going to the Boeri Lake and Chemin L'Etang trailheads, and the right-hand road going to the Freshwater Lake visitor centre and car park. See page 128 for the whereabouts of the Morne Micotrin trailhead.

WHERE TO STAY

🏠 Cocoa Cottages (5 rooms, 1 'treehouse') Shawford, Trafalgar; ☎ 767 448 0412; e cocoacottage@gmail.com; www.cocoacottages.com. Attractive accommodation with a chocolate theme (see page 76) in forest & tropical garden surroundings. The cottage rooms are rustic, cosy & romantic. All have en-suite bathrooms. Communal kitchen restaurant serving fresh local dishes & open lounge & music area with a 'TV' window onto nature. Cocoa & chocolate experience is a sweet & interesting diversion. 'Treehouse' SC accommodation sleeps up to 6. Idyllic natural setting & comfortable, relaxing accommodation for those looking to unwind or explore. Rooms **$$$**, treehouse **$$$$$**

🏠 Papillote Wilderness Retreat (4 suites & 2 dbl rooms) Trafalgar; ☎ 767 448 2287;

e papillote@cwdom.dm; www.papillote.dm. Established & popular eco-resort set in 2ha of beautiful rainforest gardens with natural hot springs, relaxing pools, & waterfalls. (See page 120 for more about Papillote gardens.) SC suites are spacious with lounge, kitchen & bedrooms. All rooms are nicely designed in wood & have en-suite bathrooms & fans. Papillote has a large restaurant overlooking the gardens serving a high standard of Creole & international cuisine. Variety of massage & reflexology therapies offered. Normal operations high season only (Nov–Apr). Low season (May–Aug) SC suites only & no restaurant. Closed Sep & Oct. **$$$**

🏠 Rainforest Shangri-La Resort (5 cabins) ☎ 767 440 5093; e shangrila@cwdom.dm; www.rainforestshangrila.com. Wellness resort along a volcanically active river valley. The resort grounds host a number of hot & cold mineral-rich pools, a natural steam sauna, & a waterfall. Along the riverbanks are naturally occurring hot springs & a large steam cave, known as the Dragon's Mouth. Accommodation consists of private wooden cabins & duplex bungalows hidden amongst tall roseaux reeds. All cabins have private bathroom facilities, hammock & veranda. The resort has a large restaurant serving international & local cuisine. Massage & yoga services offered. **$$$**

🏠 **Rainforest Retreat Cottages** (2 cottages, 3 rooms) Shawford; 767 449 9540; rachel@ ourdominica.com; www.ourdominica.com. Located in Shawford, on the road to Trafalgar. Each hardwood cottage has 1 bedroom, a kitchenette, living room, telephone, TV & ceiling fans. Main building nearby has 3 rooms, each with dbl bed & en-suite bathroom. Gated accommodation with fruit & flower gardens & spring-fed swimming pool. **$$$**

🏠 **Roxy's Mountain Lodge** (16 rooms) Laudat; 767 448 4845; e roxys@cwdom.dm; www.avirtualdominica.com/eiroxys. Traditional mountain lodge of stone & wood with a natural feel & nice views of Morne Micotrin & the heights of Laudat. 12 rooms have en-suite bathroom facilities, some have private verandas & 4-poster beds. Restaurant serves continental & full b/fast, lunch & dinner. There is a small bar & a shared TV lounge area. Great location for hiking enthusiasts. **$$**

🏠 **Chez Ophelia Cottage Apartments** (10 cottage apts) Copthall; 767 448 3438; e chezophelia@cwdom.dm; www.chezophelia.com. 5 pleasant cottages split into apts on the road to Wotten Waven. All apts have en-suite bathroom facilities & fans. Communal lounge, TV & restaurant area where b/fast & dinners are served. Cuisine is local & sometimes accompanied by the beautiful voice of 'Dominica's Lady of Song', Ophelia, who is the

owner of the cottages. Wireless internet. Closed Sep. **$$**

🏠 **Le Petit Paradis** (1 cottage & 4 apts) Wotten Waven; 767 440 4352; m 767 276 2761; e lepetitparadis200@hotmail.com; www.petitparadisdominica.com. Guesthouse & restaurant designed in bamboo & madras, traditional Creole colours. Bamboo shack is a 3-bedroom cottage with small kitchenette, Roadside apt has 3 bedrooms, kitchen & is good for families, Tangerine, Pommerac, & Bwa Bandé each have 2 bedrooms. All rooms have private bathrooms. Internet café & gift shop. **$**

🏠 **Tia's Bamboo Cottages** (3 cottages) Wotten Waven; 767 448 1998; m 767 225 4823; e tiacottages@hotmail.com; www.avirtualdominica.com/ tiasbamboocottages. Rustic bamboo cottages, hot pools & restaurant perched along the slopes of a small river gulley in Wotten Waven. 2 1-bedroom cottages & 1 3-bedroom cottage, all en suite. Nice gardens, pools & river. **$**

🏠 **Grace Apartments** (2 apts) Wotten Waven; 767 448 2934; e grace.apts@gmail.com; www.avirtualdominica.com/graceapartments. Located in Wotten Waven, 2 self-contained apts each with 2 bedrooms, kitchen & living area. Also available for long term rent. **$**

🏠 **The Secret Garden** (5 rooms) Wotten Waven; 767 448 7854. Rustic wooden house with 5 rooms & 4 bathrooms, living area, kitchen, mosquito nets, fans & shared veranda. Trail down to volcanically active river & hot sulphur springs Very simple accommodation, good for hiking groups. **$**

🏠 **Symes Zee Villa** (15 rooms) Laudat; 767 448 2494. Secluded villa-style accommodation located in the area of Baiac on a narrow ridge on the road to Laudat. En-suite rooms are simple with hot & cold water & fans. There is a bar & terrace restaurant area with great views across the Boeri River Valley. A swimming pool & restaurant are planned. **$**

CAMPING

🏕 **Mount Plézi Estate & Gardens** Laudat; 767 614 6482. Located close to Ti Tou Gorge & the Boiling Lake trailhead this campsite is ideal for hikers. Natural spring, covered pitches, cooking area, fruit & vegetable gardens, toilet & washroom facilities. **$**

🏕 **Ti Kwen Glo Cho** Wotten Waven; 767 440 3162. Natural gardens, hot & cold pools, waterfall, small bar, toilet facilities. Local food prepared by request. Handy for Wai'tukubuli National Trail hikers. **$**

✗ **Rainforest Restaurant** At Papillote Wilderness Retreat, Trafalgar; ✎ 767 448 2287. Excellent Creole & international cuisine served in open restaurant overlooking the rainforest gardens. A really beautiful setting. Open during high season only (Nov–Apr) but will accommodate large groups in low season. Closed Sep & Oct. $$$

✗ **Rainforest Shangri-La** Wotten Waven; ✎ 767 440 5093. Large restaurant serving local & international cuisine. Reservations required. $$–$$$

✗ **River Rock Café & Bar** Trafalgar; ✎ 767 448 3472. Located close to Trafalgar Falls serving Creole lunches, sandwiches & dinners on a covered veranda overlooking the river valley. A pretty setting & a great place for lunch & a cold drink. Try the passionfruit rum punch. Dinner by reservation only. $$

✗ **Le Petit Paradis** Wotten Waven; ✎ 767 440 4352; m 767 276 2761. Local eatery made of bamboo & decorated with traditional madras serving Creole lunches & dinners. No menu, they cook whatever is fresh in. Confirm prices before dining. $$

✗ **Tia's Bamboo Cottages** Wotten Waven; ✎ 767 448 1998. Pretty restaurant made of wood & bamboo overlooking a small river valley. Rainforest surroundings, hot pools & cottage accommodation. Call in advance for lunch & dinner. $$

✗ **Ti Kwen Glo Cho** Wotten Waven; ✎ 767 440 3162. Traditional food by reservation only in very rustic & natural surroundings. Hot pools. $$

✗ **IECSS Bar Grocery Snackette** Wotten Waven; ✎ 767 440 4100. Roadside bar located in Wotten Waven village serving drinks & local snacks. $

WHAT TO SEE AND DO

VILLAGES OF THE ROSEAU VALLEY Following the 1805 Battle of **Trafalgar** between the British and the French fleets, the estate at the head of the Roseau Valley was named in honour of Nelson's famous victory by the landowners from England who had settled there. The estate produced coffee and sugar. Following emancipation in 1838, the liberated workers created a settlement and grew vegetables, supplying fresh produce to the people of Roseau. At the head of the present-day village are the famous twin waterfalls, also called Trafalgar (see below). Nearby is a hydro-electric plant that uses water that runs down from the Freshwater Lake, via Ti Tou Gorge and the 'father' falls. The river that runs from the falls below the village and along the valley eventually becomes the Roseau River. The village itself is small and mostly residential with a couple of small bars. A favourite with visitors is the River Rock Café on the way to the falls (see *Where to eat and drink* above). The deck at the back has lovely views down to the river valley. There is a narrow track down to the river nearby where you will often see local people going for a river bath. Why not join them? The river pools are lovely and refreshing. As well as the waterfalls, Trafalgar is also home to the delightful **Papillote Gardens** (see below).

Wotten Waven is located in the southeastern corner of the Roseau Valley and is connected to the village of Trafalgar by a road that crosses the River Blanc and the Roseau River. In periods of heavy rainfall this road occasionally becomes flooded by the rivers and cannot be crossed. Wotten Waven is an area of substantial subterranean geothermal activity with a number of volcanic fumaroles and hot sulphur springs. In 2010 a geothermal energy project began in this area. The original estate lands produced coffee, sugar and *ground provisions*. Following emancipation, liberated slave workers established a small settlement on the estate and much of the land in the area was sold off. Today it is still a community of farmers but is fast becoming known as a natural hot spa and wellness therapy village. There are quite a number of hot sulphur pools and wellness practitioners here (see page 88) as well as small eco cottages, rustic bars and eateries. Look out for the very quaint Brenda's Shop at the junction between Tia's and Screw's. It's a great little place for home-made confectioneries and a cold drink. Wotten Waven has a tourist information centre but, at the time of writing, it hardly ever seems to be open. You may get lucky; let me know if you find anything interesting inside.

Morne Prosper is located on the top of a ridge on the southern side of the Roseau Valley. It has become known for its farmlands and high quality agricultural produce. You should take a trip up there. The road is a little narrow and winding, but once you eventually get to the top, keep going until you reach the farmlands and then get out of your car and walk. The views all around are lovely. Say hello to the farmers and perhaps even buy some produce.

Laudat is Dominica's highest village and came about as a stay-over point when people used to use the Chemin L'Etang track (see page 125) to cross the island from east to west and vice-versa. Today it is a very quiet place, very rural and mostly engaged in farming, yet its unassuming nature disguises its prominence as one of the principle gateways to the natural attractions of the Morne Trois Pitons National Park. The Wai'tukubuli National Trail also passes through the village and links it to Trafalgar down in the Roseau Valley below. People are friendly here and very used to visitors.

ACTIVITIES AND SPECIAL INTERESTS

Canyoning For the adventurous, a canyoning trip along the river between Ti Tou Gorge and the Trafalgar Falls is a great way to spend a day. Having (literally) been shown the ropes and fully kitted out, you rappel down the side of a waterfall into the gorge at a point near the Rainforest Aerial Tram. Once inside the gorge, you are accompanied along the river, rappelling down further falls and jumping into pristine pools until you come to the breathtaking Cathedral Canyon. A short hike up a tributary brings you back up to the very same place you started your adventure. For more information on canyoning and operators, see page 74.

The Emerald Pool (*Site pass required*) The Emerald Pool is a very popular attraction, especially during the cruise ship season and at weekends. The small waterfall and crystal-clear pool is perhaps one of Dominica's most photographed natural sites, and is certainly one of the most visited. Located on the northern edge of the national park, within sight of Morne Trois Pitons itself, the Emerald Pool is a very accessible and beautiful rainforest attraction.

The Emerald Pool is just off the road to Castle Bruce and the Kalinago Territory. It is signposted and very easy to find. See page 50 for information on buses from Roseau. If travelling by car from the Roseau area, once you reach the Pont Cassé roundabout in the interior, take the road towards Castle Bruce and La Plaine. After around ten minutes there is a signposted junction with the road to Castle Bruce and the Kalinago Territory to the left, which is where you should turn. After a very short distance the entrance to the Emerald Pool visitor centre is on the left. If you are not in possession of a site pass, you can buy one from the Emerald Pool visitor centre, where you will also find vendors selling souvenirs and refreshments.

Getting to and from the Emerald Pool requires a short, gentle walk in two easy sections; the first part is a 15-minute stroll through the rainforest along a well-maintained path. There is a nice viewpoint to the right and a wooden bridge across a cascading river. Some steps up, and then eventually down, lead to the waterfall and the pool. Just follow the signs. As this site receives a lot of visitor traffic, it is really important to minimise your impact as much as possible. Please do not leave any litter, nor etch your name in the rocks as many have already.

5

On the return trip, take the path that leads upwards, rather than the path to the left across the bridge. This is an old Kalinago trail and and loops back to the visitor centre. It is also now part of the Wai'tukubuli National Trail. It is a pleasant and easy walk through the rainforest.

Papillote Gardens First started in 1967, and then substantially repaired following the devastation that was wreaked by Hurricane David in 1979, Papillote is Dominica's best known private tropical garden. It is a 2ha oasis of rainforest plants and flowers, natural hot springs and pools, waterfalls, hummingbirds, butterflies, stick insects and much more. It is a delight for gardeners, photographers, horticulturalists and botanists. A 60-minute accompanied or self-guided walk takes in a variety of tropical flora including tree ferns, bromeliads, orchids, heliconias, gingers, breadfruit and calabash trees, jade vines and rare aroids. The sparkling river, terraced walkways and rest areas all complement this garden beautifully and make it a must-visit for anyone with a hint of green in their fingers. End your walk with a hot spa, an outdoor massage, or some fine local cuisine in the Rainforest Restaurant. Local crafts and souvenirs are available for purchase at the Butterfly Boutique. For more information go to www.papillote.dm. Open during the high season only (November to April).

The Rainforest Aerial Tram Dominica's Rainforest Aerial Tram is an excellent way to enjoy the island's rainforest environment without getting muddy – though you may get a little wet. It is a good option if hiking is not a possibility or your time is limited. The tram is a ride lasting around 90 minutes in eight-seater gondolas that glide slowly through the heights of the rainforest canopy. The guides who accompany each gondola are well trained and informative. The tour can also include a short rainforest hike followed by a breathtaking walk across a suspension bridge crossing the Breakfast River Gorge at a height of around 100m. Refreshments are available at the Rainforest Café and souvenirs may be purchased from the gift shop, both of which are located on site.

The Rainforest Aerial Tram is located in the heights of Laudat, close to Ti Tou Gorge (see directions above). If driving, simply follow the signs. Once you reach the entrance, drive over the bridge and follow the signs to the car park. It is a good idea to bring a light waterproof jacket with you. The gondolas have a roof but the front, back and sides are all open to the elements.

Please note the Rainforest Aerial Tram only operates during the cruise ship season (October to April). Once the cruise ships stop, so does the tram. The last gondola usually leaves at around 14.30 so you will need to plan on being there before then. For the latest information on opening times, prices and so on: ☏ 767 448 8775; www.rainforestrams.com. You can also call in at the Rainforest Aerial Tram office on Virgin Lane, Roseau.

Ti Tou Gorge Ti Tou Gorge is a very popular attraction, especially during the cruise ship season and at weekends.

Located between the Freshwater Lake and Trafalgar Falls, at the head of the Roseau Valley, there is a deep river gorge. At a point near the village of Laudat near the start of the main Boiling Lake Trail, this gorge is accessible to swimmers. Through the narrow cleft in the rock it is possible to swim through the deep, cold water to reach a small waterfall. The name 'Ti Tou' is Creole for 'small throat', a perfect description of the narrow rock funnel through which the river runs from the waterfall to emerge at a small, man-made pool.

Ti Tou Gorge was one of the set locations for the film *Pirates of the Caribbean* and, during the height of the season it may be busy with day visitors swimming up and floating downstream in buoyancy belts. Tour guides may be leaping from the cliffs above into the deep pools, or ascending the waterfall as part of the show. If you prefer to enjoy the gorge in a little more peace and serenity, it may be wise to come in the late afternoon once the crowds have died down, or early in the morning before they arrive. Ti Tou Gorge is worth a visit, so try not to let the prospect of cruise ship hoards put you off.

See page 50 for bus information from Roseau. Public buses will not take you all the way to the gorge, however. The walk there from the village of Laudat takes around 15–20 minutes and is easy going. Just follow the signs to the Rainforest Aerial Tram. Once at the entrance to the tram, the gorge is along the track that continues straight ahead. Follow the trail to a narrow bridge alongside a freshwater pipe running quite high over the river. Once across, go left and follow the path around to the wooden shelter and the gorge itself. Mind your head on the pipe.

If you are going to Ti Tou Gorge by car, take the Valley Road out of Roseau (at the eastern end of King George V Street), taking a left at the forks for Wotten Waven and then Trafalgar, and following the signs all the way to the Rainforest Aerial Tram. Park up just by the bridge and follow the directions above.

For the most part, the water inside the Ti Tou Gorge is too deep to stand up in and the walls on each side are smooth, slippery rock. Around half-way into the gorge there is a short, shallow section and an opportunity to stand and walk. It takes around five minutes of fairly gentle swimming to reach the waterfall at the end of the gorge. It is deep here too. Taking some kind of flotation aid is a great idea and allows weaker swimmers to experience the fun and excitement of passing through this lovely natural formation to see the waterfall. The water in the gorge is very cold and the waterfall at the end quite powerful. Unless equipped with something waterproof, leave cameras behind. Do not swim up the gorge in periods of heavy rainfall. Flash flooding does occur here. If the water is very high and brown with lots of floating debris, do not go.

To enter the gorge, walk down the stone steps on the left-hand side of the fairly shallow, though rocky, pool. Surf shoes are a good idea. At the far side of the pool there is a small cascade of warm water, which is a nice way to get the circulation going again after the cold water of the gorge. The entrance to the gorge is the dark opening on the right-hand edge of the pool. Yes, really, it is.

Trafalgar Falls *(Site pass required)*

The 'father' falls with a drop of around 65m, and the 'mother' falls with a drop of around 35m, make up the Trafalgar Falls. As you face them, the father falls are on the left-hand side and the mother falls on the right. The father falls used to cascade down a tall face of smooth rocks alongside a natural hot spring, but in 1996 there was a huge landslide and this unusual hot and cold water cascade was lost. The waterfall is still quite lovely, however. It has a deep pool and there are still small hot water springs nearby. The source for the father falls is a river that runs from the Freshwater Lake via Ti Tou Gorge in the Morne Trois Pitons National Park.

The mother falls are the more accessible of the two waterfalls, though it is still a very tricky scramble over large and often slippery boulders. Taking its source from the Morne Trois Pitons River (better known locally as the Breakfast River), which is crossed by hikers on the Boiling Lake Trail from Ti Tou Gorge, this thundering waterfall also has a great bathing pool. You will also come across a cascade of small warm water pools along the trail from the viewing platform.

The Trafalgar Falls visitor centre has a large car park with souvenir stalls, toilet and changing facilities, snack bar and a display room with examples of flowers and birds that may be seen in the area. It is also the entrance to the waterfall trail and where a forestry officer will ask for site passes. The Trafalgar Falls has a nice wooden viewing platform just ten minutes or so along an easy trail where you can get good photographs of both falls. This area is a rainforest habitat and it is possible to see several species of fern, epiphyte and bromeliad. Look out for large land crabs scrambling for cover as you pass. Trained guides can be hired at the visitor centre to escort you either along the trail to the viewing platform or all the way to the foot of the falls.

Volcanic Activity The area between Wotten Waven and Trafalgar, and all the way up beyond Wotten Waven right up to the Valley of Desolation, is volcanically active. Beneath the surface, and occasionally breaching it, is a source of natural energy that expresses itself in fumaroles and hot water springs. In some places the ground itself is warm. In all likelihood this energy will be exploited in the future by geothermal engineers, but for now it remains enigmatic and raw.

You don't have to hike all the way up to the Valley of Desolation or the Boiling Lake to experience it first-hand, however. The private grounds of the Shangri-La Resort and the River Blanc that runs alongside it, are both very accessible and good places to start. Quite close to the entrance of the Shangri-La Resort (look for the sign on the road that links Trafalgar with Wotten Waven) is a short path through tall roseaux reeds leading to a small wooden platform. Here you can see fumaroles bubbling up through, and heating, tiny pools of water. Pay a small entry fee and you may also explore the grounds of the resort itself by following clearly marked paths and steps. Look out for the steam cave, known as Dragon's Mouth, which you can see from the road bridge, and the naturally heated spas and saunas along the river bank. The ground is warm and you can smell sulphur dioxide in the air. This river is fairly active all the way up into the interior where it finds its source beyond the Du Mas Estate and in the foothills of the mighty Morne Watt, a tall volcano that overlooks the Valley of Desolation.

Wotten Waven Hot Springs and Wellness Sulphur is widely believed to provide positive benefits to the body including detoxification of skin cells and as a natural remedy for infection, inflammation and fungal conditions. Hot sulphur springs are said to assist with skin rehydration, joint and muscle pain, and in replenishing the body with naturally occurring minerals. For these reasons, many also claim sulphur-rich treatments such as hot baths and mud wraps aid in the anti-ageing process.

It is through the exploitation of this naturally occurring phenomenon along the southern edge of the Roseau Valley that Wotten Waven is establishing a reputation as a wellness destination. Both visitors and locals are able to combine the beauty of the natural surroundings with relaxation, rejuvenation, and of course, great fun. Take an after-hours soak under the stars in a hot sulphur pool, watching the steam rise against the moon and stars above, accompanied by the music of the river and the songs of the tree frogs, and it is easy to appreciate the growing attraction and natural mystique of the area.

There are several nice hot spas in Wotten Waven including **Screw's**, **Ti Kwen Glo Cho**, **Tia's Bamboo Cottages** and **Rainforest Shangri-La**. In addition to natural hot springs, the Roseau Valley is also emerging as a centre for a range of wellness therapies, and several practitioners operate here. See pages 88–9 for details of hot spas and wellness practitioners.

HIKES

The Boiling Lake (from Ti Tou Gorge) (Site pass required. Difficulty: T: 3; R: 2; E: 3; D: 4; Rating = 7.5)

Dominica's Boiling Lake is said to be the second-largest of its kind in the world. It is a flooded fumarole approximately 60m in diameter with a magma chamber beneath the surface, heating the fresh water to a rolling boil. The lake is fed by two small streams and once it reaches a certain level it overflows through a gap in the crater wall on the eastern side. This overflow eventually becomes the White River.

The first recorded sighting of the Boiling Lake was in 1870 when a magistrate from the east coast village of La Plaine, Mr Edmund Watt, attempted to find an alternative route to the Chemin L'Etang (Freshwater Lake road, see page 125) across the interior of the island. After several days in the forest he arrived at the village of Laudat and reported sighting a boiling volcanic crater. Mr Watt was accompanied by Dr H A A Nicholls and a number of porters and bush cutters to the location of his sighting, along the same route that the main trail follows today. The mountains of Morne Watt and Morne Nicholls bear the names of the two men.

The level of the lake has been known to fluctuate and in late 2004 it almost ran dry. There was no boiling and only a small pool of water remained at the centre of the crater surrounded by thick pungent mud. Within four months the lake was back to its normal level and boiling again. Similar events were recorded in 1887, 1900, 1977 and 1983. No satisfactory explanation has ever been produced.

The Nicholls–Watt route, the primary trail that is used to access the lake today, begins at Ti Tou Gorge and climbs up to Morne Nicholls before descending into the Valley of Desolation and then to the lake itself. The Valley of Desolation is an unfortunate name for what is essentially an area of extraordinary activity, beauty and life. This wide valley contains hot streams, bubbling mud and violent steam vents. The fumarole vegetation consists of lichens, mosses, bromeliads and *kaklen* (*Clusia mangle*). Subjected as they are to sulphurous gases and a heady concoction of mineral deposits, the rocks of the valley are painted in whites, browns, yellows and oranges.

The trailhead for this hike is located at Ti Tou Gorge (see above for directions on how to get there).

The Boiling Lake trail has changed considerably over the years. It used to be a tough, muddy scramble along a very roughly hewn trail. Today the route is much improved and far more accessible to a broader range of hikers. Nevertheless, at least three hours of walking there, and the same back, with several steep ascents and descents can still take its toll. The passage through the Valley of Desolation is much as it used to be: tricky, rough and quite difficult to follow. Straying from it can result in serious injury and should be avoided if you are not with a knowledgeable guide.

Take the stone steps to the right of the wooden hut at Ti Tou Gorge and follow the path into the forest. These steps are slippery in the wet; remember them when you return as many tired hikers end up on their backsides just here. The trail is wide and fairly easy going for the first hour, climbing gently and making its way deeper into the rainforest. After an hour or so you will descend and arrive at the Breakfast River, completing the first third of the walk to the lake. Often at this point you begin to detect the unmistakeable aroma of sulphur dioxide. You are getting closer to volcano country.

Do not hang around the Breakfast River for too long. There are always plenty of troublesome mosquitoes here and your challenge is hard enough as it is. Take it easy across the river; it is best to cross to the left of the larger boulders where the water is a little more shallow. Once on the other side, the trail gets tougher as it climbs steeply towards the top of Morne Nicholls. When you stop for a rest, listen out for jaco parrots – if you can hear them above the sound of your own breathing, that is. After about 45 minutes you will reach the top, a circular clearing where, on a bright day, there are spectacular views across the Morne Trois Pitons National Park. To the west is Roseau and the Caribbean, to the north Morne Micotrin and behind it Morne Trois Pitons itself. To the east is the ridge of the Grande Soufriere Hills and beyond it the Atlantic Ocean, and to the south is the foreboding peak of Morne Watt. If you look to the east you should also spot the steam rising from the Valley of Desolation and the Boiling Lake.

At the top of Morne Nicholls you are about halfway to the lake and at the highest point of the hike. From here you must negotiate a long series of steep steps that descend into the Valley of Desolation. Be careful, these steps are really slippery and often waterlogged. Take a moment to look at the amazing green and reds of the cliff sides. At the bottom of these steps, head left down and across a stream and a terrain of rubble and frequent landslides into the Valley of Desolation. Once in the valley the trail is difficult to make out, but it is there, meandering across the rocks alongside the stream, the steam vents and the hot bubbling pools, and exiting at the far side along the river. A guide can show you the best and safest route across the valley. If you have chosen to do this hike without a guide, now is a good time to look back at where you have just come from so you can remember it on the return journey. Many people do not do this and then have trouble figuring out the route home.

The Valley of Desolation is in two parts. After the first section, the trail follows the left-hand bank of a river then crosses it to the right where it becomes a wide stone path. Along the way you will see small cascades of water and hot pools on your left. This is where you could choose to bathe on the return leg of your hike. It is worth it. You cross the river again and come to a short but steep scramble up and over a rock face followed by an undulating hike through the forest with further river crossings. After around 30–45 minutes or so, the trail enters a second part of the Valley of Desolation. Follow the narrow track as it winds around the left-hand side to the river. Cross over it carefully and then start climbing up the steep, rocky ridge. Be careful here. There have been landslides, it is slippery and the track is very narrow and steep in places. Once at the top, take a breather and smile – you just have a few minutes to go. Follow the clear trail to the lake.

The Boeri Lake *(Site pass required. Difficulty: T: 2; R: 1; E: 2; D: 1; Rating = 3.8)*

The Boeri Lake is the highest mountain lake on the island at an elevation of 853m and 2ha in surface area. It is a crater lake located beneath the summit of Morne Micotrin within the Morne Trois Pitons National Park. The lake is thought to be around 40m deep and is fairly devoid of subsurface vegetation or life. Surrounded by large boulders and upper montane thicket, overlooked by the cloud-covered summit of Morne Micotrin, and with the only sound coming from the mountain whistler (rufous-throated solitaire), the lake is exquisitely serene.

Beyond the lake, to the west, there are two much smaller lakes. They are accessible in the dry season when the waters recede a little, though passage to them is extremely rough. From these two lakes it is possible to walk to the Middleham Falls along the source of the Boeri River, though this should certainly not be attempted without expert guidance.

To get to the Boeri Lake, follow the same directions to the Freshwater Lake (above), but turn left at the fork instead of right. The Boeri Lake trailhead is at the end of the road.

Follow the clearly marked trail uphill for around 30 minutes until the wooden steps give way to a path of rocks and boulders. Before reaching this point, if the weather is clear, there should be fine views across to the Freshwater Lake in the south and the village of Grand Fond in the east. Head down the hill and then take great care over the rocky path; this walk is often very wet underfoot and these stones can be quite slippery. Cross over the narrow and shallow Clarkes River and then two more streams including an outlet for the Boeri Lake itself. Negotiate a further rocky path that leads right up to the lake. You will come to a fork; to the right is the lake, and straight ahead the remains of a wooden viewing platform. You now find yourself in a crater between Morne Micotrin, which is above and beyond the ridge behind you, and Morne Trois Pitons which is above and beyond the ridge in front. You can almost hear a pin drop, it is so still. Take a swim to cool off; the water is refreshing, but very cold, and more than a little eerie.

Located between the Freshwater Lake and the Boeri Lake you will come across some bamboo water pipes. They are channelling water from a hot water source. This is a great spot to freshen up after your hike.

Chemin L'Etang (*Difficulty: T: 2; R: 0; E: 2; D: 2; Rating = 3.8*)

> **NOTE**
>
> The Chemin L'Etang trail suffered significant landslide damage in recent times and at the time of writing it is still impassable. The landslide is just below the Freshwater Lake. Please check on the status of this trail before attempting it.

The Chemin L'Etang trail is thought to have originally been used by Amerindians to cross the island and was later used by villagers from east and west before roads were constructed. Together with rough sea routes, this path was once an important method of cross-island transportation for people and their produce. Meaning 'lake road', the trail passes the Freshwater Lake in what is now the Morne Trois Pitons National Park at an elevation of 762m. Originally people would have walked from the mouth of the Rosalie River up to the lake, then down the Roseau Valley to the capital, and vice-versa. The village of Laudat was created by people needing to overnight on the journey. Thanks to road access, today's Chemin L'Etang Trail is somewhat shorter and more forgiving than that, with one end at the village of Grand Fond and the other at the Freshwater Lake itself.

The hike is very scenic with great views of the interior and the Atlantic coastline. At each end of the hike there is an interesting and beautiful natural feature. At the western end of the trail is the exquisite serenity of the 4ha Freshwater Lake. At the eastern end of the trail at the top of the village of Grand Fond is a short but steep trail down to the Dernier Falls (see page 167).

The trailhead at the Freshwater Lake end is just off the Freshwater Lake circular trail (see page 126). Enter the trail from the road that runs to the Boeri Lake trailhead and follow it for about ten minutes. You will see a sign for Chemin L'Etang on your left. The trailhead at Grand Fond is right at the end of the paved road at the top of the village. Follow the wide track to the right of the building and then right again.

The top of the trail can be rather steep and slippery even when not in a state of disrepair so take it steady. After this it is very easy to follow and turns into a wide track that leads all the way to Grand Fond.

Between 30 and 45 minutes from the Freshwater Lake there is a small stream and a pretty cascade running down the mountain. Take a look higher, or carefully scramble up the side of the cascade, and you should see a nice waterfall. A little beyond this point heading towards Grand Fond, look down below a river crossing and see it form another tall waterfall that tumbles down into the valley.

Within about 30 minutes of Grand Fond there is another small cascade near a wider river crossing. Across the river on the Grand Fond side, the trail emerges into a wide valley with tall clusters of ferns and creaking clusters of tall bamboo. The trail widens as you get closer to the village. If you wish to continue to the Dernier Falls, follow the paved road for about ten minutes until you see the sign. The trailhead is off to the right.

The Freshwater Lake Circular Hike (*Site pass required. Difficulty: T: 2; R: 0; E: 3; D: 1; Rating = 3.8*) The Freshwater Lake is located in a valley between Morne Micotrin and Morne Nicholls. It has a surface area of approximately 4ha and is at an elevation of 762m above sea level. This area receives some of Dominica's highest rainfall, almost 900cm a year, making it one of the wettest places on the planet. It is often cloaked in cloud and can therefore be quite a cold place. Due to the weather and location, the area around the lake is a combination of upper montane and cloud forest. The vegetation is fairly low growing, consisting of ferns, mosses, *kaklen* (*Clusia mangle*) and mountain palms. Bromeliads, colourful gingers, heliconias and orchids can also be found growing around the lake trail. Living in the lake itself are tilapia, a tropical freshwater fish species belonging to the cichlid family that was introduced some time ago. Although not blessed with an abundance of clear and sunny days, the serenity of the Freshwater Lake and the natural beauty of the environment all around are breathtaking and most certainly worth a visit. As they are located so close to each other, it is also a nice idea to combine a hike around the Freshwater Lake with the Boeri Lake, if you have the time and energy.

The Freshwater Lake is located beyond the village of Laudat, within the Morne Trois Pitons National Park. See page 50 for bus information. Please note, public buses will not go beyond Laudat to the lake. You must either pay extra, take a taxi, hitch a ride, or walk. The walk from the junction to the lake is about 30–45 minutes along a paved road. It has great views on a clear day though so it's not that bad!

By car, simply head for Laudat from Roseau (refer to the instructions on page 116) and when you reach the junction before the village, take the concrete road straight ahead rather than the road down to the right. Follow it all the way into the park, and at a fork take a right to the Freshwater Lake visitor car park.

The easiest way to do this hike is in a counter-clockwise direction. This means that you descend rather than ascend the steepest parts. It is also best if you wish to go on to the Boeri Lake.

The trailhead is beyond the visitor building and across the dam wall. It is a clear path that winds its way around the lake and up and down the peaks and ridges along the way. From the top of these ridges there are nice views of the lake and the village of Grand Fond, with Rosalie Bay and the Atlantic Ocean beyond it to the east. On a clear day it is also possible to see the island of Marie-Galante further to the northeast.

In places the trail is steep and slippery when wet, so be careful. Pay great attention when walking over rounded wooden logs or flat wooden planks and bridges. They can be covered with a thin layer of slime that makes walking on them very treacherous. There are rather a lot of these wooden logs at the beginning of the walk but fortunately tree fern trunks are used later which offer greater traction.

You will make a gradual ascent to the top of a ridge from where you can enjoy the views. Further around the loop you will find yourself on the top of a sharp peak where there is a bench to have a rest. The climb down this peak is very steep, but thankfully the steps are made of tree fern rather than wooden logs. Again, take your time and take in the awesome views across the interior. In front of you is Morne Micotrin and a little to the right, beyond it, is Morne Trois Pitons. To the left you will see two prominent volcanoes: Morne Anglais to the west facing the Caribbean, and Morne Watt a little further to the east. Whenever you see Morne Watt, think Valley of Desolation and Boiling Lake – they are located to the north east of this volcano.

Descend to the ridge and then climb up to the next peak. You will come to a small circular clearing with a rough trail heading down to the east. This is the Chemin L'Etang Trail to the village of Grand Fond. Straight ahead is the continuation of the loop trail and to the left is the Freshwater Lake itself. You will emerge on the paved road that links the Freshwater Lake to the Boeri Lake. To the right is the Boeri Lake trailhead and to the left is the Freshwater Lake and car park.

A local group used to offer kayak rentals on the Freshwater Lake but a lack of business forced them to close. There has been some talk of this service restarting, so look out for it when you visit.

Middleham Falls (*Site pass required. Difficulty: T: 2; R: 1; E: 2; D: 1; Rating = 3.8*)
When plans were being developed to create the Morne Trois Pitons National Park in the 1970s the then owner of the Middleham Estate, Mr John Archbold, an American millionaire, donated the land in its entirety to the World Wildlife Fund in an effort to encourage the formation of the park. The estate covered in excess of 400ha and was transferred to the government of Dominica when the national park was created in 1975. The rainforest vegetation in this area includes fine specimens of the buttress-rooted *chatanier* tree, *gommiers*, tree ferns, epiphytes and bromeliads. Jaco parrots, one of two endemic Amazonians, also inhabit this region and are frequently sighted.

The main trail to the waterfall actually runs all the way between the villages of Cochrane and Laudat. The most common route used by visitors is the trail from Laudat which is fairly easy and takes around an hour. This route is also part of the Wai'tukubuli National Trail. The trail from Cochrane is less frequently used though it is a little less steep and passes through very undisturbed areas of rainforest. This route takes a little over an hour and runs past Tou Santi or 'Stinky Hole', a fissure full of bats and the stench of their droppings. Both routes require small river and stream crossings (the route from Cochrane more so) and they converge at a junction just above the waterfall. The last section of the trail to the falls is a little steeper, rocky and sometimes quite waterlogged so you have to be careful. The waterfall itself is one of the tallest on the island. The pool at the bottom is deep and well worth the scramble down for a refreshing dip. This waterfall changes quite noticeably between seasons. When it is dry, the falls are very narrow and the pool extremely tranquil. In the height of the wet season the waterfall is full and thunderous, throwing out vast clouds of spray and making access to the pool almost impossible.

The trailhead from the Laudat side is well signposted, particularly as it also forms part of the Wai'tukubuli National Trail. You will see the signs on the left, just before you reach Laudat. Turn off and follow the narrow road until you come to the end. There is a small parking area and a changing facility.

For the Cochrane trailhead, follow the road next to the Old Mill Cultural Centre in Canefield, just off the west coast highway, and keep going until you reach Cochrane. Drive up the very steep road all the way through and to the top of the village. At the junction, turn right, and then left. Follow the road until you come to a second junction where you turn left again. Keep going until you reach the end of the road when there is a small area to park up.

See page 50 for information on where to catch public buses to Cochrane and Laudat from Roseau. Please note that Cochrane buses do not run very often and will only take you to the village itself. From there, you must walk. Another option is to try to hitch a ride up to the village from the Old Mill Cultural Centre.

Middleham Falls from Laudat Follow the clear path through the forest and across the shallow river. The trail winds uphill and though it is steep in places, it does not become particularly severe. After about 30–45 minutes you will reach a well-marked junction. Straight ahead leads to the village of Cochrane, the right-hand track is the continuation of Segment 4 of the Wai'tukubuli National Trail, and to the left is the route down to the waterfall.

From this point the trail becomes a little more difficult. It heads downhill via a series of switchbacks and then comes to a wooden staircase. At the bottom, be careful crossing over slippery rocks and streams, especially in the wet, and look out for a point where the trail passes over a boulder on your right. You should be able to see the viewing platform and waterfall from this point. Clamber over the boulder and make your way along the path to the wooden platform. You must make this right turn as the trail that continues downhill just comes to a dead end at a point where there was a landslide some time ago.

If you wish to bathe in the pool, exit the platform and go down to the right of it. Negotiate your way around the base and then make your way down the rocks to the pool. Take your time and be careful with your footing. Jumping into the pool from the margins can be fun, but be sure the water in front of you has no shallow, submerged rocks, and do not dive head-first.

Middleham Falls from Cochrane From the trailhead, follow the clear path downwards into the forest. This route requires you to cross a number of small rivers. They are fairly straightforward challenges but the climbs in and out of the gulleys themselves can be a little steep and slippery, so take your time.

Ten minutes or so into the trail proper is **Tou Santi** or 'Stinky Hole', a deep laval tube that is now home to bats. The rather unpleasant aroma is the scent of the bats' droppings. Should bats be your thing, this is an interesting place to be at dusk when the bats emerge from the cave in a dense cloud and fly out into the forest.

After around 45 minutes of gently undulating trail, interrupted only by more small river gullies, you should reach a signposted junction in the trail. Straight ahead is the route to Laudat (another 45 minutes or so), to the left is part of Segment 4 of the Wai'tukubuli National Trail, and to the right is the trail down to the waterfall (see directions above).

Morne Micotrin (*Difficulty: T: 3H; R: 0; E: 4; D: 3; Rating = 6.3H*) At 1,221m Morne Micotrin is Dominica's fourth highest mountain after Morne Diablotin, Morne Trois Pitons and Morne Watt (which is currently inaccessible to hikers). It is located very close to and immediately south of Morne Trois Pitons. Morne Micotrin is also known as Morne Macaque which is a very confusing name as there are no monkeys on Dominica. Perhaps there once were; introduced in a similar way to the mona monkey (*Ceropithecus mona*), also known as macaque, which can still be found in the elevated interior of Grenada, though no records exist to support this notion. It has also been suggested that the mountain is so named because you

top	The annual World Creole Music Festival takes place during the last week of October (PD) page 62
left	Carnival Queen — the festival of Carnival is a time when Dominicans party hard, 'jump up', 'free up' and really let their hair down (CS) page 25
below	Traditional Creole *bélé* dancing (CS) page 24

left Master Kalinago canoe builder, Merlin Stoute (PC) page 154

below left Kalinago tree fern mask carver – the mask is made from the bottom of a tree fern trunk that has been split and had the core carved out (PC) page 158

below Traditionally, *larouma* baskets are made by Kalinago women and you can see some of them at work at the Kalinago Barana Auté (PC) page 159

bottom Cassava bread bakery, Kalinago Territory (PC) page 161

above left Fairtrade bananas – Dominica's banana trade has faced severe difficulties in recent years (PC) page 18

above right Rastafarians are people who live in harmony with nature (PC) page 22

right *Crabback*, a traditional Creole dish made with black crab (CS) page 9

below Fishermen at Fond St Jean – every coastal village has a community of fishermen (PC) page 142

above The sisserou (*Amazona imperialis*), Dominica's national bird (GH/C) page 6

far left Purple-throated Carib (*Eulampis jugularis*), one of four hummingbirds recorded in Dominica (CS) page 7

left Torch ginger (CS) page 5

below left 75 species of orchid have been recorded in Dominica (PC) page 5

below The boa constrictor (*Constrictor nebulosa*), or *tete chien* (PC) page 8

above   The hawksbill turtle (*Eretmochelys imbriocota*) is the most common of the four turtle species observed in the waters around Dominica
(OL) page 10

right   The longlure frogfish (*Antennarius multiocellatus*) is one of the more unusual fish species found around **Dominica** (S/D) page 10

below   The longsnout seahorse (*Hippocampus reidi*)
(RD/FLPA) page 10

below right   A sperm whale (*Physeter macrocephallus*) diving
(PC) page 11

above left   Scuba diving in the Soufriere Scotts Head
Marine Reserve (DS/S) page 145

above   Canyoning beyond Ti Tou Gorge — the
waterfalls, pools and rock formations
in the canyons are quite breathtaking
(LC) page 74

left   Hiking the Jacko Steps river trail
(CS) page 224

below   Tubing on the Layou River — sit yourself
in a large inflatable tube, shoot gentle
rapids, and drift sedately along a river
through Dominica's beautiful forest
(PC) page 82

above Screw's Sulphur Spa at Wotten Waven (PC) page 89
below left Zip-lining at the Wacky Rollers Adventure Park (PC) page 90
below right Wellness practitioners offer several types of massage therapy (PC) page 86

above   **The Roseau Valley** (PC) page 113

below left   **Crossing the Breakfast River Gorge at the Rainforest Aerial Tram in Laudat** (CS) page 120

below right   **The Indian River was featured in** *Pirates of the Caribbean: Dead Man's Chest* (PC) page 199

have to be able to climb like a monkey to reach the top. Well, you are about to prove or disprove that one yourself.

The climb is steep and technically challenging. There are some large boulders to negotiate but the real effort is in avoiding hidden holes. Micotrin is a volcano that collapsed in on itself and there are places where rocks and boulders that fell together left gaps between them. These deep holes are often masked by grass and other foliage, so it is absolutely paramount that when you are hiking the upper section of the mountain you pay attention to this. Though steep and certainly demanding, it is more a technical and mental challenge to get up and down this mountain. No twisted or broken ankles please; you have to really watch out for this.

Aside from this potential hazard, Morne Micotrin is a great mountain to climb. Unlike the others, it is very open, especially towards the top, where rocky crags and ferns make the terrain seem more like the highlands of Scotland than the tropics. There are two peaks; one higher than the other. Both have communications masts at their summit and the views are excellent on a clear day.

To get to the trailhead, follow the same directions to the Freshwater Lake (above) but look out for a ladder on your left-hand side, propped against the steep embankment, halfway between the steel bridge and the road junction that separates the Freshwater Lake from the Boeri Lake trailhead.

At the top of the ladder, the track goes immediately to your left and then you will find a wide uphill path ahead of you. The terrain here is a little tricky; lots of loose rocks, so be careful with your footing. The first hour or so is simply a straight uphill slog and there are not many views. After that it becomes more interesting. You are soon rewarded with wonderful vistas, including a bird's eye view of the Freshwater Lake. From now on the climb is much more open, there are boulders to negotiate, and you have to look out for those troublesome holes. It is more a climb than a hike at this point, but the open surroundings more than make up for your growing tiredness and paranoia about slipping down a dark fissure, never to be seen again.

You will eventually reach a junction. The trail to the left goes to the lower peak, the trail straight on goes to the higher peak. Both will take a further 20 minutes or so. The terrain continues to be challenging so please take care. Do not attempt to climb the masts nor any of the structures. Be careful of the debris you will see lying around (these peaks are often the victims of lightning strikes). I prefer to pick a spot a little away from the masts and embrace the absolute stillness and serenity of it all.

Morne Prosper to Morne Nicholls (and then perhaps the Boiling Lake) (*Site pass required only if you go on to the Boiling Lake. Difficulty to Morne Nicholls: T: 3H; R: 2; E: 3; D:2; Rating: 6.3H*) This hike takes you from the farmlands of Morne Prosper, on the southern margins of the Roseau Valley, to the peak of Morne Nicholls where it meets up with the Boiling Lake trail. From here you can either hike to Ti Tou Gorge and Laudat, or you can hike to the Boiling Lake and then head on to Ti Tou Gorge and Laudat. This description and difficulty rating covers the section from Morne Prosper to Morne Nicholls only. Please see the Boiling Lake trail (above) for a description of that hike and its associated difficulties.

A word of advice, and perhaps warning: if you are just interested in hiking to the Boiling Lake, take the standard route from Ti Tou Gorge described above. The journey from Morne Prosper is much longer and more difficult, in fact at the time of research and writing, I would suggest it is for extreme hikers only.

This trail was opened up by the Wai'tukubuli National Trail project team as an optional extra to Segment 3, from Morne Prosper to Laudat. Some used to tell me this trail is shorter and easier than the usual Boiling Lake route, but now I know those people have never hiked it. The first two-thirds of this route are indeed easy going along a wide trail within a beautiful rainforest environment. It is the final third that makes this hike the challenge it is.

The trailhead is at a junction with the Wai'tukubuli National Trail Segment 3 in the farmlands of Morne Prosper. Look for a sign indicating the Morne Hill Farm Access Road and start from there. Segment 3 continues down the hill towards Wotten Waven; our optional hike to Morne Nicholls follows the high ridge.

From the sign, take the rough vehicle track. It improves for a short distance and then becomes quite rough again. Pass farmlands on both sides and keep going straight, following the blue and yellow paint markers which you will see all the way to Morne Nicholls, either on rocks or the trunks of trees. If you cannot see one either in front or behind, retrace your steps until you find one again. These markers are helpful and quite frequent, so finding your way should not really be a problem. But please pay attention to your route; this is not a good place to get lost.

Follow the old road that runs to the Du Mas Estate before it eventually reaches a plateau, the highest point of the old estate, and then begins to descend. Pass through a flat and rather boggy area before climbing again. Cross a small wooden bridge and a pretty little tributary of the River Blanc. Once over it, follow the trail through the trees as it bypasses an area of marshland. After returning briefly to a wide path, the trail narrows and stays this way for the remainder of the journey. Pick your way through the trees, following the markers, and begin climbing in earnest. You are now making your way up the side of and to the top of a series of ridges that are part of Morne Watt, one of the island's tallest volcanic peaks. The rainforest is impressive, with large *gommier* and *chatanier* trees. You may well hear jaco parrots here too.

The trail gets steeper and trickier as it continues to climb across and up the ridge. A firm footing is difficult so take your time and use trees to help you. Once you make it to the top of the ridge, follow it for a while and take a little breather before heading steeply downhill again. Eventually you reach a clearly marked trail junction. To your left is a trail to Wotten Waven, to your right is the trail up to Morne Nicholls and by far the most difficult section of the hike.

The trail remains quite flat for a while but then begins to climb up and over several sharp ridges and narrow river gullies. It is very steep and muddy, especially in the wet season. You must really take your time here as a slip could easily result in injury. This last section is also very tiring. If you reached the trail junction in around two hours, you still have one more to go; and it is punishing.

At the time of writing there were no steps at all here and this section really needs them. Some areas are very difficult to climb and traverse, and establishing firm footholds requires a lot of concentration and an equal measure of strength. Be patient and positive. The environment has changed now. Notice how you are in montane thicket with hints of cloud forest and fumarole vegetation. One of the river gullies you must cross is most definitely volcanic in nature.

Eventually you will catch sight of the main Boiling Lake trail. Look for a wooden hut off to the left. You may even hear hikers. Somewhat tired and probably very muddy you meet up with the Boiling Lake trail on the mid section between the summit of Morne Nicholls and the descent into the Valley of Desolation. The summit of Morne Nicholls, Ti Tou Gorge and Laudat are to your left (about 90 minutes away), and the Boiling Lake is to your right (also about 90 minutes away). Think carefully about which way you are going to go now. How tired are you, what time is it, and how much water do you have? Remember, if you decide to go to the Boiling Lake and then back to Ti Tou Gorge and Laudat, it is a further 4½ hours of hiking altogether (1½ to the Boiling Lake then three all the way back to Ti Tou Gorge).

Morne Trois Pitons (*Site pass required. Difficulty T: 4H; R: 0; E: 4; D: 3; Rating = 6.9H*) At 1,342m Morne Trois Pitons is the second tallest mountain in Dominica. Named after its three peaked summit, this magnificent volcano dominates the southern landscape and includes three main vegetation types: rainforest, montane thicket and cloud forest, or elfin woodland (see page 4). It is also possible to see all four species of endemic hummingbirds on this hike (see page 7), especially as you get closer to the summit.

It is a strenuous climb to the first summit of Morne Trois Pitons, but great fun and really worth the effort. It is possible to continue to the middle summit (add at least another two hours to the hike), though not recommended at all. The trail from the first peak is in very poor shape and quite treacherous. It is not a place to become stuck or indeed lost. Satisfy yourself with your achievement to reach and enjoy the awesome views from the rocky crag of the first piton.

The trail itself is clear and very easy to follow. In a couple of places towards the summit it is steep and the ascent involves climbing up and over rocks, tree roots and branches. Many of the steps you have to climb are round wooden logs rather than the tree fern trunks which offer greater traction. These wooden logs are slippery, especially in the wet, and on descent. There are also three places where you have to scale short but steep slopes using ropes. All of these factors combine to give the terrain its hazard rating. One or two sections are quite precipitous so vertigo sufferers may wish to think carefully before taking on this hike. A clear day makes for the best views, of course, so check the weather before starting out. Regardless of the forecast, it is always a good idea to carry a light waterproof to protect you from the elements. Depending on conditions, the summits of Dominica's mountains can sometimes be very cold places.

The trailhead is located a short distance along the road from Pont Cassé to Castle Bruce and Rosalie. From the Pont Cassé roundabout, look for a sign on the right-hand side of the road.

The first 15 minutes of the hike is a steady ascent through rainforest. After that the climb becomes much more severe and you have to cope with what are often very slippery wooden steps, so be careful. After around 45–60 minutes there is a tricky little traverse across a narrow rock followed by more steep steps and rock scrambles.

About halfway up you will notice that the environment transitions from montane thicket to elfin woodland and you are rewarded with your first clear sight of the summit. There are also magnificent 180° views of the west, north and east. To the west, you can see the ridge of Warner and beyond it the Caribbean Sea. Directly to the north is the cloud-covered summit of Morne Diablotin, Dominica's highest peak. On a clear day you can even see as far as the island of Guadeloupe. Down below and in front of you is the roundabout of Pont Cassé, the Layou Valley, Bells and the particularly pointed summit of Morne Laurent (also known as Morne Negres Marrons after the Maroon camp that was once there) which is located on the fringes of the Central Forest Reserve.

Your next challenge is to negotiate three quite short though very steep and slippery rock faces. Use the ropes and take your time. These rocks have very few good foot holes and they are often running with water, so take care. Tree roots on either side can help, but check that they are secure before trusting them with your weight.

5

Once you have successfully negotiated these rock faces in one piece, the final stretch is a tough but fun climb through *kaklen* (*Clusia mangle*) trees. Take it very slowly and test each branch before risking your full weight. The trick here is careful and thoughtful movement rather than a rush to get through it. Part of this last section is very steep, wet and muddy. It deserves your full attention. Your reward is the view, which is fantastic along this stretch.

You should get to the summit in around 2½–3 hours. It is a crag of moss and *kaklen* covered rocks. Hopefully the skies are clear for you. If not, be patient and wait for a window to appear in the clouds. Break out your picnic and enjoy being where you are.

6

The South

In this chapter we explore the mountain villages of Giraudel, Eggleston and Bellevue Chopin. We travel through the fishing villages of the southwest coast to the Soufriere Scotts Head Marine Reserve, and we head to the historic area of Grand Bay where Europeans established their first settlements on the island.

GETTING THERE

BY BUS Information about public bus stops in Roseau can be found on page 50. There is a good service between Roseau, Pointe Michel, Bellevue Chopin, Grand Bay and Soufriere. Buses that go on to Petit Savanne and Scotts Head, or up to Giraudel and Eggleston, operate a little less frequently and you may have to hitch a ride if you are in a particular hurry. A good place to get a lift up to Giraudel is from behind the Texaco garage in Castle Comfort. For Scotts Head, you can usually get a ride from Soufriere or you can walk along the sea wall.

BY CAR The road to the two mountain villages of **Giraudel** and **Eggleston** is a loop with both ends located on the coastal road south of Roseau. Head south from the capital down Victoria Street, and pass through Newtown until you come to a junction with a road heading up to the left. This steep winding route passes through the community of Fortune (pronounced 'fort-né') and then up the side of a steep ridge overlooking the Roseau Valley. There are great views from here. Exercise caution as the road is narrow and there are several blind corners. Remember to use your horn. After around ten minutes or so the village of Eggleston appears. Continuing through Eggleston the road climbs further and curves around towards the south. To the left is Morne Anglais and to the right are nice views of the Caribbean Sea down below. After a short distance the road passes through the flower village of Giraudel before turning to the west and beginning a steep descent down the mountainside. The road bisects the residential community of Castle Comfort before emerging on to the main coastal road once more. To access the loop road from its southern end, take the road alongside the Texaco petrol station in Castle Comfort and then turn to the right around the back of it.

To get to **Pointe Michel**, **Soufriere**, and **Scotts Head**, take the southern coastal road from Roseau that passes Fort Young, the Public Library and the House of Assembly, and through Newtown. At the junction over the small bridge in the village of Loubiere, continue straight ahead along the west coast. The road is very narrow through Pointe Michel so pay attention to oncoming vehicles and look out for places to pull over and pass. When you arrive in Soufriere, there is a junction. The road immediately to the left goes to Soufriere Sulphur Springs, the road next

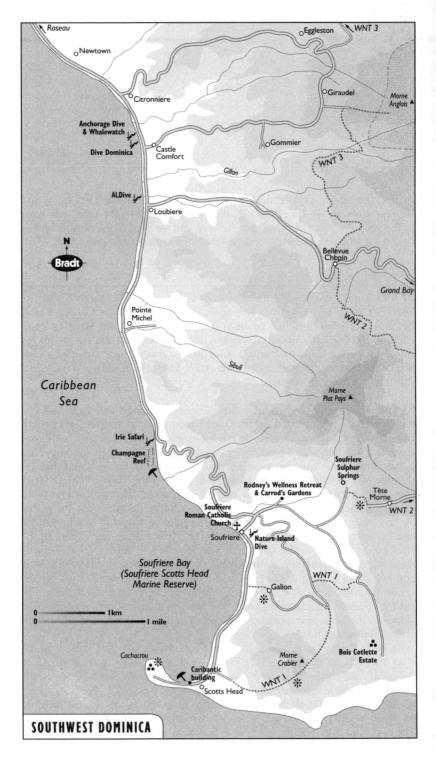

to it goes up to Galion, the road ahead just goes into the back of the village, and the road to the right continues along the coast to Scotts Head. Go down this road and at the bottom use your horn before making a very sharp left turn. A right turn at this junction takes you to the very pretty Soufriere church.

To get to the elevated village of **Galion**, take the narrow road to the right of the Sulphur Springs road at the junction in Soufriere and follow it as it snakes up the mountain. The road ends in the village.

To get to **Bellevue Chopin**, **Grand Bay**, **Fond St Jean** and **Petit Savanne**, take the southern coastal road out of Roseau through Newtown and Castle Comfort. Immediately over the small bridge in Loubiere is a road to the left. This road goes to Grand Bay via Bellevue Chopin and Pichelin. Just after Loubiere the road passes through Fond Baron, the Everton Estate and Snug Corner, home of Kubuli beer. After around 15 minutes the road reaches the high elevations of Bellevue Chopin before descending again through the small village of Pichelin towards the coast. Upon reaching the only major junction, the road to the left goes east along the south coast past the Geneva Estate, Dubuc, Stowe, Fond St Jean and Petite Savanne, and the road to the right goes to Grand Bay Village and on to Tete Morne. There are road signs, so don't worry.

WHERE TO STAY

🏠 **Zandoli Inn** (5 rooms) Stowe; 📞 767 446 3161; e zandoli@cwdom.dm; www.zandoli.com. Luxury hideaway hotel located in 6 acres of forest gardens on the beautiful coastline of Stowe. Exquisite rooms, tastefully furnished with en-suite bathrooms, fans, mosquito nets, jalousie windows & verandas with ocean views. Restaurant serves haute cuisine & caters for resident guests only, either outside on the patio or indoors in the dining room & bar area. A number of trails run through the coastal forest belonging to the hotel, including a path down to a small sun deck & pool which continues down to the rocky shoreline. A peaceful escape in a great location. **$$$**

🏠 **Exotica Cottages** (7 cottages) Gommier, Giraudel; 📞 767 448 8839; e exotica@ cwdom.dm; www.exotica-cottages.com. Attractive, spacious & comfortable wooden cottages in the natural surroundings of Gommier near Giraudel. Each cottage has a living area with sofa bed, a bedroom with 2 dbl beds, en-suite bathroom & kitchen, TV, fans & verandas overlooking the gardens. Organic produce grown on the grounds & owner, Mrs Fae Martin, will prepare Creole meals on request. Very comfortable location with great views & ideal for exploring the south. **$$–$$$**

🏠 **Chez Fie Doudou** (1 cottage) Giraudel; 📞 767 448 7719; e marvlynr@cwdom.dm; www.chezfiedoudoucottage.com. Cosy 2-bed SC cottage located in expansive tropical flower & fruit gardens. Living area, fully equipped kitchen & wrap-around porch. Great views & idyllic mountain village setting. **$$**

🏠 **The Hide-Out Cottage** (1 cottage) Geneva Over River, Grand Bay; 📞 767 446 4642, 767 277 8750; e seedatriva@yahoo.com; www.hideout.ch. Rustic wooden cottage hidden away in beautiful natural surroundings beside the Geneva River. Rastafarian husband & wife team Rahel & Octave Joseph live nearby & are happy to share their vegetable produce & knowledge of local plants & herbs with their guests. Octave is also an excellent tour guide. The cottage comfortably sleeps 2 & has bathroom & kitchenette. A short track leads to the Geneva River. Peaceful setting in a very natural environment. **$**

🏠 **Ocean View Apartments** (3 apts) Scotts Head; 📞 767 449 8266; e oceanview_apts@ hotmail.com; www.avirtualdominica.com/ oceanview_apts. Located high in the village with views of the Atlantic & Martinique, 3 SC ground-floor apts with combined living & sleeping areas, kitchen & bathroom. Each apt is equipped with ceiling fans, mosquito nets & private terrace. Patio gardens where the owners grow fruit for guests. **$**

6

✘ **Sea Lounge** Loubiere; ☎ 767 440 6973; 🕐 Thu–Sat, evenings only. Fine dining by the waterfront. Fresh salads, vegetables, seafood & more in pleasant surroundings. $$$

✘ **Chez Wen** Scotts Head; ☎ 767 448 6668. Fresh local cooking, good seafood. Located on the shoreline. $–$$

✘ **Rodney's Wellness Retreat & Carrod's Gardens** Soufriere; ☎ 767 245 4725; 🕐 daytimes & evenings. Relaxing gardens, restaurant & bar. Try the traditional one-pot braf on Sat. $–$$

✘ **Roger's** Scotts Head; ☎ 767 448 7851. Local cuisine, fresh fish a speciality. $–$$

✘ **Melvina's** Champagne, Pointe Michel; ☎ 767 440 5480. Local bar & eatery. Very popular on Fri nights. $

WHAT TO SEE AND DO

VILLAGES OF THE SOUTH The south coast is where European settlers first gained a foothold in Dominica. Despite an agreement between Britain and France concluding that the island should remain the possession of the indigenous Kalinago, prospectors from Martinique soon began to venture across the channel to begin small lumber enterprises in what is now known as Grand Bay. These settlers succeeded in living alongside the indigenous people and they soon spread around the coast to the Kalinago settlement of Sairi, now known as Roseau.

The influence of France has always been strong in the south, indeed it was with the co-operation of villagers from La Pointe (now Pointe Michel) that the French were able to mount an invasion in 1805, sacking Roseau and forcing the outnumbered British to retreat all the way to Fort Shirley at the Cabrits. Today people from Grand Bay, Pointe Michel and tiny hamlets such as Dubuc are fine exponents of Creole traditions, particularly in music and dance.

Farming and fishing play an important part in the life of these southern villages. Fond St Jean, Soufriere and Scotts Head are noted for their fishermen, and Bellevue Chopin is becoming prominent as a centre for organic farming. In the southeast, around Petit Savanne and beyond to Delices, you will see and smell bay trees growing on the hillsides. Though no longer as prominent as it once was, bay remains a cash crop in these parts and it is harvested and processed for its oil.

Eggleston and **Giraudel** are small mountain villages located at an elevation of around 450–500m on the western slopes of Morne Anglais. Looking down on Roseau and the Caribbean Sea, the height of the villages usually means temperatures are a little cooler and beautiful panoramic views along the west coast are guaranteed. Eggleston runs along a narrow ridge between two river valleys and is a small community of residential houses. Giraudel is also a small village, located

GIRAUDEL & EGGLESTON FLOWER GROWERS INC

This small community group is responsible for the organisation of the Giraudel and Eggleston flower show and is also involved in the growing and selling of plants and flowers in the area. The group also helps to organise community tours of gardens as well as Creole cooking classes. A tour of the Alfred's mature gardens, or those at Chez Fie Dou Dou, some hands-on cooking with the Eugenes or a demonstration of haute Creole cuisine from Mrs Fae Martin are all certain to keep enthusiasts both interested and entertained. For further information email: e giraudeleggleston@communitytourism.dm.

to the southeast of Eggleston. Both communities come alive with colour in May when the flower show usually takes place. Giraudel is also known for its traditional jing ping music (see page 24).

Loubiere is a small village south of Castle Comfort on the southern coastal road. It is the home of Kubuli beer and Loubiere mineral water, which are produced using natural spring water at Snug Corner – a little further inland along the road to Bellevue Chopin and Grand Bay. Loubiere itself is predominantly residential.

The original Kalinago name for **Pointe Michel** was Sibouli, the name of a fish presumably caught in abundance in the area. The French settlers of the early 18th century who arrived from Martinique named the area La Pointe and a number of estates growing coffee, sugar and limes were established on the hillside of Morne Plat Pays behind the village. The Union Estate still has one of the last surviving wooden estate houses.

The Pointe Michel of today is a lively community of farmers, fishermen, and returnees. The main road through the village passes a number of lively snackettes and bars including the Fish Pot, which is very popular on a Friday night, the Barrel and Bamboo Bar, and several other small roadside bars along the seafront selling beer, spirits, fried chicken, fish and *bakes*. The road becomes very narrow as it winds through the village and close to the water's edge, where its residents can be seen socialising or mending fishing baskets and nets. Standing at the centre of the village above the cemetery, and looking out across the sea, is the pretty stone Roman Catholic Church of St Luke. The coastal road passes the cemetery and several more seafront houses, convenience stores and bars.

Soufriere is a seaside village located between Pointe Michel and Scotts Head. Soufriere Bay, home to the **Soufriere Scotts Head Marine Reserve**, is a submerged crater formed by the eruption of a large volcano millions of years ago. The steeply sloping hillside behind the village, with active hot springs and sulphur deposits, is testament to this creation.

Soufriere's Roman Catholic Church of St Mark is perhaps one of the most photographed landmarks in the south and is particularly pretty when viewed from the sea or from around the bay towards Scotts Head. Completed in 1880, the church is currently undergoing a long overdue programme of restoration. Funded partially by Rome and subsequently by private donations, a new ceiling has been built, and wooden pews and gallery railings carved and installed. Funding is still required to replace the broken stained-glass windows, to add further wooden pews and to undertake additional structural repairs. Visitors to the church are encouraged to make a small donation to this cause.

The interior walls of the church are decorated with pretty murals depicting simple village life. On either side of the altar there are colourfully painted scenes of villagers dancing the *bélé* and men fishing from small wooden boats. Along the sides of the church are wooden louvre windows and decorated arches. Outside are the convent and presbytery buildings, and at the foot of the cliffs where the church grounds meet the shoreline is a cave where it is believed the original settlers may have sheltered. Above the cave is a shrine and in front of it an altar for open air services.

On the shore in front of the church a small bath has been constructed by local people. This bath has been designed to capture and retain the warm sea water that is heated from volcanic vents beneath the sand. It is a popular spot for villagers and visitors to relax and have fun after a hard day at work or perhaps during the surface interval between scuba dives. You may also see the very simple *pwi pwi* fishing rafts of those not yet able to upgrade to a wooden or fibreglass boat. These

6

basic wooden rafts hark back to the past and the kind of vessels some of the earliest settlers may have used to catch fish from inshore waters.

Soufriere Bay is a place where both Amerindian and French settlers found haven and home. In the 1970s archaeological excavations at a number of sites around Soufriere uncovered artefacts dating back to the earliest Amerindian settlers as well as their Arawakan successors. Carved *zemi* stones and conch shells depicting earth spirits were also found here.

In the heart of the village, behind the Nature Island Dive building, are the ruins of Rose's lime factory. Established in Scotland in the 1860s, the L Rose and Lime Company, manufacturer of Rose's Lime Juice Cordial and lime marmalade, was a prominent business in Dominica in the early part of the 20th century. Several estates in the west were purchased by the company for the production of lime products including Bath Estate, Picard Estate, St Aroment Estate, Canefield Estate and in 1950, Soufriere Estate. Economic and social circumstances forced the company to withdraw from Dominica in the late 1970s and the estates were either sold off or presented to the Dominican government.

In July Soufriere becomes very busy during the island's annual Dive Fest. Traditional canoe races are held here on the final Sunday of the festival. You can try a range of freshly cooked fish, there is of course plenty to drink, and you can even take part in the canoe races yourself.

The village of **Scotts Head** is named after Colonel George Scott who was lieutenant governor of Dominica from 1764 to 1767. Scott was part of the British invasion force that captured Dominica from the French in 1761 and was responsible for the construction of some of the island's military installations, including a fort on the prominent isthmus beyond the village. This headland also bears his name as well as the original Kalinago one, **Cachacrou**, whose literal meaning is 'hat which is being eaten', presumably by the surrounding swells of the convergence of Atlantic Ocean and Caribbean Sea. Scott's fortifications on top of Cachacrou have mostly slipped down the cliffs beneath the waves, though some ruins remain visible today.

Predominantly a fishing village, you cannot fail to notice the number of brightly painted wooden and fibreglass fishing boats resting along the shore or moored in the bay. Towards Cachacrou is a colourfully painted building where fishermen keep their tackle and boat equipment, and all around this area it is possible to see people sitting along the shoreline mending nets and fish traps. The sound of

THE SOUFRIERE SCOTTS HEAD MARINE RESERVE (SSMR)

The Soufriere Scotts Head Marine Reserve was established by an Act of Parliament to manage and balance the demands placed on the natural resources of Soufriere Bay by recreational watersports and local fishermen. The SSMR is managed by the Local Area Management Authority (LAMA) which has its office along the shore in Soufriere. The LAMA employs wardens to monitor the reserve, its marine life and reefs, as well as maintain moorings and collect user fees. The SSMR is sectioned into four zones: the fishing priority zone, which is the largest of the four; the scuba area; the nursery; and the recreational area. Encompassing the submerged vents at Champagne Reef all the way through to the dramatic drop-offs at Scotts Head, the SSMR attracts scuba divers from around the world. For more about the dive sites of the SSMR see page 82.

BELLEVUE CHOPIN ORGANIC FARMERS GROUP

The Bellevue Chopin Organic Farmers Group was founded in 2004. It offers a range of organic farm products and also has its own organic composting facility. As part of a drive to develop the new agrotourism sector in Dominica, this community group also offers a variety of one-hour tours to visitors interested in this subject. It is a great initiative and definitely worth supporting.

The **Broad Meadows Tour** takes you on a trip around Mr Gordon Royer's vegetable and herb garden, and a tour of the organic composting facility; there are also nice views of the surrounding area. The **Harmony Garden Tour** is a walk around Mr Roy Ormond's organic herbal farm where you can also learn about the traditional uses of herbs and natural medicines. On the **River Farm Tour** you can see Mr Petronel Green's organic pineapple and anthurium gardens as well as enjoy the river and beautiful scenic views. Mr Delroy Registe's **Mountain Creole Garden Tour** gives you an insight into traditional planting methods and natural landscaping. You can also see organic vegetables, citrus and bananas.

If you plan on taking all four tours, the group will also arrange a traditional lunch for you.

For more information: ✆ 767 316 2710 or 767 315 1175; e bellevue@communitytourism.dm or bcofmi@hotmail.com.

a conch shell being blown is a signal to the village that a fisherman has brought his catch ashore and is ready to sell. Depending on the fisherman, his boat and the tactics he has employed, this catch may be anything from a string of small snapper to a large tuna, dorado or marlin.

The village itself is nestled on the slopes of Morne Crabier and is a delightful labyrinth of narrow, twisting alleyways and small roads. It is really worth taking the time to wander up the hill, along these narrow paths and roads, although a little steep in places, to see the pretty houses and absorb some of the village life. Scotts Head villagers clearly take pride in the appearance of their houses and gardens, regardless of their size. On a clear day, either from the heights of the village, or from the shoreline, it is possible to see the outline of Martinique some 30km to the south.

Located at the beginning of the Cachacrou isthmus is the **Caribantic** building. This building marks the starting point of Dominica's Wai'tukubuli National Trail (see *Chapter 10*). Used as a meeting place and interpretation centre, the Caribantic has information about the national trail, a shower, toilet and changing facility, and also a small bar serving drinks and snacks.

Visiting snorkellers heading to the seaside cove beneath Cachacrou should pay a US$2 per person **Marine Reserve Fee**. This fee is collected on a rather inconsistent basis by fisheries wardens. On the Cachacrou headland there is a rough and somewhat overgrown path leading up to the ruins where there is a small cannon. Just along the wall by the radio mast is a further trail that goes right up to the very top of Cachacrou where there are excellent views of the bay. At the bottom, along the Caribbean shoreline, there is a path to the right leading to a sheltered cove. This is a popular spot for bathers and snorkellers with the Scotts Head Drop-off dive site within easy swimming distance (the red dive buoy marks the spot).

The South   WHAT TO SEE AND DO

6

The village of **Bellevue Chopin** is located on a ridge between the peaks of Morne Anglais, Morne Canot and Morne Eloi. Morne Canot was the source of minor earthquake swarms in 1998, and tremors were felt throughout the south of the island. Dominica has a high concentration of dormant volcanoes and seismologists and vulcanologists from the Seismic Research Unit of the University of the West Indies constantly monitor this area.

Located high above Roseau and Grand Bay, the area around Bellevue Chopin was a place of Maroon encampments during the 18th and 19th centuries. Today it is a small farming community and, with the assistance of EU funding, is developing as an agrotourism centre. You can now take a tour to learn about and gain first-hand experience of organic farming in Dominica (see box on page 139).

The bus stop area at the top of the ridge is a nice place to stop and take a break. There are a couple of small shops selling drinks, cooked food, snacks and fruits, and the view down to Roseau is fabulous.

Grand Bay stretches between Pointe Tanama and Carib Point and is surrounded by the peaks of Morne Vert and Morne Plat Pays to the west, Morne Anglais to the north and Foundland to the east. The Amerindian settlers who arrived in this natural bay on the south coast are thought to have named the area Bericoua, a name which survives today though is often written 'Berekua'. This is also the area where the first French settlers arrived from the neighbouring island of Martinique, and set up small plantations and timber works. Jeannot Rolle was a free black from Martinique who purchased land and established the first significant plantation here. He invited Jesuits to the area and erected a large stone cross, known as **La Belle Croix**, which can still be seen standing in the cemetery today.

Often referred to as **Grand Bay Village** or **South City**, the settlement of Berekua is to be found on the western edge of the bay. When approaching from Roseau via Bellevue Chopin, a right turn at the junction a little beyond the Perdu Temps trailhead takes you into the heart of Grand Bay Village. The junction is well signposted. The road passes through a residential area before joining the main thoroughfare of Lallay. This is the very lively main street of Grand Bay Village and is lined with small colourful bars and snackettes as well as a number of galvanised steel nightclubs. This area has a certain degree of notoriety. Once considered quite violent, Grand Bay village had a reputation for existing almost outside the laws of the country. Things have cooled down considerably these days, however, though the blocs and shanties off Lallay together with the Grand Bay Carnival still have a lingering reputation for trouble. Such acts of aggression, should they take place, are always fuelled by local rivalry and are never directed towards visitors.

The Lallay road runs from the seafront all the way up through Grand Bay Village to **Tete Morne**. The road is steep, narrow and full of hairpin bends so take care and use your horn on blind corners if driving. As you enter the hillside community of Tete Morne, the road becomes lined with small wooden houses as it nears the heart of the village and there are pleasant views across the valley as well as down to the bay below. The village is located on a ridge between Morne Plat Pays and Morne Vert. From Tete Morne there are trails across the Palmiste Estate to the summit of Morne Vert and from there down to the estate at Bois Cotlette near Soufriere (see page 148). Segment 2 of the Wai'tukubuli National Trail also passes through this village.

At the foot of the Lallay road where it meets the sea there are several small wooden houses, some ruins and the impressive Grand Bay Roman Catholic Church. The church is large and quite beautiful, built from stone with a bright galvanised steel roof. Tall stone arch windows are opened to let in the Atlantic breeze and above them are modern stained-glass windows decorated in a kaleidoscope of

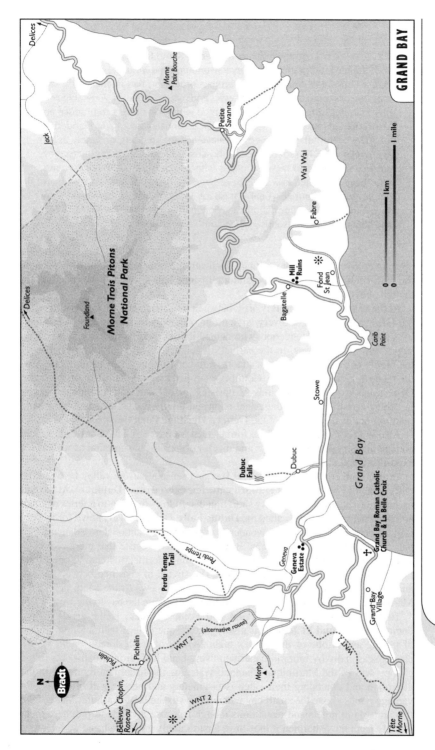

GRAND BAY

abstract colour. The church is situated beneath the cemetery, within which stands the 18th-century La Belle Croix, and a tall stone bell tower that stands proud on the hill above.

At the heart of the Grand Bay area, between the village and the Geneva River, is the **Geneva Estate**. Once a very large estate originally owned by Jesuits and then by a family of Swiss Huguenots who named it after their home town, it produced sugar, rum and molasses. In the early 19th century it was sold to the Lockharts, the family of novelist Jean Rhys's mother. In her 1966 novel, *Wide Sargasso Sea*, the Geneva Estate features as 'Coulibri' and, just as with the estate of the book, Geneva has experienced periods of uprising, arson and violence in each of the last three centuries. Today the estate is owned jointly by the state and by private holdings and is the location of the **Geneva Heritage Park** (see page 144).

Also within the grounds of the former Geneva estate is **The Coal Pot**, a local cottage industry producing soaps and oils for domestic consumption as well as for export (see box above).

On the northern edge of the Grand Bay and set in a narrow valley between the cliffs is the tiny settlement of **Dubuc** (sometimes also written **Dubique**). At the end of this pretty little village is a very short trail that follows the river to a series of small and quite narrow cascades called the **Dubuc Falls**. Dubuc is also known for its very talented cultural group who are wonderful exponents of traditional *bélé* dancing (see page 24). To the east of Dubuc is **Stowe**, a once large estate that produced sugar and rum. Stowe Estate was also the site of a gun placement defending one of the few accessible landing places in the bay. The stretch of coastline between Stowe and Carib Point is quite breathtaking, with superb views to the south across the Martinique Channel and to the rugged Morne Fous across the bay to the west.

To the east, between Carib Point and Point Retireau, is the small fishing community of **Fond St Jean**. It is a very picturesque village with a long tradition of fishing and is one of the south's main sources of fresh dorado (*mahi mahi*), caught seasonally by intrepid fishermen using hand lines from small boats in the choppy seas of the Martinique Channel. Watching the fishermen returning in the afternoon and unloading their catch is fascinating and people will often take up vantage points above the small bay where the boats are hauled ashore. Most of the fish are sold to hotels and restaurants though it is also possible to purchase them directly from the fishermen if they have a particularly good catch.

The narrow road to Fond St Jean runs alongside a beautiful terracotta-coloured cliff face that has been shaped by weather and sea. The road enters the village and passes the small stone beach behind the buildings on the right-hand side where the brightly painted fishing boats are lined up along the water's edge. It then exits the village and winds its way steeply up to **Fabre** from where there are breathtaking views of Fond St Jean and the coastline all the way westwards to Point des Fous. This area is stunning, with steep hills, deep valleys and lush greenery. The hillsides are spotted with bay trees and along the road in Fabre there is a bay distillery shed, one of many in the area. At the end of the road is a small coconut-lined rocky beach where the waves of the Atlantic roll ashore creating a deep thundering sound as the smooth rocks are tossed around beneath the surface. The isolated valley between Fabre and Fond St Jean is **Wai Wai**, a former Kalinago settlement.

Bagatelle is a small village running alongside the main road, located just above Fond St Jean. Midway through the village is a snackette and next to it a small spur road that runs down to some houses above the Malabuka River, ending at the ruins of an old mill. The road is called the **Bagatelle Old Mill Road** and the ruins are really worth visiting. They are accessed via some large brightly painted wrought-iron gates and include a number of pieces of machinery and a large waterwheel that would have powered the cane-crushing machinery in the production of sugar and molasses for rum. The Bagatelle village council has been very keen to develop the mill in an attempt to retain and promote the area's cultural heritage. The council would also like to develop a heritage walking trail that would incorporate the mill and several bay distilleries in the area around Fond St Jean and Bagatelle.

The Cool River Shop and Bar can be found on the apex of a bend above Bagatelle. Located next to a small river, it is a nice place to stop for some refreshments and perhaps watch the domino games that occasionally take place here.

Beyond Bagatelle on the southeastern corner of Dominica is the settlement of **Petite Savanne**. This area is bay country and the major cash crop is bay oil. The work is unforgiving – cultivating and harvesting the bay tree crop along the steep slopes of Foundland, and then distilling the oil for returns that are less than 10% of those typical of banana production – already very low themselves. Look out for the bay sheds and distilleries that are dotted around this area and all the way to Delices on the east coast. Petite Savanne itself is a charming village perched on the steep coastal hillside. The Rogiste Road descends to the lower part of the village where there are tracks to the shore. It is a very steep road with superb views.

BAY LEAF PRODUCTS

The leaves of the bay tree, or *bois d'Inde*, are strongly scented and are used to season foods, aromatise Bay Rum and produce essential oils. Village farmers harvest their bay leaf crops on the slopes of the mountains, then bind the branches together and send them rolling down to the bottom. These bundles are then assembled and taken to a distillery. A fire is set beneath a large vat and the bay leaves are cooked until they release their oil. It is a basic, yet productive system. The organic manufacture of bay oil has traditionally been one of the prime income sources for the farmers of the villages in the southeast of Dominica. The methods remain very simple and traditional, and bay farmers can often be seen transporting their crops to small village distilleries for oil production in this area.

ACTIVITIES AND SPECIAL INTERESTS

ATV Jungle Ride Highride Nature Adventures (*Bellevue Chopin;* ✆ *767 448 6296;* e *highriders@cwdom.dm; www.avirtualdominica.com/highrideadventures*) offer the chance to take an all-terrain vehicle (ATV) ride through the rainforest on a fully guided tour. The vehicles are automatic and are capable of dealing with all kinds of terrain and weather conditions. Each tour is preceded by a training and practice session so no experience is necessary. The ATVs can carry one driver and one passenger per vehicle. Call or email for prices and advance bookings.

Bellevue Chopin Organic Farm Tours Support the local community of Bellevue Chopin, as well as satisfying your own thirst for knowledge, by taking one or several of the organic farm tours that are organised by the Bellevue Chopin Organic Farmers Group. For more information and contact details see box on page 139.

Cachacrou Viewpoint The views of Soufriere Bay from the top of Cachacrou are definitely worth the short climb. On the spit of land that separates the Atlantic from the Caribbean, a path to the right follows the sea around into the corner where the bathing and snorkelling are good. To the left, a path goes straight up to the top of the point. Follow it through the clusters of wild lemon grass until you reach the unsightly communications mast that has been unceremoniously planted almost right on top of the shrine to lost mariners. The path to the right, away from the mast, runs to an old wall and to the right of this is a short, somewhat overgrown trail to a viewpoint with an old cannon overlooking the bay. Just behind the painted wall at the gateway to the communications mast, there is a narrow track that runs all the way to the very top of Cachacrou. The climb is steep and a little slippery on the crumbling ground, so take it steady, but the views from the summit are wonderful and definitely worth the effort of getting there. On a clear day you can also see Martinique to the south. Sit there long enough and it is not that unusual to catch sight of dolphins surfacing in the bay.

Geneva Heritage Park Located on the Geneva Estate (see page 142) this community tourism project has been a rather stop-start affair over the years. Amongst the impressive ruins of this historic estate you will find the home of **Coal Pot Soaps** (see box on page 142) and a rather nice art gallery where Hillroy George displays his wood carvings as well as pieces by other local artisans. Do support them if you can, and also offer some encouragement to develop this project further; it has a lot of potential. A trail behind the ruins leads to farmlands and the pretty Geneva River.

Giraudel and Eggleston Garden and Cooking Tours The Giraudel and Eggleston Flower Growers Group organises garden and cooking tours in these two very pretty mountain communities. For more information and contact details see the box on page 136.

Kayaking The sheltered Soufriere Bay is ideal for ocean kayaking. With calm blue waters overlooked by lush green mountains, ocean kayaking, whether undertaken independently or as part of a guided tour, is a nice way to spend a few hours in the south. A popular excursion is from Soufriere all the way around to Champagne. (See page 81 for information about kayak rentals.) You may also come across kayak and pedalo rental along the shoreline at Scotts Head.

Dive Fest is an annual celebration of scuba diving and watersports organised by the Dominica Watersports Association. The event takes place over one week in July and includes introductory scuba experiences for adults and children, underwater treasure hunts, canoe racing, boat excursions and parties. Events are staged at various venues along the west coast with Soufriere hosting the canoe racing and closing party along the shore. For further information contact the **Dominica Watersports Association** (*www.dominicawatersports.com*).

Scuba diving (*SSMR fee payable*) Operators in the south offer daily boat-diving tours of sites within the marine reserve as well as to sites on the Atlantic side of Scotts Head. Dive site tours are led by qualified divemasters or dive instructors. In addition to basic dive rates, operators in this area must also charge a Marine Reserve Fee of US$2 per diver. (See page 82 for information about dive sites and dive operators in this area.)

Snorkelling (*SSMR fee payable*) 1km south of Pointe Michel, at the very first bend in the coastal road, is Champagne Beach. There is a small parking area with a path to the right. Next to the path is Irie Safari (◊ *767 440 5085;* e *underwater@iriesafari. com; www.iriesafaridominica.com*) which has a refreshments area, showers and toilets. You can rent snorkelling equipment here or alternatively book a guided snorkelling tour. (See page 86 for other scuba dive and snorkelling tour operators in this area.)

Continue down the path to the shore and along the boardwalk to the far side of the beach. It is a very pleasant area, popular with both visitors and locals, and the water is usually very calm and clear. Right at the very southern end of the beach before a small rocky volcanic outcrop is the area of Champagne Reef, a broad formation that starts at the shore and heads out into deeper water. In the shallow area at the end of the volcanic outcrop, near a white marker post, is a submerged active fumarole. All around this area bubbles emerge from vents in the rock creating an impression of champagne bubbles in a glass. The vents themselves are warm, and in places quite hot. It is really quite beautiful when the sea is clear and the sun reflects off the streams of bubbles.

Although the best corals are deeper, the shallow area along the shore is often alive with fish and other marine creatures. Visitors should see parrotfish here as well as smaller reef fish such as damselfish, blue tang, bluehead and surgeonfish. It is also possible to see hawksbill turtles cruising by. Take care not to touch black sea urchins or fireworms, small hairy worms that crawl across rocks. Both cause skin irritation and require attention. Located beyond the bubbles and a little to the south are the encrusted remains of cannon and iron chains.

The site is very popular with snorkellers and scuba divers, and when cruise ships are in it can be quite a busy place. Due to its popularity it is very important to take care of the area and not damage it. When snorkelling or scuba diving try not to stand on or touch the bottom. Be careful not to damage yellow tube sponges or any other marine life.

To snorkel at Champagne Reef visitors must pay a US$2 per person Soufriere Scotts Head Marine Reserve (SSMR) fee. This is collected by staff at Irie Safari.

To go snorkelling at **Scotts Head,** walk to the Cachacrou isthmus and take the wide vehicle track to the right along the shoreline and into the sheltered cove. This

6

area is great for bathing and is also an interesting place to go snorkelling. The red dive buoy is the mooring for the Scotts Head Drop-Off dive site and is easily accessible from the shore. Snorkellers can follow the beautiful line of corals and sponges along the top of this dramatic formation. The occasional barracuda, eagle ray or school of jacks may be seen in addition to numerous colourful reef fish. Snorkellers and bathers swimming out to the drop-off should take note of prevailing currents which, though rare in this area, are likely to run along shore towards the open ocean, making the swim back a little more taxing than the swim out to the reef itself. Please bear this in mind, particularly if you are not an especially strong swimmer.

Visitors snorkelling at Scotts Head should pay a US$2 per person Soufriere Scotts Head Marine Reserve (SSMR) fee. This fee is collected by fisheries wardens on a rather ad hoc basis.

Soufriere Sulphur Springs (*Site pass required*) At the Canal junction at the top of the village of Soufriere is a sign indicating the road to the Sulphur Springs. The road heads inland towards the valley for a short distance before coming to an end at the Sulphur Springs car park and reception centre. Visitor passes can be purchased at the site itself.

Recent redevelopment work has seen a number of improvements to this long-established attraction. From the car park there is a tree-lined path to the reception building, a stylised wooden cabin, where a forestry officer will collect your pass. These trees have name plates and the reception centre has an imaginative and informative display describing the history and geological formation of the area. From here the path crosses a warm water cascade to a small junction. To the left is the original, large sulphur pool and to the right is a path leading to three further pools and a trail that takes you to scarred areas of hillside where volcanic activity creates steaming, pungent deposits of sulphur. Straight ahead at the junction is a changing facility, a covered picnic area and refreshments building.

The path leading to the three higher pools also takes you to the trailhead of the climb to the top of the Soufriere ridge and across to the village of Tete Morne (see page 147). Like the hot sulphur springs in the area of Wotten Waven (see page 89), bathing in the mineral-rich waters is considered to be a rejuvenating and healthy activity.

Rodney's Wellness Retreat and Carrod's Gardens (*Soufriere;* \ 767 245 4725; e *relax@rodneyswellness.com;* *www.rodneyswellness.com*) This idyllic sanctuary is just off the road to Soufriere Sulphur Springs (follow the signs and turn left before the school). It boasts relaxing gardens, a restaurant and a bar, and offers organic produce, organised walks around the area and a hot mud pool. Try the traditional one-pot *braf* on Saturdays. It is a nice escape for those looking for a little peace and a place to hang out with a fresh fruit juice and a good book. Open daytimes and evenings.

HIKES
Morne Anglais (*Difficulty: T: 3; R: 0; E: 4; D: 3; Rating = 6.3*) This is a steep walk and in places quite a tricky climb through deep mud and tree roots. In certain sections the trail can also be quite difficult to follow. The summit of Morne Anglais is often clear of cloud cover and, because this peak is slightly offset from the others, the views are awesome. You can see from Roseau all the way up to Salisbury on the west coast, Grand Bay in the south, and even Delices in the east – all from one spot.

The trailhead is in the pretty village of Giraudel (see page 50 for information on buses and page 133 for driving directions). The best route to take is directly up through Castle Comfort from the Texaco garage on the west coast highway. When you enter the village of Giraudel, one of the first buildings you meet is the small schoolhouse (it has a mural painted on the side). There is a small parking area here.

To the left of the school there are two side roads heading steeply uphill. Take the rougher one to the left past a couple of houses. Don't worry about the dogs. Follow it all the way up until you reach a junction with a new road. Keep going straight and follow this road around the bend to the left. You then come to another junction. There is a rough track heading uphill on the right. Follow it up past a couple of small farms on the left and a concrete water tank on the right. Keep going until you come to a large, abandoned water catchment, surrounded by a wire fence. As you face it, head for the bottom left-hand corner. Standing at the bottom left-hand corner of the old catchment, follow the fence all the way to the top left-hand corner. The bush on your left may be a little overgrown and there may also be one or two rather curious goats in your path, but keep going. Ignore the spur trail to the left and stick to the fence.

When you get to the top of the catchment you should see a trail heading up and away from the corner. Follow it uphill. It can be steep and rather slippery here and sometimes the trail disappears a bit, but keep going until you come out at the bottom right-hand corner of a large open field.

If there is a farmer working here, please offer a greeting. If there are cows grazing, give them a wide berth. Your task is to head up to the very top left-hand corner of the field. You may be able to make out a faint trace through the grass. Halfway up, cows permitting, turn around and take in the view.

When you reach the top left-hand corner, look for a trail running up and away from the field. It may be difficult to spot in the bush, but it is there. When you find it, follow it up through the forest. The trail is now a lot easier to see but you should still pay attention. There are some areas where the path seems to disappear around a sharp corner or behind a tree. You are climbing a narrow ridge that curves around towards the summit, so you cannot go too far wrong. It has some steep and narrow stretches and you will be able to enjoy a couple of good viewpoints. To your right (the south), the village you can see is Bellevue Chopin. To your left (the north), you can see Morne Micotrin and occasionally Morne Trois Pitons and the Freshwater Lake if the weather is clear.

The trail then starts to descend and it is from this point that the terrain becomes a little more challenging. Once you reach the bottom of this incline, you climb again, all the way to the top. It will be very muddy and you must use your upper body strength from time to time to help you climb up a few steep sections. Eventually you reach the top and as you do so you are greeted by razor grass. Lovely. The path through the grass may be a little overgrown, but it is there. Pick your way through it as best you can, trying not to get too cut up by it, and aiming for the radio mast. Watch out for hollows in the trail beneath your feet.

You will come out at a clearing, the lower summit of the two, where there is a solar panel and ham radio equipment. The trail to the upper summit ahead of you is no longer passable. Enjoy the fabulous views.

Soufriere–Palmiste Loop (*Difficulty: T: 3; R: 0; E: 4; D: 2; Rating = 5.6*) This is a
loop hike that begins and ends at Soufriere Sulphur Springs. It takes in the historic Bois Cotlette Estate and includes a very steep climb to the summit of Morne Vert. The views of Grand Bay from the top are fabulous. The descent to Soufriere is much easier than the climb and you can reward yourself further with a hot sulphur spa or a refreshing dip in Soufriere Bay.

BOIS COTLETTE

The Bois Cotlette Estate was established by French settlers in the early 18th century and is considered to be the best-preserved example of plantation buildings existing in Dominica today. The estate is named after the Bois Cotlette tree (*Citharexylum spinosum*). Thanks to ongoing preservation work, the results of which are quite beautiful, the planter's house and surrounding land and buildings paint a vivid picture of the past when coffee, sugar, limes, rum and molasses were produced there.

To the south of the estate is the windmill tower. When functioning, it would have faced the trade winds which powered its sails enabling it to turn the rollers and crush the sugarcane. This windmill tower is the only one of its kind in Dominica. At the centre of the grounds is the pretty wooden planter's house and on either side are industrial buildings such as the boiling house and distillery where sugar, rum and molasses were produced, and the coffee house where the dried coffee was stored and prepared for shipping.

South of Bois Cotlette is Morne Rouge Estate, another of the first French estates established in the south. It produced sugar, cocoa, coffee and limes and until the mid 20th century was still owned by the original French family. The estate building stands today and is thought to be one of the oldest surviving on the island. A privately owned house, it is quite beautiful, located on the cliffs above the sea with a view across to Martinique.

For more information about the Bois Cotlette Heritage Plantation contact Michael Didier (767 448 3279; e *michaeldidier@hotmail.com*). Dominican historian Lennox Honychurch also has detailed content on his website www.lennoxhonychurch.com.

See page 50 for information about buses to Soufriere and page 133 for driving directions. If you are on a bus, get off at the junction at the top of Soufriere and follow the signposted road to the springs. About three-quarters of the way there, beyond the houses, you will see a wide vehicle track next to a bar on your right. This is the trailhead. If you are driving, park at the Soufriere Sulphur Springs car park and then walk back down the tree-lined avenue a couple of hundred metres until you see the vehicle track and bar on the left. You are actually walking part of Segment 1 of the Wai'tukubuli National Trail, but in the opposite direction – that is why you may see signs pointing to where you have just come from.

Follow the wide vehicle track for 20–30 minutes until you come to the Bois Cotlette Estate (see box on page 148 for more information). A little further along the road, beyond the main buildings, you will see the ruin of the windmill tower.

Retrace your steps to the wall at the entrance to the estate grounds and look for a painted marker. With your back to Bois Cotlette, the trail is over the wall on your right. Follow it through the woodland, over some loose stones and into a rather dark gulley until it begins to climb. The ascent is severe and it is often difficult to find a firm footing. Be prepared to slide and crawl. Take regular breaks and tell yourself when you get to the top that everything is downhill from then on! It is a steep and long climb. If the trail is occasionally difficult to make out, pause and look for ribbons in the trees. Once you start to see bamboo thickets, you can comfort yourself with the thought that you are about three-quarters of the way there and the trail starts to get a little easier. You will come to an old water trough in a gulley and you will probably see evidence of cows. Keep to the main trail until you pass through some tall grass and then emerge by farmlands. You will probably see farmers working here and they may come and greet you. Let them know you are on your way down to Tete Morne and Soufriere and they will happily show you the way.

When you see these fields, you need to head over to the right, to the sloping grasslands where you will pick up the clear trail again. There are fabulous views of Grand Bay here and it is a lovely spot to sit down, relax, recover from the climb and just enjoy being where you are.

Follow the trail. The views should be on your right and the hillside on your left. Ignore a wide spur that heads down to the right and keep going straight. In fact ignore all spurs and just stick to the main trail as it meanders quite steeply down the side of the Palmiste Estate towards the village of Tete Morne. There are some nice views across the village to the mountains of the interior. You will see some shacks and ruined buildings on your left just before you emerge at a paved road. Take a left and follow the road up through the top of the village until it comes to an end and turns into a rough track. This is part of the Wai'tukuli National Trail Segment 2 and, yes, you are walking it in the opposite direction again! But keep going. You will reach the crest of the hill. Way down below you is the village of Soufriere and the Caribbean Sea.

The trail continues as a series of switchbacks that winds down the mountainside. It is very easy to follow, though it is a little steep in places. Enjoy the views. Towards the bottom, on your right, you will see the active sulphur deposits above the Soufriere Sulphur Springs. When you reach a trail junction, access to the springs is to your right, across the small stream. If you wish to bypass the springs and go down to the car park, just follow the wide track straight ahead of you. Please remember that if you do wish to use the springs, a site fee is payable.

Galion and Morne Crabier (*Difficulty: T: 2; R: 0; E: 3; D: 2; Rating = 4.4*)

This hike takes you from Scotts Head up to the village of Galion where you can enjoy great views of Soufriere Bay. After passing through the village, you pick up the Wai'tukubuli National Trail Segment 1, but do it in reverse, all the way down to Scotts Head again where you can reward yourself with a swim, a fresh fish lunch and a cold drink.

The trailhead is located near a small stone building with a red galvanised steel roof on the side of the road between Scotts Head and Soufriere. Look for a small public convenience; it is near there. To the left of this building is a wide track heading uphill. This is the start of the walk. Follow this track all the way up to the village of Galion. It takes around 30 minutes of steep climbing to reach the top where there is a wonderful view of Soufriere Bay.

Walk through and out of the village, following the main road for about 15–20 minutes. Note the volcanic nature of the landscape beyond the village. The escarpments to your right have volcanic activity and you may notice the distinctive smell of sulphur dioxide from time to time. Look at the ridges around you; you are clearly inside a crater. This road is also lined with cashew trees.

You will reach a sharp hairpin bend with an old stone building quite nearby on the left. A track runs directly into the forest at the apex of the bend – look for Wai'tukubuli National Trail signs. You are now going to follow part of Segment 1 in the opposite direction all the way to Scotts Head.

After about ten minutes or so the trail splits. Take the right-hand fork. After another five minutes the trail splits again with a spur going off to the left. Take the right-hand fork once more. After only another 15m or so there is a third fork. The trail to the right goes to a house, so take the one to the left. Keep following the

National Trail signs, but in reverse, of course. Very shortly the trail emerges at a small clearing. Walk straight across it and follow the steep track up into the woods on the other side. Follow this path up to the top. It will take around 30–45 minutes of fairly tough climbing. Take a breather and a drink at the top and, when you are ready, begin your descent.

Down the south side of the mountain there are good views across the channel to Martinique. The section from the summit is quite steep so take care with your footing. You will soon come out at a beautiful clearing that looks more like Yorkshire Dales pasture land than the Caribbean. Walk down the right-hand side to the very end and pick up the trail again. The clear track winds down the mountainside in a series of switchbacks until it reaches the village of Scotts Head.

When you reach a road junction, take the road to the right and then the next to the left. Follow the signs and the narrow road as it meanders down through the pretty fishing village to Soufriere Bay.

At the bottom, the road to the left heads out to Cachacrou where the waves of the Atlantic break on the left and the warm, still waters of the Caribbean lap gently against the shore to the right. This is a great spot for a swim after your tough walk. The road to the right heads towards Soufriere and the small stone building where the hike began. There are a couple of great little local bars here; Chez Wen and Roger's.

Perdu Temps (from Pichelin) *(Difficulty: T: 3; R: 3; E: 2; D: 3; Rating = 6.9)* This beautiful rainforest hike starts on the main road between Pichelin and Grand Bay and ends up near the village of Delices on the southeast coast. It follows a trail once used by people in the south to cross the island before roads were constructed. Near Pichelin there used to be a small settlement called Perdu Temps and a paved road leading to it. In 1979 Hurricane David forced people to abandon the settlement after the Pichelin River Bridge was washed away and houses were destroyed.

Poor signage and numerous river crossings make this trail difficult to follow. For this reason a guide is essential; without one, you will almost certainly get lost – it has happened to plenty of people. A good contact is **Octave Joseph** of the Hide-Out Cottage in Geneva (✆ 767 446 46 42). You could also try **Bumpiing Tours** (✆ 767 315 0493), or **KHATTS** (✆ 767 448 1660). If you are staying at Jungle Bay, they may also offer a guided hike. The trail can be started from either end, of course. Give yourself plenty of time and do not attempt this hike if there has been heavy rain. The White River crossing at the Delices end is dangerous when it is in full flood.

The trailhead is located between the hamlet of Pichelin and the Grand Bay junction. Look for the sign. Use a Grand Bay bus to get here (see page 50), or by car follow the directions to Grand Bay described on page 134.

From the clearing on the main road head left to pick up the trail and follow it across flat land for a short distance until it reaches the Pichelin River. This is the first crossing of many and is quite easy. The trail then runs along an old stone road that once led to the settlement of Perdu Temps. Soon you will reach the Geneva River, which you must also cross. It is a pretty river and the countryside in this area is quite beautiful. Take care with the crossing; the river is deep in places and the rocks are slippery. From the other side, the trail passes through open countryside and farmland. It crosses a number of small streams and rivers and begins its gradual ascent up the valley. At the sign to Pomme's place, take the right-hand fork and continue the steady climb. You will pass alongside some small wooden buildings and a clear area of pasture land. There are good views behind you of the villages of Grand Bay and Tete Morne, with the Martinique Channel beyond.

A sharp turn to the right, followed by a steep climb through the forest, brings you to the summit of a ridge. This is roughly the halfway point. There is a fairly steep descent from this ridge down into very dense rainforest. You will come across a number of plant species native to this kind of habitat such as the *chatanier* with its buttress roots, the *gommier*, tree ferns, mountain palms, *zel-mouch*, *bwa riviere*, wild anthuriums and several varieties of orchids. The ground on either side of the trail is covered in an emerald blanket of *pawasol agouti*, and if you are lucky enough, you may even disturb an agouti and see it scuttling off into the forest. Jaco parrots may also be heard calling from high up in the canopy here, especially in the vicinity of *gommier* trees. A good guide, with knowledge of forest plants and animals, can really enhance this hike for you; and, for the next stretch, will spare you the stress and embarrassment of getting lost.

From now on the trail makes a series of river crossings and the route becomes very difficult to follow. The rivers are usually quite shallow but the continuation points are difficult to find as they are not necessarily located on the bank directly opposite. Nevertheless, the rivers, streams and cascades you see here are quite beautiful. The trail turns out of the dense forest to a ridge with views across a river valley to **Jacks Falls** which is particularly impressive in the wet season. You will continue your descent towards the River Jack which you cross several times in quick succession. The crossings are usually shallow and fairly easy.

From here you have to look for a continuation of the trail on the left bank which passes behind a tree and heads uphill towards a flat area of woodland, pasture and bay trees. To the south you will see the summit of Foundland, the tallest mountain in the southeast. The trail then begins its final descent towards the White River. Crossing the White River can be tricky as it is fast-flowing and quite deep in places. Your guide can help you. It is a lovely place to just sit in a pool and cool down, or perhaps have a picnic. The source of this river is the Boiling Lake (see page 123). Once on the other side, you will meet the trailhead for the Victoria Falls which forks to the left, and which is another 30–45 minutes upriver (see page 174). The trail straight on emerges at a clearing, some houses and Zion Valley, a bush bar and gardens owned by the very friendly Moses. It is a nice place to stop for a drink. The vehicle track takes you uphill to the main road south of Delices.

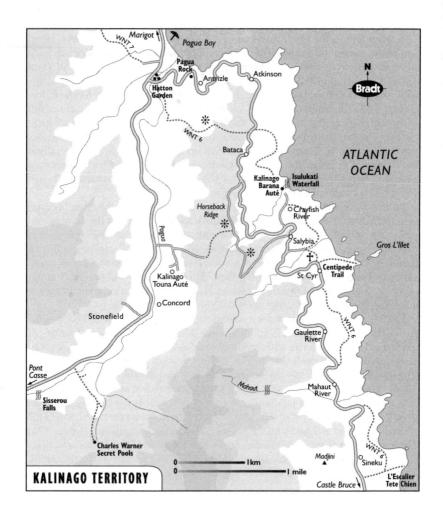

KALINAGO TERRITORY

7

The Kalinago Territory and the East

THE KALINAGO

'Carib' is a word you may hear a lot during your visit. It was the name used by Europeans to describe the Amerindian people of the Greater and Lesser Antilles island chain. Very controversially and probably quite unfairly, this name had connotations of cannibalism and it is one of the reasons why Dominica's indigenous people do not like it very much. Indian tribes had travelled by canoe from South America and arrived in islands such as Dominica as early as 5000BC. They are thought to have populated large parts of Central and North America as well as the islands in between. The Taino people settled in the Greater Antilles and the Igneri in the Lesser Antilles. The Kalinago were also an Arawakan-speaking people from South America who arrived in the Lesser Antilles in the 12th and 13th centuries, eventually displacing the Igneri. When the Spanish arrived in the Greater Antilles in the 15th century they set to work enslaving and killing the Taino people until none remained. The Kalinago who had settled in Dominica fought against the Spanish and, quite incredibly, resisted all attempts to take the island for around 200 years. Unfortunately this constant battle over several generations had a high price and the number of Kalinago living here seriously declined. By the time the first French settlers arrived in the early 18th century, the Kalinago had little choice other than to accept their fate and share Wai'tukubuli, the name they gave Dominica, with these new people.

The European colonialists created small estates and claimed more and more land as their own. The Kalinago were consequently forced further and further into the more remote reaches of the island. West African slaves brought from other islands to work on the French and subsequently British estates often escaped into the rainforest where they either clashed or collaborated with the Kalinago against the Europeans. Following emancipation in 1838 and the later arrival of more west Africans liberated from slave ships, many of the estates declined and new settlements were created in their place. The population of liberated slaves grew and farming and fishing villages were established throughout the island.

During this time Kalinago numbers were in serious decline and in 1903 Crown Colony administrator Hesketh Bell secured a reservation for them on the east coast. This land became known as the Carib Reserve and, more recently, the Carib Territory. The people currently living in this territory are descendants of the Kalinago. Though racial and social integration, together with the influences of North America, Europe and Africa, have significantly affected the development of the Kalinago, there is a contemporary movement that aims to arrest the decline of their cultural heritage, and it needs your support.

Throughout this book I refer to Dominica's indigenous people as Kalinago and do not use the word Carib. I urge you to do the same, even though you will hear

Kalinago themselves use the word Carib occasionally. You will surprise and please them by using the name they prefer.

The development of tourism in Dominica offers the Kalinago people an opportunity to raise the profile of their cultural heritage as well as generate an income from it. Throughout the territory you will see a number of stalls selling traditional crafts and two very innovative projects, the Kalinago Barana Auté and the Kalinago Touna Auté, complement each other as showcases for both historic and contemporary Kalinago life and culture.

GETTING THERE

BY BUS See page 50 for information on buses from Roseau. Please remember that buses tend to stop running in the early evening and that you should be prepared for longer waits in more remote places such as San Sauveur, Petite Soufriere, and Delices.

BY CAR To get to the Kalinago Territory by car you either approach it from the north at Hatton Garden junction or from the south near Castle Bruce. From Roseau it is easier to get there via Castle Bruce. Take the Imperial Road from Canefield up to Pont Cassé and then take the right-hand exit, following the signs to Castle Bruce. About ten minutes down this road you will come to a second junction. Take the road to the left past the Emerald Pool and, at the end of the long Castle Bruce stretch, just before you reach the coast, take another left.

If you are heading to the rest of the east coast from Roseau you have two options. The first is to go via Pont Cassé as described above, but instead of turning

CANOE BUILDING

The Kalinago were master canoe builders, carving out vessels from single tree trunks, usually *gommier* (*Dacryodes excelsa*), and using them to catch fish, migrate between islands and for warfare. Unfortunately the art of canoe building is no longer as strong as it once was though there are still one or two builders in the Kalinago Territory who are trying to keep it alive.

The method of creating a canoe has changed a little with the introduction of modern tools, but the process itself is still very much the same. The hull of the canoe is carved out from a large *gommier* tree – either in the forest, or after it has been dragged out to the workshop, depending on how big it is. Sometimes fire is used to speed up the hollowing-out process together with simple hand tools. In former times, sharp volcanic rock would have been the cutting tool of choice. Hot rocks and steam are also used to stretch out the canoe, with tree branches acting as props. The bordage along the top of the canoe is also made from the *gommier* tree and is sealed using soft *gommier* sap blended with black sand to produce a tough, water-resistant sealant and resin that the builders refer to as *putty*. The ribs, bow and rowlock pins are usually made from white cedar. As a finishing touch, canoes are painted in bright colours according to the wishes of the customer.

When you are passing through the Kalinago Territory look out for Merlin Stoute and his two sons who may be working on a canoe by the roadside. Merlin is in his 70s and has been building canoes and fishing for a living for over 50 years.

left towards Castle Bruce and the Emerald Pool, go straight. This will take you to Rosalie, Riviere Cyrique and beyond. You can also get there via Grand Bay and the south coast (see page 134). The road beyond Petit Savanne climbs to the top of Paix Bouche and then sharply back down again towards Delices, Boetica and La Plaine.

To get to Good Hope and San Sauveur you take the road that runs next to the playing field in Castle Bruce. A new road is under construction at the time of writing that follows the old trail from Rosalie to Petite Soufriere.

WHERE TO STAY

HIGH END

🏠 **Rosalie Bay Resort** (28 rooms) Rosalie; ☎ 767 446 1010; e info@rosaliebay.com; www.rosaliebay.com. Eco luxury resort located beside the Rosalie River & the black volcanic sands of the Atlantic coastline. 28 rooms & suites to match all preferences, each very stylishly designed & furnished offering comfort & privacy. King & queen beds, en-suite bathrooms with organic products, fans & verandas with either ocean, river or garden views. Restaurant offers a full service of haute Creole & international cuisine, there is a fully equipped gym, a spa offering a range of wellness services, a unique freshwater bathing pool, cabana bar & colourful tropical gardens. A state-of-the art conference centre has audio-visual technologies, stage, bar & other amenities. Eco sensitivity is demonstrated by the large wind turbine & the promotion of leatherback turtle nesting site & education activities. Perfect for romantics, business retreats or those who simply wish to escape & indulge. Nature tours, weddings, retreats, airport transfers, wireless internet. **$$$$$**

🏠 **Jungle Bay Resort & Spa** (35 cottages) Delices; ☎ 767 446 1789; e info@junglebaydominica.com; www.junglebaydominica.com. Delightful hardwood cottages located in over 20ha of forest in the southeast. Each private, thoughtfully designed cottage sleeps 2 & has en-suite bathroom, semi-outdoor shower & private veranda. Close attention to detail. Large open-air restaurant serves local & international dishes. Other facilities include bar, games & TV room, yoga centre, health spa, gift shop & pool. Friendly & professional service. Hikes & island

tours offered. Wedding & honeymoon packages available. Complementary airport & ferry transfers. Minimum stay 3 nights. **$$$$$**

🏠 **Beau Rive** (8 standard rooms, 2 cottage rooms) Castle Bruce; ☎ 767 445 8992; e info@beaurive.com; www.beaurive.com. Elegant & intimate hotel with traditional feel set in tranquil gardens with beautiful ocean views. Each tastefully designed & decorated room sleeps 2, has en-suite bathroom, ceiling fan & veranda looking out on the Atlantic Ocean. Lounge & library, restaurant, bar & open terrace. Swimming pool & sun deck. Internet access. Cool sea breezes & a perfect balance of design & comfort gives this hotel its distinction. Very popular & with an excellent reputation for standards & service. **$$$$**

🏠 **Silks** (5 rooms) Hatton Garden, Marigot; ☎ 767 445 8846; e info@silkshotel.com; www.silkshotel.com. Charming hotel on historic estate grounds at the convergence of Pagua & Hatton Garden rivers. Stylish, well-furnished rooms have AC, 4-poster & king-size beds, en-suite bathroom, private terrace garden. Swimming pool, river access. Restaurant offers international cuisine. Sat BBQ & river tubing. Laid back, welcoming, & hiker friendly. Camping pitches available. **$$$**

🏠 **Atlantique View Resort & Spa** (40 rooms) Anse Du Mai; ☎ 767 445 6719; e atlantisofdom@yahoo.com; www.atlantiqueviewresortandspa.com. Under construction at the time of writing but worth checking website for updates. Located on the main Portsmouth to Calibishie road, near the pretty coastal hamlet of Anse Soldat.

MODERATE

🏠 **River Rush Eco Retreat** (5 cottages) Stonefield, nr Concord; ☎ 767 295 7266; e mo@river-rush.com; www.river-rush.com. Simple

but comfortable wooden cottages located in a magical forest & river setting. 4 cottages sleep 2, 1 cottage sleeps 4. All have double bed, mosquito netting, en-suite bathroom. Larger cottage has big open windows looking out on to Pagua River. Large communal bar & lounge hosts the popular 'Jazz in the Jungle' event every Sun (Mo, the owner, is a saxophonist). Garden trails lead to the river & pools. Weddings & events catered for. Peaceful & private, beautiful natural surroundings. B/fast inc. **$$$**

⌂ **Roots Jungle Retreat** (4 cottages) Pagua Hills, nr Concord; ✆ 767 275 6000, 767 265 3806; e rootsjungleretreat@gmail.com; www.rootsjungleretreat.com. Eco retreat located in remote forest surroundings with nearby rivers, waterfall & pool. Each thoughtfully designed wooden cottage has private composting toilet & shower & galley-style kitchen. Some can comfortably accommodate more than 2 people. Bar & restaurant, BBQ & stone bread-oven. Welcoming hosts also offer a range of interesting day tours. Great location for those looking for a peaceful escape. B/fast inc. **$$**

⌂ **Mermaid's Secret** (2 cabins, 3 Mongolian yurts) Rosalie; ✆ 767 295 6299; e mermaids.secret@gmail.com;

www.mermaidssecret.com. Located on the banks of the Rosalie River, 2 self-contained wooden cabins have bedroom, private bathroom, kitchenette, lounge area, covered deck, fans & wireless internet. One cabin is designed for a family of 4, the other for a couple. Mongolian yurts add a colourful twist for those looking for a little camping luxury. Yurts have shared facilities. Communal BBQ area & pretty Mermaid's Pool nearby. Camping also available. Friendly, personal service, handy & affordable location for exploring the east. Cabins & yurts: **$$**

⌂ **Hibiscus Valley Inn** (4 rooms, 3 bungalows) Concord; ✆ 767 445 8195; e info@hibiscusvalley.com; www.hibiscusvalley.com. 3 simple, rustic wooden bungalows divided into 6 rooms on a landscaped hillside near the village of Concord. Each bungalow room has private bathroom, fan, hammock & veranda. Main house has 4 en-suite rooms with dbl bed, TV, AC, fridge & private veranda. Restaurant serves meals by request. Additional wooden family house available for rent. Enquire for details. Bungalow rooms **$**, main house rooms **$$**

BUDGET

⌂ **Kai Woshe Guest House** (5 rooms) Delices; ✆ 767 446 1688; e kaiwoshe@hotmail.com; www.kaiwoshe.hotels.officelive.com. Simple accommodation located in a large house on the road to Jungle Bay Resort. 4 rooms share 2 bathrooms, the master room is en suite. Fans & shared veranda. Internet access & gardens. Friendly owner is an organic farmer. **$**, master **$$**

⌂ **Domcan's Guesthouse & Restaurant** (6 self-catering suites) Castle Bruce; ✆ 767 445 7794; e domcanrestaurant@hotmail.com; www.domcansguesthouse.com. Each SC suite sleeps 2 & is fully equipped with galley-style kitchen, living & dining area, bedroom & en-suite bathroom. Roll-out cots are available for an extra adult or children. Each suite has ceiling fans, TV & verandas at the front & back, with fabulous ocean views to the rear. Wireless internet access, bar & full-service restaurant, including al fresco dining deck. Neat & tidy accommodation that is handy for exploring the east coast & Kalinago Territory. **$**

⌂ **Gingerlily Cottage** (2 bedroom house) Riviere Cyrique; ✆ 41 32 724 2607; e gingerinfo@hotmail.com; www.ginger-lily.com. Fully

furnished clean & tidy house located in Morne Aux Frégates, just above Riviere Cyrique. Large balcony with great mountain & ocean views. Meals can be ordered from Ti Mam's Bar at the foot of the hill. Good value. **$**

⌂ **Carib Territory Guesthouse** (8 rooms) Crayfish River; ✆ 767 445 7256; e charlohotel@yahoo.com; www.avirtualdominica/ctgh. Simple dbl rooms with fans, 3 with en-suite bathrooms. Shared terrace on upper floor with ocean views. Bar & restaurant also with ocean view serves b/fast & dinner to guests by reservation. Fully equipped gym, wireless internet, shared lounge with TV. Extra bunk rooms available. Airport transfers. Close to KBA, Horseback Ridge & handy for National Trail hikers. **$**

⌂ **Rosalie Forest** (3 cottages, 3 bamboo treehouses, 8-bed dormitory) Rosalie; ✆ 767 275 1886; e info@rosalieforest.com; www.rosalieforest.com. About as back-to-basics as it gets. 2 bamboo treehouses located in dense woodland up a steep 15–20min trail. Each has dbl bed, composting toilet, cold shower & use of shared cooking area. Also up the mountain is an 8-bed wooden dormitory with composting toilet & shower. 3 wooden cottages located at the foot of the mountain sleep up to 3 persons & have bathroom, kitchen, balcony, hammock. Camping available. Reclusive, no frills eco accommodation. Treehouses **$**, cottages **$$**, camping **$**

HIKING AND YOGA RETREATS

🏠 **Hiker's Retreat** (4 dbl rooms) Fayal, Rosalie; ✆ 767 446 1076, 732 213 5459; e hikersretreat@hikingdominica.com; www.hikingdominica.com. Lovely homestay accommodation for hiking enthusiasts who wish to explore & enjoy Dominica in the company of knowledgeable guides. Upper floors each have 2 dbl bedrooms, bathroom, living area & large veranda. Thoughtfully designed & furnished with fabulous views of Rosalie Bay. Healthy meals prepared & various hiking options available.

Picturesque location & friendly hosts. Prices are per person per night & include b/fast, dinner, picnics & all hiking tours. **$$$$$**

🏠 **Rasta Yoga Nurture Retreat** (2 cottages) Rosalie (on the Grand Fond Rd); ✆ 767 446 2247; www.dominicarastayoga.com. Yoga Ashram with 2 wooden cottages & main house for yoga & *ital* meals. Each cottage has 2 dbl bedrooms, toilet & shower, fridge, DVD player, internet access. Various yoga packages available. See website & contact for further info.

CAMPING

⚑ **Mermaid's Secret** Rosalie; ✆ 767 295 6299. Approx 10 pitches with shared facilities, communal kitchen & BBQ area. Mongolian yurts also available. Tent pitches **$**, Mongolian yurts **$$**

⚑ **Rosalie Forest** Rosalie; ✆ 767 275 1886. Approx 10 pitches with shared facilities in riverside location. 2- & 4-man tent rental available. **$**

⚑ **Zion Valley** Victoria. Located at the Victoria Falls trailhead, Moses provides simple pitches, *ital* food, bush teas, juices & a warm & friendly welcome. Located on the banks of the White River. Moses offers guided tours to the waterfall & invites you to 'see, touch & smell' his vegetable & herb garden. Tent rentals also available. **$**

✖ WHERE TO EAT AND DRINK

CREOLE AND INTERNATIONAL RESTAURANTS

✖ **Rosalie Bay Resort** Rosalie; ✆ 767 446 1010. A fusion of Creole & international cuisine with a hint of Belize. High quality full-service dining at this top class eco luxury resort. **$$$**

✖ **Silks Hotel** Hatton Gardon, Marigot; ✆ 767 445 8846. International dishes, b/fast, lunch, dinner, 7 days a week. Sat BBQ & live music by the riverside. All welcome. Reservations required. **$$$**

✖ **River Rush Eco Retreat** Stonefield, nr Concord; ✆ 767 295 7266. No regular dining

but every Sun there is 'Jazz in the Jungle' where owner & jazz saxophonist, Mo, is accompanied by local musicians. Everyone is welcome to enjoy drinks & Sunday Brunch. **$$$**

✖ **Jungle Bay Resort & Spa** Delices; ✆ 767 446 1789. Large open-air restaurant serving a variety of local & international cuisine. Continental b/fast, lunch & dinner always available. Picturesque setting. **$$–$$$**

KANKI

Kanki is a traditional Kalinago dish made from cassava roots (*Manihot esculenta*). The roots are peeled and grated then soaked in water before being strained through muslin. The water is left to settle in a bowl until a starchy residue has collected at the bottom. The excess water is poured away and the starchy residue mixed up with the grated cassava, sugar and a variety of spices until it becomes sticky. Portions of the mixture are wrapped in banana leaves and tied up with string before being boiled in a pot of water. After around 15 minutes the *kanki* is ready to serve.

✗ Riverside Café Citrus Creek Plantation Taberi, La Plaine; ✆ 767 446 1234. Lovely restaurant serving high quality French & Creole lunches & snacks. Fresh juices, wines, coffee. Wireless internet & pretty riverside setting. $$–$$$
✗ Domcans Guesthouse & Restaurant Castle Bruce; ✆ 767 445 7794. Serving Creole &

international dishes. Deck restaurant has lovely coastal & sea views. $–$$
✗ Beau Rive Castle Bruce; ✆ 767 445 8992. Dining is reserved for hotel guests only but everyone is welcome to come for a drink & enjoy the terrace & the views. $

CREOLE AND KALINAGO EATERIES

✗ Islet View Restaurant Castle Bruce; ✆ 767 446 0370. Very popular restaurant with both visitors & locals, serving traditional Creole dishes & an unparalleled range of homemade rum fusions. Bamboo & banana leaf decor with great views of St David's Bay from the dining deck. $–$$
✗ Kalinago Barana Auté Crayfish River; ✆ 767 445 7979. Traditional lunches served in calabash bowls. Handy place for a bite & refreshments if exploring the Kalinago Territory. $
✗ Ocean Sea View Restaurant Carse O Gowrie, La Plaine. Good local lunches & refreshments. Handy for budget travellers in the southeast. Located just off the main highway. $

✗ Ti Mam's Located on the east coast highway at the foot of the Morne Aux Frégates road, serving good local food & drinks. Handy eatery if staying at Gingerlily Cottage or exploring the southeast on a budget. $
✗ Cassava Bakery Salybia. Traditional Kalinago cassava bread made at this roadside bakery in Salybia. Great just to try or to nibble on your hikes or road trips. $
✗ Lynnworth Bakery Riviere Cyrique. A handy place to pick up fresh bread, cakes & more for your river or beachside picnic on the east coast. Just follow the lovely smell of fresh bread or look for the brightly painted yellow & white building on the south side of the village on the main highway. $

VEGETARIAN

✗ Chez Juliana Livity Venue Rosalie (on the Grand Fond Rd); ✆ 767 446 2247. Part of the Rasta

Yoga Ashram & serving *ital* foods such as fresh fruits & vegetables but also fish & seafood. $–$$

WHAT TO SEE AND DO

THE KALINAGO TERRITORY The Kalinago Territory covers 1,530ha on the east coast of Dominica from the village of Bataca in the north to the village of Sineku in the south. It was established in 1903 by Dominica's first Crown Colony administrator, Hesketh Bell, who governed Dominica between 1899 and 1905. The Kalinago Territory is administered by the Kalinago Council which is headed up by

TREE FERN CARVINGS

You may come across hand-carved masks made from a dark, fibrous material. This is actually the bottom of a tree fern trunk (known locally as *fwigè* or *fougère*) that has been split, the core carved out, and the remaining two halves shaped into various types of mask. There are several very competent exponents of this craft in Dominica, some of whom are Kalinago. One such person is Israel Joseph (Nom Fwigè, featured in a short documentary film of the same name) who has a small and truly unique roadside shop made from newspaper printing plates by the side of the road in Mahaut River. He makes high quality masks, plant holders and reliefs. Israel's wife, Victoria, is an accomplished *larouma* basket weaver.

The Kalinago are excellent basket weavers. Their beautiful products can be purchased from stalls and craft shops around the island and they are also exported to overseas markets. Traditionally, basketwork would have been used to carry food and to catch fish and crustaceans. Today a variety of wares are available, including beautifully shaped baskets, bottles, mats and finger traps.

They are made from the *larouma* reed (*Ischosiphon arouma*) which was probably brought by Amerindians from the Amazon River basin several thousand years ago and planted as a crop. The Kalinago word for the reed was *oualloman*, but it underwent a transition to French Creole and became *l'arouman*. It is a tall reed which, after harvesting, is split and the pith removed. The strips of reed are laid out in the sun to dry and turn a reddish brown. Some reeds are coloured black by covering them in mud and leaving them for a few days. White reeds are created simply by using the underside of the reddish-brown reeds that have been left out in the sun. Baskets were traditionally lined with the leaves of the *z'ailes mouches* (*Caludovica insignis*) plant which is found growing in the rainforest and which provides a natural waterproofing.

Traditionally, *larouma* baskets are made by Kalinago women and you can see some of them at work at the Kalinago Barana Auté (KBA). Kalinago basketwork is sold at the KBA, at a number of roadside stalls and craft shops throughout the Kalinago Territory, and in gift shops and boutiques in Roseau.

the Kalinago Chief. Both council and chief are democratically elected by residents of the villages within the Kalinago Territory every five years.

The Kalinago Territory is communally owned. No one person can buy or sell part of the territory nor use it as collateral at a bank. Any Kalinago resident may stake a claim to a vacant portion of land, however, and so long as no-one else has already claimed it, and the Kalinago Council approves the claim, then that resident may build a house there and work the land. Any land which has been left untended for more than a year may be claimed by someone else, subject to approval by the Kalinago Council.

There are eight hamlets within the Kalinago Territory: Bataca, Salybia, Concord, Crayfish River, Mahaut River, St Cyr, Sineku and Gaulette River. In appearance these hamlets resemble any other rural settlements in Dominica, consisting of small houses of wood and concrete, flower gardens and vegetable plots. Along the roadside visitors will come across stalls selling traditional *larouma* basketwork and other hand-crafted gifts. Much of the territory is uninhabited, stretching from Sineku westwards across a high ridge and up to the banks of the Pagua River in the area of Charles Warner.

The administrative centre of the Kalinago Territory is **Salybia** which is home to the Kalinago Council and the police station. Heading north through Salybia there is a road to the right that goes down to the Salybia Catholic Church which was built in 1991. Its steeply pitched roof and the anchor poles that are driven deep into the ground are designed to protect the church from hurricanes. Both the exterior and interior have murals depicting Kalinago life and the arrival of Europeans. The church altar is a small hand-carved canoe.

Located in Salybia Bay are two islets referred to as either the Salybia Isles or **Petit L'Ilet** and **Gros L'Ilet**. According to Kalinago legend, each islet was once a ship that was used to transport the spirits of dead Kalinago out to sea. It is said that on at least one of the islets there is a large steel anchor chain emerging from the rock down to the ocean floor.

On a high ridge overlooking the hamlet of **Bataca** and the Pagua River Valley is **Pagua Rock**. This volcanic rock formation, some 20m in height, is said to be the home of a benevolent spirit and the steps leading up to it were once used by the people of Bataca in search of good fortune, which could be found in the form of charms on the top of the rock itself. According to legend, if you are very lucky, you may find a small white flower that only blooms one day of the year. If it is in bloom, you should rub it into the palm of your hand and then point your palm at any person you wish to command. Upon calling their name, that person will do as you wish. There is a catch, however. The rock has a number of cracks and if you were to ever catch sight of the spirit living within, you could be sure someone you knew was going to die.

Kalinago Barana Auté (*Crayfish River;* \ *767 445 7979;* e *admin@ kalinagobaranaaute.como; www.kalinagobaranaaute.com;* ☉ *daily (Kalinago guides are available by request)*) Kalinago Barana Auté (KBA) translates to 'Kalinago village by the sea'. Located down a very steep paved road in the hamlet of Crayfish River, the village is well signposted from the main road and therefore easy to find.

This showcase village was opened in April 2006. It is a representation of a pre-Columbian Amerindian village and attempts to recreate and promote greater awareness of the Kalinago tradition and former way of life. The KBA was made possible through funding by the government of Dominica and the involvement of local people within the Kalinago community. It is a very interesting place where visitors are able to experience and learn about the Kalinago traditional way of life as well as purchase crafts and souvenirs.

A circular trail begins at the reception centre where you pay an entrance fee. You can either choose to walk the trail by yourself or pay for a Kalinago guide to accompany you. The latter is absolutely the best way to make the most of your visit.

Passing through a tall thatched archway there are craft stalls on the left where Kalinago women are busily creating *larouma* basketware. On the right are toilets and refreshment facilities. The **Old Mapou Tree Trail**, or Binalecaall Mapou Wêwê, takes you to the cliff side where there is a viewpoint, or Barana Neupatae, over the Atlantic. Curving back inland, the path crosses the Crayfish River before heading back to the coast again. There are further viewpoints of the rugged coastline as well as the **Isulukati Waterfall** as it cascades down the smooth rocks, through a pool and down into the sea. The pool beneath the falls is known locally as Basin Bleau and is a nice place to bathe. Signs along the route point out plants and trees that have been traditionally used by the Kalinago for both herbal medicine and shelter construction.

The trail ascends and passes a number of thatched huts called *ajoupas* and *mwenas*. You can see examples of Kalinago canoe building and demonstrations of cassava

---

POTTERY

Kalinago women traditionally fashioned earthenware pots from clays found across the island. Some of the items they created were entirely functional, such as the *canalli* which was used to ferment *ouicou*, a beer made from cassava. Other pottery items were more ornate, decorated with images from both nature and legend, and were used as ceremonial bowls. Traditional pottery making can still be seen today at the Kalinago Barana Auté.

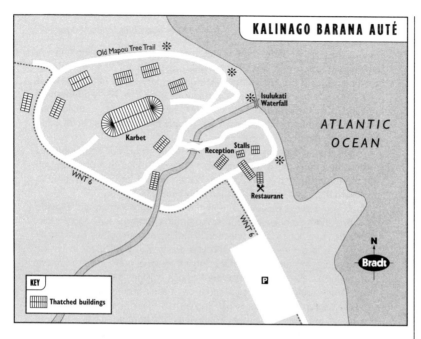

processing (see box on page 157 for more about cassava, and below for the cassava bakery). On the way back towards the Crayfish River the trail meets the impressive Karbet. Traditionally, a *karbet* was a large thatched hut that was located in the centre of an Amerindian village with the smaller *ajoupa* huts surrounding it. The word *karbet* is actually a French term that was used to describe this structure. The original Kalinago word was *taboui* but sadly it has been rather lost over the years. Only Amerindian men were allowed in the *karbet*, which would probably have been around 20m long and 10m wide. It was a place where they kept their weapons and slept in hammocks strung up between the beams. The women and children of the village slept in their *ajoupas*, which the men visited from time to time. The replica *karbet* in the KBA is used for presentations of Kalinago culture as well as for dance performances by groups such as the Carina Cultural Group and the Karifuna Cultural Group.

The old coastal road brings you back across the Crayfish River to the reception building and the vendors. The basketwork crafts sold at the gift shops are great value for money and unique souvenirs of your visit. Try to support them if you can.

Cassava Bakery (*Salybia*; ☏ 767 276 5618, 767 445 8050) Cassava (*Manihot esculenta*) was brought to the island by Amerindian settlers. It is extensively cultivated in many subtropical regions of the world where it is a food staple for both humans and animals. Also called manioc, the root must be cooked thoroughly to rid it of its toxins. It is very rich in starch but is quite bereft of protein and other nutrients. It can be cooked in many ways; as puddings (*tapioca*) or sweet cakes (*kanki*), but is also used to make a basic bread. There are three notable cassava bakeries in the Kalinago Territory: at the Kalinago Barana Auté, at Kalinago Touna Auté, and along the roadside in Salybia. The latter is a functional bakery as well as a visitor attraction. If they are operating when you are there, stop and see how it is made, then try some. It is actually pretty good.

Touna is the smallest of the communities that comprise the Kalinago Territory but it is unique in several ways. It is the only one that is not along the Atlantic coastline, situated instead on the western boundary of the beautiful Pagua River. The community name, Touna, actually means 'water'. The residents here hunt and fish in the river and they cultivate their small farms for a subsistence living. The community has less than 100 people and they are all involved in different occupations.

We felt it would be an interesting idea to open up our community to visitors, and I think this is the only experience of its kind that provides you with the opportunity to meet families in their homes, and give you time to speak with them and learn about their daily lives.

When you arrive, I welcome you at the community Karbet, and provide you with a short overview of both the community and the Kalinago people. Afterwards, I take you to visit a selection of families at their homes. Each family is involved in a different activity and you are free to participate in basket weaving, squeezing sugar cane juice using a traditional press, making cassava bread, taking a walk and learning about herbal medicines, farming and foods.

Two families offer basic accommodation at their homes for visitors who would like the further experience of living with us. Play dominos or cards with a neighbour, or try out some night fishing if it is the hunting season. The next day participate in other activities such as making castor oil, cultivating cocoa and coffee into chocolate sticks flavoured with cinnamon and nutmeg. Enjoy some home cooking, making dishes from food grown around the home, like bananas, dasheen, ripe plantains, calalou, coconut tablet and jam, while listening to stories of growing up and folkloric legends.

Mabrika. Welcome to Kalinago Touna Auté.

Touna Auté is located near Concord (☏ *767 285 1830, 767 316 7655;* e *onenicepeople@gmail.com*). To get there, head along the Imperial Road from Pont Cassé to Hatton Garden and the east coast. In the village of Concord you will see a sign for Touna Auté on the right. Follow the road over a bridge and then turn right at the next junction along a rough vehicle track. Ask for Irvince.

L'Escalier Tete Chien

L'Escalier Tete Chien is an impressive lava dyke that emerges dramatically from the sea to the foot of the coastal cliffs in Sineku. These dykes are formed by lava forcing its way up through cracks in a volcano and then hardening to form impermeable rock. Water cannot push its way through this rock at all and so the dyke becomes increasingly impressive and prominent as the rock around it is slowly eroded by the ocean. Locals who have tried free-diving down the formation report that they see it plunging to depths beyond their breath-hold limits.

The Kalinago legend that gives the formation its name tells of a giant snake climbing up the volcano from the deep, churning up the rock along the way. Upon reaching the top of the cliff the snake made its way to a mountain called Madjini overlooking Sineku, where it now resides in a large cave. The snake was said to resemble a boa constrictor, hence the French Creole name Tete Chien. The lava dyke has become the boa's staircase and the snake itself is said to be one of three gods residing in the Kalinago Territory. The other two are a giant centipede in the area of St Cyr and a smaller snake locally called a *koulèv* in the Pagua area near Hatton Garden. Legend has it that if you take a carved canoe paddle, some tobacco and a rooster to the snake god in his cave at Madjini, a man will appear and grant you a wish.

The track to L'Escalier Tete Chien has some interesting flora which have a number of medicinal uses in the Kalinago Territory. The leaves of the glory cedar may be mixed with those of the guava to make a cold tea which is said to act as a revitalising drink. The glory cedar is a fast-growing tree and is often planted along boundary lines. There are several types of bromeliad along the way as well as a grass known locally as *bartad lapit*, which has a white powdery substance on its underside. According to the Kalinago this powder may be used as an antiseptic, traditionally for the severed umbilical cord of a baby.

L'Escalier Tete Chien is located along the rugged Atlantic coastline off the village of Sineku. If you are coming from the south, look to the right-hand side when you are near the centre of the village, opposite a calabash tree. You should see a sign and a vehicle track running along the left-hand side of a bar. Unfortunately this bar is an area where visitors are often subjected to rather unwanted attention. Politely decline offers of a guide from the drinkers at this bar; you do not need one. If you are in a car, just drive up the track to the newly constructed reception building and park up there.

From here it is a very short distance to the formation. Follow the track until it reaches the rocky coastline and turns into a narrow, and rather steep, path. You will soon see L'Escalier Tete Chien and can therefore decide how far, if at all, you would like to go down to get a better look. It is a little steep and slippery but it is just fine if you take your time. Be very careful if the sea is rough.

EAST COAST VILLAGES Amerindians arrived on the black sandy shores of **Castle Bruce** some 2,000 years ago and built a settlement there. They named it **Kouanari** and probably lived off fish and shellfish caught from the bay and the brackish water of the lagoon at the mouth of the river. On the fertile land of red soil they would have planted cassava and other root crops until the Europeans turned up and changed their existence forever.

By the time the French and British arrived, the flat and extremely fertile lands stretching inland from the bay became sugarcane and coffee plantations. In 1761, when the British captured Dominica from the French, the bay was named St David's Bay and Royal Engineer Captain James Bruce, who built some of the island's fortifications at the time, purchased all 600ha of the river valley and named the area after himself. Bruce imported over 150 west African slaves to work his cane and coffee plantations. After emancipation in 1838 the estate was abandoned and the slaves began to settle in the valley and further to the north in the area of Richmond Estate. A village eventually began to develop up the hillside overlooking the bay. Access to Roseau was by ship or on foot. People walked tracks from the

---

KALINAGO CULTURAL GROUPS

The **Karifuna Cultural Group** and the **Carina Cultural Group** are dedicated to preserving and teaching the cultural heritage and traditions of the Kalinago people. You will see them performing at the Kalinago Barana Auté and at the village of Concord on cruise ship days, as well as at cultural events throughout the year. The groups also travel abroad occasionally, promoting and developing relationships with people sympathetic to or with a common interest in the perpetuation of Kalinago cultural heritage. Try to see and support them if you can during your stay in Dominica.

village across the interior, either through the area of Pont Cassé (now Segment 5 of the Wai'tukubuli National Trail) or via the Chemin L'Etang trail from Rosalie. A motorable road connecting Castle Bruce was constructed in 1963.

As with many settlements that were isolated from the capital for so long, a strong village identity emerged and is still evident today. Castle Bruce has depended upon agriculture for its existence ever since the estates broke up and free people began tending to their own smallholdings. The predominant crop for a long time has been the banana and, though you are presented with a wide corridor of dense banana plantations along the entire stretch of the valley to the shores of St David's Bay, this is one of those communities that has been impacted by WTO (World Trade Organisation) rules affecting the banana trade. Farmers have been forced out of agriculture and those remaining have had to rethink their whole approach to production, farm management and trade. Thanks to organisations such as The Fairtrade Foundation, Dominica's small banana producers still have hope.

Before arriving at the shore, there is a school on the left and playing fields on the right. The road ahead leads to Castle Bruce village, the road to the left goes north along the east coast through the Kalinago Territory, and the small road to the right winds south along the coast to the villages of Saint Sauveur and Petite Soufriere. Castle Bruce is a patchwork of small dwellings perched along the slopes overlooking the ocean below. The quaint Roman Catholic church stands at its centre.

The beach along St David's Bay is both pretty and wild. Smooth driftwood of all shapes and sizes litters the black sandy shoreline all the way to the mouth of the river. At the southern end of the bay are two islets and at the mouth of the Castle Bruce River is a brackish water lagoon where local families are often seen bathing in the late afternoons.

The journey south from Castle Bruce along the coast to Petite Soufriere is a beautiful one. It passes through several settlements that capture the essence of rural life in Dominica and there are also some excellent viewpoints and photo opportunities of the rugged Atlantic coastline along the way. The road is narrow and winding, sometimes high above the sea, sometimes down alongside it. At the time of writing the road ends in Petite Soufriere and there is very little traffic. A drive along this stretch of coastline is therefore a peaceful and interesting way to pass an afternoon. A road is planned, however, that will connect Petite Soufriere with Rosalie, following the route of an existing trail.

Just where the road from Pont Cassé reaches the sea at St David's Bay, there is a small road to the right opposite Castle Bruce School that runs alongside a playing field. This is the road to Petite Soufriere.

The road passes through fields crowded with banana plants then crosses some marshland and goes over the Castle Bruce River. From the area of Tronto and Depaix

TÉWÉ VAVAL

Vaval is the spirit of Carnival and Téwé Vaval is the symbolic burial or burning of an effigy representing the spirit of Carnival that takes place on Ash Wednesday. In the west coast village of Dublanc and also in Bataca in the Kalinago Territory, these effigies are paraded through the streets before being burned at sunset. This ritual symbolises the end of Carnival and the beginning of the Lent period. These days, instead of marking the end of festivities, Vaval appears to be a good excuse to make the Carnival jump-ups last one more day, for those who still have the strength left, that is.

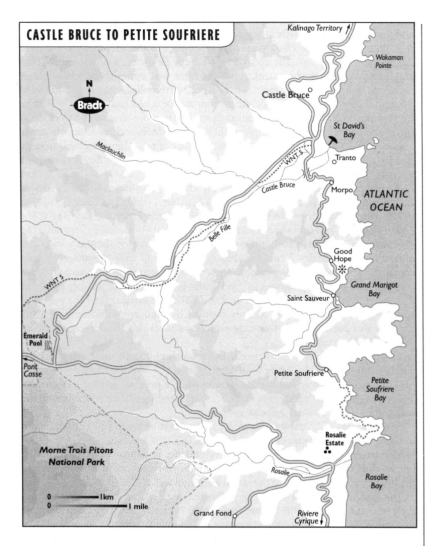

and the cliffs of Pointe Zicac, the road climbs up towards the small settlement of **Morpo**. From here there are some beautiful views of St David's Bay, the Castle Bruce River and the twin islets on the southern tip of the bay. The journey continues along the cliff side towards the village of **Good Hope**, where it descends quite sharply down a narrow road lined with colourful crotons. From Good Hope there are nice views of Grand Marigot Bay and the pointed outcrop of L'Ilet just offshore along the southern tip of the cove. Near Good Hope there is a cassava processing plant where ground manioc or farine is produced for island-wide consumption as well as for export abroad. Also along this stretch are bay sheds for storing and drying bay leaves ready for boiling to extract their oil. Looking inland it is possible to see a number of young bay trees growing on the steep slopes of Morne Aux Delices. From Good Hope the road continues its descent to the pretty fishing village of Saint Sauveur.

Saint Sauveur is located along the shore in the southwest corner of Grand Marigot Bay. Upon entering the village, the scene is dominated by the new school and Roman Catholic church sitting on a rare piece of flat ground next to the ocean. It is thought that over 2,000 years ago this area was the site of a pre-Kalinago Amerindian settlement. The church was rebuilt following a hurricane in 1916 and is undergoing refurbishment. A narrow stone road opposite the school passes between some residential properties until it reaches the village cemetery. If the word 'beautiful' could ever be considered appropriate for a cemetery then it would be for this one. Volcanic rocks protruding from the ground, surrounded by colourful plants and flowers, complement makeshift wooden crosses and headstones to create a scene of simple but stunning beauty in this place of rest. Hummingbirds in large numbers, including green and blue-crested Caribs, dart between flowers alongside the narrow path up to this place.

A road between the new school and the church leads down to the bay itself. At the end of the road is the heart of Saint Sauveur. Fishing has been a tradition in this village ever since the first settlers arrived here. From the **Bay Bar** at the end of the road, villagers await the return of the fishing boats each afternoon. The spectacle of their return and of the villagers eagerly awaiting them is a snapshot of tradition and history. 'I cooking chicken tonight, oui!' calls a woman to a boat captain with a disappointing catch. When the dorado are running, usually from November to February, these men can easily bring back over 20 fish apiece in their brightly painted boats, which look so fragile and small against the powerful waves of the Atlantic Ocean as they round L'Ilet and return home across the bay. The Bay Bar is a perfect vantage point to witness this scene each afternoon throughout the year.

Heading south from Saint Sauveur the road climbs again until it reaches the rural farming hamlet of **Petite Soufriere**. Due to the severe terrain it was never part of a working estate but instead developed as a peasant farming community. Today you can see the villagers of Petite Soufriere tending to their root crops on the vertiginous slopes above the ocean.

Some of Dominica's most captivating coastline is to be found from Rosalie south to Carib Point. The drama of rugged cliffs, rocky islets, crashing waves, sea stacks, hidden coves and volcanic outcrops is breathtaking. Settlements of pretty wooden houses cling to the steep hillsides above the cliffs, and rivers running from deep in the interior plummet down to the ocean as coastal waterfalls.

The Rosalie River is formed by the convergence of several other rivers that find their source deep within the Morne Trois Pitons National Park. It is along this river that one of Dominica's largest estates was once located. Covering an area of over 840ha, the Rosalie Estate produced sugar, limes, cocoa, bananas and coconuts. In the 1780s, during a period of conflict with bands of well-organised Maroons, the estate was attacked and plundered. Chief Balla, one of the most prominent Maroon leaders of the time, led an assault during which several estate workers were killed, including its manager, and much of the estate was burned down. This action led to a greater intensity and focus on the part of the planters' legion to capture and kill the bands of marauding Maroons. Thanks to tip-offs from captured Maroon women, several leaders were taken, including Balla, who was shot and then exposed on the iron frame of a gibbet, taking, it is said, a week to die. (For more on the Maroons see pages 14 and 210).

Today the ruins of the estate buildings can still be seen near to the river mouth, including an aqueduct and sugar works. The church has been restored and is now the Rosalie Diocesan Centre.

Immediately to the south of the Rosalie River bridge, opposite the Rosalie Bay Eco Resort, is a road that runs steeply up into the interior and the elevated village

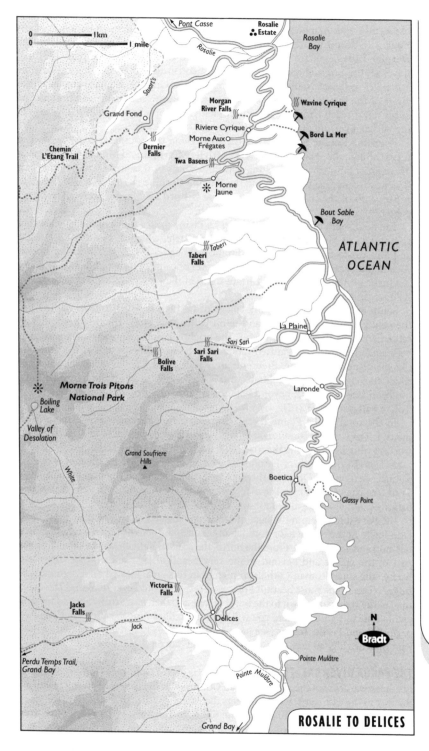

ROSALIE TO DELICES

of **Grand Fond**. At a height of around 400m, the small settlement lies on a narrow ridge with deep river valleys to the north and south. The village is known for the **Dernier Falls** (see page 167) and the **Chemin Letang Trail** (see page 125) that traverses the lower elevations of Morne Micotrin to the Freshwater Lake in the Morne Trois Pitons National Park. The road up to Grand Fond has some beautiful views of the interior and the deep river valley on the south side of the ridge. As buses rarely reach Grand Fond, expect plenty of people to ask you for a ride up to the village if you are driving. It would be nice of you to oblige.

From the Rosalie River bridge, the road along the southeast coast twists and turns through the small communities of **Riviere Cyrique** and **Morne Aux Frégates**. There are a number of interesting natural features in this area including the **Twa Basens** cascade (see page 169) and the **Wavine Cyrique** coastal waterfall (see page 175). South of the trail to Wavine Cyrique is **Bord La Mer** or **Secret Beach** (see page 170), a lovely cove and dark sand beach.

The road south of Riviere Cyrique to La Plaine passes the very pretty mountain community of **Morne Jaune** and the Taberi Estate, which was once a large sugar and lime estate and got its name from the Kalinago word *taboui*, meaning 'house'. Also in this area, along the shoreline, is the very beautiful **Bout Sable Bay**. This bay is a turtle nesting site where, at certain times of the year, giant leatherbacks can be seen returning to lay their eggs.

South of Bout Sable Bay is the village of **La Plaine**, which gets its name from the gently sloping area of flat land upon which it is built. The original Kalinago settlement here was called Koulirou. The brightly painted Roman Catholic church with small bell tower, galvanised roof and arched windows stands at the centre of the village near the school. Predominantly residential, La Plaine has a number of small convenience stores and bars, and is also the location of the **Sari Sari Falls** trailhead (see page 173), beyond which is a more remote and tougher hike to the **Bolive Falls** (see page 212).

To the south of La Plaine there is an area called **Laronde**, where there is an inauspicious concrete monument along the roadside dedicated to five construction workers who died building the road here. Each one of the short columns represents a life lost. To the south of Laronde is a small village called **Boetica**, also once a Kalinago settlement. Opposite the Roman Catholic church is the start of the **Glassy Trail** (see page 172), which is a nice walk to the cliffs and the interesting salt water bathing pools along the dramatic and very rugged eastern coastline.

The very quiet farming village of **Delices** is located at the southeastern tip of Dominica. At the end of a long stretch of road from Boetica there is a junction by a bus stop and a pay phone. From the north, the road straight ahead goes to the upper part of the village and beyond to the very beautiful farmlands of the Belvedere Estate. The small Roman Catholic cemetery in this area, located on a high narrow ridge, is one of the most beautiful places of rest you could ever imagine. The main road to the right runs down to the lower village and then past arrowroot and banana plantations to Victoria where you will find the trailhead for the **Victoria Falls** (see page 174) and **Perdu Temps** (see page 150) trails. This is also the road that crosses Paix Bouche ridge to Petite Savanne and Grand Bay on the south coast.

THE PAGUA RIVER VALLEY The Pagua River is one of Dominica's longest and runs northeastwards from the area of D'Leau Gommier in the Central Forest Reserve all the way to the east coast, where it meets the Atlantic Ocean at Pagua Bay. The river also marks the western boundary of the Kalinago Territory. It is a very pretty river and has a number of accessible bathing pools.

Both river and road pass through the small village of **Concord** on the northern edge of the Central Forest Reserve. From the main road you should see a sign to **Kalinago Touna Auté** (see page 162) where you can experience a little of contemporary Kalinago life. The tall ridge you can see to the southeast of the village is Horseback Ridge in the Kalinago Territory (see page 172). On the north side of the village, where the road narrows and climbs a high ridge, there are wonderful views down the Pagua River valley.

To the north of Concord, where the Pagua River meets the sea, is **Hatton Garden**. This was once a British-owned estate that produced sugar, rum and limes. It had a watermill and was worked by around 200 slaves. The ruins of the factory are now part of the Silks Hotel. When you emerge from the interior to meet the sea at Hatton Garden, you are greeted by the beautiful and dramatic Pagua Bay. At the junction before Silks, the road to the right goes south along the coast through the Kalinago Territory and the road straight ahead follows the coast to Marigot, Melville Hall Airport and the beaches of the northeast.

On the northern edge of Pagua Bay is Marigot and on the southern edge is the village of **Atkinson**. The original Kalinago name for this village was Warawa, but it was renamed in the 1760s after William Atkinson, a British landowner in the area. It is a small farming community overlooking the bay on the northern boundary of the Kalinago Territory. Right next to Atkinson is the tiny hamlet of Antrizle. Look for a bus stop and a sign to Antrizle Beach, a very pretty Dominican secret.

On the road between the village of Concord and the northern boundary of the Central Forest Reserve is an area called **Deux Branches**. Along the side of the road there are several colourfully painted signs for the **Sisserou Falls** (sometimes also called Diamond River Falls). In actual fact these falls are a series of large river rapids and pools rather than a waterfall, but it is a pretty and interesting natural site nevertheless. The tallest river rapid can be seen from the road but a short series of steps down to the river takes less than five minutes to complete and is very easy. The land owner may appear and greet you. He will ask for a few dollars to pass over his land (about US$2 each is enough).

At the bottom of the steps you are greeted by a beautiful stretch of the Pagua River with some of the biggest boulders you may ever have seen. Volumes of white water gush over and through these boulders, rushing down through the forest towards the sea. A further trail above the cascades (you have to access it from the road) takes you to a really lovely bathing pool. It is definitely worth stopping here to freshen up if you have time.

ACTIVITIES AND SPECIAL INTERESTS

Horseriding The **Cool Runnings Farm** (*Rosalie;* ✆ *767 285 6987; www.mermaidssecret.com (follow link to Cool Runnings Farm)*), a small livestock and organic farm, offers horseriding for both beginners and the experienced. Practice sessions and guided excursions on forest trails are followed by fun on the farm and lunch over a wood fire.

Twa Basens This is a series of three pools and pretty cascades located on a shallow river near the village of Riviere Cyrique. The first pool is very accessible and follows a short walk. The pools above it require a short but wet and slippery climb up each cascade. All three pools are fairly deep, very pretty and make an excellent spot for a refreshing river bathe, especially if you have just been climbing Wavine Cyrique (see page 175).

To get to Riviere Cyrique from Roseau, take the Imperial Road via Pont Cassé and follow the signs to Rosalie and La Plaine. For bus information see page 50.

On the south side of Riviere Cyrique, right next to the sign for the village and a road bridge that crosses a river, you will find the rather overgrown trailhead for this short walk. The track is next to the concrete block, heading inland. Follow it for a short distance until you reach the river, which you should simply follow upstream. You will come to the first pool and cascade in no more than five minutes. The track runs along the left-hand side of the first pool right up to the cascade, which you must then climb if you wish to go up to the two higher cascades and pools.

Morgan River Falls This is a very pretty cascading waterfall located close to the main road on the north side of the village of Riviere Cyrique. It is a short and interesting diversion if you happen to be in this area and is best in the wet season. On the apex of a bend crossing a small river just before you enter the village of Riviere Cyrique from the north, there is a narrow track heading inland. If you reach the sign for Wavine Cyrique, then you have gone too far. Go back to the last sharp bend crossing a river and look on the inland side of the road.

Follow the rather overgrown and muddy track up river for about ten minutes until you see the waterfall. To get a closer look you need to cross to the left-hand side of the river and climb up the rocks to the base of the waterfall. Watch your footing.

Turtle watching At certain times of the year (usually from late March to October) it is possible to see endangered giant leatherback turtles coming ashore to lay their eggs, and then baby turtles returning to the sea. This usually occurs at night time. Contact the organisations below for information and organised viewings. It is really important to protect and respect this natural phenomenon. Please be sure to view it as unobtrusively and respectfully as possible. Noise, bright headlights and direct human interaction must be avoided at all costs.

Dominica Sea Turtle Conservation Organisation (Sea Turtle Hotline) ☏ 767 616 8684

Forestry, Wildlife & Parks Division ☏ 767 266 3817

HIKES
Bord La Mer 'Secret Beach' (*Difficulty: T: 1; R: 0; E: 1; D: 0; Rating = 1.3*) Locally known as Bord La Mer, meaning 'beside the sea', this natural site requires a short downhill walk to a secluded sandy cove. It is very pretty, bounded by littoral woodland and coconut palms. It has black sand and rolling waves and is a nice spot to relax with a picnic. Unfortunately the sea has strong undertow and rather unpredictable cross-currents making it rather unsuitable for bathing. If you do decide to take a dip to cool off, please bear this in mind.

There is a sign for the trail on the main road passing through the east coast village of Riviere Cyrique. It is a little to the south of the sign for Wavine Cyrique. Follow the wide track down to the playing field, where you will see a second sign at the top of the trail on the right-hand side of the field.

Follow the clear, wide track down the steps for around 10–15 minutes or so until you reach a steeper slope. Follow the narrow track as it winds its way down. After another 15 minutes you will emerge on to the black sand of this pretty beach and cove.

Charles Warner 'Secret Pool' (*Difficulty: T: 2; R: 2; E: 1; D: 2; Rating = 4.4*) This is a very nice trail through rainforest in the Pagua River Valley to some hidden pools, which are a very pleasant location for bathing and for a riverside picnic. The trail is clear but is often quite muddy and involves a river crossing.

Charles Warner was a British landowner, descendant of Sir Thomas Warner and relative of Kalinago Chief Thomas 'Indian' Warner, who was murdered by his half-brother in the infamous massacre of 1764 (see page 218). Charles Warner purchased a number of properties in Dominica, his main estate being in the parish of St Paul on the west coast between Mahaut and Layou, and now called Warner. His name is also used to describe the area around the Charles Warner River, a tributary of the Pagua River south of the settlement of Concord within the Kalinago Territory.

The trailhead is quite difficult to find. You have to look for it about halfway between the Sisserou Falls at Deux Branches and the village of Concord. If you are travelling from the Sisserou Falls towards Concord, it is on the right-hand side. Just after a bend, look for a rectangular concrete footing where a banana shed may have once stood. Just beyond this platform there is a clear trail lined with ginger lilies.

To get to this point by bus you would have to be *en route* from Roseau to Marigot (see page 50 for Roseau bus stops). By car, head towards Marigot and Melville Hall from Pont Cassé and pass right through the Central Forest Reserve.

Not far from the beginning of this hike is the very pretty Pagua River which the route crosses and then resumes on the far bank. The crossing is usually shallow and safe, however, during periods of heavy rain the river level rises and the flow becomes a little stronger. Let common sense be your guide here. If conditions are good, the river is also a great place for a river bath.

On the far side of the river you will come to a fork. Take the right-hand spur and follow the trail through banana fields and an open area of land with nice views of the valley. Continuing through more banana plantations, the path runs to a little stream before going up and over a small ridge. Descending into a gulley, the trail then picks up the Charles Warner River and runs along its southern bank for a short stretch before turning away to the right into a beautiful area of rainforest. The trail then rejoins the Charles Warner River and comes to a lovely pool and small cascade. The rocks beneath the cascade are smooth and in fairly shallow water, though the pool itself is deep. With caution it is possible to climb up the right-hand side of this cascade to a further pool above. Both pools are excellent for bathing and this secluded area of rainforest is the perfect place for a picnic. Trails you may see continuing from here are primarily used by hunters.

Chemin L'Etang (from Grand Fond) (*Difficulty: T: 2; R: 0; E: 2; D: 2; Rating = 3.8*)
For details on this historic hike please see page 125. The trailhead in Grand Fond is at the very top of the village. Where the road ends and then forks, simply keep following the wide track to the right (use the communication poles as your guide). Now follow the instructions given in *Chapter 5*; but in reverse of course!

Dernier Falls (*Difficulty: T: 2; R: 0; E: 3; D: 1; Rating = 3.8*)
The Dernier Falls is an interesting waterfall within a circular cavern in the river valley to the south of Grand Fond. It has a deep pool that is suitable for bathing. The trail down to the river is quite short but also fairly steep. No climbing is involved as steps have been cut all the way down. The riverbank at the entrance to the pool and cavern is a nice place for a picnic.

Buses to Grand Fond run very infrequently (see page 50 for information on where to catch a bus) and you will often see people at the bottom of the road, near the Rosalie River bridge, waiting and hoping for a ride up to this elevated community. If you are travelling by car, head for Rosalie and La Plaine from Pont Cassé and, once you cross the Rosalie River, take a right and follow the road all the way up to the village. You will see a signpost near the top on your left.

An alternative way to get here is to hike the Chemin L'Etang trail from the Freshwater Lake (see page 125).

Follow the rough track along the back of the village for around five minutes, passing a small banana field and some bay trees until you reach some steps that run steeply down the side of the valley. Descend for around 15–20 minutes. At the bottom is the wide, stony river bank. The pool and waterfall are hidden within a very pretty cavern to your right.

Glassy Point (*Difficulty: T: 2; R: 0; E: 1; D: 1; Rating = 2.5*) This is a fairly easy hike from the village of Boetica to a cliff top and then down to a volcanic outcrop where there are small salt water pools.

Boetica is located on the east coast between Delices and La Plaine. To get there from Roseau you can either take the road from Pont Cassé to Rosalie and La Plaine, or you could choose the route via Grand Bay and Delices. In terms of time and distance, it is about the same. See page 50 for bus information.

The Glassy Point trailhead is opposite the Roman Catholic chapel in Boetica and is clearly signposted. Pass by a ruined building to your left and through woodland towards the coast. There are views of the ocean and of L'Îlet, a rocky islet just offshore. The trail heads inland and descends at a gentle gradient through the woods to a dark gulley where it turns sharply back towards the ocean. Take care here as it is quite damp and wet with loose rocks and fallen leaves making it a little greasy underfoot. After following the rocky river bed for a short stretch the path heads up the right-hand side of the gulley towards the ocean. The cliffs come into view after around 30 minutes from the start and the trail reaches a point where it follows the very narrow ridge of Glassy Point. Cliffs and ocean are now on either side of you. Upon reaching a freshwater tap there is a fabulous viewpoint down to the left. From here the main trail is also to the left. You may see an old spur trail to the right. This track leads down to another section of Glassy Point and is very rough, overgrown and not worth the exertion. Follow the main path down towards the sea. The trail continues around Glassy Point to a volcanic outcrop. The outcrop has a couple of small sea pools. This kind of lava formation can be quite sharp so take care of hands and footing. On a clear day there are nice views to the north and south along this particularly beautiful stretch of coastline.

Horseback Ridge (*Difficulty: T: 1; R: 0; E: 2; D: 1; Rating = 2.5*) Horseback Ridge is the name given to a narrow stretch of road that runs along a high ridge behind the villages of Salybia and Bataca. It can either be driven in around 15 minutes or walked in around 45 minutes or so. It is an extremely beautiful route that was originally designed as an access road to the farms above Salybia. The end of the road emerges in the village of Bataca, at the northern boundary of the Kalinago Territory. A nice way of doing this hike is to walk it in a loop, starting and finishing in Salybia. It is a lovely walk with great views and a chance to interact with Kalinago villagers and farmers. The loop will take around 90 minutes.

If you are coming here by bus, please see page 50 for bus stops in Roseau. Set off early. By car, head for Castle Bruce from Pont Cassé and then follow the signs to the Kalinago Territory. A good place to park is opposite the Salybia police station, close to the entrance of the Kalinago Barana Auté. The southern end of the Horseback Ridge road is signposted.

Walk up the paved road and pass the Kalinago Council office on your left. Keep going. It is a steady climb all the way to the top of the ridge. You will pass a few small houses and shacks, one of which has its own little wooden bench out front where the owner must sit and enjoy the view down to the sea from time to time. Indeed the views here are gorgeous. You can see the villages of Salybia, Crayfish River and Bataca as well as the rugged coastline, the Atlantic Ocean and the very flat French island of Marie-Galante on the horizon.

At the height of the ridge here is a picnic shelter and a viewpoint where you can look down upon the Pagua River valley, the village of Concord and Touna Auté (see page 162). Across the valley are the high mountain slopes of the interior, the Northern Forest Reserve and the cloud covered peak of Morne Diablotin. You will see a small and very steep track heading down the northern slopes of the ridge. This is called the **Fond Trail**, a 30-minute walk down to Concord and Touna Auté. This was the escape route used by frightened villagers and the place they hid during the events of the so-called 'Carib War' (see box on page 239).

Continuing around the ridge, enjoy the great views and hopefully bump into local farmers tending somewhat vertiginous plots on either side of the track. They grow bananas, peppers, yams, and a variety of other vegetables and fruits. The thin, rather needle-like grass you may see growing along the margins of the path is called *veti ver* which the Kalinago utilise in two ways: they thatch their *ajoupa, karbets* and other shelters with it; and they also use it in areas where soil is prone to erosion from rains. Also along this ridge you may see numerous butterflies dancing around the wildflowers of the path and verges.

The path curves and descends towards Bataca. When you reach the top of the village, follow it downhill past pretty gardens, small houses and shacks until you meet up with the main road. Head right and simply follow it for 30–45 minutes through Bataca, Crayfish River and the beginning of Salybia until you arrive back at the police station. As you are close to the Kalinago Barana Auté, why not head down there for a drink and a bite to eat before taking the Old Mapou Tree Trail around the 'model' village (see page 160).

Perdu Temps (From Delices) *(Difficulty: T: 3; R: 3; E: 2; D: 3; Rating = 6.9)* This

hike is described in detail in *Chapter 6*, page 150. The route from Delices is exactly the same, but in reverse, of course. You must take a guide as signage is very poor and sections of the trail are very difficult to follow. Guides for this hike are also suggested on page 79.

Sari Sari Falls *(Difficulty: T: 3; R: 2; E: 2; D: 2; Rating = 5.6)* This is a beautiful,

tall waterfall located on the Sari Sari River near to the village of La Plaine. The hike is quite short and fairly easy though it does involve two river crossings, a little wading, and scrambling over quite slippery boulders. You should not attempt this hike if it is or has been raining heavily. Flash flooding can and does occur on this river.

There are two ways to get to La Plaine from the Roseau area. One is via Pont Cassé, Rosalie and Riviere Cyrique, the other is via Grand Bay, Delices and Boetica. Both take about the same amount of time. For bus information see page 50.

There is a sign to the Sari Sari Falls on the main coastal road once you enter La Plaine. Follow it past the school and the church. At the junction go left and at the next one, which is signposted, take the right-hand turn. At the very end of the road there is a track that curves to the right by a small building. This is the trailhead.

Follow the track along a field and then down a series of steep steps until you reach the river. Cross the river using the rope as an aid. Follow the track along the right-hand side of the river for a short distance and then cross back again before reaching quite a large cascade. The track then climbs steeply upwards above the left bank of the river.

Follow the track as it runs back down towards the river. There are some nice views of the river and several of its cascades as you head down. You will reach a spur which is usually signposted. Take the trail on the right and follow it down to the river. The rest of the way is simply a walk upriver, sticking to the left-hand side. Around a curve you will see the waterfall.

To get to the pool, carefully make your way over the boulders until you reach some very tall ones. On the left, between two large rocks, is a small hole through which you can pass and climb up. Once through it, be very careful with your footing. The rocks from here to the pool are very slippery. At the pool you will feel the full force of the waterfall. It is deep and great for a refreshing bathe.

Victoria Falls (*Difficulty: T: 3; R: 3H; E: 1; D: 2; Rating = 5.6H*) If it is raining, you should pick a different hike. Flash flooding does happen here and negotiating the White River can be difficult even in the dry season. The trail is not particularly obvious: it makes several tricky river crossings and it involves a few awkward scrambles over rocks, especially at the end. A guide to help and provide safety is a prudent idea.

The Victoria Falls trail begins on the southern outskirts of the village of Delices. The quickest way to get here from Roseau by road is via Grand Bay and the south coast. See page 50 for bus details.

The trailhead is located to the south of Delices and is usually signposted. From the sign, either walk or drive down the rough vehicle track to the clearing at the bottom. If you park here, you must pay a small fee at the Zion Valley bar. Say hello to Moses; he is a lovely man and can take you to the waterfall if you prefer to have some very knowledgeable and good company. His bar is also a nice place to relax on the way back; treat yourself to a cold beer, a fresh fruit juice or a bush tea. Camping pitches and tent rental are also available here.

The trail continues from the clearing down to the river and then almost immediately splits. Facing the river, the Victoria Falls trail is to the right.

Follow the trail along the bank and down to the river where you must make your first crossing. A good tip on this trail is to look across to the far bank before crossing. Try to see where the trail continues and then pick the easiest route across to that point. On the other side climb up the bank and follow the trail past small buildings and through farmland to reach the river again. Wade across to the other side, keeping the rapids to your right. Follow the clear trail through the trees as far as it goes. The trail will bring you down to the riverbank. It is sandy and rocky. Stick to it as far as you can safely go and then make your way across the river to the left-hand bank.

On the other side follow the trail along the shore for a short distance. You will have to scramble over a few rocks and boulders before you are forced back across the river to the right-hand bank. Follow the trail over the rocks to a final river crossing. This last crossing is easier as the water is usually not very deep. Once on the other side it is a tricky and slippery scramble over large boulders upriver to the waterfall which you should soon see in front of you. You can either choose to stay here or try to make it to the pool. You really ought to have a guide for this last bit as it is a little troublesome. The route is along the left-hand side, over the large boulders. Be careful, it is slippery.

Wavine Cyrique (*Difficulty: T: 4H; R: 0; E: 4; D: 1; Rating = 5.6H*) Many people mistakenly refer to this site as the 'Secret Beach'. Actually the Secret Beach is a different place a little further south (see Bord La Mer on page 170). If you see photographs of a waterfall shooting from the top of a high cliff down into the sea, you are actually looking at Wavine Cyrique.

Whatever people may tell you, please be under no illusions: this is a challenging and potentially dangerous hike. But it is also unique and quite unforgettable. It requires a steep climb from the top of a cliff to the bottom using ropes and tree roots. Though you are not exposed and cannot see the full extent of the climb, if you suffer from vertigo this may not be for you. It is a physically challenging hike because you have to use upper and lower body strength on the short climbing section, but moreover it is a mental challenge. Conquering your apprehension and fear is certainly half the battle. However, the good news is that it is probably not quite as terrifying as the horror stories some may tell you. You will find that most people are embellishing the stories they have heard rather than speaking from first-hand experience. This happens a lot here. In actual fact, the rope and root climb is only about one-third of the overall descent; the rest is just a steep track. A guide is a good idea on this one because, as it is unfamiliar to you, it may be tricky to figure out the best way down, where to put your feet and so on. A guide also provides a great sense of reassurance because (hopefully) he or she has already done it (if you see their legs trembling you will know different, of course).

To find the Wavine Cyrique trailhead, take a bus or drive to the small village of Riviere Cyrique on the east coast (see page 50 for bus information). There is a very clear sign on the main road towards the centre of the village. Do not confuse it with Bord La Mer (Secret Beach, see page 170). When you have found the sign, follow the narrow, croton-lined road through a pretty residential area until the paved road ends. A vehicle track takes you a short distance to the main trail. If you are in a car, find a spot that will not block the road or impede access for others.

Walk for around 10–15 minutes down a trail with steps. It will bring you to the top of the cliff where all you will see is the end of a rope tied to a tree. Make your way down and you will come to a second rope. The climb is vertical now and you must use a combination of rope, tree roots and branches to get down. Take your time. Going down is much harder than coming up because it is difficult to see where you are putting your feet and, as you have never been here before, your imagination is running riot. Be sure you have a firm footing and are secure before lowering yourself or letting go of anything! You will come to a rock face and a rope ladder. Most people think this is the hardest part because the rope ladder is a little wobbly and you do not have the security of lots of trees to hang on to. At the bottom of the ladder shift yourself to your right across the rock face. This is a bit tricky. Follow the ropes and breathe!

There are two more rope segments but they are very short and easy by comparison. The trail is narrow and steep so keep your concentration levels high until you reach the shoreline. Facing the sea, go left over the coastal rocks until you come to a black sand beach and the Wavine Cyrique waterfall. If conditions allow, go and stand underneath it, but keep a watchful eye on the waves, the surge and the currents.

Hopefully your legs have stopped shaking by now.

Remember to save a little energy as you have to climb all the way back up again. You will find it is not the cliff climb that gets you on the return journey, however, it will be the steps and trail back up to the village. A good place to go when you have finished this hike (aside from the nearest bar – Riverside Cafe at Citrus Creek is a good idea) is Twa Basens (see page 169).

8

Portsmouth, Cabrits National Park and the North

In this chapter we explore the town of Portsmouth and the historic Cabrits National Park. We head to the remote coastal villages of the north, crossing the Morne Aux Diables volcano, and see how people eke out a living from fishing and farming. Then we travel to Calibishie and Marigot, exploring beaches and dramatic coastal formations along the way.

GETTING THERE AND AWAY

BY CAR The west coast road from Roseau gets you to Portsmouth in about an hour. After passing through Picard the road curves towards the sea at Glanvillea where you must take a right turn along Michael Douglas Boulevard (named after a Dominican political leader, not the Hollywood actor) and over the Indian River. The first junction is a mini roundabout. The road ahead goes through the town and on to the Cabrits, the northwest and the road across Morne Aux Diables to Pennville. The road to the right goes to Borne, Vieille Case, Calibishie and the northeast coast.

To get to Marigot and Melville Hall Airport from Roseau, take the Imperial Road through the interior, passing Pont Cassé and the Central Forest Reserve, emerging at the Atlantic coastline via Concord and Hatton Garden. Heading north along the coastal road, you pass through the hilly village of Marigot. Melville Hall Airport is just a little further along the coast. It usually takes 60–90 minutes to reach the airport from Roseau.

BY BUS See page 50 for information about buses in Roseau and Portsmouth.

WHERE TO STAY

HIGH END

🏠 **Villa Passiflora** (3 bedroom villa) Calibishie; ✎ (US) 423 718 1842; e parkneur@ comcast.net; www.villapassiflora.com. Located to the southeast of Calibishie, between Pointe Baptiste & Hodges Bay, Villa Passiflora is one of Dominica's most exquisite accommodation options. A beautifully designed & managed home in a tranquil & private setting, it has 3 bedrooms each with en-suite bathroom, open plan living, dining & kitchen area, study & library, large veranda decks, an infinity pool,

hammocks, 4-poster beds with mosquito netting, & wonderful sea views. Housekeeping services include cooking if required, & on-site caretakers. Beaches nearby. Rooms can be rented on an individual basis but the owners prefer to rent the whole villa. 3 day minimum rental. **$$$$$**
🏠 **Red Rock Haven Hotel & Escape Beach Bar** (2 1-bed cottages, 1 2-bed villa) Pointe Baptiste; ✎ 767 445 7997; e info@ redrockhaven.com; www.redrockhaven.com. Luxurious, thoughtfully designed accommodation

perched above the beach at Pointe Baptiste. The cottage rooms have 1 bedroom, en-suite bathroom & private verandas. The villa has 2 bedrooms each with en-suite bathroom & plunge pool. Communal open living, dining & kitchen area, large veranda with pool. Escape Beach Bar & Grill serves haute French & Asian dinners as well as casual cabana lunches. **$$$$$** (both cottages & villa)

🏠 **Pointe Baptiste Estate** (1 main house, 2 cottages) Pointe Baptiste, Calibishie; ☎ 767 225 5378, 767 445 7368; e manager@ pointebaptiste.com; www.pointebaptiste.com. Very charming historical wooden estate house sleeps 6 & has 4 bedrooms, bathrooms, sitting room, kitchen, dining area, library, ceiling fans, mosquito nets & very large veranda. Home of the Napier family since 1930 (see *Black & White Sands* box on page 201), the main house is a traditional design with antique furniture, books & artworks. Guests have included Somerset Maugham & Noël Coward. Small wooden cottages sleep 2 & have kitchen area, 1 bedroom, bathroom, ceiling fan, mosquito net & veranda. Located in 10ha of landscaped private grounds with herb & organic fruit & veg gardens, trails to Red Rocks (see page 200) & secluded black & white sand beaches. House **$$$$$**, cottages **$$$**

🏠 **Secret Bay** (2 villas, 2 bungalows) Petite Baie, Portsmouth; ☎ 767 445 4444; e info@ secretbay.dm; www.secretbay.dm. Luxury accommodation under construction at the time of writing. Located between the Cario River & 'Secret Beach' to the south of Picard. Mapou & Ti-Fey are bungalows with a treehouse feel. They sleep 2, are fully equipped,have en-suite bathroom & views. Zing-Zing Villa has 2 bedrooms & sleeps up to 4, is fully equipped & has 2 en-suite bathrooms, AC, & sun deck. Zabuco Honeymoon Villa has 1 bedroom, is fully

MODERATE

🏠 **Manicou River Resort** (2 cottages, 1 villa) Tanetane, Portsmouth; ☎ 767 616 8903; e manicou_river_resort@fastmail.fm; www.manicouriverresort.com. Located on the hillside above Douglas Bay, overlooking the Caribbean coastline, the Cabrits National Park & Portsmouth. Each wooden cottage sleeps 2, has bathroom, shower, SC facilities & veranda. The spacious & airy villa also sleeps 2. It has living

equipped & has fabulous views of mountains & sea. **$$$$$**

🏠 **Villa Vista** (2 or 3 dbl rooms) Hodges Bay, Calibishie; ☎ 767 235 5760, 767 295 7520; e villavistadominica@gmail.com; www.villavistadominica.com. Modern & attractive villa accommodation with lovely views of Hodges Beach & Bay. En-suite bathrooms, fully equipped kitchen, laundry, veranda & pool with ocean views. Wireless internet & TV. A trail alongside the villa leads down to the river & bay. Relaxing, peaceful & private. Great for couples & families with children above 12yrs. **$$$$$**

🏠 **Comfort Cottages** (4 cottages) Blenheim; ☎ 767 445 3245; m 767 616 3325; e comfortcottages@cwdom.dm; www.comfortcottages.com. Gated community of modern, well-furnished cottages with great views of the northeast coastline. 3 cottages have 1 bedroom, 1 cottage has 2 bedrooms. All have alarm systems, TV, music system, wireless internet, lounge, fully equipped kitchen, private deck with plunge pool. Bedrooms have AC. Grounds have manicured gardens with coastal views, BBQ area, covered gazebo with hammocks. There is a restaurant & bar for guests only. Discounted rates for long stays & vehicle hire. Complimentary airport transfers. **$$$$**

🏠 **Coffee River Cottages** (1 cottage) Melville Hall Estate, Marigot; ☎ 767 613 4696; e coffeeriverdominica@gmail.com; www.coffeeriverdominica.com. Lovely SC cottage in 5 acres of beautiful gardens, working farm & river setting. Thoughtfully designed & fully equipped, the cottage comfortably sleeps a family of 4 but is also a romantic hideaway for couples. Off-grid, secure, peaceful & with all you need. Stroll through the gardens, bathe in the river & explore the east coast with ease. **$$$$**

area, bathroom, shower & kitchen, plus a large open deck with panoramic views. Expansive forest gardens have walking trails & the pretty Manicou River borders the property. Cottages **$$$**, villa **$$$$$**

🏠 **Pagua Bay House** (7 rooms) Pagua Bay, Marigot; ☎ 767 445 8888; e paguabayhouse@ cwdom.dm; www.paguabayhouse.com. Designed to look like simple banana sheds on the outside, but very chic & modern on the inside. Each of Pagua Bay's simple but spacious rooms have ceiling fans, AC, TV, mini bar, safe, oversized private bathroom & shower, dbl beds & luxurious soft furnishings. Located close to the ocean enjoying cooling breezes & home-grown produce. Wireless internet throughout. Handy for the airport & exploring the north & east. Complementary airport shuttle. **$$$**

🏠 **Picard Beach Wellness Eco Cottages** (18 cottages) Picard; 🝷 767 445 5131; e picardbeach@cwdom.dm; www.picardbeachcottages.dm. Eco-friendly resort with private wooden cottages in pleasant & private beachside grounds. Each solar-powered cottage has en-suite bathroom, TV, AC, ceiling fans, private veranda with deckchairs, telephone & SC facilities. Wireless internet. All cottages face the sea; some are directly on the beach front. Wellness therapies including massage are offered. Organic gardens. **$$$**

🏠 **Calibishie Cove** (4 apt suites) Hodges Bay, Calibishie; 🝷 (US) 813 417 8448 or (Dominica) 767 265 1993; e calibishiecove@gmail.com; www.calibishiecove.com. Spacious SC suites overlooking Hodges Bay. Mid-sized suites have 1 bedroom, private bathroom, patio veranda, living area, kitchenette. Penthouse suite has 1 bedroom, spacious kitchen & living area, plunge pool, sun deck & wrap-around veranda. Kayak & snorkelling equipment rental, & island tours arranged. Wedding services & catering. Mid-sized suites **$$$**, penthouse suite **$$$$**

🏠 **Comfortel De Champ** (5 rooms) Picard; 🝷 767 445 4452; e info@godominica.com; www.godominica.com. Modern, well-furnished accommodation on hillside position above Picard with fabulous views of Prince Rupert Bay & the Cabrits National Park. Clean & tidy rooms have 1 bed, en-suite bathroom & shared veranda. Leisure & jacuzzi area includes loungers, hammocks, hot tub, waterfall shower, TVs & bar service. Fruit & tropical flower garden with sun deck. De Champ Restaurant & Bar offers panoramic vistas, Creole & international cuisine, bar snacks & Sunday sunset dinner. Great location for academics & families visiting Ross University students. **$$$**

🏠 **Calibishie Lodges** (6 lodges) Calibishie; 🝷 767 445 8537; e info@calibishie-lodges.com; www.calibishie-lodges.com. Popular

accommodation choice on the eastern edge of Calibishie. Each thoughtfully designed lodge has 1 queen bed & 1 queen-size sofa bed, en-suite bathroom, fans, SC facilities, TV, living area & private veranda. Upper lodges have ocean views. Wireless internet. Bamboo Restaurant offers a full service of b/fast, lunch & dinner. Sun terrace & pool. **$$$**

🏠 **Windblow Estate** (3 suites) Calibishie; 🝷 767 445 8198; e islandtwo@ windblowestate.com; www.windblowestate.com; Skype: islandtwo. 3 fully furnished SC suites located on a ridge overlooking Calibishie. 2 suites have 1 bedroom & the third has 2 bedrooms. En-suite bathrooms, ceiling fans, internet access, TV, fully equipped kitchen & verandas with excellent panoramic views of the ocean. Cool breezes keep it comfortable. **$$$**

🏠 **Bay View Lodges** (2 SC apts) Calibishie; 🝷 767 245 8705; e enquiries@ bayviewdominica.com; www.bayviewdominica.com. Tastefully designed, bright, airy & clean rooms with awesome views of the very pretty Hodges Bay & 'Treasure Island'. Each lodge has 1 bedroom, dining & living area with sofa bed, bathroom, kitchenette, & private veranda. Nice gardens. **$$**

🏠 **Dominica's Sea View Apartments** (5 apts) Calibishie; 🝷 767 445 8537; e info@dominicasseaviewapartments.com; www.dominicasseaviewapartments.com. 1-bedroom upper apts sleep 2 people & ground floor 2-bedroom apts sleep 4. All have en-suite bathrooms, queen-sized beds, fully equipped kitchens, living area, TV, fans & veranda. Panoramic views of ocean & coastline from shared upper floor veranda. Tastefully designed & furnished. Wireless internet. Sister accommodation to Calibishie Lodges & shares facilities there. Long term rents also available. **$$**

🏠 **Sea Cliff Cottages** (5 cottages) Calibishie; 🝷 767 445 7008, 767 445 8998; e seacliff@ dominica-cottages.com; www.dominica-cottages.com. Pleasant self-contained cottages in large gardens sleeping 2–7, fully equipped with en-suite bathrooms, kitchen, seating areas & balconies. Panoramic sea & mountain views. Wireless internet & TV. Mobile phones provided to guests. Nearby trail runs down to the beach & river at Hodges Bay. Good value SC accommodation in a nice location. Suitable for couples & families. **$$**

8

🏠 **Veranda View Guesthouse** (2 rooms) Calibishie; ☎ 767 445 8900; e reserve@ lodgingdominica.com; www.lodgingdominica.com. Lovely guesthouse accommodation located right on the water in Calibishie village. Each room has bed, lounger, en-suite bathroom, a small kitchenette & a large shared veranda with gorgeous sea views. Terrace bar & restaurant, dinner cooked by reservation, small gift shop selling local products. Delightfully decorated & a warm welcome. **$$**, discounts for longer stays

🏠 **Portsmouth Beach Hotel** (80 rooms) Picard; ☎ 67 445 5142; f 767 445 5599; e pbh@cwdom.dm; www.avirtualdominica.com/pbh. Double-block hotel complex on beachfront that serves both visitors & students from the nearby Ross University School of Medicine. Each room has en-suite bathroom & AC. 30 rooms have SC facilities. Le Flambeau beachfront restaurant offers local & international cuisine. **$$**

🏠 **Sister Sea Lodge** (6 cottages) Picard; ☎ 767 445 5211; e sangow@cwdom.dm; www.sistersealodge.com. Self-contained cottage accommodation located on the beach at Picard. Cottages have stonework en-suite bathrooms, kitchenette, living area & porch, & are situated in tropical gardens of flowers, banana plants & coconut palms. Beachfront bar & restaurant specialises in fish dishes served on banana leaves with fresh locally grown vegetables. Indian River boat tours pick-up available from the beach in front of the restaurant. 3-night min stay. **$$**

🏠 **Heaven's Best Guesthouse & Restaurant** (7 rooms) Savanne Paille, Portsmouth; ☎ 767 445 6677, 767 277 3952; e reservations@heavensbestguesthouse.com; www.heavensbestguesthouse.com. Very friendly guesthouse & restaurant located in the village of Savanne Paille near Douglas Bay. Rooms sleep 2 & have en-suite bathroom, AC, TV & small kitchenette. Swimming pool & internet access. Restaurant serves high quality local & international dishes. Friendly with good service. **$$**

🏠 **Jacoway Inn** (2 rooms) Calibishie; ☎ 767 445 8872, 767 613 2908; e jacowayinn@ gmail.com; www.calibishie.net. Located in lush banana & plantain farmlands on the ridge above Calibishie. Rooms have dbl bed, en-suite bathroom, fridge, microwave, dining & seating area. Upper room has private veranda, ground floor room has private terrace. Ocean views, gazebo & gardens. B/fast inc. **$$**

BUDGET

🏠 **My Father's Place** (3 apts, 3 rooms) Marigot; ☎ 767 445 7215; www.myfathersplaceguesthouse.com. Self-contained apts with private bathroom, kitchen & AC sleep up to 3. In main house 2 dbls & 1 sgl room have fans & shared bathroom. Bar & gardens. Located above Sandy Beach in Marigot. Apts **$$**, rooms **$**

🏠 **Brandy Manor** (1 cottage, 2 rooms) Brandy, Bornes; ☎ 767 235 4871, 767 612 0978. Very pretty, back-to-nature, eco-friendly accommodation in a woodland & river setting along the Wai'tukubuli National Trail. Attractive wood & stone cottage perched on the banks of the Brandy River sleeps 2 & has washroom facilities. Cosy, comfortable & rustic rooms in the main lodge each sleep 2 & have shared bathroom facilities & lounge. Brandy Manor is off-grid but has a generator & paraffin lamps for the evenings. Yasmin cooks local & international dishes in a very pleasant open restaurant & bar area. Organic gardens, horses, dog kennels & hiking trail to Brandy Falls. Horseriding with Brandy Manor Equestrian is a treat (see page 199). Continental b/fast inc. **$–$$**

🏠 **Casaropa Apartments** (5 apts) Bay St, Portsmouth; ☎ 767 445 4475; e casaropa@ cwdom.dm. Self-contained apts located in the heart of Portsmouth. En-suite bathrooms, TV, AC & fans. Each apt is wired for internet access, some have sea views. **$**

CAMPING

🏕 **Brandy Manor** Brandy, Bornes; ☎ 767 235 4871, 767 612 0978. Located alongside the Brandy River & near to the end of Wai'tukubuli National Trail Segment 11. Camping pitches, shared facilities & dining. Please call ahead to make a reservation. **$**

PORTSMOUTH AND PICARD AREA Portsmouth has a number of small snackettes serving local dishes. The majority of restaurants are located outside the town in Picard and in Lagoon. The restaurants in Picard offer a host of international as well as local cuisine. Those along the beach in both Picard and Lagoon also have an international menu and tend to specialise in fish and seafood dishes.

If you are looking for good value takeaway food then one of the best places to go is the covered market area next to Ross University School of Medicine in Picard. You will find local lunches, pizza, wraps, *rotis*, barbecues, subs, sandwiches, curries, salads, fresh fruit juices and more.

Creole and international restaurants

✖ **Adaj** Bay St, Portsmouth; ✎ 767 445 6535. Located in downtown Portsmouth, serving a range of French Creole, Italian & American cuisine. $$

✖ **Heaven's Best Guesthouse & Restaurant** Savanne Paille; ✎ 767 445 6677, 767 277 3952; ⏰ closed Sun. High quality Caribbean & American cuisine from chef Heskeith Clarke. Dining by advanced reservation only. No bar, so bring your own wine. $$

✖ **Comfortel De Champ** Picard; ✎ 767 445 4452. Located on the hillside above Picard with fabulous views of Prince Rupert Bay & the Cabrits. Creole & international dishes, appetisers & popular Sunday sunset dinner (by reservation). Lively with a good atmosphere. $$

✖ **Big Papa's Restaurant & Sports Bar** Lagoon, Portsmouth; ✎ 767 445 6444. Bar & restaurant located on the beach serving a range of Creole & international dishes & refreshments. Occasional live music. $$

✖ **Blue Bay** Lagoon, Portsmouth; ✎ 767 445 4985. Hidden away at the end of a narrow alleyway in Lagoon & perched right against the shoreline is the pretty Blue Bay restaurant serving a combination of international & local cuisine. $$

✖ **Le Flambeau** Portsmouth Beach Hotel, Picard, Portsmouth; ✎ 767 445 5142. Pleasant beachfront restaurant offering a range of local & international cuisine. $$

✖ **Purple Turtle Beach Club** Lagoon, Portsmouth; ✎ 767 445 5296. Beach bar & restaurant serving drinks, lunches & dinners. Good value & ideal location for bathers, sailors & sun-worshippers. $$

✖ **Iguana Café & Restaurant** Michael Douglas Blvd, Portsmouth; ✎ 767 445 277 0815. Offbeat-looking restaurant offering an authentic Dominican cooking experience. Seafood, pasta, salads & local vegetables & provisions. A warm welcome from Jennifer & Cartouche. $$

✖ **Riverside Restaurant & Bar** Picard; ✎ 767 445 5888. Located just off the west coast highway serving a variety of international dishes. $$

✖ **Tomato Fresh Food Café & Deli** Picard, Portsmouth; ✎ 767 445 3334. Serves fresh deli sandwiches, subs & entrées including steaks, ribs & seafood. Wireless internet. Follow the signs. $–$$

✖ **Junction** University Drive, Picard; ✎ 767 445 4505. All day sandwiches, tacos, wings & drinks, including coffee. $

Creole eateries

✖ **Big Mama's Kitchen** Harbour Lane, Portsmouth. Cosy eatery serving local b/fast, lunches & dinner. Good for fresh juices. $

✖ **Douglas Snackette** Bay St, Portsmouth. Large eatery & take-out popular with locals in busy bus stop area on Bay St. $

Potter's Kitchen Picard. Located off the west coast highway, opposite Ross University Medical School. Local cooking. $

✖ **Prince Rupert Tavern** Cabrits National Park. Located at the historic Cabrits serving drinks, local lunches, soups & snacks. Octopus, goat & fish water a speciality at w/ends. $

Asian

✖ **Brother's Restaurant** Picard, Portsmouth; ✎ 767 445 3755. Chinese restaurant located near Ross University. $$

✖ **Hai Rong Yuan Chinese Restaurant & Bar** Picard, Portsmouth; ✎ 767 445 6612. Chinese restaurant just off the west coast highway. $$

Vegetarian

✘ **Natural Livity** Picard; 🔾 767 613 4860. Wholesome vegetarian & vegan food &

Fast food

✘ **KFC** Picard. Located on the main highway. The name says it all.

Coffee shops

💻 **Cabrits Dive & Café** Lagoon, Portsmouth; 🔾 767 295 6424. Located by the water, serving coffee, beer, wine & juices.

Venues

☆ **Azille Valley Country Club** Bornes; 🔾 767 445 5568. Live entertainment, bar & dining.

refreshments. Located opposite Ross University. $–$$

✘ **Perky's Pizza** Picard, Portsmouth; 🔾 67 445 3281. Pizza restaurant & takeaway located opposite Ross University.

💻 **Rituals** Picard; 🔾 767 445 4223. Coffee shop franchise also serving sandwiches, wraps, pastries & desserts. Wireless internet.

Call or pass by for information about what's on when.

NORTH EAST
Creole and international restaurants

✘ **Escape Beach Bar & Grill** Red Rock Haven Hotel, Pointe Baptiste; 🔾 767 445 7997, 767 275 7998; ⏲ from noon Wed–Sun. High-quality French & Asian fusion dinners, casual lunches & light bites at this lovely beachside location in Pointe Baptiste. Dinner reservations recommended. $$$

✘ **Pagua Bay Bar & Grill** Pagua Bay, Marigot; 🔾 445 8888; ⏲ closed Mon. Modern bistro style restaurant with indoor & outdoor dining, a great deck & fabulous views of the bay. For lunch try burgers, sandwiches, pizza, tacos or salads, for dinner treat yourself to a steak, fresh fish or pasta dishes. Lunch $–$$, dinner $$$

✘ **Randy's Restaurant & Bar** Hunt Rd, Wesley; 🔾 767 315 7474. A combination of Creole & international fare served up at this quaint

& popular bar & eatery on the hillside above Wesley. Try the chicken curry. $$

✘ **Calabash Restaurant** Calibishie; 🔾 767 445 8438. Waterside restaurant with indoor & open deck dining. An interesting mix of Creole & international dishes on offer. Reservations for dinner preferred. $$

✘ **Bamboo Restaurant** Calibishie; 🔾 767 445 8537. Calibishie Lodge's restaurant serves local & international dishes. B/fast, lunch & dinner. Advanced dinner reservations preferred. $$

✘ **Coral Reef Restaurant & Bar** Calibishie; 🔾 767 445 7432. Out of sight behind the Coral Reef Supermarket on Main St, Calibishie, this waterside bar & restaurant really feels like a hidden treasure. Simple but tasty Creole & international food. Lovely views & good value. $–$$

Creole eateries

✘ **Black Pearl** Calibishie. Snackette on the main road in Calibishie serving traditional snacks & lunches. $

✘ **Chez Patsy Rock Site Restaurant & Bar** Calibishie. Local eatery in the heart of Calibishie serving traditional lunches with fresh fish, seafood & homemade quiche a speciality. $

✘ **Glenda's Restaurant & Bar** Calibishie. Rustic wooden roadside eatery on the west side of Calibishie with nice views of the coast. Local cooking & refreshments. $

✘ **Warrow's Seaside Lounge Bar & Restaurant** Calibishie. Waterside bar serving Creole food with occasional live music. $

SHOPPING

Shopping in Portsmouth is a bit of a struggle. There are not many shops, but if you are prepared to look hard you should find the bare essentials. For many years the town has been quite a run-down place though there is talk of rejuvenation and investment, which will hopefully lift it from the doldrums. Three main streets run in parallel but it is only Bay Street (the one closest to the water) that has much to offer in the way of shops and services. If you cannot find what you are looking for in Portsmouth, then you should try Picard, which benefits from the presence of the Ross University School of Medicine and has more to offer.

FOOD, DRINK AND ESSENTIALS In the middle of Bay Street is the **Portsmouth market**, which is at its busiest on Saturday mornings when hucksters and farmers from the north come to sell their produce. There are a couple of small supermarkets on and just off Bay Street in Portsmouth. Though a little more spread out, Picard has a better selection.

Duverney's Supermarket Picard. Small supermarket, located opposite Ross University.
HHV Whitchurch IGA Picard. Large supermarket with a good range of products.

James Store Picard. Small, well-stocked supermarket & general store.

GIFTS AND SPECIALITY PRODUCTS

D's Tropical Fruits & Flowers Picard. Located opposite the main entrance of Ross University, D's stocks a wide range of Creole gifts, crafts, fruits, wines, spirits, cigars & speciality foods such as yoghurts, soya milk, cheeses & honey. Flower arrangements & baskets also made to order.

Cabrits Cruise Ship Berth On cruise ship days the Cabrits has a number of vendors selling a range of gifts & souvenirs.
Indian River Visitor Centre Gifts & souvenirs, T-shirts, flags etc.

OTHER PRACTICALITIES

PHARMACIES
✚ **Bayside Pharmacy** Bay St, Portsmouth; ☏ 767 445 4751. Located on the south side of town, opposite Courts.

✚ **Bulls Eye Pharmacy** Ross Blvd, Picard; ☏ 767 445 3600. Located opposite the main entrance of Ross University School of Medicine.

BANKS
$ **National Bank of Dominica** Bay St, Portsmouth; ☏ 767 445 5430. Located on the south side of Portsmouth near the Indian River. Car parking & ATM.

$ **Scotiabank** Picard. Small banking unit with ATM located opposite Ross University School of Medicine.

OTHER SERVICES
Couriers
DHL Express Bay St, Portsmouth. Located on the south side of town near Courts.

FedEx Bay St, Portsmouth. Located on the centre of Bay St, near the market.

Money services
Cambio Man Bay St, Portsmouth. Currency exchange in the heart of town near the market.
Moneygram Bay St, Portsmouth. Wire services located next to Cambio Man.

Western Union Bay St, Portsmouth. Wire services located near Courts on the south side of town.

Travel agencies

Whitchurch Travel Bay St, Portsmouth; ✆ 767 445 4331. Domestic tours & overseas travel services located near Courts on the south side of Portsmouth.

Tourist information

🛈 **Calibishie Tourist Information** Brightly painted building along the roadside as you enter Calibishie from the west. Accommodation, dining & tours information, local crafts, books, magazines, leaflets & general advice.

WHAT TO SEE AND DO

THE CABRITS NATIONAL PARK (*Site pass required*) The 525ha Cabrits National Park was established in 1986. The twin peaks of the Cabrits are thought to have been formed from the same volcano that collapsed and eroded over time. East Cabrit is 140m above sea level and West Cabrit stands at a height of 171m. Located within the park, and its most prominent feature, is the ruined 18th-century **Fort Shirley Garrison**. The park is connected to the mainland by Dominica's largest wetland, the Cabrits Swamp, and it also includes some 421ha of marine environment. The name 'Cabrits' is derived from the French word *cabri*, meaning 'young goat'. It is said goats were brought here for food and allowed to roam freely around the headland.

In 1990 the government of Dominica established a cruise ship berth at the Cabrits on the site of the dockyard that would have served Fort Shirley Garrison some 200 years before.

On arriving at the Cabrits National Park there is car parking on the left just before the cruise ship berth arrivals building. Beyond this is the visitor centre which houses an exhibition room and snackette. The exhibition room displays an interesting and informative interpretation of the geological formation of the Cabrits as well as the history of the garrison.

A site pass is required for the Cabrits National Park, which can be purchased at the snackette. The stone archway and path in front of the visitor centre forms the entrance to the park and leads up to the garrison and the trails. The trails are very pleasant walks through the park and include garrison ruins (see *Hikes* below). They also have excellent views of the surrounding area.

The Cabrits habitat is dry coastal woodland. Trees found here include teak (*Tectona grandis*), the silk cotton tree (*Ceiba occidentalis*), the bay tree (*Pimenta racemosa*), the naked indian tree (*Bursera simaruba*), the mahogany (*Swietenia mahogani*) and the savonnet (*Lauchocarpus latifolus*). In the grassy area above the Fort Shirley powder magazine you can see Dominica's national flower, the *bwa kwaib* (*Sabinea carinalis*).

The Fort Shirley Garrison Despite the fact that Portsmouth was no longer an appropriate location for the island's capital, the natural harbour of Prince Rupert Bay still needed defending from invaders. British Governor Sir Thomas Shirley began the task of constructing a military garrison on the headland of the Cabrits, based on the plans of Captain James Bruce who designed many of the island's fortifications at the time. All of the forest was cleared from the area, and a fully functional and quite impressive 80ha military stronghold of over 50 buildings was created.

Other than witnessing the Battle of the Saints in 1782, the fort experienced no military conflict. Due to its location next to a large swamp, many of the troops stationed there fell ill and died. The garrison's problems were confounded by the escalating costs of defending an island that was producing little by way of income.

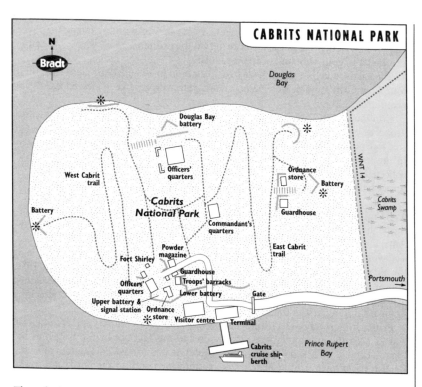

The solution was to create regiments of African and Creole slaves who were more accustomed to the testing climate and who were also considerably cheaper. These troops formed the Black West India Regiments, or the 'Black Regiments'.

In 1802 the 8th West India Regiment staged a revolt at the Fort Shirley Garrison. Their commander-in-chief was Governor Andrew James Cochrane, who took it upon himself to use the regiment to work his private estates without pay. On 9 April the regiment took over Fort Shirley for a number of days though troop reinforcements and attack from HMS *Magnificent* resulted in many deaths. Those who survived fled into the forest where they joined up with bands of Maroons.

In 1805 French forces attacked Dominica from the south and a fierce battle raged off Roseau. The French fleet gained ground in La Pointe (Pointe Michel) and cannon fire from Fort Young resulted in flames drifting on the wind towards the town. Roseau was burned to the ground and the remaining British troops under Governor Sir George Prevost retreated to the garrison at Fort Shirley. He refused to surrender and the French, perhaps no longer relishing the fight, withdrew from Dominica.

Following the defeat of the French the requirement for military fortifications gradually receded and in 1854 the garrison of Fort Shirley was abandoned to nature. In 1983 restoration began and, whenever funding becomes available, is continuing under the professional guidance of historian Lennox Honychurch (see page 29).

From the clearing above the visitor centre, walk up the stone causeway to the fort. The entrance passes between two stone buildings. On your left is the **guardhouse** and on your right the **powder magazine**. The guardhouse has small windows through which guards would have been able to observe and fire at intruders entering the fort. To the left of the guardhouse are the **troop barracks**, beyond which is the restored **lower battery** with seven cannons pointing out across Prince Rupert Bay. At the rear of the lower battery is the **ordnance store** where you can see cannonballs, grapeshot and ordnance tools.

The garrison is thought to have had 35 cannon in all and 17 of them can still be found here. The cannon were 32 pounders, each with a range of around 2.4km and accuracy to 1.2km.

Continue up the causeway past the bottle palms to the upper section of the fort. This area is dominated by the restored **officers' quarters**. Beneath the large mango tree in front of the building is an iron pump. This is a **cistern**, one of three located in the garrison, that would have provided the troops with fresh drinking water collected from roofs and a water catchment. To the left of the officers' quarters is the **upper battery** and **signal station** with cannons pointing out across the bay.

PORTSMOUTH AND ENVIRONS The broad and beautiful bay that stretches from the Cabrits headland south to Morne Espagnol was called **Ouyuhayo** by the Amerindian settlers who lived there and then later **Grand Anse** by the French. Today it is named after Prince Rupert of the Rhine, a Royalist commander during the English Civil War (1642–51) who is said to have taken refuge here in 1652. Following defeat by the Parliamentarians of Oliver Cromwell, the man he named 'Ironside' at the 1644 Battle of Marston Moor, Rupert took to piracy, attacking English shipping first in the Mediterranean and later in the West Indies.

Prince Rupert Bay was a natural harbour for ships, both military and commercial, and in 1765 the area along its eastern shoreline was laid out by the British as the island's capital. As it was to be a major seaport, it was named Portsmouth after the English naval town. Unfortunately large swamplands both to the north and to the

THE RESTORATION OF FORT SHIRLEY   *Dr Lennox Honychurch*

Fort Shirley and the Cabrits Garrison, abandoned to the forest since 1854, has been undergoing significant restoration in recent years. A team of skilled carpenters and masons has been piecing together the ruined buildings. The focus has been on the garrison headquarters at Fort Shirley where cast iron cannons that were once scattered in the forest are now pointing out to sea again on restored ramparts and gun carriages. The restored officers' quarters are popular for events such as weddings, small conferences and dinners. In the main hall is an exhibition of reproductions of 18th century paintings of Dominican scenes, while old maps and artefacts are displayed in the Powder Magazines. The Troop Barracks have been converted into a hostel for groups on heritage and ecology study tours. The troops' kitchen has been restored and the former parade ground, where soldiers attended drill practice each day, has been cleared for recreation. For those who prefer ruins, a loop trail follows the military roads through the forest to make a circuit of the main army buildings in the valley. It includes a viewpoint towards the French islands overlooking the site of the Battle of the Saints fought between the French and British fleets in 1782.

Dr Lennox Honychurch, D.Phil, M.Phil, is a historian and educator who takes an active role in the preservation of Dominica's architectural heritage. One of his many roles is to oversee the restoration of Fort Shirley and the Cabrits Garrison. For more information: www.lennoxhonychurch.com.

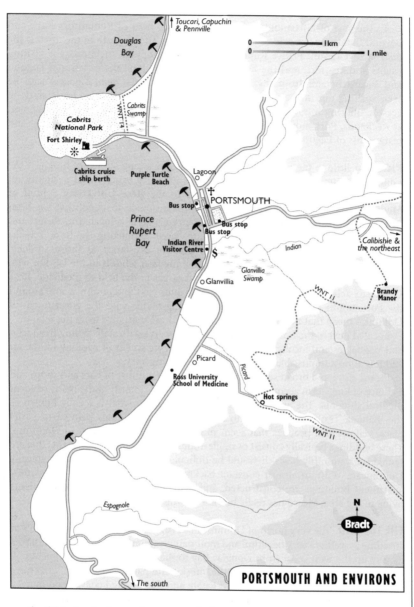

PORTSMOUTH AND ENVIRONS

N

Bradt

8

south of this developing settlement resulted in too many cases of malaria and yellow fever for this to be a practical plan. Just three years later the project was abandoned and the settlement of Roseau in the south was made Dominica's capital instead.

Today Portsmouth still has the feel of a town that has never really fulfilled its potential. This would appear to be changing, however. An ambitious redevelopment plan for Portsmouth exists which could potentially include a marina, boutique hotel and golf course. All of this is dependent on the requisite funding being made available, of course. These plans also include the removal of the numerous rusting hulks that seem to have been resting along this coastline for an eternity.

To the east of Portsmouth is the large playing field of **Benjamin's Park** and beyond that there is a grid of residential housing. To the north of the town is the district of **Lagoon**. Prince Rupert Bay is a very popular anchorage for visiting yachts and cruisers, and the bars and restaurants along the beaches at Lagoon and Picard benefit from the arrival of these visitors. 'Yacht Chasers' can be seen rushing out in their small boats or canoes from Lagoon to greet arriving vessels, offering mooring services, shopping, gifts and tours. At night time and at weekends, Portsmouth becomes livelier, especially around the beach, bars and restaurants of Lagoon.

Picard A little to the south of Portsmouth, beside a long stretch of beach, is the rapidly growing community of Picard. This area has experienced a significant expansion over recent years primarily due to the **Ross University School of Medicine** that is located here. Ross is a US-based medical school that has been in existence for over 25 years. Its Basic Science Campus is located in Picard and medical students typically spend 16 months here completing the basic science curriculum. The university functions to provide assistance to those students who have not succeeded in securing places at medical schools in the US but who wish to continue to pursue an education and career in the field of medicine. Ross University School of Medicine is a major contributor to the economy in and around the Portsmouth area and mutual benefit arrangements with the government of Dominica mean that the island also receives medical assistance from the school.

Located next to the university is a small market area with stalls selling fresh fruit and vegetables and locally cooked food. The alluring smells of cooking fill the air and it is almost impossible to resist giving something a try.

Picard also has a broad selection of restaurants, a number of bars and shops and a choice of long-term accommodation that is aimed primarily at the many resident medical students. The area opposite the campus along what is locally known as the 'Banana Trail' is crowded with large apartment buildings painted in pastel lilacs, yellows and peaches that seem more fitting to Florida than to Dominica. These buildings typically consist of single-room, self-contained apartments that are rented on a monthly basis. It would be difficult to describe this area as typically Dominican. With an almost constant background sound of hammering as new apartment buildings are constructed, and with the number of medical students living in the area, Picard has really become a 'little America'.

THE TOP END The very north of Dominica has rugged and interesting stretches of coastline as well as a very beautiful and mountainous interior. A narrow road snakes its way up the west coast from Douglas Bay to the remote village of Capuchin. A road from Savanne Paille cuts across the interior and passes over a northern crater of Morne Aux Diables to the Delaford Estate and the elevated coastal community of Pennville. From the northeastern hamlet of La Haut, the road meanders along the east coast through the village of Vieille Case down to Thibaud where it joins the main road from Marigot to Portsmouth.

To the north of the Cabrits is **Douglas Bay**, once called Malalia by Amerindian settlers, then renamed after Sir James Douglas, an 18th-century admiral of the British navy. With the twin peaks of the Cabrits to the south and the headland of Douglas Point to the north, this calm and tranquil bay is very picturesque. Unlike the beaches further to the south, the narrow stretch of sand near **Tanetane** is rarely visited. Beyond Tanetane the road curves around the bay and offers a choice of routes. To the left, the road goes up through the hamlets of Savanne Paille, Morne

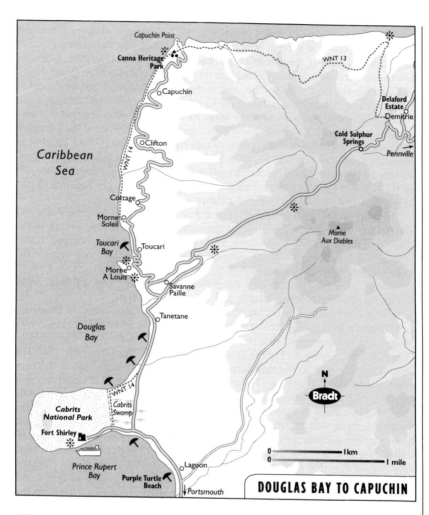

DOUGLAS BAY TO CAPUCHIN

A Louis and then down into the very pretty Toucari. The road to the right is the way across Morne Aux Diables to Pennville.

Taking a left at this junction and ascending to Savanne Paille and Morne A Louis presents you with superb views of Douglas Bay and the Cabrits. The narrow road then heads steeply downhill into Toucari Bay. Take care during this descent as the road is very steep, very narrow and has a number of sharp corners.

The sheltered and beautiful bay at the village of **Toucari** is quite idyllic. The bay is also an interesting site for snorkellers and scuba divers, though it is rarely visited. It also serves as a natural anchorage for sailboats. Hidden beneath its waters is a reef formation with hard and soft corals, an abundance of aquatic life and a number of small caves and shallow caverns. Small cottages and dwelling houses, together with snackettes, bars and coconut palms, line the road along the bay. To the north, perched on the hillside above the road, is Toucari Roman Catholic Church.

The road north from Toucari hugs the west coast until it reaches the most northerly village of **Capuchin**. *En route* it passes through the hamlets of **Cottage** and **Clifton**. Both are pretty with small convenience stores, colourfully painted wooden houses and well-tended gardens. In 1567 a number of Spanish treasure ships were wrecked in a storm off the coast of Capuchin. The Kalinago are said to have salvaged some of the valuable cargo and stashed it in a secret cave. Stories of lost treasure are rife in this area though as yet none of it has ever been found. North of Capuchin the road ends and becomes a dirt track. This track passes Capuchin Point, or Cape Melville, and arrives at the Canna Heritage Park. In addition to a gun battery placement, cannon and some stone ruins, there is evidence that this area was also once a small Amerindian settlement and a missionary site of the Capuchin religious order. The track that runs eastwards from this point is the Capuchin to Pennville Trail, now Segment 13 of the Wai'tukubuli National Trail (see page 250), a pretty and ancient coastal track that ends in the small farming village of Demitrie on the Delaford Estate, a little to the west of the village of Pennville. Segment 14 also begins here and runs all the way to the Cabrits (see page 251).

The road up the western side of Morne Aux Diables from Savanne Paille and Toucari has some spectacular views of Prince Rupert Bay and Portsmouth to the south, and the Saints to the northwest. Once over the ridge you enter a wide crater of what was once a large volcano. At the base of the crater there is a sign for the **Cold Sulphur Springs** (see page 198).

Following the road up and over the crater's eastern ridge, you will soon enjoy wonderful panoramas of the Atlantic and the eastern coastline.

Descending Morne Aux Diables through the farming community of **Demitrie** and **Delaford**, look for the second turning on the left. The first will be near Edrick's Tavern and is a dead end. This is also the eastern trailhead for the Capuchin to Pennville Trail, Segment 13 of the Wai'tukubuli National Trail (see page 250). The second turning goes to the tiny hamlet of **La Haut** which is located at the very northeastern tip of Dominica. Follow this road past a number of small wooden houses until it ends. There is a trail running to the right of the house immediately in front of you down to **Point Jaco**. You should ask one of the villagers of La Haut for directions as well as permission to pass alongside their houses and gardens. They are very friendly and should be more than happy to help you. The rough trail is easy to follow but it is quite tough in places. Though fairly short, it runs very steeply downhill and can be quite slippery. Follow it through some coastal woodland and small clearings until you reach the open grassland and rocky outcrops of Point Jaco. The trail runs down the steep grassy slope right to the rocky outcrop itself.

This area is also known as **Carib** because there was once an Amerindian village here. It is believed that many of the people who currently live in the area are descendants of those original settlers.

On the lower slopes of Morne Aux Diables you arrive at the coastal village of **Pennville**. The village is in two parts, Upper Pennville and Lower Pennville. Located on the main road between Lower Pennville and the small community of **En Bas** to the south is a short river trail to the **Bwa Nef Waterfall** (see page 200).

In 1646, Father Raymond Breton, a French priest of the Dominican order, gave the island's first Christian Mass at the Amerindian village of Itassi in the *karbet* of Chief Kalamiena. Unfortunately for Father Breton, it was not for another hundred years that Christianity gained a firm footing in Dominica. A mural of his first Mass is painted on the wall of the parish hall at the top of the village, now called **Vieille Case**.

In November 2004, an earthquake 27km north of Dominica, measuring 6.3 on the Richter Scale, shook the island and caused damage to several buildings in the north, including the Vieille Case Catholic Church. The quake was followed by a

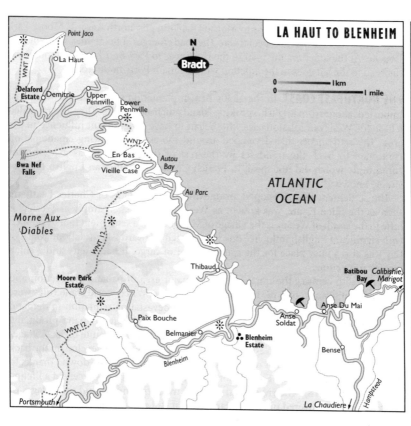

series of aftershocks and torrential rains. This very unusual church – completed in 1869, constructed from volcanic rock and with a beautiful Spanish façade and shingle roof – unfortunately could not be saved. A new, more modern replacement has been erected.

Vieille Case is built on a steep slope overlooking the bay at **Autou**. This charming cove serves as a landing place for local fishermen and is accessed via a steep and narrow road at the bottom of the village. The road emerges at a small pasture where you may encounter cows or horses. On the left-hand side is a wide grassy path leading to the boat landing. Watch the waves rushing into the bay from the open ocean and imagine how tricky it must be to both set out and land at this point. At the end of the pasture is a narrow track leading out to a rocky volcanic outcrop. There are great views along the coast from here. There was once a rite of passage challenge for the children of Vieille Case called '*decouvé l'église*'. The children, usually young boys, had to swim out from the shore at Autou until they could see the roof of the church high up above the village.

Along the coast from Autou is another nice cove called **Au Parc**.

South of Au Parc is the small farming and fishing community of **Thibaud**, named after a French settler who purchased land from the Amerindians here in the 18th century. The school and playing field are located on the shoreline of Sandwich Bay. This area is the site of the original village.

Before arriving at a junction with the main route between Portsmouth and the east coast, you will come across a sign to Blenheim along a small road to the right. From this road the views south across to Morne Diablotin and north towards Moore Park and Morne Aux Diables are spectacular. The road emerges at Belmanier, south of Paix Bouche. At the junction, the road to the right goes to Paix Bouche and Moore Park, the road to the left goes to the junction with the main Portsmouth road.

THE NORTHEAST COAST In the 1830s British plantation owners in the northeast imported labour from English-speaking islands such as Antigua. They also provided a base for Wesleyan missionaries who began to have a significant influence in the area. The settlements that developed around the estates following emancipation continued to buck the trend set by the rest of the island. It was a Methodist community which did not speak in French Creole, but rather an English form of Creole known as *kockoy*.

The settlement that developed around the former estates of Charles Leatham, such as the Eden Estate, was known as Wesleyville and later simply as Wesley. A little to the south of Wesley is the village of Marigot, also a settlement that developed with significant English influence due to imported Leeward Islands labour. Marigot Bay was also a busy place for the transhipment of cargo. It had a jetty and a small fort for protection.

In the 20th century the northeast was a major area of banana production and received significant economic benefit from this trade. When world trade rules were changed, the area was on the receiving end of a devastating reduction in demand for small island bananas. Unable to compete with the huge banana-producing companies of the Americas, the outlook in this area appeared quite bleak. Villages such as Woodford Hill and Wesley, places that had just begun to develop on the back of a banana boom, suffered a reversal of fortune and became run-down. Thanks to the efforts of The Fairtrade Foundation, the banana industry has received a lifeline (see box on page 18). The ridges and elevated tracts of land behind the villages of the northeast are covered in banana farms and it still remains an important source of income for the people of this area.

The sprawling village of **Marigot** developed around the plantation of John Weir who brought in slave labourers from Antigua and the Leeward Islands. The modern village stretches from Pagua Bay to Melville Hall and consists of several small districts, including one called Weirs after the former plantation owner. The main road runs through the heart of the village and is where most of the bars, shops and eateries are to be found.

Located on the southern edge of the village is an area called North End which was once a small community in its own right. In 1795 there was fighting in North End between the British and the French and in the mid-19th century there was a small Kalinago village here. As the village of Marigot expanded southwards, the Kalinago crossed the Pagua River and settled in what is now the Kalinago Territory.

The impressive Marigot Fisheries complex on Marigot Bay was funded by Japan. (Though it is always denied, most fisheries funded by the Japanese in the Caribbean region have been linked with favourable voting at the annual Whaling Commission. Dominica used to abstain but has recently been lauded by Greenpeace for voting against commercial whaling.) You can purchase fresh fish here most days of the week.

There is a hidden beach and cove to the south of Marigot Fisheries called **Sandy Beach**. On a hairpin bend on the main road above the fisheries you will see a guesthouse called My Father's Place at the end of a short track behind a large iron gate. To the left of this gate is a track that winds around the building where it joins a wider one, before reaching some steep steps that have been cut into the side of

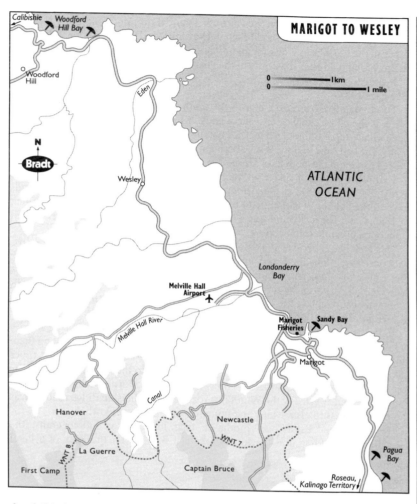

ATLANTIC
OCEAN

N

Bradt

Calibishie   Woodford
Hill Bay

Woodford
Hill

Eden

Wesley

0 _____ 1km
0 _____ 1 mile

Londonderry
Bay

Melville Hall
Airport

Melville Hall River

Marigot
Fisheries   Sandy Bay

Marigot

Canal

Hanover   Newcastle

WNT 7

WNT 8   La Guerre

First Camp   Captain Bruce   Roseau,
Kalinago Territory

Pagua
Bay

the cliff. Take care descending. The beach here is beautiful and the sea is great for swimming and snorkelling as it is protected by a reef.

North of Marigot is the expansive and dramatic Londonderry Bay where waves roll along the sandy and rocky shoreline in front of **Melville Hall Airport** (see page 37).

The village of **Wesley** lies to the north of Marigot and Melville Hall Airport. Standing quite majestically above the predominantly residential village is the Our Lady of Assumption Roman Catholic Church. The church has commanding views of the village, the brightly painted Anglican church, and beyond the ridges where bananas grow in abundance. On the northern edge of Wesley towards the Eden Estate, you may see people working on the production of *copra* (dried coconut kernels).

The banana farming community of **Woodford Hill** is located in the area of a former sugar-producing estate, one of the largest on the island in the 19th century. The area also had a harbour and a small fort for protection. Before the Europeans arrived, it is believed there was an Amerindian settlement here. Behind the village there are large tracts of banana farms where the present-day villagers grow and sell the bulk of their produce via The Fairtrade Foundation. Along the shore is one of the nicest stretches of light sand beach in Dominica; indeed it is comparable to any other in the Caribbean. Look for an unmarked road running to the shore from the main coastal road near the centre of the village.

A little to the north of Woodford Hill is another pleasant beach at **Hodges Bay** (see page 198).

Pointe Baptiste is located a little to the south of Calibishie and is a very beautiful place. It should certainly be on your agenda. It has a lovely white sand beach and a quite wonderful coastline of red rock formations that will keep photographers happy for hours. The best time to come is late afternoon when you can catch the sun setting over the red rocks and the foothills of Morne Aux Diables. See page 200 for more details.

Calibishie is a small village on the coast with a very pretty shoreline and views across the sea to the Saints, Guadeloupe and Marie-Galante. A shallow reef extends beyond the light sand shoreline to breakers and the rock formation Port D'Enfer, or Hell's Gate. The formation was once a natural arch through which water surged from open ocean to calmer shore.

This area has experienced a small wave of overseas investment in recent years, with ocean view lots developed and sold to small private hoteliers and speculators. The sandy beaches, panoramic ocean views, sea breeze and proximity to the Melville Hall Airport have seen tourist accommodation and ancillary services both supplement and replace the banana as a source of local income. There are a number of very good hotels, lodges and cottages here.

To the back of the village are coconut palms and banana farms covering a series of tall ridges in a blanket of green. A network of farm feeder roads runs along these ridges and makes for a superb hike or drive. The roads are a little rough at times but the scenery is beautiful, with views over the ocean to the north, and across the rainforest interior of the Northern Forest Reserve and Morne Diablotin National Park to the southwest. Try the Windblow road or the Calibishie Ridge road and, as these farm access roads are long and numerous, try not to get lost!

The **Hampstead Estate** once produced sugar, limes, cocoa and coconuts. The ruined estate building and machine works can be seen on the apex of a bend

FROM COCONUT TO COPRA

The flowering of the coconut palm produces *drupes*, which are large green fruit growing in bunches high in the tree. Each fruit is surrounded by a tough fibrous husk up to 15cm thick which is called the *pericarp*. Beneath this is a thin, hard brown kernel containing the *albumen*, or coconut milk, which transforms itself into a white flesh as the fruit matures. Young coconuts are often referred to as *jellies*, in reference to the soft, sweet jelly-like flesh that is beginning to form. The albumen of these young coconuts is often called coconut water and is a refreshing drink.

Mature coconuts are harvested and their dried fibrous husks removed to extract the tough, thin shell of the kernel. This in turn is cracked in half to expose the white flesh of the coconut. Each coconut half is thoroughly dried either by exposure to the sun or by cooking in an oven for up to two days. The dried flesh is then extracted from the kernel. This dried flesh is *copra*.

The *copra* is bagged, sold locally or exported. Copra products include coconut oil and skin care products. Low grade *copra* is often used as fodder for fattening horses and cattle.

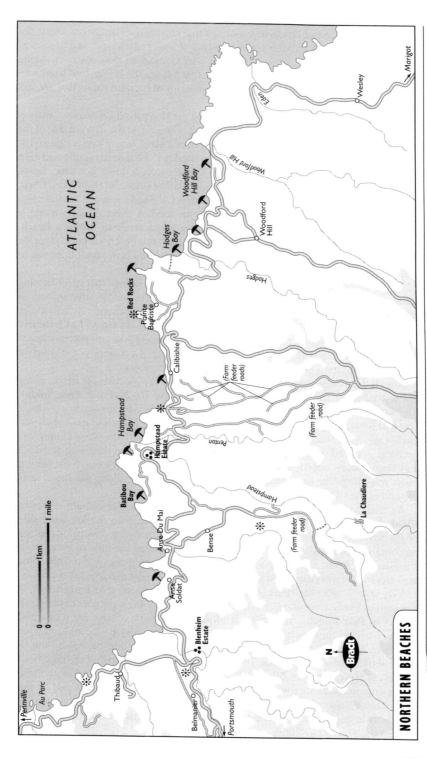

NORTHERN BEACHES

between Calibishie and Bense, near a bridge that crosses the Hampstead River. The ruins consist of stone buildings, several items of heavy machinery and presses as well as a waterwheel which was driven by water channelled from the river. Along the side and to the rear of the ruins is a track that follows the Hampstead River into the depths of the former estate, through plantations of coconut palms that are still harvested for *copra*.

On the road from Calibishie, before reaching the Hampstead Estate ruins, there is a vehicle track that runs to **Hampstead Beach**. It is located on the seaward side of the road, oppostite the Windblow Road, on the apex of a bend. It may have a sign saying 'Number 1 Beach'. This track can become very muddy if it has been raining and even in a 4x4 it can be a challenge. It only takes 15 minutes to walk down. It is a nice beach and was one of the locations for the movie *Pirates of the Caribbean: Dead Man's Chest*.

Beyond Hampstead Beach, heading away from Calibishie, you will see the ruins of a small church on the right-hand side of the road. A short distance along is another vehicle track running down to the sea which leads to **Batibou Beach**. Batibou is the original Kalinago name for the area and this beach is a good place for bathing. The vehicle track is very broken up and it may be a better option for you to walk down. It will take about 20 minutes.

To the west of Batibou Beach is the signposted road to **Bense**. This small farming village is located on the slopes of a narrow ridge that extends inland towards the foothills of Morne Diablotin. Through the village the route makes the transition to farm feeder road and continues to the area of Ti Branches. *En route*, there is a sign to **La Chaudiere Pool**. The trail winds down the ridge to a river, an effervescent pool and a pretty cascade that is surrounded by dark rocks, giving it the appearance of a cooking pot. It is a great spot for bathing and a picnic. See page 201 for more information.

Anse is the Creole word for bay, and to the west of the junction for Bense, along the coastal road, are the two fishing villages of **Anse Du Mai** and **Anse Soldat**. The former has a concrete jetty, a pretty cove and beach, fishing boats and a customs house. It is one of three ports of entry for private boats and has a sheltered anchorage. Anse Soldat is quite beautiful, its tranquil bay perhaps one of Dominica's prettiest. A paved road leads into the village and the sheltered cove with its beach and clear shallow waters. There is a bar from where local people watch the fishing boats returning. The fishermen sell their catch from a table along the shore, near the end of the village road.

As the road leaves the coast and heads west towards Portsmouth it passes **Blenheim Estate**. You will see the ruins of the sugar mill on the left-hand side of the road, behind the shell of a house. The somewhat overgrown ruins contain machine works, a sluice canal that would have controlled the flow of water from the Blenheim River, and a large waterwheel. The machinery, cogs and presses show how river water was channelled to rotate the wheel and turn the cane roller presses.

Very shortly after the ruins on the right-hand side, heading to Portsmouth, is the road to Vieille Case and Pennville. The next road on the right goes to the small hamlet of **Paix Bouche**, and above it **Moore Park**. Both villages are residential with one or two convenience stores and snackettes. Paix Bouche means 'shut your mouth' in reference, it is said, to walkers climbing up the steep hillside having to stop talking to save their breath. The road that runs straight up and through both hamlets is a nice drive or hike on a clear day. It continues beyond Moore Park, past a communications tower, before turning into a farm track and part of the Wai'tukubuli National Trail Segment 12 (see page 249). The road, though somewhat narrow, is in good condition and has good views of Morne Distinée, Morne Aux Diables and Morne Diablotin.

The road between Portsmouth and the east coast passes through the villages of Dos D'Ane and Bornes. Near the village of Bornes there is a signposted track to Brandy Manor. This track leads to a trail and then on to the cascade of **Brandy Falls**. Ask Yasmin at Brandy Manor for directions or a guide. It is a rough trail and a guide is a very good idea. Also in this area you may come across the remains of the only railway the island has ever had. Rails used to run from Brandy Ridge to the Indian River, transporting timber for the 1910 Forest Company Ltd. From here the timber was taken by river to the coast. The company went bankrupt just three years after starting the endeavour and the rails were salvaged by construction workers for buildings in Portsmouth. The small steam train that transported the timber was sold overseas, though remains of discarded rolling stock can still be seen around Brandy Manor. The route of the railway is part of Wai'tukubuli National Trail Segment 11.

ACTIVITIES AND SPECIAL INTERESTS

Beaches Though it is known more for its greenery than it is for its sand, Dominica has some lovely beaches, bays and sheltered waters that are great for bathing. Most of the best ones are located in the north. Here is a selection.

Anse Soldat Located on the northeast coast, this tiny fishing village is nestled on a pretty bay that is protected from the Atlantic by a shallow reef. A thin strip of white sand, calm, shallow waters and the occasional fishing boat coming in to land, make this a gorgeous and very peaceful spot. Follow the main road through the village all the way to the shoreline.

Batibou Taking its name from the Kalinago word for 'bay', Batibou is accessed via a rough vehicle track on the main coastal road from Blenheim to Calibishie. It is unmarked, so difficult to find. Look for it on the seaward side of the road, close to the apex of a bend, near to a ruined church school. It is between this building and the turn-off for Hampstead Beach (often marked with a sign saying 'Number 1 Beach'). The road is rough and it is better to walk down. It will take about 20 minutes. The bay is very pretty and the beach quite long and sheltered.

Calibishie The village of Calibishie has a narrow but very pretty stretch of white sand beach running almost its entire length. You can access it from a number of places. There is a reef system that protects the inshore waters, which are very shallow. At low tide you may see local people wandering around in the surf looking to catch a supper of octopus and sea eggs. A great spot is near the Coral Reef Supermarket where you can also enjoy good food and drink at the beachside restaurant at the back. This is a real gem. To the south of Calibishie is **Pointe Baptiste** (see above) where you can also enjoy Escape, a very nice beach bar and restaurant.

Douglas Bay This very beautiful and tranquil bay is located on the north side of the Cabrits peninsula. It has a very narrow strip of sand with access just before the bridge and sea wall at Tanetane. It is great for bathing too.

Hampstead Just along the coast from Batibou is Hampstead Bay. Look for a sign saying 'Number 1 Beach'. The vehicle track is located on the apex of a sharp bend opposite the Windblow Road, so watch out for traffic. Also be careful of the deep drainage gutter. The track down to the beach can be very muddy so if you are driving it may be prudent to park a little higher up and then walk down. It takes about 20 minutes on foot. Hampstead Bay is broad and the black sand beach very long. For *Pirates of the Caribbean* fans, this beach was where the cannibals were chasing Captain Jack Sparrow and friends back to the *Black Pearl*.

Hodges Bay To the southeast of Calibishie and Pointe Baptiste is Hodges Bay. Infrequently visited, this is a very lovely place. The bay is quite sheltered making it safe for bathing and the beach is very long and clean. To find it, look for the signs to Sea Cliff Cottages and follow the road down towards Calibishie Cove. Before reaching it, you should see a track on the right-hand side of Villa Vista that goes down to the beach. It is short but quite steep. At the bottom you have to cross the small river mouth to get to the beach proper. The islet offshore is accessible to good swimmers and those with kayaks, and there is a track that runs along its spine and goes right to the end. If you have a mask and snorkel, there is a large bank of sea fans between the shore and the islet that is worth a look. Be careful of sea surge and currents when you get close to the islet.

Purple Turtle Located north of Portsmouth in the area called Lagoon (sometimes Lagon) on the road to the Cabrits National Park and the 'top end'. A mixture of light and dark sand with shallow and calm bathing make this a great spot. It is especially good for children. The Purple Turtle Beach Club has good local and international food, cold drinks and a toilet. Shower facilities are located a little to the south of the bar.

Sandy Bay An unofficial 'secret beach', Sandy Bay is a lovely spot, located just off Marigot. Just above the Marigot Bay Fisheries you will see a sign for My Father's Place. Running along the wall on the left of the gate is a track that joins up with a wider one a little further down. This leads to some rather steep steps that you have to navigate down to the beach, which is actually in two parts, separated by a rocky outcrop and cave. The inshore waters are protected by a reef system that is actually not bad for snorkelling though you should stick to the inshore side. The beach is quite popular with local people at weekends.

Toucari Bay A picture postcard village and bay located along the very northwest coast of the island. The bay has a black sand beach and is very calm. Bring your snorkel and investigate the reefs and shallow sea caves.

Woodford Hill Perhaps Dominica's most beautiful stretch of sand, Woodford Hill Beach was the subject of some controversy in recent times when a luxury hotel chain wanted to make it private. Fortunately this never happened and this is a must-visit spot. There is no sign for it but it is quite easy to find. Along the coastal road that passes through the village of Woodford Hill, look for a narrow paved road on a bend that goes down towards the sea. The verges are usually quite overgrown, disguising it a little, but you should see it. Go down to the bottom and, if you have come by car, park up under the trees. Be sure to leave your valuables locked away out of sight as there have been very occasional incidents of opportunist theft on this beach. Do not let this put you off though. This is as nice a beach as any in the Caribbean.

Cold Sulphur Springs At the base of the crater on Morne Aux Diables you should see a sign for the **Cold Sulphur Springs** (sometimes called Cold Soufriere). A very easy 15-minute walk takes you along a track and a series of small steps down to the base of the crater. You reach a small wooden viewing platform over the cold springs. Though not especially photogenic, this area is fascinating, with a number of bubbling freshwater pools and streams that are effervescent with the release of sulphurous gas bubbles from beneath the ground. A volcanic Zen garden of large rocks, bright green mosses and clear pools, the springs are surrounded by *kaklen* (*Clusia mangle*), a very typical species of fumarole vegetation found at most volcanic sites in Dominica.

Farm feeder roads
The feeder roads to the banana farms along the ridges behind Calibishie are very accessible and offer some excellent scenery. Good starting points are the Windblow Road to the west of Calibishie, and the Calibishie Ridge road from the east of the village. The roads wind around the ridges and hook up with each other, eventually looping back down to the village itself.

If you are driving, you should have a 4x4 as the terrain is a little rough in places. It is also a nice place to hike or take an evening stroll. The views are good, the area interesting, and there is always a chance you will be able to meet and chat with farmers. Finish off with a trip to the beach.

Horseriding
Horseriding trips are offered by **Brandy Manor Equestrian** (*Brandy, Bornes;* ↘ *767 235 4871, 767 612 0978*). Whether you are a novice or a seasoned rider, enjoy the trails through semi-deciduous woodland and rainforest, climb Sugarloaf Mountain and enjoy superb views of Prince Rupert Bay and the Morne Diablotin National Park. 90-minute and 150-minute excursions are available and these can be combined with an outdoor picnic and barbecue or a hike to the Brandy Falls. You can also enjoy a short section of the Wai'tukubuli National Trail on horseback. They have well-cared-for, stabled horses. **Rainforest Riding** (*Portsmouth;* ↘ *767 445 3619, 767 265 7386*) also offer accompanied horseriding in the Indian River area.

Indian River Boat Trip
(*Site pass required; prices pp US$15 plus US$2 for the site pass*) Boat tours along the Indian River begin at the visitor centre near the Indian River bridge to the south of Portsmouth on Michael Douglas Boulevard. Small, colourful wooden fishing boats carry up to eight passengers each along a one-mile stretch of the Indian River. The boats are owned by their guides, who are trained and certified by the Discover Dominica Authority, and they provide a running commentary on the flora and fauna that may be seen *en route*. This area of the Indian River actually lies below sea level making it quite deep and therefore one of the few rivers in Dominica that is accessible by boat. It is lined with a type of mangrove, known locally as the bloodwood tree because of its reddish sap and which has large buttress roots that extend in interesting contortions along the banks of the river before disappearing beneath the water. This is a great place for birdwatching. Common water birds seen here include the green heron, the mangrove cuckoo, both the belted and ringed kingfisher, the common moorhen and the Caribbean coot (see page 6 for more information on Dominica's birds and page 71 for more on birdwatching).

The Indian River runs along the northern edge of the **Glanvillia Swamp**, one of two large areas of swampland in this region. For fans of the *Pirates of the Caribbean* films, the Indian River was the location of the hideaway of Tia Dalma (Calypso) in *Dead Man's Chest*. The river tour calls in for refreshments at a wooden river bar before returning to the visitor centre.

Indigo Art Gallery
Located in the northern village of Bornes is the Indigo Art Gallery (↘ *767 445 3486; www.indigo.wetpaint.com; visits to the gallery are strictly by reservation only & there is a charge of US$10 pp*). The treehouse gallery is a masterpiece of natural design, originality, simplicity and great beauty. It has

8

expansive views of the forest canopy, and birds regularly fly in and out. Decorating the gallery walls is the colourful artwork of **Marie Frederick**, a roots artist who was born in France and who now finds her inspiration in the daily life of Dominica, its natural environment and simple wooden houses. Marie works in pen and ink, water colour, acrylics and oil pastels. For a really special treat, ask Marie to show you her guest cottage. It will take your breath away.

Red Rocks at Pointe Baptiste

Pointe Baptiste is located on the northeast coast, a little to the south of Calibishie. It has two areas that are certainly worth visiting. The first is the Red Rocks, a very unusual coastal formation of smooth red earth that has been compacted and shaped by both ocean and weather. As well as the beauty of the formations themselves, you can explore a cave, short trails along the coast to further formations and a black sand beach along the margins of the Pointe Baptiste Estate, and fabulous views back across the bay to Calibishie, Morne Aux Diables and the northern interior. This is a magical spot at dusk when the sun sets behind the mountains.

The second area worth visiting at Pointe Baptiste is the white sand beach at Pointe Baptiste Bay. It is a good place to chill out and you can also enjoy the offerings of the Escape Bar and Grill, hidden in the trees behind.

To get to Pointe Baptiste you have to follow the coastal road southeastwards out of Calibishie towards Woodford Hill. Very shortly after leaving Calibishie village, look for a small sign on your left (the sign for Red Rock Haven should also help). A sharp turn up a small road brings you into Pointe Baptiste village. To get to the beach, take the first right turn down a rough road. Follow it as it curves to the right and then left all the way down to the beach. If you plan on visiting the Escape Bar and Grill as well as the beach, follow the signs for Red Rock Haven and go down the private road to the very end. Park up and then follow the trail down to the bar and the beach.

To get to Red Rocks, drive straight through Pointe Baptiste and keep going. The road becomes a vehicle track and curves through grassland to the right where it ends at a small parking area. As this land is private, you will be asked to pay a visitor's fee of US$2 per person. Follow the track behind the wooden hut and keep going straight. Ignore the spurs for now, you can explore them afterwards. The trail passes through coastal brush and then down a few steps to the formation. Have fun exploring.

Scuba diving

The northwest coast from Prince Rupert Bay to Capuchin has some interesting, dramatic and quite challenging dive sites. The calm, shallow water along its beaches also make it a good place to learn. For information about dive sites in the north see page 84.

Cabrits Dive Centre Picard Estate, Portsmouth; ☏ 767 445 3010; e cabritsdive@yahoo.com; www.cabritsdive.com. PADI 5-star Centre offering boat diving & a range of courses.

HIKES

Bwa Nef Waterfall (*Difficulty: T: 2; R: 1; E: 2; D: 1; Rating = 3.8*) This is a fun little river hike to an interesting waterfall that is inside a tall, narrow canyon. It is tricky to get to the trailhead by bus as they travel very infrequently along this stretch of road. You really need a car or you could hitch a ride from Pennville or Vieille Case. For bus information from Portsmouth see page 50.

To find the trail, head south from Pennville and stop at the second hairpin bend on a river gulley. The road passes over the river and on the right-hand side of the road, a little to the right of the apex of the bend, you should see a sign and a narrow trail leading down to the river. By some cruel twist of fate, or perhaps a little bad planning, you can only see this sign from the north.

Follow the river upstream. From time to time you will see the trail appearing on each bank, but ultimately you are brought back to the river again. There is a very short section that passes through some private land and the owner may request a small 'contribution' (do keep it small because this stretch is really very short). Eventually you will come to a tall, narrow canyon where you will see the cascading waterfall. Once inside the cavern, take a look up above you at the large boulder perched precariously over the waterfall. When the sun shines between the falls and the boulder, it is as if someone has switched on a light, completely illuminating the cavern.

La Chaudiere (*Difficulty: T: 2; R: 2; E: 2; D: 1; Rating = 4.4*) On the main road between Blenheim and Hampstead you will see a sign for the village of Bense and La Chaudiere Pool. Drive through the village until you come out the other side to a feeder road that heads out along Hampstead Ridge. This road is quite broken in places and so a 4x4 will certainly help. If you are travelling by bus, you will have to walk here from the village. For bus information from Portsmouth see page 50. Continue along this road until you reach a sign for La Chaudiere pointing down to the left-hand side of a wooden hut with a galvanised steel roof. It is quite a distance along the rough road, so stick with it and enjoy the views. Park up opposite the hut if you have a car. There may well be banana farmers working here so be sure you are not blocking the road or obstructing them in any way.

Walk down the path until you reach a spur. You should stick to the track on the right. The other track is the original trail which heads straight down the side of the valley to the river below. It is extremely steep and as the walk is a fairly short one anyway you should take the alternative route to the right. Follow this path as it meanders steadily down the valley, turning occasionally into steps as it gets a little steeper, through groves of coconut and palm trees. After around 20 minutes or so you will be at the foot of the valley and have the Hampstead River before you. You have to cross the intersection of two rivers. Cross the first river over the rocks and rapids where it narrows on your right. Once across, walk to the left around the headland and then stick to the right. You will see La Chaudiere around the corner.

You can access the pool from either the right- or the left-hand bank. You will also see that the pool does indeed resemble a cooking pot (which is what La Chaudiere means), with high rock walls and foaming water combining to create the image of a large boiling cauldron. The water is far from hot, however. The pool is great fun for bathing, but be careful – it is very deep and the current is quite strong. If you decide you cannot resist the temptation to jump in from the sides, then please do it feet and not head first.

Douglas Bay Battery and Garrison Ruins (Site pass required. Difficulty: T: 2; R: 0; E: 2; D:1; Rating = 3.1) Follow the signposted trail to the Douglas Bay battery from the clearing and footpath below Fort Shirley. After a short distance you will reach a sign pointing to the commandant's quarters up a spur trail to the right. Take this trail up to the partially restored ruins of the commandant's quarters. From here continue northwards along the main trail until you see the impressive ruins of the officers' quarters to your left. Walk down to them and take a look around. Trees and vines embrace and weave themselves around the stone ruins. Three cannon lie abandoned by the ruins of the defensive wall and a gateway leads to the remains of the battery. Take care when exploring the ruins as there are many sharp rocks and plenty of objects to trip on underfoot. The woodland area to the south of the ruins of the officers' quarters was once a parade ground. Also in this area and at the foot of East Cabrit, there were stables, further troops' barracks and a cistern.

To the west of these impressive ruins, heading steeply uphill, are some steps. Climb up to the top where you meet a wide path. Head to the right for 15–20 minutes around the northern edge of West Cabrit, along the partially restored ruins of a wall, until you come to the end of the path. There are nice views across Douglas Bay and along the coast towards Capuchin. To the north you can usually also see The Saints and Guadeloupe.

Walk back along the wide track all the way to Fort Shirley.

East Cabrit Trail (Site pass required. Difficulty: T: 2; R: 0; E: 2; D:1; Rating = 3.1) This is a really nice trail with excellent panoramic views from the summit of East Cabrit. In the clearing below Fort Shirley follow the signposted trail to the Douglas Bay battery. When you reach the sign pointing up to the commandant's quarters, follow it. At the ruin, the wide trail running north leads to the officers' quarters and the Douglas Bay battery (see above), but there is also a narrow spur trail on the north side of the ruin that heads upwards through the trees. This is the East Cabrit Trail. It is a pretty walk that gradually climbs up East Cabrit in a series of long but fairly gentle switchbacks. It takes around 30–45 minutes or so to reach the ruins of the East Cabrit guardhouse, ordnance store and powder magazine. Up the stone steps are the ruins of a battery position with views across to the east. Take time to explore then continue along the East Cabrit Trail until you reach the end at the ruined northeast battery emplacement. From here there are panoramic views from Douglas Bay to Prince Rupert Bay. Immediately below is the patchwork swamp of the Cabrits with its distinctive clumps of ferns and sedges. This trail is also a good place to encounter the *kouwès* grass snake, hermit crabs, and tree and ground lizards.

West Cabrit Trail (Site pass required. Difficulty: T: 2; R: 0; E: 2; D:1; Rating = 3.1) From the top of Fort Shirley, behind the restored officers' quarters, a sign indicates the start of the West Cabrit Trail. The track passes through dry coastal woodland and climbs gradually to the top of West Cabrit via a series of fairly

THE BATTLE OF THE SAINTS

One of history's most famous naval battles was fought off the northwest coast of Dominica. In 1782 Admiral the Comte de Grasse set sail from Martinique with 35 warships and a plan to meet up with a Spanish fleet of 12 warships who together would attack the British-held island of Jamaica. De Grasse was pursued by 36 ships of the British fleet that had set out from St Lucia under the command of Admiral James Rodney. On 12 April the fleets lined up for battle off Les Îles des Saintes, a small group of islands between Guadeloupe and Dominica.

It is said a sudden shift of wind allowed Rodney's flagship, *Formidable*, and several others to break the French line in two places, firing upon and scattering them as they did so. The resulting confusion and disorder of the French fleet ended in defeat and de Grasse surrendered on his flagship, *Ville de Paris*. No-one can be certain whether the manoeuvre to break the French line was deliberate or just pure luck, but it became a tactic that was repeated in later battles. The French and Spanish failed to capture Jamaica and Rodney was made a peer.

gentle switchbacks. You will see some fine examples of the naked indian tree, known locally as *gòmyé wouj* (*Bursera simaruba*), and the savonnet (*Lauchocarpus latifolius*), which is the most common tree found growing on the Cabrits headland. It is also highly likely that you will encounter one of Dominica's grass snake species, the *kouwès*, along this trail, as well as hermit crabs, land crabs and tree and ground lizards. After around 30–45 minutes of steady climbing, you reach the cannon emplacement of the West Cabrit battery. There is a nice view westwards out over the Caribbean Sea.

In addition to the battery placement, West Cabrit was also the location for a hospital and surgery, surgeons' quarters, further troops' barracks, artillery quarters and the commandant's bungalow.

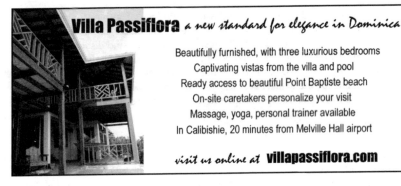
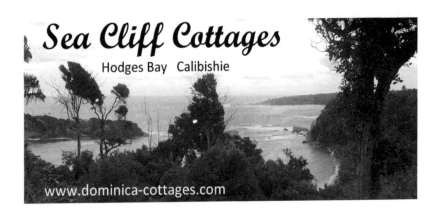

9

Northern and Central Interior, Morne Diablotin and the West

In this chapter we will explore the very beautiful forest and parrot habitats of the Morne Diablotin National Park and head south along the Caribbean coastline towards Roseau, passing several fishing villages along the way. We follow the magnificent Layou River inland to the Central Forest Reserve and the farming settlement of Bells where we discover waterfalls, a 'miracle lake', and Maroon legends.

GETTING THERE

BY CAR It takes about an hour to travel the west coast highway between Roseau and Portsmouth. The road crosses the Layou River just before it meets the sea and there is a junction offering you a route along the Layou River valley to Pont Cassé, Bells and the Central Forest Reserve. Bells is located on the main road to Melville Hall and Marigot from Pont Cassé. To get there from Roseau take the Imperial Road from Canefield. Syndicate and the Morne Diablotin National Park are accessed from the west coast highway. Look for a clearly signposted turn-off near the village of Dublanc. It takes about 15–20 minutes to reach the Syndicate visitor centre from the coast and the road passes through picturesque lands of forest and citrus farms.

BY BUS Buses run frequently along the west coast highway though they rarely travel along the Layou Valley road and they do not travel at all up the road to Syndicate and the Morne Diablotin National Park. For more information see page 50.

WHERE TO STAY

HIGH END

Harmony Villa (4 bedrooms) Pont Cassé; (UK) +44 (0)7976 785739; e carlaarmour@ hotmail.com; www.harmonyvilla.com. Exquisite open-plan wooden villa in a secluded forest location. Beautifully designed & constructed with wide verandas, living area, fully equipped kitchen, 4 bedrooms & bathrooms. Tall wooden ceilings & spiral staircase. Decorated with the original artwork of owner Carla Armour. Beautiful & luxurious getaway. Min 2 nights' stay. Price includes welcome dinner & drinks, b/fast on the first morning, pantry stocked with groceries, daily housekeeping. Night security on call. **$$$$$**

Ramelton Estate (3 bedrooms) Layou Valley; +1 246 425 2788; e edp@caribsurf. com; www.rameltondominica.net. Plantation-style accommodation in 22 acres of beautiful garden & forest surroundings. Each room has large private bathroom with shower, there is a kitchen, a lounge with open fire, & a large veranda with lovely views. A long trail leads down to a river. Internet access. Caretaker lives in the grounds & there is a daily maid service. Peaceful & private. Ideal for couples or a group of friends. Weekly stays preferred, discounts for longer. **$$$$$**

MODERATE

🏠 **Sunset Bay Club & Seaside Dive Resort** (12 rooms, 1 suite) Batali Beach, Coulibistrie; ☎ 767 446 6522; e sunset@cwdom.dm; www.sunsetbayclub.com. Well maintained accommodation in coastal garden surroundings & located on the beach at Batali Bay. Each dbl room has ceiling fans, en-suite bathrooms, mosquito nets, fridge & safe. Family rooms have bunks to sleep 4. Spacious honeymoon suite also available. Laundry, large swimming pool, poolside showers & sauna. Wireless internet. The hotel has its own dive centre with instructors & 2 dive boats. The Four Seasons Restaurant serves local & international cuisine daily. Various all-inclusive & family packages available. Anchorage & provisioning service for visiting yachts. **$$$**

🏠 **The Tamarind Tree Hotel & Restaurant** (12 rooms) Salisbury; ☎ 767 449 7395; e hotel@tamarindtreedominica.com; www.tamarindtreedominica.com. Swiss & German-owned hotel located along the cliffs to the south of Salisbury. 6 standard & 6 superior rooms. All rooms have en-suite bathrooms, solar-heated water, refrigerator & ceiling fans. Superior rooms on the upper floor also have AC. Shared spacious verandas on each floor with great views of the sea & the coastline to the north. Some rooms can be joined to create family suites. Wireless internet. Terrace restaurant & bar in gardens by swimming pool & jacuzzi serves local & international cuisine. German, Swiss, Italian, Spanish & French as well as English spoken. Hiking & scuba diving packages are available using local guides & the nearby East Carib Dive Centre. Closed Sep. **$$$**

🏠 **Crescent Moon Cabins** (4 cabins) Riviere La Croix; ☎ 767 449 3449; e jeanviv@cwdom.dm; www.crescentmooncabins.com. Perched on a hillside above a river are 4 wooden cabins, tastefully furnished with dbl bed, en-suite bathroom & verandas overlooking the valley towards the sea. Cabins sleep couples & families of 4. Dining terrace, communal lounge with library & internet connectivity. Organic farm & greenhouse, tropical gardens, hot bath & plunge pool. Natural spring provides clean drinking water. Owners make goats cheese, soap, essential oils & balms. All

dietary needs catered for & the food is excellent. On-site, fully-equipped Montessori classroom for guest families & local children. Very hands-on, sensorial & natural accommodation with personal service. Great for families with small children. Peaceful, wholesome & welcoming. **$$$**

🏠 **Caribbean Sea View Apartments** (6 apts, 1 villa) Mero; ☎ 767 449 7572; e info@caribbeanseaview.com; www.caribbeanseaview.com. Located in the heights above Mero with nice coastal & sea views. Well furnished SC apts with fully equipped kitchen, dbl bedroom with 4-poster bed, bathroom, living area, private veranda & AC. The cosy SC villa has 1 bedroom, kitchen, private bathroom & veranda. **$$–$$$**

🏠 **Zen Gardens** (3 cottages) D'Leau Gommier, Bells; ☎ 767 449 3737; m 767 612 5128; e zengardens37@gmail.com. Remote & beautiful location in the heart of Dominica, 3 rustic & pretty cottages set in colourful gardens with 5 sparkling rivers. Shared shower & toilet facilities. Cottages have running cold water from a local spring. Harmony Massage service also on site. A great escape & about as laid back as it gets. **$$**

🏠 **Elegant Suites** (30 suites) Check Hall Estate; ☎ 767 448 0474, 767 220 3100; e reservations@cis.dm; www.elegantsuites.dm. Large SC apt complex in residential area south of Massacre, just off west coast highway. Each suite has 3 bedrooms, en-suite bathrooms, AC, TV, kitchen, lounge & dining area. Shared use of swimming pool. Bar & grill located on site serving a range of local & international food. **$$**

🏠 **Morning Bird Suite Hotel Bar & Restaurant** (5 suites) Mero; ☎ 767 449 7401; e morningbirdhotel@gmail.com; www.morningbirdhotel.dm. Located in the heights above Mero, a short distance from the main coastal highway. Well-presented & spacious modern suites with en-suite bathrooms, living area & kitchen. Private verandas offer excellent views of the sea & mountains. 4 suites have 2 bedrooms, 1 suite has 1 bedroom. Rooms have TV & ceiling fans. The restaurant bar offers local & international cuisine with views from the open terrace. B/fast inc. **$$**

BUDGET

🏠 **Suite Pepper** (2 apts) Jimmit; ☎ 767 440 4321; e askpepper@pepperscottage.com;

www.pepperscottage.com. Located in Jimmit on the Warner road, 2 modern apts each with 2 beds, bathroom, AC, TV, kitchenette & laundry facilities. Owner is a taxi & tour operator. **$**

🏠 **Cozy Inn Motel** (13 rooms) Mero; ↘ 767 449 6844, 767 449 6969. Basic but clean budget

accommodation with en-suite bathroom, fans & verandas. TV in shared lounge. Located very close to Mero beach. **$**

✖ WHERE TO EAT AND DRINK

✖ **Four Seasons Restaurant** Sunset Bay Club, Batali Beach, Coulibistrie; ↘ 767 446 6522. Serving local & international cuisine in very pleasant surroundings. Lobster a speciality. **$$–$$$**

✖ **Mirage** Mero; ↘ 767 449 6676. Located on the hillside above Mero beach. Covered terrace restaurant with open views of the sea. Offers French cuisine with fresh local ingredients. **$$–$$$**

✖ **Morning Bird Suite Hotel Bar & Restaurant** Mero; ↘ 767 449 7401. Pleasant restaurant with great mountain & sea views serving local & international cuisine. **$$**

✖ **The Tamarind Tree Hotel & Restaurant** Salisbury; ↘ 767 449 7395. Extensive lunch & dinner menu serving local & international cuisine in a pleasant terrace restaurant. **$$**

✖ **West Central** Salisbury; ↘ 767 449 7979. Modern restaurant & bar located on the west coast highway near Salisbury, serving a range of international dishes. **$$**

✖ **Chez La DouDou** East Carib Dive, Salisbury; ↘ 767 449 6575. Rustic beach bar & restaurant serving local & international dishes, fruit juices & rum punches. **$–$$**

✖ **Double House Restaurant & Bar** Mero; ↘ 767 245 0089. Located on the west coast highway above Mero, serving drinks, local & international food. Great sea views. **$–$$**

✖ **Romance Café** Mero Located on the beach at Mero, serving drinks, tapas, pastries, homemade ice-creams, coffee & more. **$–$$**

✖ **Connie's Mero Beach Bar** Mero; ↘ 767 449 6513. Located on Mero Beach, serving local lunches, snacks & a variety of beverages. Sun loungers for rent. **$**

✖ **Mam's Restaurant & Bar** Massacre; ↘ 767 449 0892. Popular local eatery on the west coast highway south of Massacre. Good for take-out snacks, lunches & dinners. **$**

✖ **Merokai Beach Bar** ↘ 767 615 5723. Located on Mero beach, offering a variety of local & international dishes & snacks. Sun loungers for rent. **$**

WHAT TO SEE AND DO

THE MORNE DIABLOTIN NATIONAL PARK When it was formed in 1977, the **Northern Forest Reserve** covered 8,900ha of mountains and rainforest. In January 2000 3,335ha were taken from the reserve to form the **Morne Diablotin National Park**, which was created primarily as a sanctuary to protect the natural habitat of Dominica's two endemic parrots, in particular its national bird, the sisserou (*Amazona imperialis*). Morne Diablotin gets its name from the French name for the black-capped petrel (*Pterodroma hasitata*), a bird that used to inhabit the cliff faces of the mountain. The name translates to 'little devil' and was given because of its apparent demonic sounding call. The petrel typically nests on high cliff faces, burrowing a hole or using natural clefts. Sadly it is rarely observed in Dominica these days.

The higher elevations of Morne Diablotin are cloaked in elfin woodland. Low-growing *kaklen* (*Clusia mangle*) dominates the terrain, growing in a dense, tangled blanket some 2–3m above the ground. The *palmiste moutan*, or mountain palm (*Prestoea montana*) pushes its way through the *kaklen*, together with other low-growing trees and ferns. The lower elevations give way to montane forest and then dense swathes of rainforest. Trees such as the *gommier* (*Dacryodes excelsa*) and several species of *chatanier* (*Sloanea dentata*, *Sloanea caribaea* and *Sloanea*

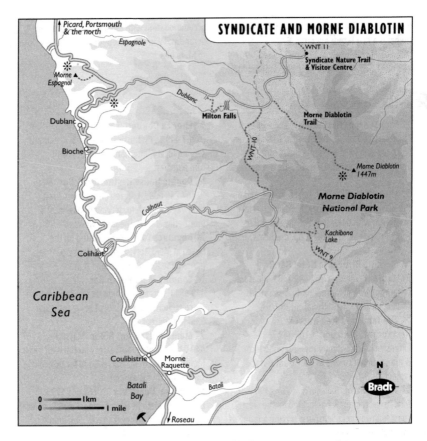

berteriana) can be found here, its unmistakable buttress roots reaching out across the forest floor. Other trees known locally as the *mang blanc*, *mang wouj*, *bwa kanno* and *kwé kwé* can also be found in this habitat and have prop roots. The karapit (*Amanoa caribaea*) produces both buttress and prop roots and is one of the most abundant species of large tree growing in the rainforest.

Within the Morne Diablotin National Park is the Syndicate Nature Trail, one of Dominica's most popular hiking and birdwatching trails (see details on page 221). There is also a tough trail to the 1,447m summit of Morne Diablotin (see page 222).

The visitor centre was opened in October 2006 and has an interpretation centre where visitors can learn about the rainforest habitat, including the trees, animals and birds that may be seen within it. The centre also has toilets and a small shop selling refreshments.

THE CENTRAL FOREST RESERVE The 410ha Central Forest Reserve is Dominica's oldest forest reserve, established in 1952. As the name suggests, it is located centrally, between the Morne Trois Pitons National Park and the Northern Forest Reserve. It has a rich biodiversity and consists of dense tropical rainforest, rivers, streams and waterfalls. It also provides a habitat for free-roaming fauna such as the agouti, and birds such as the endemic jaco parrot (*Amazonia arausiaca*). The *gommier* trees that grow in abundance in this dense forest have traditionally been used by the Kalinago for canoe building.

To date, the reserve has no established visitor sites though there are a number of bush trails, rivers and small waterfalls.

Bisecting the Central Forest Reserve is the main artery for vehicle traffic passing between Melville Hall Airport and the capital, Roseau. Located along this road is the village of **Bells**, a farming community to the south of the Central Forest Reserve and along the Layou River. There are a number of accessible natural attractions around this village as well as sites of historical interest. They include the Layou River itself, the Spanny Falls (see page 224), the Jacko Falls (see page 219) and the very interesting Jacko Steps (see page 220).

THE LAYOU RIVER The Layou is Dominica's longest river, originating in the heights of the Northern Forest Reserve in the area of Mosquito Mountain, and emptying into the Caribbean Sea just south of St Joseph. It is a beautiful river that runs through deep gorges and wide expanses of rainforest. It is alive with mountain mullet and crayfish, and many species of birds, including herons and kingfishers, can be seen along its banks or buzzing across its surface for insects. The river has stretches of rapids as well as both shallow and deep pools that are perfect for bathing and, more recently, river tubing.

In 1997, on a section of the river where it is joined by one of its tributaries, the Mathieu River, there was a series of dramatic landslides that changed the shape of the landscape forever. The two rivers meet in a gorge where the cliffs are easily 100m tall. Upstream from this junction, in the region of Carholm, valley walls of the Mathieu River collapsed, sliding into the river and passing into the gorge where the two rivers join. A landslide dam was created, plugging both rivers. Water backed up behind the dam and three days later it was breached, sending wave upon wave of water and mud racing down the Layou River to the sea. A second landslide took place on the Mathieu River the following week, creating exactly the same effect at the same river junction. The Mathieu River was plugged more solidly this time but it was only three days before the backed-up volume of river water along the Layou breached the dam again. The Mathieu River was plugged a final time, however, and a large lake formed in the river valley behind the landslide dam. That lake, known as Lake Mathieu (or Miracle Lake) is still there today (see page 219).

There are lots of great places to go bathing along the Layou River and on a hot and steamy Dominica day, a river is much more refreshing than the sea. If you take the Layou Valley road from the bridge on the west coast near St Joseph and follow it all the way to a second bridge, pull over on the right-hand side where there is a place to park. Directly opposite you should see a trail through some banana plants and bamboo. It is very short and ends at a nice spot on a bend of the river. Over the other side there is a hot water spring. Another good place can be found by continuing past the bridge for another five minutes or so until you see a vehicle track on the left. If you have found the right one, it meets the river at a large and fairly deep pool. To really experience the river properly, if you are adventurous enough and it is not the wet season, you should try the Jacko Steps trail (see page 224). You will hike a really beautiful stretch of the Layou River, cross rapids, swim in deep pools and even discover a hidden waterfall.

WEST COAST VILLAGES Located along the shoreline between the communities of Picard and Dublanc, **Morne Espagnol** is a 365m-tall peak. There is a communications mast on the summit and a rough and steep access track has been built to maintain it. A walk up to the top is a very steep climb but the views are

9

THE MAROONS

'Maroons' is the name given to the runaway slaves of 18th- and 19th-century Dominica. Before the French arrived on the island, bringing with them their own slaves, it is thought that a number of runaways from other islands had already arrived in Dominica and had either befriended the indigenous Kalinago or were living in remote forest locations. Once the Europeans had established a foothold, the slaves that were brought to Dominica to work on estates soon outnumbered their colonial masters. Some of them escaped and lived in camps in the interior. These Maroons, or *negres marrons*, used the island's rugged terrain to their advantage, protected by tall peaks, deep ravines and dense rainforest. They cut trails across the island to other Maroon encampments and to estate settlements which they raided for ground provisions and livestock. The Maroons were led by a number of prominent chiefs including Robin, Hill, Quashie, Battrebois, Pharcelle, Clemence, Nico, Congo Ray, Moko, Zombie, Jacko, Goree Greg, Balla, Sandy, Juba, Elephant, Cicero, Soleil, Nicholas, Diano, Lewis and Jupiter. Areas of the interior of Dominica where these chiefs had their camps still retain their names today.

By the late 18th century the number of camps and the network of trails stretched the entire length of the island's dense interior. In 1785 a co-ordinated effort by the European planters attempted to drive the Maroons out of hiding and either kill or recapture the slaves that were now causing them so much trouble. A legion of around 500 men tried but largely failed to curb the increasingly daring raids of the Maroons. It was not until coerced information provided by captured Maroon women, Angelique, Marie-Rose and Victorie, gave away the location of encampments that this legion made any progress at all. But armed with this new information, however, they managed to kill or capture many Maroon chiefs.

excellent. If driving north to Picard and Portsmouth, the track can be found on the left-hand side once you are beside the mountain.

The two villages of **Dublanc** and **Bioche** are situated between Colihaut and Picard to the south of Portsmouth. The road into Bioche follows the small river to the shoreline where fishermen land their catch. The road across the bridge is a dead end. The village of Dublanc is also located on a river, the source of which is high up in the area of Syndicate in the shadow of Morne Diablotin. It is along this river in Syndicate that the Milton Falls are located. Dublanc is a residential community with a small primary school and playing field located along its shoreline. A road loops through the village from the main coastal highway.

The French Roman Catholic priest, Father Raymond Breton, who visited Dominica between 1642 and 1650 in an attempt to convert the Kalinago to Christianity, built the first church on the island in a settlement at **Colihaut**. In 1795 Colihaut was the scene of a revolt when settlers who were sympathetic to the French attempted to aid an invasion from the north. Unfortunately for them the invasion failed and the British military captured and deported a number of people from Dominica.

Colihaut is located at the foot of the Colihaut River valley. From the coastal highway heading north, the main part of the village is to the left, between the shore and the road, though residences have spread further up the valley to the right. A narrow street lined with large mango trees takes you alongside the river and into the heart of the village where the Roman Catholic church dominates the small houses,

Those who were taken alive were tried, tortured and condemned to awful deaths, often publicly gibbeted.

Stories and songs of Maroon chiefs such as Balla and Jacko made them the source of legend. In the area around the present-day village of Bells there are steep stone steps in the cliff face leading up to the flat summit of the former camp of Chief Jacko. These steps, cut by the men of his camp, enabled Jacko to retreat quickly to the heights of his natural fortress and defend himself from attempts at taking him. (See page 224 for details of the Jacko Steps hike.)

Following the capture of a number of prominent chiefs, the planters legion was eventually disbanded. The Maroons had not disappeared, however, and they continued to live in the depths of the forest and use their network of tracks to move across the island, thwarting attempts to capture or prevent them from raiding estates. Between 1812 and 1815 everything came to a head in what is referred to as the 'Last Maroon War'. Regular troops were used in an attempt to rout the Maroons from their camps. Local rangers who knew the forests well were used to help locate the camps of their former companions. It was this knowledge that enabled the troops to ruthlessly evict, capture and kill the remaining Maroons in a series of successful attacks. Jacko, who it is thought spent over 40 years hiding out in the forest, was shot in 1814 after a bloody assault on his camp.

Of the prominent Maroons captured during this final series of raids, several were decapitated and their heads exposed on tall stakes across the island. Others were flogged or imprisoned. Without their strong leaders, the Maroons dispersed and disappeared. With the abolition of the slave trade via the Abolition Act in 1808 and full emancipation in 1838, the story of the Maroons became part of history and their chiefs people of legend and folklore.

convenience stores and bars. Built in 1950, the Church of St Peter is constructed from stone with large wooden louvre windows and a tall bell tower. On the north side of the church is a small garden and in front of the entrance gate a message of love has been tiled into the pavement.

Painted on a nearby wall is a mural of the *ban mauvais* parading through the streets in their *sensay* costumes accompanied by a band playing their *la peau cabwit* goatskin drums at carnival time (see box on page 214). A little further down the road is a beautiful old wooden house belonging to the Shillingford family. The house has large verandas with intricately carved decorative fretwork, jalousie windows and large wooden hurricane shutters. There are a number of bars and snackettes in this area as well as a traditional stone oven bakery. Towards the sea you may see colourful boats pulled up and fishing traps scattered along the rocky shoreline.

Like many coastal villages, **Coulibistrie** sits either side of a river (the Coulibistrie) that runs from the interior down through a deep valley and to the sea. The river is fast-flowing with small rapids and bathing pools higher up. Coulibistrie has several small residential houses, snackettes and convenience stores located each side of the river. The Coulibistrie Roman Catholic Church is a pretty stone building with wooden framed windows that are half stained glass and half louvre. A makeshift belltower hugs the building on one side. An interesting feature of this pretty little community is the way the houses have been built around the numerous large boulders that cover the base of the river valley. These huge rocks are everywhere

When I write a guide to Dominica I have to think about you, the visitor; who you are, and what you can realistically and safely do during your short stay on the island. This means I have to be quite selective about the places I describe and the details I include. I want to tell you about more than the main tourist spots but at the same time I don't want to send you off into the bush in search of a hidden waterfall, never to be seen again. It is a fine balance and difficult for me to resist the urge to tell you about absolutely everything because I love exploring the island so much myself. I think my guidebook should be as comprehensive as possible for the majority, but also act as a useful starting point for people who would like to take their Dominica experience a step or two further. And so this is how I have tried to pitch it. Whether this means getting to know people or places better, learning a bush craft, or doing some extreme hiking, I hope I have managed to point you in the right direction.

So for the people who email me about all those 'secret places' that I am keeping to myself, this box is for you. And in the spirit of having to look hard for hidden treasures, I have deliberately buried these pointers at the back of the book! Whether you decide to follow them up or not, I think it gives you an idea of how much more there is to discover on this extraordinary island. And by the way, please do not try to find these places alone – do yourself a big favour and hire a local expert. No matter how many survival shows you may have watched, the dense rainforest is a disorienting place and people have been lost here. Local knowledge and expertise is invaluable.

I wish you the best of luck with your exploring. Go to updates.bradtguides. com/dominica and tell me about your adventures.

BEYOND BOERI There are two small lakes beyond the Boeri Lake. Though diminutive, they are very atmospheric, locked away in the heart of Dominica's interior. They form part of the Boeri River that runs all the way to the west coast via the Middleham Falls. The track is rough and there is a continuation to the Middleham Falls though it is extremely muddy.

BOLIVE (BOLI) FALLS Although this waterfall appears on some tourist maps, it is a very long and challenging hike and you must take a guide. Your reward is a three-stage waterfall deep in the forest above La Plaine and the Sari Sari River. The trail arrives at the top of the second section where there is a great bathing pool.

BOETICA RIVER GORGE There is a dramatic gorge, rock formation and waterfall along the Boetica River. A second very beautiful section of the gorge runs all the way down to the sea.

BOILING LAKE FROM FRESHWATER LAKE This is a gorgeous hike in good weather. It follows a ridge above the Freshwater Lake, the Valley of Desolation, and reaches a high peak above the Boiling Lake. The hike ends at this viewpoint, a landslide destroyed the descent. The trail also passes a junction with a route down to the elevated east coast village of Morne Jaune. This is a great hike, one of my favourites, but you need company.

FOND ENGLAND WATERFALL This waterfall is located in a deep river gulley off the Middleham Falls trail in the Tou Santi area. Best viewed in the wet season when it is bigger, access is via a steep climb that requires ropes.

KACHIBONA LAKE Located in the heights above the west coast village of Colihaut is an area called Kachibona which was once a Maroon encampment. The lake was once quite large but a landslide reduced it to the size of a pond. Although the destination itself may not be that impressive, the hike here is beautiful and you pass some of the largest specimens of *gommier* tree on the island. Still tricky to follow, this route is occasionally walked by the people of Colihaut during cultural celebrations.

MARAQUE FALLS In the opposite valley to the Dernier Falls near Grand Fond is a very impressive, but extremely difficult to reach, waterfall along the Stuart's River.

MAHAUT RIVER WATERFALL Very deep within the bush above the Kalinago village of Mahaut River is a tall waterfall that cascades down a flattish rock face into a small pool. There are also several small rivers, streams and bathing pools in this area. Access is very difficult, however, and the climb up the river to the waterfall is quite a challenge.

SOLTOUN WATERFALLS Located between the village of Campbell and the Soltoun Estate in the Layou Valley, there is a series of waterfalls and river cascades. A fabulous river hike from Campbell takes you past them. A final set of five waterfalls near Soltoun (which can also be accessed via a short hike across private land from the main Layou road) are extremely beautiful. I would not be at all surprised if these waterfalls become more mainstream sites one day in the not too distant future.

TABERI RIVER WATERFALL A two-hour hike up the very pretty Taberi River on Dominica's east coast brings you to a fabulous 25m waterfall.

TAFFIA FALLS A pretty waterfall on the northwest tip of the island that, rather like Wavine Cyrique (see page 175) tumbles from the cliffs on to the shoreline.

WHO TO ASK Well, not me, sorry. Although I am always exploring Dominica and have done all the hikes described here, I am not a hiking guide or a tour operator. A very good person to ask is Ken Dill, owner of KHATTS. Ken has explored Dominica extensively and should be able to help you get to some of these places and perhaps some others he may have found (ask him about his Layou River hike). Richard Metawi of Extreme Dominica certainly knows about Boetica River Gorge as well as several other interesting places he has discovered on his canyoning trips. David Victorin can take you to the Fond England Waterfall and a few other places in the Trois Pitons area. Elvis Stedman is forever exploring the Morne Trois Pitons National Park area and he also knows the whereabouts of a couple of nice waterfalls and pools in the Laudat area. You could also ask him about the Freshwater Lake to Boiling Lake hike. Octave Joseph knows Soltoun and is a good guide for Perdu Temps. And finally, it is also really worth getting in touch with Mike Rabess of the Hiker's Retreat – you can even stay there. He and his wife hike around the island very often and they know lots of Dominica's trails. Ask him about the Freshwater Lake, Bolive Falls or Morne Jaune to Boiling Lake hikes. See pages 74 and 80 for contact details.

SENSAY, BAN MAUVAIS AND LA PEAU CABWIT

The French and Creole term for Carnival is *masquerade* and it is from this word that *mas* is derived, an abbreviated form which is used by Dominicans to describe the period of carnival (you may come across the term 'Mas Domnik'). This two-day festival before Lent combines costume, music and dance with origins in west Africa and French Creole. Following emancipation in 1838 the festivities of *mas* moved to the streets of the capital, where bands from villages all around the island would come to celebrate. Each band had its own distinct style of music, dance and costume. One such costume is the *sensay*, which is a full dress of long strips of material with a headpiece that may include horns and a mask. The mask is of tribal origin and many demonic variations exist. The costumes of these groups, called *ban mauvais*, were deliberately intimidating, threatening terror with whips, sticks and batons. Today one of Dominica's best-known *ban mauvais* groups hails from the village of Colihaut.

During the Carnival season there is always a *ban mauvais* parade accompanied by the drums of a *la peau cabwit* (goatskin drum) band through the streets of Roseau, and sometimes also in Colihaut itself. It is always atmospheric and stirring as the *sensay* dance their way through the streets accompanied by a cacophony of drums, horns and whistles. If you are visiting Dominica during Carnival, be sure to experience the *ban mauvais* and *la peau cabwit* parade at *jouvert* in Roseau, from around 04.00 on Carnival Monday.

and, instead of being moved, have simply been left as part of the village. A petrol station and handy convenience store is located on the opposite side of the river next to the Coulibistrie police station.

The name of the village of **Morne Raquette** is derived from the French word for prickly pear cactus, which grows wild in the area. The Kalinago word for the cactus is *bata* and the original name for the settlement below Morne Raquette was Batali, a name still given to the area today. The beach at Batali is predominantly used by local fishermen to store their boats and fish traps. A little further to the south at Sunset Bay Club, the beach is much nicer and the sea excellent for bathing and even snorkelling.

The village of Morne Raquette is a small community located high up on the slopes of Morne Jalousie above Batali Bay and Coulibistrie. Access to the village is via a small road that joins the main coastal highway on the southern edge of Coulibistrie. The road is well signposted and is a steep climb. The village itself is pretty with excellent views of the Caribbean Sea. The road climbs up through the village and into dry coastal woodland and scrub that is dominated by the yellow blossoms of *kampech* trees (*Haematoxylum campechianum*) until it reaches the summit of the mountain. The views along the coast to the south are superb and it is possible to see the unmistakable shape of Scotts Head when the weather is clear. The drive along this road really requires a 4x4 vehicle because of its gradient and also because the surface deteriorates in places. From the summit, the road descends a little and runs high along the side of the river valley. As it heads inland the views of Dominica's interior are breathtaking and, on a clear day, it is possible to see the peaks of several volcanoes as well as nearby Mosquito Mountain. The road continues on through banana plantations and becomes part of the island's web of farm access roads.

Salisbury is a village that until fairly recently was still commonly called Baroui, its original Kalinago name. The Kalinago village was located in the area of the present

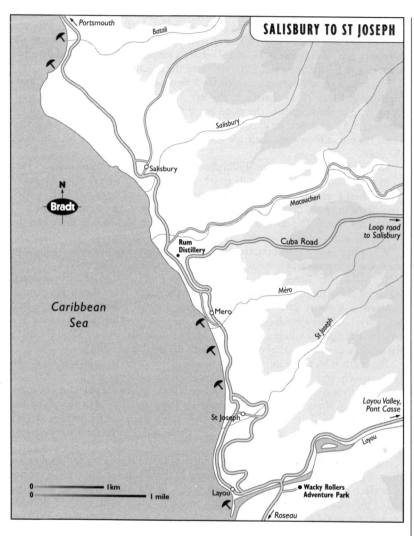

Caribbean Sea

Portsmouth
Batali
Salisbury
Salisbury
Macoucheri
Loop road to Salisbury
Rum Distillery
Cuba Road
Méro
Mero
St Joseph
St Joseph
Layou Valley, Pont Casse
Layou
Layou
Wacky Rollers Adventure Park
Roseau

0   1km
0   1 mile

Salisbury cemetery. The name Salisbury of course reflects the British influence on the island. Following emancipation, a settlement was established on the slopes of the Salisbury (or Baroui) River valley and now extends to the heights of Grande Savanne and along the southern ridge of the Batali River valley. Bananas and citrus fruits such as oranges and grapefruit are grown above the village, all the way up to Petit Macoucheri beneath the peak of Mosquito Mountain. The feeder roads up to these heights that are used extensively by local farmers make for an excellent drive into the interior, with impressive views from up above the river valleys. Such a trip also gives an interesting insight into the rural farming activities of the people in the area, and passing along rough vehicle tracks through orchards and banana plantations, seeing farmers hard at work cultivating and harvesting their crops, offers a truly vivid impression of the life of some Dominicans.

The Roman Catholic Church of St Theresa at Salisbury was built in 1929 and has been recently renovated. It is a beautiful stone church situated above the main coastal highway to the south of the village. A rough vehicle track directly opposite, on the other side of the coastal highway, leads down to Salisbury beach, where the Salisbury fish landing site is located. There is a small concrete jetty and usually a scattering of fishing boats and fish traps along the beach.

The village of Salisbury is accessed via a signposted road that leaves the main highway and then turns sharply to the left. The road through the village heads straight up to the heights of the ridge above the river valley. On each side of the narrow road are houses, small convenience stores and several bars and snackettes. From the top of the village there are good views down towards the sea and along the coast.

Macoucheri is home to the Shillingford Estates distillery which produces rum from sugarcane that it grows on its estate. The distillery produces several types of Macoucheri Rum which is consumed domestically, as well as exported. It is often considered to be the best base for the many variations of rum punch that are sold around the island. The distillery is located next to the Macoucheri River and the H D Shillingford Cricket Ground.

When rum is in production, the distillery offers short tours demonstrating how the home grown sugarcane is turned into bottled rum (✆ 767 449 6409).

The Macoucheri River has several nice pools for river bathing and can be accessed via the road that joins the main coastal road on the north side of the cricket ground.

Mero is a pretty little seaside community located between St Joseph and Salisbury. Look for a small one-way road off the west coast highway that runs in a crescent through the village and back out again. Residential areas of Mero extend to the inland side of the coastal road up towards the heights of Cuba.

The beach at Mero is a long and very beautiful stretch of dark volcanic sand. The sea is usually very calm and clear and excellent for bathing. The people here are very friendly and very used to visitors, indeed it is a stopping-off point for a number of cruise ship shore excursions. At weekends there are often activities along the beach such as barbecues, music and volleyball. It is a nice place for families to relax and enjoy the sea. There are some good bars, cheap and cheerful food, sun beds and ocean kayaks for rent.

The village of **St Joseph** is located just north of Layou at the base and around the steep slopes of a river valley that runs down to the sea. It has the distinct feeling of neglect, probably because most people pass it on the highway above, along the top of the valley, and few make the turn into the village itself. But it is perhaps because the world passes it by that St Joseph is such an interesting place. Walking around the village is an experience of the senses. Observing life as it is played out, walking along the narrow twisting lanes, passing small convenience stores and rum shops, tiny church schools, wooden homes and repair shops, hearing the sounds of conversation and singing from villagers in the street or sitting out on porches, the aroma of cooking drifting through the air, you feel as if you are enveloped by everyday Dominica.

Commanding the heart of St Joseph is the large Roman Catholic church, built in the late 19th century and dedicated to Saint Gerard. A walk along the river and through the village takes you past small bars and grocery stores but little more.

Tarou is a tiny fishing and farming community located along a small river valley beneath the dry scrubland slopes of Desjardin and Warner. In the summer time the area becomes vulnerable to wild fires that scorch the dry bush along the slopes above the village, forcing locals to abandon their houses and stand helplessly along the shoreline in the hope that the quickly spreading fires can be subdued before they reach their homes. The name of the village is thought to be derived from the Kalinago

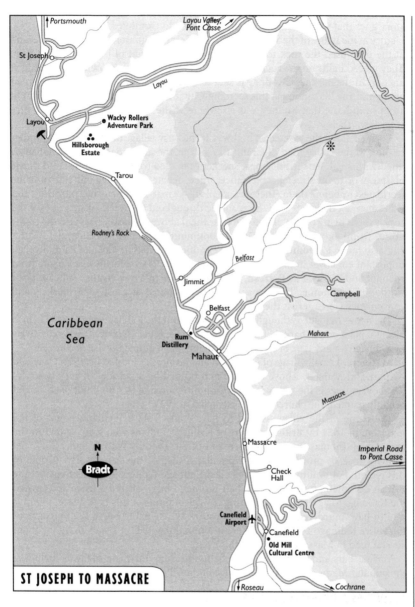

ST JOSEPH TO MASSACRE

name for a seabird that nests in the face of the nearby cliffs. In the late afternoon you may come across the fishermen of Tarou retrieving their seine nets. This involves a line of people pulling hard on a rope that extends right across the main road. The traffic halts and the catch is brought a little nearer to the dinner plate. From time to time, to let the traffic pass and to take a well-earned breather, the fishermen tie off the seine rope on a pole by the side of the road before hauling once again.

A little to the south of Tarou is Tarou Point, more popularly known as **Rodney's Rock**. A reminder of the island's volcanic history, this large lava formation is an interesting natural feature as well as the source of rather dubious local legend. The story goes that when Admiral Rodney returned to Dominica following the British victory at the Battle of the Saints in 1782, the French who were occupying the island at the time used the rock to delay his continued pursuit of their retreating fleet. They placed lights on the rock and dressed it up to give the impression of a ship at anchor. In the darkness, Rodney is said to have been completely fooled and spent all night firing his cannon at this seemingly invincible foe. Historical records would seem to indicate that Rodney was elsewhere at the time however, but it is a nice story nevertheless.

Located along the west coast highway is the busy village of **Mahaut**. In a similar fashion to the Lallay road of Grand Bay village, the main road through Mahaut is lined with small bars, rum shops, snackettes and convenience stores. Loud music blasts out on to the street, people dance, argue, debate or just hang out, watching the world pass by before them. There is a small village market on Saturday mornings and fishermen sell their catch on the roadside throughout the week – listen out for the conch shells being blown, if you can hear them above the heavy bass and the traffic noise. To the north of Mahaut is the community of Belfast, a residential district and also home to **Dominica Coconut Products**, owned by Colgate Palmolive, an important employer in the area. The factory produces wonderful soaps made from coconut and branded as **Refresh**, which should be in every visitor's suitcase prior to the journey home. These soaps can be purchased at most supermarkets and convenience stores across the island.

The name 'Mahaut' is thought to be derived from the Kalinago word *maho*, which means a plant or tree bark that can be used to make rope. *Maho* was used extensively by Kalinago for any type of work, tool or fixing that required the use of cordage.

Massacre, a small village of fishermen and farmers, is located between Canefield Airport and Mahaut. Above the road and framed by a number of very beautiful flamboyant trees is the pretty Roman Catholic church of St Ann. Built of stone and brightly painted, the church was constructed in 1921.

The name of the village is said to have come from a French account of the massacre in 1674 by British soldiers of Kalinago Indians who were settled in the area. Chief Thomas 'Indian' Warner, son of Sir Thomas Warner and a Kalinago woman, rose to prominence as a popular leader of the Amerindian people of this region. For a number of years he led Kalinago fighters in conflict against the British occupying forces until his half-brother, Philip, offered a truce and invited the Kalinago to agree a treaty. During the celebrations of this new peace, Philip is said to have murdered his rebel half-brother as a signal to begin the massacre of the entire Kalinago settlement. There is a mural painted on a wall along the main coastal road in Massacre depicting this event.

Various bars and snackettes are to be found along the main highway including the popular Mams on the southern edge of the village.

ACTIVITIES AND SPECIAL INTERESTS

Birdwatching (*Site pass required at Syndicate*) The Syndicate Nature Trail is located within the Morne Diablotin National Park. It is exceptionally beautiful and a very accessible introduction to the elevated rainforest environment of the island. The forest-covered hillsides of Morne Diablotin and Morne Turner have become one of the last remaining habitats for the endangered sisserou parrot (*Amazonia imperialis*), an Amazonian that is endemic to Dominica. This unspoilt and very beautiful habitat has become a real draw for birdwatchers visiting the island.

Birds you may encounter at Syndicate, in addition to the jaco and the sisserou parrots, may include the four species of hummingbird that are found in Dominica, including the endemic blue-headed hummingbird (*Cyanophaia bicolor*). Other sightings may include the forest thrush (*Cichlerminia lherminieri*), the scaly-breasted thrasher (*Margarops fuscus*), the trembler (*Cinclocerthia rufcauda*), and the plumbeous warbler (*Dendroica plumbea*).

The Layou River and the Pagua River are also excellent places to watch water birds such as the ringed and belted kingfisher (*Ceryle torquata* and *Ceryle alcyon*), the green-backed heron (*Butorides striatus*) and the least sandpiper (*Calidris minutilla*). Along the riverbanks you may see the cattle egret (*Bubulcus ibis*) and the snowy egret (*Egretta thula*).

For birders who would like the company of an expert guide, see page 71. For more about Dominica's birds, see page 6.

River tubing The Layou River has become a popular location for river tubing. From close to the coast you are taken upstream where you are fitted out with buoyancy aid, paddle and inflatable tube. Once in the water you are accompanied by guides back downstream to the starting point. The journey is pretty and for the most part very sedate. There are one or two short stretches of rapids to negotiate but nothing too serious and the water is fairly shallow. It is a great trip out for families. For operator details see page 82.

Zip-lining in Wacky Rollers Adventure Park Located just to the south of the Layou River bridge, along a track next to the ruins of the Hillsborough Estate, there is an adventure park with tree-top rides including zip-lining and canopy walks along suspended platforms. The course includes a hair-raising zip-line across the Layou River itself. There is also a kids' park for small children. Look for a sign on the main west coast road just to the south of the Layou River bridge. For more information contact **Wacky Rollers (WRAVE) Ltd** (↘ *767 449 8276;* e *wackyrollers@yahoo.com; www.wackyrollers.com*).

Jacko Waterfall Just before you get to the village of Bells from Pont Cassé, there is a small but pretty waterfall that is very accessible. Look for colourful signage, and a wooden shelter selling fruit and souvenirs. The waterfall is located within a deep river gully which you can view from a platform at the top. If you wish, you can also go down to it. There are concrete steps leading to the river, the waterfall and the pool. It is a nice place for a refreshing bathe. The surroundings are pretty; there is a cave, rainforest vegetation, moss covered boulders, tropical flowers and bird life. The owner of the roadside land you cross to access the pool charges a small fee of around US$1 per person. The waterfall is not particularly tall but, like the Emerald Pool, its draw is its accessibility for those who do not wish to do much walking or hiking.

Scuba diving The central west coast of Dominica has some excellent dive sites which have beautiful, healthy coral reefs, steep vertical walls and an abundance of interesting marine life. They are less visited than those in the Soufriere Scotts Head Marine Reserve and are in good condition. See page 84 for more details about the dives sites and dive operators in this area.

Lake Mathieu ('Miracle Lake') Located in the heights above the Layou River, in an area called Carholm, is a magnificent freshwater lake. It was formed as recently as 1997 following a series of dramatic landslides (see page 209). There are several viewing points as well as an accompanied hike down to the lake itself. Some of the best views are from a fairly short circular trail. Mr Christborne Shillingford

9

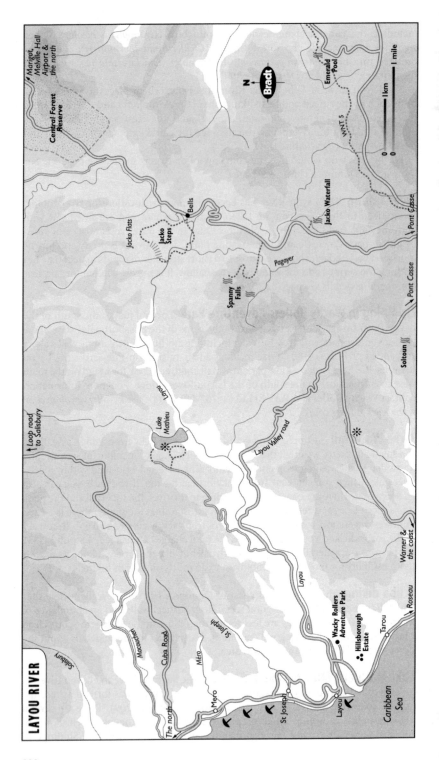

is a landowner in this area and he charges a small fee to accompany you either on the circular walk or on the short but steep trek down to the lake. His fees vary, are negotiable, and depend on the group number. He is a nice guy so just talk it over with him. He is also very passionate about the lake and its 'miraculous creation'.

To get there, take the Layou Valley road from the west coast, just by the bridge, and follow it for about 1.5km. Before you reach the second bridge, you will see a vehicle track on the left, heading uphill. You should see signs for 'Miracle Lake' or 'Miracle Valley'. A 4x4 is a good idea as the road is badly broken up in places. Just follow it as it climbs high up above the Layou River and turns inland. Stick with it all the way to the end. Park up when you come to a barrier that Mr Shillingford has placed across the road for safety. If he is around, he will probably notice you and come to greet you. He has also posted his telephone number on one of several very interesting signs.

You can just view the lake from the road. Pass around his barrier (it is a public road) and walk to the end. You will see where the road fell away with most of the hillside during the landslide, and you will of course also see the lake itself. It is very large and beautiful.

Back down the road, about 50m from the barrier, there is a trail (facing the lake and the road end, it is on your right). This is a loop trail that passes over Mr Shillingford's land and he will expect some sort of fee. Follow it straight down, ignoring the spur to your left (this is where you will return). It is quite a nice walk through the woodlands and relatively easy except for a couple of sections where you cross a shallow gully. It brings you to two rather makeshift and quite toe-curling view points. Be careful, stay away from the edge and please do not lean on the fencing. Follow the trail in a loop back. Where you come to the junction, take a right and walk uphill back to the road. Please do not attempt to hike down to the lake by yourself.

Lake Mathieu has so far not been adopted as an official site; in fact it has largely been ignored by the authorities. The reasons for this are unclear and probably complex. This may be resolved over time, of course, but until you see any official-looking signage, you should assume that the trail is privately managed, and that the view points are not reinforced platforms. It is a very beautiful and impressive natural site; it is Dominica's largest fresh water lake, and it really ought to be on the official tourist map. So watch this space.

HIKES
Syndicate Nature Trail (*Site pass required. Difficulty: T: 1; R: 0; E: 0; D: 1; Rating = 1.3*) The Syndicate Nature Trail is a loop through the rainforest habitat of the Morne Diablotin National Park. It is very popular with bird enthusiasts as this area is considered a parrot habitat. It also has a wide variety of other birdlife as well as some magnificent tree specimens. The trail is well-marked and there are signs by many of the most prominent trees along the route, giving you both the standard as well as the local name. The visitor centre has an interpretation room, washroom facilities and a small snack bar. You can also buy your site pass here.

To get to Syndicate, look for a very obvious sign along the west coast highway, a little to the north of Dublanc. The narrow road climbs uphill and passes a number of small farmsteads, many of them growing citrus. The road is quite long and fairly narrow. Use your horn on bends as you may well encounter farmers' vehicles. Pass the sign for the Milton Falls and also for the Morne Diablotin Trail. Keep going until you come to the visitor centre and car park. It is quite a way in, so do not become anxious that you may have gone the wrong way. The road is simply longer than you probably expected it to be.

Public buses do not go up this road. You could get off on the west coast highway and walk. It will take 45–60 minutes to get here. It is actually a very beautiful and scenic walk.

Pass through the visitor centre to reach the start of the trail and follow the signs. As it is a loop, you can choose which direction to go. There are also a couple of short diversions. If you stick to the main trail, you cannot get lost. At some point during your hike you will come to a viewpoint across a river valley to Morne Turner. This is a popular place for birdwatchers and there is always a good chance of seeing parrots in flight above the forest canopy. Sit and wait here for a while and you are sure to be rewarded. In all likelihood the parrots you see will be jacos. They are large, green and have a distinctive yellow tail-feather. They tend to fly in pairs and have the kind of call you would expect from parrots. The sisserou is larger and looks more ungainly in the air. It does not have the yellow tail-feather and has a much more high-pitched call.

If you walk the loop trail without stopping, it will take less than an hour. You should try to take longer, however, as this rainforest habitat, the tree species and the birdlife are all very special.

Morne Diablotin (*Site pass required. Difficulty: T: 4H; R: 0; E: 4; D: 4; Rating = 7.5H*) The hike to the 1,447m summit of Morne Diablotin is great fun, but it is also very difficult. It involves a relentless uphill hike, a scramble up steep rocks and a lengthy climb through branches and roots. For the most part the trail is very obvious, and, if you get a cloudless sky when you reach the summit, the views across the island and beyond are spectacular. Before you begin the hike, it is important to be prepared to get wet and very muddy. Also, as the summit is often windy and cloud-covered, it can be quite cold. Bring something to keep you warm, protect you from wind and rain, and ensure you have a change of clothes and somewhere to keep them dry.

You will find the trailhead on the road to the Syndicate visitor centre (see above). It is on the right-hand side, about three-quarters of the way there, and there is a sign.

From the very beginning, the trail lets you know you are climbing a mountain. The first hour is a steep climb up steps made from wood or tree fern, through the dense rainforest of the mountain's lower elevations. The forest is raw and untouched, full of magnificent *chatanier* trees with their giant buttress roots, tall and incredibly straight *gommier* trees, *bwa mang* with their prop roots, giant tree ferns and an abundance of epiphytes. The first hour of the hike also has a background symphony of birdsong, including those of both species of endemic parrot, the sisserou and the jaco. If you take a break and stand still beneath their calls, you may be lucky enough to see them flying above the canopy.

After the first hour of climbing the trail becomes a combination of steps, roots and rocks. It also begins to get muddy and, for the next 30 minutes, you will have to scramble up a number of boulders and steep slopes. As you do this, take a look around at the vegetation. You should notice that it is beginning to change from rainforest to montane forest, with the girth of the trunks smaller and the trees themselves shorter than at lower elevations.

After around 90 minutes or so you will encounter yet another change. You are now emerging into elfin woodland, or cloudforest, and you begin climbing over and under the branches of *kaklen* (*Clusia mangle*), a tree that is prolific in Dominica at these higher altitudes. The *kaklen* has twisting branches and roots with broad, fattish green leaves. The climb through them is tricky. Take care with your footing and look out for sharp branches at eye and chest level. The chances are it will be very wet now and so the *kaklen* branches and roots will be greasy and moss-covered. Take your time. Use your hands and arms to support your legs, and test each branch before giving it your full weight. The floor beneath the branches can be very boggy, even during the dry season, so be careful not to lose your hiking boots.

For the remainder of this climb, you are required to use both upper and lower body strength to get you to the rocky bluff at the top of the trail, known as Imray's View after Dr John Imray who made the first recorded ascent in 1862. The bluff is a little to the southeast of the actual summit of the mountain, and marks the end of this long and difficult hike. Hopefully your views are not obscured by clouds but if they are, be patient, wait a while and perhaps you will be fortunate enough to catch a break and enjoy the wonderful panoramas from the top of Dominica's highest mountain. Congratulations, you did it.

Milton Falls (*Difficulty: T: 2; R: 2; E: 1; D: 1; Rating = 3.8*) The Milton Falls, also known as Syndicate Falls, are found in the Syndicate area. The waterfall is attractive and very accessible. The trailhead is at the end of a rough vehicle track that begins on the road to the Syndicate visitor centre, next to a large mango tree. You will see a big red-and-white sign informing visitors that the waterfall is a water source for the settlements in the area. This means that introducing foreign substances or pollutants to the falls and river may have a detrimental effect on the people who rely on its water, particularly the villagers of Dublanc on the west coast. A fine and imprisonment await those found guilty of this offence. For this reason you should simply view the waterfall and not bathe in the pool or river.

The track to the Milton Falls passes through private land and the owner will request a fee of around US$2 per person.

To get there follow the road to Syndicate from the west coast road (see above) and look for the sign on the right-hand side about halfway to the Syndicate visitor centre. The rough vehicle track immediately forks. Go left and follow it through tall grass until you come to another junction with a rough vehicle track going quite steeply uphill to the left. You will need a 4x4 for this. If you do not have one, park by the sign at the very bottom and walk. It will only take you about 15–20 minutes to the trailhead. At the top of the steep hill there is a small parking area and another large sign. This is the start of the trail.

From the small parking area follow the vehicle track to a building. This is where you will be asked for your entry fee. The farmer is really nice and he will be happy to give you a tour of his land and tell you about the things he grows – if he is not busy working, that is (you should pay him a bit extra for this service). From the building follow the wide track downhill. You will see an open valley on your right that is fringed with banana plants with grapefruit trees beyond. If you wish to see parrots, just hang around here – sightings of the endemic jaco are almost guaranteed.

At the bottom of the hill the wide track appears to end, but pick up the trail on the left and follow it down to a river. The water is fairly shallow and it is easy to negotiate. Just stick to the right of the rocks. Follow the trail along the side of the river and then along a smaller tributary. The trail along this right-hand bank comes to a dead end. Before it does, you should see a trail appear on the opposite bank. Cross the shallow river and follow the trail over the little boulders of the left bank until you reach the waterfall.

In order to prevent people bathing in the pool, the water authorities decided it would be a fabulous idea to erect the ugliest fence they could think of all the way around it. The fence catches so much debris from flash flooding that it is unlikely to last very long and this very pretty natural attraction will be probably be left with concrete blocks and steel poles to decorate it. But do not let this put you off. It is a nice waterfall, the surrounding forest is very pretty – as are the farmlands and the views – and sightings of jaco parrots are common.

Spanny Falls (*Difficulty: T: 3; R: 0; E: 3; D: 1; Rating = 4.4*) Two great waterfalls separated by a steep ridge make up Spanny Falls (sometimes called Penrice Falls, or Spanny Twin Falls). It is the climb up and down this ridge that gives this very short hike a moderate rating. If you do not fancy the climb, you can satisfy yourself with just visiting the first waterfall which is very easy to reach.

Spanny Falls takes its name from the owner of Spanny's Disco, a bar and snackette that is located on the western edge of the village of Bells in Dominica's interior. To get there from Roseau, take the road to Marigot and Melville Hall from Pont Cassé. The bar is on the left, about 15 minutes' drive from Pont Cassé. For information about buses passing along this route see page 50.

If you are driving, park up near Spanny's Disco and pay him a visit. He is a really nice guy and he charges the usual US$2 or so for crossing his land and trail maintenance. His little bar is also a good spot for a drink afterwards.

About 20m to the south of Spanny's Bar (to the right as you exit, to the left as you face it), there is a rough vehicle track heading into the woods. This is the start of the trail.

Follow the track past a farm for around ten minutes until it ends with a spur straight ahead and another to the left. Take the trail to the left into the woods, over a couple of small rickety wooden bridges, until you reach some steps with a wooden hand rail. Follow the steps down. Be careful with your footing as this trail is often wet and the steps can be slippery. After another ten minutes you should reach the first waterfall. Surrounded by greenery, and in particular tree ferns, this pool is a lovely spot to cool off.

To get to the second waterfall, walk down to the pool and follow the small concrete path to the right. Negotiate the boulders, the log and the river, and then use the rope and tree roots to help you climb up to the top of the ridge. It is steep and a little tricky, but quite short and good fun. At the top and along and down the ridge to the second waterfall, again use the rope to support and help you. Watch your footing on tree roots and be careful on the last part down to the boulders near the pool.

Jacko Steps (*Difficulty: T: 3; R: 3H; E: 3; D: 2; Rating = 6.9H*) You should engage a guide for this hike, especially if you intend taking on the full loop (see below).

Jacko was one of the most prominent chiefs of the Maroon slaves in the late 18th and early 19th centuries. He fled from captivity into the interior from the estate at Beaubois near Castle Comfort and established a camp on a high plateau near the present-day village of Bells. This plateau, called Jacko Flats, has steep cliffs on three sides, making it a very effective natural fortress. It is from this elevated camp that Jacko directed operations during the Maroon wars of the 1780s and 1810s. The Maroons of Jacko's camp cut a series of high steps out of the cliff face. These steps made ascending the plateau a little easier, but, because they were so steep, made defending the camp easier too. Chief Jacko was eventually captured and killed during an attack by Governor Ainslie on 12 July 1814. The steps to his camp are still there and may be climbed today.

There are two ways to take on this hike. The first is to hike to the steps, descend them down to the river, and then come back the same way. The second way is to make a loop. Once at the bottom of the steps, hike through the Layou River to near the beginning. The latter is the most fun, but it is also the most challenging and should not be attempted in the wet season when the river level is high. There is no way out of the Layou River until you reach the end, so you do not want to take any risks at all with flash flooding or rising water levels. If you decide on the loop, take along a guide. This is really not a good place to get lost or find yourself trapped by the river.

The trailhead is in the village of Bells. If you are coming from Pont Cassé, take the road to Marigot and Melville Hall and, when in Bells, look for the school (on the left) and a snackette decorated in the colours and logos of telecommunications company LIME (on your right). Park up somewhere near the snackette, off the road. For bus information see page 50. Opposite the snackette you will see a wide vehicle track running downhill into a field and towards a building by the river. This is the start.

Follow this track about halfway to the building and look for a spur running towards the river on your right. You should find it roughly where the track curves. Go down to the river and look towards the opposite bank, slightly to the left, and you should see a trail. Cross the river towards it. Watch your footing and look out for deep sections.

Climb up the opposite bank; it is a little steep, but short. At the top follow the trail, but as you look down towards a building look to your right; the trail turns sharply back uphill. It comes to a small clearing and you may see a small wooden gate on your right. Ignore this and head downhill to the left. The trail now runs alongside the grounds of a house and ahead you will see another small wooden house on a hill. Walk right up to it.

This is the home of Mal and Eunace, a lovely Rastafarian couple. Eunace sometimes has freshly picked herbs, juice or bush tea for sale. It is a nice place to relax and enjoy the scenery before heading on your way. If you do not have a guide and are regretting it, speak to them about it.

The trail continues behind their house. It is a steep uphill climb. Stick to the fence on the left and make your way up to the top. You will come to a small clearing with two large trees on either side. Take the track to the left and follow it through the rainforest. At a spur, head to the right. You should come to a deep gully. Follow the track down to the right, cross over it carefully and then climb straight upwards. It looks like there is no track, but this is the way. At the top, you will see the trail again.

Follow it as it meanders through the woodlands of Jacko Flats, where the Maroon leader had his encampment. Sometimes the trail is difficult to follow. If in doubt, stop, look around, and stick to the right. The track now follows a tall, narrow ridge and there are steep drops on either side. Follow it all the way along the ridge. Take your time and watch your footing. The trail will start to head downhill. Look down to your left; you should be able to see the Layou River.

At the end of the ridge you reach the top of Jacko Steps. They are tall and often slippery with fallen leaves. Be careful negotiating your way down. On the second section there is a rope to help you. Follow the steps all the way down to the bottom and then pick up the trail again. It leads you to a small tributary. Head left and you will come out on to the Layou River. Now you must decide whether to head back the way you came or to continue along the river.

Following the river requires crossing it from side to side in order to find the easiest route. It can be deep and the current can be strong in places. River hiking can be quite disorientating and so a knowledgeable guide is essential. Basically, you are walking upstream, back towards Bells. The route back has three straight sections. After the first section it bends to the right, after the second section it turns to the left (it also splits into two for a short distance around the bend), and the last turning is also to the left. As a rule of thumb, always keep the left bank in sight. If you do this you should be fine.

After the first bend to the right, look across the rapids to the left bank. Hidden within a tubular cavern is a waterfall. There is also a great pool near here. This first right turn is deep and an indicator of whether you should continue or not. The best route is to hug the rock face on the right. On the first left turn, where it splits, stick to the river on the left, but take it along the right-hand side. The final segment is quite long but eventually you will reach a sharp curve to the left. You should now also see a field above the left bank. Stick to the left around the corner and, once around it, you should see a building over on the far bank. A little to the right of it is a trail near a large wax apple tree. Head for this, it is your exit point.

Pass the building and greet the owners if they are around. It is only polite to do so and ask permission to pass through their land. They are nice and will let you. Why not ask about buying some wax apples if they are in season? You are now on the wide track that you walked down at the very beginning of the hike and soon you will emerge at the main road by the snackette once again.

10

The Wai'tukubuli National Trail

The Wai'tukubuli National Trail runs from the south of the island at Cachacrou to the northwest at the Cabrits National Park. It is about 200km in length and is split into 14 connected segments. Each segment has its own unique set of challenges as well as areas of historic, cultural and natural interest.

TRAIL STATUS AND UPDATES

At the time of writing the National Trail was nearing completion though practicalities such as a fee system, emergency procedures, contact details, maps and literature were not yet finalised. You can check the National Trail website (*www.trail.agriculture.gov.dm*) and my own for updates (*updates.bradtguides.com/dominica*).

The trail has signposts, regular blue and yellow paint bands, and red segment markers showing you the way. Assuming you will also pick up official trail maps and other such paraphernalia when you come, you should not have too many problems following the route.

SEGMENT 1: SCOTTS HEAD TO SOUFRIERE

(*Difficulty: T: 3; R: 0; E: 4; D: 2; Rating = 5.6*)
Segment 1 follows a route from the isthmus of Cachacrou, up through the village of Scotts Head, and over the peak of Morne Crabier. It passes the historic Bois Cotlette Estate (see page 148) and several farm holdings before finally emerging at the Soufriere Sulphur Springs (see page 146). Crabier will seem a fitting name when you see the number of land crabs you could conceivably catch here, especially on the southern slopes which, at certain times of the day and year, almost seem alive with them. These crabs are used to make the seasonal Creole dish, *crabback*, which is eaten around Creole and independence time.

PRACTICALITIES Segment 1 is a short but challenging beginning to the Wai'tukubuli National Trail. The severe ascent and descent of Morne Crabier is tiring and in places the terrain is loose and uneven. The farmlands and dry forest countryside between the foot of Morne Crabier and the historic Bois Cotlette Estate are, however, very scenic and (almost) make the mountain climb worthwhile. Take plenty of water with you. This is a very dry part of the island and you will certainly need to rehydrate on the climb.

See pages 135 and 136 for places to stay, eat and drink in the south. Public buses pass fairly regularly through both Scotts Head and Soufriere during the daytime.

ATLANTIC
OCEAN

Londonderry
Bay

Pointe
Baptiste

Pagua
Bay

Wesley

Melville Hall
Airport

Marigot

WNT 7

Kalinago
Touna Auté

Concord

Bataca

Crayfish River

Kalinago Barana Auté

Salybia
St Cyr

Gaulette
River

WNT 6

Mahaut River

Sineku

Castle Bruce

Kalinago
Territory

Central
Forest
Reserve

Calibishie

Woodford
Hill

Bense

La Chaudiere ⌇

Northern
Forest
Reserve

Morne Diablotin
National Park

Mosquito
Mountain ▲

DOMINICA

Bells

Jacko Steps ▪

Mathieu
Lake

WNT 8

Thibaud

Pennville

Paix
Bouche

WNT 12

Vieille
Case

Bwa Nef
Falls

Morne
Aux Diables ▲

Bornes

Syndicate
Nature Trail

Syndicate

Morne Diablotin
1447m ▲

Kachibona
Lake

WNT 11

WNT 10

WNT 9

Capuchin

WNT 13

Clifton

WNT 14

Toucari

Cottage

Douglas
Bay

Cabrits
National Park

Fort Shirley

PORTSMOUTH

Prince Rupert
Bay

Picard

Dublanc

Bioche

Colihaut

Coulibistrie

Salisbury

Mero

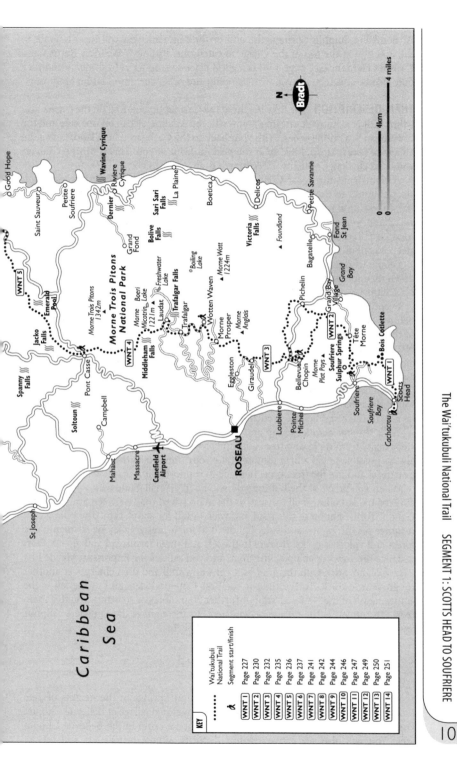

*Caribbean
Sea*

KEY

········· Waï'tukubuli
National Trail

⚑ Segment start/finish

WNT 1	Page 227
WNT 2	Page 230
WNT 3	Page 232
WNT 4	Page 235
WNT 5	Page 236
WNT 6	Page 237
WNT 7	Page 241
WNT 8	Page 242
WNT 9	Page 244
WNT 10	Page 246
WNT 11	Page 247
WNT 12	Page 249
WNT 13	Page 250
WNT 14	Page 251

St Joseph

Mahaut

Massacra

Campbell

Pont Cassé

Soltoun

**Spanny
Falls**

**Jacko
Falls**

**Emerald
Pool**

WNT 5

Good Hope

Saint Sauveur

Petite
Soufriere

Dernier

Wavine Cyrique

Rivière
Cyrique

Grand
Fond

*Morne Trois Pitons
1342m*

**Sari Sari
Falls**

La Plaine

Boetica

Delices

Petite Savanne

**Bolive
Falls**

Freshwater
Lake

*Morne
Micotrin*
1221m ▲

**Middleham
Falls**

*Morne
Boeri*

Laudat

Trafalgar Falls

Trafalgar

*°Boiling
Lake*

▲ *Morne Watt
1224m*

**Victoria
Falls**

▲ *Foundland*

*Morne
Prosper*

Wotten Waven

▲ *Morne
Anglais*

Eggleston

Giraudel

WNT 3

WNT 4

**Morne Trois Pitons
National Park**

Pichelin

Bagatelle

Fond
St Jean

Loubiere

Pointe
Michel

■ **ROSEAU**

✈ **Canefield
Airport**

**Bellevue
Chopin**

*Morne
Plat Pays* ▲

**Sulphur
Springs**

WNT 2

Grand Bay
Village

*Grand
Bay*

**Tête
Morne**

Bois Cotlette

WNT 1

Soufriere

*Soufriere
Bay*

Cachacrou

Scotts
Head

⚑

⚑

N

Bradt

0   4km

0   4 miles

At Soufriere Sulphur Springs, the end of the segment, you will have to walk to the junction at the top of the village to catch one. Rodney's Wellness Retreat and Carrod's Gardens (see page 146) is a good place to stop for refreshments and they may also be able to assist you with camping and other accommodation options.

TRAIL DESCRIPTION The hike begins at the Caribantic building on the Cachacrou isthmus. It is a dramatic starting point with the Atlantic Ocean on one side and the Caribbean Sea on the other. With your back to the Cachacrou headland, facing the village of Scotts Head, look up at the peak in front of you. This is Morne Crabier; your first challenge of many. Deep breath then, ready to go?

A right-hand turn near Chez Wen and Rogers (good local eateries) takes you steeply uphill to the very top of the village. Once there, take a right and then a left, following a rough vehicle track up the mountain slope. Passing through dry woodland, you come to a crest by a dry stone wall where you may be lucky enough to catch a breeze. From here the trail goes downhill for a while before beginning the steep ascent of Morne Crabier via a seemingly endless series of switchbacks.

People who use this trail include charcoal burners who you may meet coming down the mountain with very heavy sacks on their heads. Often you see them early on a Saturday morning when they take their charcoal to Roseau market.

Eventually the switchbacks get shorter and soon a rather special place unfolds before you. An area of lush pasture land, planted rather incongruously on the side of the mountain, seems like an oasis of peace and tranquility. It is a lovely place to rest and catch your breath. To pick up the trail again, you have to head for the top left-hand corner of this field. Look for the track between a large mango tree and a coconut palm. A short but steep section takes you through a patch of banana plants followed by a sharp right turn up a dirt track to a small, tree-covered plateau at the top of the mountain. Before you get there, look to the south. If it is clear, you may be able to catch sight of the French island of Martinique.

Walk straight across the top and begin a very steep descent. Though there are steps made from rocks and tree roots, the ground can be slippery here and it is not always possible to get a firm footing. Take your time, resist the urge to go quickly, be careful and use the trees on either side to support you.

When you arrive at the bottom you will be in a small glade with a wide, grass-covered track. Follow it all the way to the main paved road between Soufriere and Galion. Turn right on to this road and walk uphill for about 1km. The hiking trail resumes on the right-hand side. Follow it along a pretty valley of farmland, dry forest and volcanic rocks. It veers to the left at a small farmstead and after a short distance the views open up a little more and you can see the impressive Morne Plat Pays volcano. Stick with this trail as it runs downhill and then emerges at another rough vehicle track. To the right is the Bois Cotlette Estate and to the left is the continuation of the National Trail. A further 20 minutes or so brings you to a main road. To the left is the village of Soufriere, to the right is the Soufriere Sulphur Springs where Segment 1 ends and Segment 2 begins.

SEGMENT 2: SOUFRIERE TO BELLEVUE CHOPIN

(*Difficulty: T: 2; R: 0; E: 3; D: 4; Rating = 5.6*)
Segment 2 is a long hike from Soufriere Sulphur Springs to the heights of Tete Morne and then across the mountainside to the elevated village of Bellevue Chopin. Parts of this trail were used by Maroons who had a camp in the Bellevue Chopin area. You will also see active sulphur deposits, simple farmsteads and lots of

aromatic bay trees. Just as you may have met charcoal burners and villagers using the trails on Segment 1, here you may well meet people on the way to or returning from their 'gardens'; small allotments or pieces of land where they grow vegetables and *ground provisions*, perhaps rear pigs, goats, graze cows and so on. It is a trail that is functional for many people and allows you, the visitor, to look through a window into every day Dominica.

PRACTICALITIES Segment 2 is quite challenging because it has some steep climbs and it is also quite long. You need to give yourself plenty of time and it is imperative that you carry sufficient water.

Buses frequently pass along the main road at Bellevue Chopin *en route* between Roseau and Grand Bay. Accommodation is limited in this area and so making the trip to Roseau, Geneva or Stowe are your main options (see page 50). It is a short, 20-minute bus ride either way. The area around the bus stop has a couple of small shops and snackettes.

TRAIL DESCRIPTION This segment begins at Soufriere Sulphur Springs. You can either start inside the springs and walk up to the top and then right, or you can follow the wide track at the end of the road, next to the car park. Both meet at the same point. Follow the track up the mountain. On your left you can see the large volcanically active area above the springs. You will also be able to smell the sulphur dioxide in the air.

The trail climbs to the top of the ridge in a series of switchbacks through dry forest and thickets of bamboo. From time to time you are rewarded with great views down to Soufriere. If conditions are good, you can actually see reef formations in the bay.

When you reach the top of the ridge, pass over it and walk down into the village of Tete Morne. Up to your right is the Palmiste Estate and Morne Vert (see page 147 for hike directions). Walk down the village road past the stone cross and look for the trail sign on the left. Follow this side road a short distance to a rather pretty avenue of bay trees and look for the trail sign, once again on the left, in between the bay. If you have never come across bay before, take a leaf, crunch it up in the palm of your hand and then smell it.

Follow the trail downhill and cross over a dry river gully. The trail undulates a little and comes to a small glade. Stick to the left and enjoy views of the interior and the southeast. Skirt around the perimeter of a second glade and then descend very steeply down a narrow ridge. If you suffer from vertigo it may be a good idea not to look down to your left at this point. The track down this ridge is tricky and it is important to take your time and be sure of your footing. At the bottom you will arrive in another dry river gully. Follow it and walk through a small farmstead before coming to a paved road. Go left and then look for a continuation of the trail on your right, running along the left-hand side of a large house.

Follow the track to a junction and veer left, ignoring the more beaten trail to the right. It may be a little overgrown around here. Stick to the wide path and pass beneath some dangling ficus vines. Eventually the track will curve to the right near a house and become a paved road. Walk down it for a short distance to a junction and then take the trail to the left along a dirt track. To your right you should see fields of yams or dasheens and have good views of Grand Bay beyond. Continue along this well used farm trail, skirting plots of vegetables and *ground provisions*. Look out for sorrel, low-growing bushes with deep red flowers that are used to make a seasonal drink at Christmas time. To your right you should be able to see the Atlantic Ocean and ahead of you the verdant mountains of Dominica's interior.

10

At a sharp turn, follow the trail down a steep hill and alongside more fields of dasheen until you come to a paved feeder road. Go right and follow it downhill to another paved road where you must turn left. Walk uphill to a junction. You have a choice of taking a right and following an alternative (and slightly longer) route to Bellevue Chopin via the communities of Pichelin and New Florida. I recommend going left via Morpo, but it does involve a rather long and steep climb up the feeder road. Morpo is a peak to the south of Grand Bay that was once the domain of escaped slaves and is now where local farmers eke out a living. Follow the road all the way up to the top – it will take you at least 30 minutes to get there. The views from the rest area are great. Take a seat and look down on the Grand Bay coastline. If it is a clear day you can also see Martinique to the south.

Opposite the benches you will see an old feeder road. This is the route to Bellevue Chopin. Starting quite wide and then narrowing to a trail, the journey through lush woodland is an enjoyable one. Formerly a Maroon trace, this track has a bit of history. Follow it upwards past a small cave and around the edges of a river gully that is crowded with tall tree ferns. Some sections of the trail are very narrow where they cling to the steep mountain slopes of Morne Plat Pays. You will come to the apex of a bend where the route passes through a cleft and then heads back along a pretty woodland trail and down some rather steep steps. Views of the mountainous interior open up ahead of you. The very pointed peak is Morne Anglais which is the southernmost volcano of the Morne Trois Pitons National Park (see page 146). To the right of it are Morne John, Morne Watt and Foundland.

The small clearing below, with what looks like a wall, is the remains of an old quarry, or a 'tarrish pit'. The trail widens and runs downhill and turns into a rough feeder road. As it reaches the outskirts of Bellevue Chopin it becomes a paved road all the way to the main junction and bus stop which marks the end of this hike.

SEGMENT 3: BELLEVUE CHOPIN TO WOTTEN WAVEN

(*Difficulty: T: 3; R: 1; E: 3; D: 4; Rating = 6.9*)
In terms of distance, this is one of the longest segments of the National Trail. It begins in the elevated community of Bellevue Chopin and introduces you to some of the organic farming for which this area has become known. Following a Maroon trail you walk from Bellevue Chopin across the foothills of Morne Anglais to the flower village of Giraudel. From there you drop down into the River Claire Valley and then climb up to the farmlands of Morne Prosper. The final stretch is a descent to the volcanically active spa village of Wotten Waven. Along the route you can enjoy great views of Roseau, the Roseau Valley, the west coast and the peaks of the Morne Trois Pitons National Park. You will also meet villagers and farmers, giving you a little insight into the lives of people who live and work here.

PRACTICALITIES Duration and the steep River Claire Valley combine to give this hike its high rating. It is certainly long so you should set off early and take plenty of water. You can also pick up refreshments in Giraudel *en route*. The descent into the River Claire Valley is long and steep; there may be ropes to help you in places. The climb out and up to Morne Prosper is a little shorter but no less steep and there may also be ropes to assist you.

Public buses run frequently between Roseau, Wotten Waven and Trafalgar. There are several accommodation choices at the end of this hike, including camping, and you will find them on page 116. The Roseau Valley has a number of restaurants, bars and local eateries and, if your legs are aching after your long hike, you can enjoy a natural hot bath or even a massage here (see page 89).

TRAIL DESCRIPTION The trailhead for Segment 3 is located on the main road through Bellevue Chopin by the bus stops and snackettes. Follow the wide vehicle track from the sign. It is an easy and pleasant introduction to the walk. Notice the rainforest vegetation: tree ferns, bromeliads, ginger lilies and heliconia. You will also pass several bamboo thickets and thick clusters of *impatiens* that fill the verges with vivid colours. At the first junction, stick to the main track and go down, rather than up to the right. The rainforest vegetation becomes even more prevalent as you move away from the village and further into the bush.

Soon you will come to an organic composting facility. This is an integral component of the Bellevue Chopin organic farming community (see page 139 for details). The production of organic pesticides and fertilisers is small and only serves the local farmers at present. With investment the composting facility could become a more commercial enterprise. If you get a chance to come back, you should take the tour. It is very interesting and well worth supporting.

You will come to a three-way junction. Take the track that goes straight up. There are a few gentle ups and downs and it becomes a little overgrown in places, but it is fairly easy going. Eventually the track comes to a T-junction. Take the trail to the right. You now move from wide feeder road to forest trail and an environment of semi-deciduous forest mixed with rainforest vegetation.

The trail begins a long uphill climb through the forest to the brow of a hill where you can rest for a while before heading down again. Take another break where the trail evens out for a stretch and enjoy the serenity of the forest.

The terrain gets a little muddy in places and you have to negotiate a few loose stones and tree roots. Be careful not to stumble. It is always best to step between tree roots rather than on them as they can be surprisingly slippery. Follow the steep slope down to a dry creek, be careful on the rocks, and then walk alongside some bamboo thickets. Soon you will come to a bridge over another dry river bed. It is rare, but this river can flood quite violently after heavy rains. Once you are over the bridge, look out for all the colourful ginger lilies and anthuriums.

Another climb begins. It is quite steep and the terrain is a little troublesome in places. You will see anthuriums growing all around as you follow the contours of the mountainside and climb up to the village of Giraudel. Views begin to open up on your left; you can see the pointed volcanic peak of Morne Canot and the larger Morne Plat Pays further to the left as you look back towards Bellevue Chopin.

A short but steep climb brings you to the outskirts of Giraudel. At the road, head uphill to the right and follow it to a T-junction. Go left and, when you reach the main village road, turn right. Follow the main road through the charming village of Giraudel. You will pass a couple of snackettes where you can take a rest and top up with liquids if you need them. Follow the main road right out of the village and continue along it for about 1km until you see a sign pointing to a road on the right. From this road there are good views of Roseau and the west coast. Pass the church and keep going, following the main road all the way as it curves around to the left and continues to wind its way uphill. After a while the paved road ends and a rougher vehicle track continues. Very soon it levels out again and you can take a breather whilst enjoying more great views; this time of Morne Trois Pitons, Morne Micotrin and the west coast. If you look carefully you should be able to make out a village on a high narrow ridge between you and the mountains beyond. This is Morne Prosper, where you are heading next.

Stick to the main track and head downhill until you reach a fork. Take the track to the left and follow it downhill. After about 20 minutes or so you should come to a sign pointing to the right. Climb the bank and pick up the forest trail.

You are now making a rather long and steep descent to the River Claire. A series of switchbacks and rather severe slopes finally brings you to the bottom of this valley. Notice how the vegetation shifts from rather dry semi-deciduous woodland at the top to much wetter rainforest vegetation at the bottom. Your legs will be tired after the long hike so it is important you control your descent and make your way steadily and carefully down.

You will reach a trail junction. To the left is a wide track that runs to the community of Elmshall in the Roseau Valley (about 45 minutes away). The National Trail continues to the right. Very soon you will arrive at the river crossing. So long as the day is not closing in on you, this is a fabulous place to stop for a rest. The River Claire is really beautiful and the series of cascades and pools upstream are a real joy. Refresh yourself before moving on. You have a steep climb ahead, but try to comfort yourself with the fact that it is the last major climb on this segment.

Over the bridge, pick up the trail and climb the ridge up to Morne Prosper via a series of switchbacks and rather steep steps. The ascent is hard but it is shorter than the descent down to the river. You will know when you are close to the top of the ridge when you begin to smell the lemon grass.

Catch your breath on the benches at the top and enjoy the view of Morne Anglais. The houses you see along the western slopes of the mountain are actually Giraudel, where you have just come from.

If you are sitting on the bench looking at the view, you must now follow the trail to your left. Where it forks, go left again and you will come to a paved road and some houses. Follow the road to the junction. This is the main road through Morne Prosper. Turn right and follow the main road uphill to a four-way junction. Go straight on up the rough feeder road. Stick to this track as it runs alongside farmlands and then around a bend to the left, where you come to another junction at a sign for the Morne Hill Farm access road. To the right is the optional trail to Morne Nicholls and the Boiling Lake (see page 129) which you may not have the time and energy for right now! A cold beer and a hot sulphur bath probably sound far more appealing so take the road straight ahead down the hill. You should have great views of farmland, Morne Micotrin and the village of Laudat across the Roseau Valley.

The feeder road soon ends and turns into a rough track. A short, steep climb up the hill brings you to more farmland. Head along the edge of the fields until you reach a fork. Go left and walk alongside another vegetable plot to another fork. Follow the track to the left along the edge of the field to the tree line. Follow the wide woodland path downhill. It is quite steep in places and there are some steps to negotiate. The woodlands are beautiful, however. Can you smell the sulphur yet? You will soon, and this is a good sign; it means you are near the end of the journey.

This area is very picturesque. Look at the vegetation to your left. You should see a whole forest of tree ferns and colourful ginger lilies. The village of Wotten Waven also comes into view now. As you approach, you begin to get a sense of how volcanically active it is around here; the smells, the colour of the soil.

A short downhill stretch brings you to a stream. Cross over and climb the short but steep hill on the far side. You will now arrive at the rear of some houses. Follow the fence and the signs to the main road. The end of the trail and the main village junction (and bus stop) are to your left.

(Difficulty: T: 2; R: 1; E: 3; D: 3; Rating = 5.6)

Segment 4 runs from the spa village of Wotten Waven at the head of the Roseau Valley all the way to Pont Cassé in the interior. It connects you with some of Dominica's most notable hiking trails and natural attractions. Optional additions to this segment therefore include Trafalgar Falls (see page 121), Ti Tou Gorge (see page 119), the Boiling Lake trail (see page 122), the Freshwater Lake (see page 126), the Boeri Lake (see page 124), Morne Micotrin (see page 128) and Middleham Falls (see page 127).

From Wotten Waven the trail leads you to Trafalgar and then it climbs steeply up to Dominica's highest village, Laudat. Primary gateway to the Morne Trois Pitons National Park, Laudat is a village where most hikers end up sooner or later. From here the trail passes through the Middleham Estate and skirts the Morne Trois Pitons National Park, winding its way through a truly beautiful area of rainforest until it emerges at Pont Cassé in the shadow of Morne Trois Pitons itself.

PRACTICALITIES There are a couple of steep ups and downs on this hike but many stretches are in fact quite flat or gently undulating. River crossings are few and do not present much of a hazard. A great optional diversion is to visit the Middleham Falls which are just a 15–20 minute hike from the main trail.

Buses are frequent at Pont Cassé and run in all directions to and from the capital. Accommodation, food and drink are very limited, however. One option would be to make advance arrangements with Crescent Moon Cabins in Sylvania (see page 206). Harmony Villa (see page 205) is not far away but perhaps a little beyond the budget of most hikers. Another option is to stay in Castle Bruce (Domcan's is an affordable option, see page 156) and then bus it back to this spot the following morning.

TRAIL DESCRIPTION From Wotten Waven, follow the paved road across the Roseau Valley to Trafalgar, passing Screw's Sulphur Spa and the Shangri-La Resort along the way. When you reach the road junction, left is Trafalgar and the continuation of the trail, right is Trafalgar Falls and Papillote Gardens, both just 15 minutes or so away. Follow the road left into Trafalgar and look for signs on the right leading you up through the narrow backstreets of the village. The paved road climbs and then ends, turning into a trail and then ascending very steeply via a series of switchbacks. When you reach the top of the ridge there are good views down to your right (you are up above Papillote). The trail evens out for a stretch before making a final short climb to the farmlands of Laudat. Follow the signs to a paved feeder road which heads into the village. You will come to a junction by a bar. To the right is Ti Tou Gorge and the Boiling Lake trailhead. The National Trail continues to the left. At the next junction go right and follow the road uphill until you reach the Lake View Lodge and another road junction. To the right are the Freshwater Lake, Boeri Lake, Chemin L'Etang and Morne Micotrin (see references above). The National Trail continues along the main road to the left. Follow it until you see the signs on your right for both the National Trail and the Middleham Falls.

Follow the long feeder road all the way to the Middleham Falls trailhead. Once on the trail proper you will come to a shallow river crossing. Take the trail uphill via a series of steps and switchbacks until you come to the flat. Continue all the way to the sign-posted trail junction. To the left is the trail down to Middleham Falls, straight on goes to Cochrane, and to the right is the continuation of the National Trail.

10

The next section is very beautiful. Though there are no views, the rainforest is quite magical. Listen out for jaco parrots and the distinctive call of the mountain whistler. The forest contains a wide variety of tree species and a lack of dense undergrowth means that you can see quite far into it. Stop and rest; listen to the sounds of nature. Look for movement; perhaps you will see an agouti foraging for fallen fruit or woodland birds such as the trembler or the forest thrush. Seeds dropping beneath *gommier* trees is a sign parrots are feeding in the canopy above; they are usually in pairs and the sudden sound of squawking means they are likely to take flight.

The trail climbs very gently up a ridge in the heart of the Middleham Estate before descending again. You will come to a junction where there is a shelter and rest area. Straight on is Sylvania and the main road between Roseau and Pont Cassé; it takes about 20 minutes to get there. To the right is the continuation of the National Trail. The route follows the national parks boundary for a distance before leaving it near a very large *gommier* tree (see how people have been bleeding it for its sap) and then heading quite steeply uphill. As you climb you will pass the large buttress roots of magnificent *chatanier* trees. Pay attention to the route; it is easy to stray off track if your head is down. Take a breather on the benches and complete the ascent by squeezing through tall trees and huge boulders and finally using ropes to help you get to the top. Here you will find another covered rest area. Now follow the trail sharply down the other side of the ridge until you come to a bridge spanning a deep gorge. Once over the other side, there is another river gully and rather pretty cascade to negotiate. After this the trail is very easy-going all the way to Pont Cassé where it emerges at the traffic island. Segment 5 continues to the right along the road to Castle Bruce.

SEGMENT 5: PONT CASSÉ TO CASTLE BRUCE

(*Difficulty: T: 2; R: 2; E: 1; D: 3; Rating = 5.0*)
Segment 5 follows a historic route that was originally used by the indigenous Kalinago, then by bands of escaped slaves (Maroons, or *negres marrons*), and more recently by people travelling from the east coast village of Castle Bruce to Roseau where they would meet the newly constructed Imperial Road at Pont Cassé. One of the many benefits of the Wai'tukubuli National Trail is that it keeps historic routes like this one alive and allows both residents and visitors to experience and enjoy the journey taken by many before them.

PRACTICALITIES This is a fairly easy trail, gently undulating with few steep inclines. The main challenges on this journey are the river and stream crossings, of which there are many, though few are especially deep. At the time of writing few of these crossings had bridges of any kind. This may well have changed by the time this book goes to print. (See *updates.bradtguides.com/dominica* for updates on the Wai'tukubuli National Trail.)

Buses pass through Castle Bruce fairly frequently to and from Roseau. Accommodation is reasonably limited (see page 155) though Domcan's is certainly an affordable option for hikers (it is located on the highway above the village). You can also eat there. Castle Bruce has a number of small shops, bars and snackettes. See page 157 for information about where to eat and drink.

TRAIL DESCRIPTION From the trailhead near Pont Cassé, head down into the rainforest. It is a very typical rainforest environment; usually quite wet and with dense vegetation on either side of the route. It is easy to imagine how runaway slaves (Maroons) managed to hide out in forests like this for as long as they did.

The trail emerges from the forest for a brief period and offers views across the interior to the north where you will see the conical peak of Morne Negres Marrons (also known as Morne Laurent), so named because it was once the location of a Maroon camp. The trail continues through the forest, interrupted briefly as it passes across a feeder road and the remains of a farm. After crossing numerous small rivers and streams, you will eventually meet up with the Emerald Pool trail where you have the option of taking a very short diversion to enjoy this frequently visited natural attraction (see page 119). Follow the National Trail signs, passing a viewpoint, until you come out into an area of grassland that runs alongside and eventually meets the main highway to the east in an area called Fond Melle. Follow the road for about 1.5km before heading back into the forest. (Look for a sign on the right-hand side of the road).

The trail descends rather sharply down to the L'Or River after leaving the road. Look to the left and you will see where this pretty waterway joins the Fond Figues River to create the Belle Fille. This convergence of several rivers and streams is quite lovely and, if you are feeling a little hot and bothered, is a great place to cool off. Across the other side of the river the trail continues through rainforest vegetation and there are nice views of the river down to your left. Follow the undulating track as it continues along the course of the river. It will even out and cross a paved road by a bridge. Keep going straight, sticking to the river. Look out for all the tree ferns and heliconia. It is a lovely forest and river environment.

You will come to a river crossing with some gorgeous cascades and pools. Make a short diversion to the left to take a look at the river gorge. Over the other side, the trail climbs quite high above the river before descending again, crossing a couple of small streams along the way. You will come to a croton-lined path that runs through a small farmstead where they grow yams and seasoning peppers. Pass by the small wooden house (don't worry about the dogs) and greet the owners if they are around. Crossing some rather rough ground, head back into the bush and then return to the river where you must make a crossing. On the other side you will arrive at Mr Cooper's farm. He is a lovely man and his family has lived and farmed this area for generations. Follow the trail around and through his farm, crossing a small stream and heading towards a tiny white house. Pass through the gardens and to the right of the house. You will come out on to the main highway once again.

Head right towards Castle Bruce and follow the road for about 2km. Once on the straight section, look for a small bridge. Around 100m beyond it, on the right, the trail leaves the road and heads into banana plantations. Follow the wide feeder road in a straight line all the way through these farmlands. It is completely flat and very easy going. Soon you may hear the sound of the ocean. Cross a small river and come to a paved road. The Atlantic is in front of you, the road to San Sauveur is to your right, and Castle Bruce is to your left. Head left and at the junction go right (if you have had enough, this is a good place to catch a bus). Follow the road past St David's Bay and into the village. Just after the old Roman Catholic church, take the road downhill on the right and follow it for about 3km as it meanders through and around the lower part of the village. Eventually it joins the main highway again. To the right is the beginning of Segment 6.

SEGMENT 6: CASTLE BRUCE TO HATTON GARDEN

(*Difficulty: T: 2; R: 2; E: 2; D: 4; Rating = 6.3*)
This segment passes through the Kalinago Territory (see page 158). It brings you either through or very close to most of the Territory's villages and it also incorporates the

Kalinago Barana Auté (see page 160) and L'Escalier Tete Chien (see page 162). The route follows woodland, village and farm tracks that offer great views of the east coast, and it also follows sections of the main highway through the Territory. You will meet Kalinago people at work or at rest, you will have an opportunity to see and perhaps purchase craft products such as tree fern carvings, calabash bowls and *larouma* basketware, and you will get a taste of what life is like for Dominica's indigenous people.

PRACTICALITIES This is not an especially difficult hike, it is just long. There are a few small river and stream crossings, there are some short but steep ups and downs, and in a few places the terrain is a little slippery. Start very early. This is key, especially if you wish to take your time and enjoy the views, the crafts, and meeting people as well as visit the Kalinago Barana Auté and L'Escalier Tete Chien.

The trail emerges at Hatton Garden where buses run fairly frequently between Marigot and Roseau. Silks Hotel is hiker friendly and camping pitches are available. Pagua Bay House is not exactly budget but it is nice and very convenient.

TRAIL DESCRIPTION The trailhead is at the Richmond Estate to the north of Castle Bruce, just before you enter the Kalinago Territory. Look for a sign on the right and a wide section of old paved track that was actually the original coastal road. Pass alongside plantains, coconut palms and breadfruit trees until you come to some gates and a house. Note the trespasser sign; it seems a bit harsh. Pass to the left of the gates and follow the track downhill through woodland. It gets quite steep, muddy and slippery in some places so watch it. At the bottom of this slope you come to a river. Cross over it carefully and climb up the short hill before heading downhill again. Soon you will hear the sound of the ocean and then you will see it on your right-hand side.

The trail levels out for a stretch. Ignore spurs and stick to the main track as it meanders downhill through coastal woodland and coconut palms towards the sea. Continue downhill, again it is quite steep, until you come close to the shoreline. The National Trail continues to the left but you will also see a track on your right that goes down to the sea at Raymond Bay. Walk alongside the pretty Madjini River and cross the bridge. Chill out for a while and catch your breath before continuing up the clear trail. Notice how all the trees and shrubs have been shaped by the trade winds. This is very typical of the littoral woodland all along the exposed east coast. Climb a short, rocky and rather muddy path that can be quite slick in the wet until it becomes paved and meets up with the main highway through the Kalinago Territory.

At the road, go right and head to Sineku. A short walk brings you to the trailhead for L'Escalier Tete Chien, which is also your turning point. By the way, if you are asked by the drinkers at the bar if you need a guide, you don't. Follow the wide track down to the L'Escalier Tete Chien reception buildings. Walk past them and look for a trail sign on your left. If you know your trees, it is near a large mango. The track straight ahead continues to L'Escalier Tete Chien (ten minutes away – see page 162).

The National Trail continues through coastal woodland with occasional views on your right. Again some of the downhill stretches can be a little steep and slippery. You will come to a junction. The National Trail goes to the left and there is a track down to the sea on your right. You will be able to see the volcanic formations that are very typical along this coast.

Stick to the left and follow the signs. The trail now follows the coast, up and down a series of river gullies. It is a bit of a plod and not very interesting, but you are rewarded with nice coastal scenery from time to time. You will also cross a couple of small streams. Eventually the trail widens and you find yourself walking away from the sea through fields of bananas, coconut palms, paw-paw and mango. And then you arrive at the main road again, this time near the village of Mahaut River.

Turn right and follow the road downhill. You will pass the craft shop and home of Israel and Victoria Joseph. Israel carves tree ferns (known locally as *fougère*, or *fwigè*) into masks, plant holders and reliefs. His work is excellent. Victoria makes traditional *larouma* basketware (you can see a short film I made about them on *updates.bradtguides.com/dominica*).

At the bottom of the hill, just around the bend, pick up the trail again on the right-hand side. Follow the wide track downhill to the Mahaut River. Cross over and then follow the trail uphill until you come to the rear of the Sineku Primary School. Up above the school you will see the roof of the Mahaut River Church. On the right-hand side of the school you should see a sign. Pass between two large thickets of bamboo and follow the trail to a small river. Cross and head uphill again. Ignore spurs and continue straight until you come to some houses. Follow the paved road. Enjoy the heliconias, crotons, ginger lilies, and banana plants that fill the verges with colour. Once again, you will arrive at the main road.

Turn right and follow the highway. Look out for further craft stalls as well as fresh fruit and vegetables for sale. Try a jelly coconut; the water is refreshing and it may give you the burst of energy you probably need by now. Continue along the highway to the community of Gaulette River and look for a trail sign on the right-hand side near a bus stop. Follow the paved vehicle track downhill. The track curves to the left around a playing field and becomes a trail that runs downhill for quite a distance towards the sea. Enjoy nice coastal views of Pointe Belair and Gros L'Ilet before arriving at the very pretty Gaulette River. Take care crossing and then follow the trail uphill. Watch your head. At the top of the ravine keep left and keep going uphill. The landscape opens up to farmland and you will come to some dwelling houses. Take the route uphill to the left and rejoin the main highway in the settlement of St Cyr.

Go right and, just after the Salybia Primary School, look for a trail sign on the right. A wide vehicle track runs quite steeply downhill. At a junction, go straight and continue downhill towards the sea until you come to the farm of Mr and Mrs Francis. Hopefully they are around because they are a lovely couple. They have some picnic tables on a piece of flat grassland next to their house which has nice coastal views and is the perfect place for a rest and refreshments. Mr or Mrs Francis may have fresh fruits and juice for sale. Mr Francis likes to tell visitors about the area as well as explain a little about Kalinago history and culture. Offer a little 'contribution' if you can.

THE 'CARIB WAR'

On 19 September 1930 a rather heavy-handed attempt by armed policemen to search for and confiscate contraband, namely smuggled rum and tobacco, turned into a pitch battle with local people. The police retaliated by firing their weapons, killing two Kalinago and injuring two others. Incensed, the Kalinago beat the policemen, who somehow managed to escape. The Crown Colony Administrator perpetuated the heavy-handedness of the affair when he decided to call on a British naval vessel, *HMS Delhi*, which was in the area, to lend assistance. The *Delhi* arrived firing flares across the coastline to frighten the Kalinago and landing marines to round up those who were suspected of being the troublemakers. The incident became known as the 'Carib Uprising' or the 'Carib War'.

Continue downhill and pass a memorial to the 'Carib War' of 1930 (see box on page 239). Follow this coastal bush and woodland stretch, ignoring spurs and sticking to the main track.

Be careful on the rocks as you approach the pretty Salybia River. Cross the bridge. Notice the small shrine cut in the rockface and follow the track to a junction. The road to the right comes to a dead end at the river mouth. It is worth a short trip down to see the views of the coast. Follow the road uphill. You will soon catch sight of a cemetery. On your left you may also see the ruins of the original Roman Catholic church that was built in the latter half of the 19th century. It has been engulfed by bush which is unfortunate as it has some interesting architectural features as well as a pretty mural that is still largely intact on an internal wall.

Follow the track uphill to the new church. It is a very interesting building, also with murals inside and out. Look out for Faustulus Frederick's Unique Souvenir Shop. Mr Frederick is a former Kalinago chief and is one of the best exponents of calabash bowl carving and design on the island (along with Hilroy Fingal, see page 27). Pay him a visit if you can.

Look for a trail sign to the right of the church, opposite the mural. Follow it uphill and go right at a junction. You will come to a very interesting wooden dwelling house on stilts. The trail passes to the left of it and then up the bank on the far side. You will come to more houses. Bear left along the wide track. This settlement is Crayfish River.

The road becomes paved as it climbs uphill and then joins up with the main road leading down to the Kalinago Barana Auté. Turn right at this junction and follow this rather steep road all the way down to the reception building. You now have a choice of touring the Kalinago Barana Auté (see page 160 for details) or continuing on your journey. (Not that I would ever deliberately lead you astray on these hikes but I feel it is only right to inform you that the KBA has a bar.)

The National Trail continues up the road to the left of the reception building, across the Crayfish River and up past the *karbet*, *ajoupa* and cassava press structures to the very end of the paved road. Look for a trail on the left through a field which can sometimes be quite overgrown. Notice all the colourful wild flowers, a variety of heliconia, as you pass through. Stick to the main track as it curves away from the sea and heads inland and reaches a brook. Cross over and follow the uphill path until you come to the Buluku River where there are some pretty cascades. Cross over and follow the trail to a small clearing by a house. There is a junction here. Ignore the trail immediately to the left and take the one on the right of it, on the outside. On your right you will see a large field of passionfruit vines; on your left are plantains. At another clearing the track becomes paved and continues to the left. Follow it all the way uphill until it comes to the main highway at Bataca.

Take a left (yes, left) and follow the main road for about 1km. Look for a sign on the right and follow the road uphill. Keep going straight up the Horseback Ridge Road towards the Bataca water tower where you will see a junction. Go right up to the tower and then look for a trail on the left just before you reach it. Follow it downhill. Look for a spur on the left and keep going down. Now look for another spur, this time on the right. Some parts of this descent can be very steep so take care. The views across to the north are great. (Look for some communications masts in the distance. You will come to them on Segment 7.) Follow the stream down to the bottom of the hill where the trail widens and crosses some rather rough open terrain. At a junction take the wide track to the right and follow it alongside the Pagua River which should be on your left. The track climbs for a short stretch but then flattens out. It can be swampy around here. After passing through a banana plantation you come to a main road. To your right is the road to Antrizle, Atkinson and the Kalinago Territory. To your left is Hatton Garden, the end of this segment and the start of Segment 7. Take a left, cross the bridge, then take a right at the junction. The start of Segment 7 is on your left. This road heads towards Marigot

SEGMENT 7: HATTON GARDEN TO FIRST CAMP

(*Difficulty: T: 2; R: 2; E: 3; D: 3; Rating = 6.3*)
This segment of the National Trail runs between the Hatton Garden Estate and the farmlands of Hanover in the forested hillsides to the southwest of Marigot. It passes through farmland, wet and dry forest habitats, and over rivers. Regions in this area such as First Camp, Captain Bruce, La Guerre, Gregg and Newcastle reflect a history of exploration, battles, Maroon leaders and lands that were named after places back home during colonial times. The trail itself is a combination of old hunting tracks, farm feeder roads, and historic traces. You can expect to see and hear jaco parrots as well as meet farmers and learn a little about what they are growing. There are also some nice views of the northeastern coastline as well as westwards across the interior.

PRACTICALITIES The most difficult parts of this trail are the rather steep ups and downs where it crosses ridges and river gullies. When crossing farmland please do not help yourself to anything you see growing there, nor leave the trail for a closer look.

At First Camp there are no hotels, buses, shops or restaurants. There may be plans to set up a campsite here in the future but at present your only real option is to opt for accommodation in the northeast (see page 177) and then get a ride back here if you plan to continue on Segment 8. Look out for updates on updates.bradtguides.com/dominica.

TRAIL DESCRIPTION This segment begins in Hatton Garden, close to the shoreline of Pagua Bay. Look for the trailhead between the river bridge and the sea. Follow the vehicle track to its end, ignoring any spurs, and cross over the Marechal River which has been running towards the ocean on your right-hand side. The forest trail climbs gradually and emerges into an open valley of abandoned farmland. Round a corner and cross a small brook. Pass between some cocoa trees and then carefully cross another small stream before climbing up a steep hill. It can get a little overgrown here. Stick to the tree-line on the left. The trail heads back into the forest and climbs through deciduous woodland and rainforest via a couple of switchbacks. Around a corner descend with care into a second, rather pretty river valley and cross over a small river.

After passing through more overgrown and abandoned farmland, head back into the forest and begin climbing up a ridge. The views start to open up a little more. Pass through a small banana plantation and come to a feeder road. Go right and follow it for about 500m, keeping an eye out for a sign on your left. Take the steep trail uphill towards a line of coconut palms along the ridge line. You come to another vehicle track at the top. Go left and then left again after just a few yards. It is a short but steep climb. There are good views of Melville Hall Airport and the northeast coastline on your right.

You will come to a communications mast. Walk around the perimeter and follow the feeder road. At the junction go left and walk towards another mast. There are good views all around. As you face the mast: Morne Diablotin is at 3 o'clock; Morne Aux Diables is at 4 o'clock; Pagua Bay is at 9 o'clock; and at 12 o'clock, behind the mast, is Horseback Ridge in the Kalinago Territory (if you hiked Segment 6, this is where you came from). Follow the road. On your right is a banana plantation. Say hi to Alex if he is working his land. The track becomes paved and there are cocoa trees on your left. At the main feeder road junction, go left and then almost immediately right.

The trail now passes through a farm belonging to the Walter family. It is a large citrus and banana farm that also has lots of cocoa and breadfruit trees as well as less common fruits such as golden apple, known locally as *pom sitè*, which makes a very refreshing drink. Creeping along the ground between fruit trees and banana plants you may also see pumpkins. A major attraction to hikers, yet a pest to the farm itself, is the number of jaco parrots in this area. You are guaranteed to see and hear them flying around so have your camera or binoculars at the ready. Whilst they are an attraction to visitors, you may wish to spare a thought for citrus farms like this one. They can lose fairly substantial portions of their crops to marauding jaco parrots.

As you exit the farm and descend into a river gully you will notice a dramatic transition from farmland to a wet forest habitat. This area has some very large heliconia species growing alongside the trail. Cross over the Manitipo River and begin a steep ascent to the top of a ridge where you will notice the habitat changes once again. Here the forest is a drier woodland habitat that reflects its proximity to the coast. A short descent brings you to a viewpoint where you can see the Atlantic Ocean, Melville Hall Airport and the very flat French island of Marie-Galante. Descending further you will reach a junction where the National Trail heads inland once again. The vehicle track to the right is a feeder road that will bring you to the coastal village of Marigot.

Back in the forest the trail makes a gradual ascent. Look out for torch ginger on your right-hand side. As the trail becomes a little steeper, the views behind you open up and you can see the island's northeastern coastline. At a junction with some farmland, the National Trail heads to the right. To the left you can see the depths of the interior and the ridgeline running up to Mang Peak. Curving back around into the forest, the trail climbs steeply to the top of a ridge. Notice the *gommier* trees (they are tall and straight with rounded trunks and occasionally seeping white sap), *balata* (the bullet tree, known for its strength), *bwa bandé* (Dominica's now notorious 'natural Viagra'), and the *savonette* whose roots used to be used by the Kalinago to stun river fish before catching them.

Begin a long descent into a river valley. It is steep in places. Pass through an environment of wet forest, tree ferns and tall *gommier* and enjoy views to the north. The trail continues descending until it finally reaches a junction. The National Trail continues to the left. After a flat stretch the trail meanders downhill to a lovely river. Across the river it is a short but steep climb up the ridge, followed by a downhill trail through the forest until you reach open farmland. The trail now turns into a feeder road that passes between farms. Please do not stray from the path and on to these farmlands.

The vehicle track runs downhill until it fords the Coffee River. On the other side, it climbs all the way up to a junction with another feeder road. To the left is First Camp and the start of Segment 8. To the right, the feeder road passes through the Vauxhall and Sanderlea estates before rounding the back of the Melville Hall Airport runway and emerging at the Atlantic coast.

SEGMENT 8: FIRST CAMP TO PETITE MACOUCHERIE

(*Difficulty: T: 4H; R: 2; E: 4; D: 4; Rating = 8.8H*)
Running right across Dominica through the Northern Forest Reserve, this segment is about as remote and unspoilt as it gets. It begins in the farmland of

Hanover and First Camp on the east coast and ends in the elevated farmland of Petite Macoucherie, high above Mero, on the west coast. The rainforest *en route* is beautiful with magnificent specimens of *gommier, chatanier, karapit* and other trees, and the canopy sometimes seems alive with parrots; mostly jaco, though sisserou have also been heard here. The trail reaches its highest point at the summit of Mosquito Mountain where rainforest is replaced by montane thicket and a wet covering of mosses and lichens.

This is a trail that really began as a hunter's trace. You will come across pits that were dug to trap wild pigs and you may even see signs of the animals themselves. Look for evidence of digging in wet soil around tree roots where they have been looking for worms. You may also see trees where moss or lichen has been worn off the bark from pigs rubbing themselves against it for a good scratch. Notice how high the marks are; big pigs. You are unlikely to meet them, however, as they are elusive and very easily spooked. Hunters still operate in this area but they no longer use pit traps.

PRACTICALITIES The ratings indicate this to be Dominica's toughest hike and I think this is right. It is very long; between seven and nine hours, meaning you must set off at first light in order to reach the end before darkness falls. The first four hours are fairly easy going; the trail undulates without too much severity and there is a cluster of river crossings around a third of the way. The ascent and descent of Mosquito Mountain is severe and very draining after four to five hours of remote rainforest hiking. It is very steep and you must use both upper and lower body strength, together with a very focused mind, to make it. From the summit a very narrow ridge line with tricky terrain maintains your altitude and concentration for a further hour before dropping you back down into the rainforest. From there, thankfully, the trail is easier again.

This segment needs proper planning; do not take it lightly. I recommend a guide for all but the most experienced and well-equipped hikers.

The starting and ending points of this segment are also remote. There are no public buses and even farm vehicles are rare. You must therefore arrange for a drop-off, pick-up or carry camping gear. At the time of writing there are plans to establish simple camping pitches at the beginning, mid-way, and end points, together with a couple of simple wooden shelters at the eastern base of Mosquito Mountain. Check online for updates. The rivers and streams you cross *en route* are all good for drinking but be sure to refill bottles from fast flows and not still pools.

TRAIL DESCRIPTION Follow the feeder road in Hanover uphill to a junction. Go right, and at the next junction take the uphill feeder road to the left. After a short distance the road narrows to a trail. There are good views of the interior to your left. The trail undulates and meanders through the semi-deciduous and rainforest habitat of First Camp, so named because in 1964 it was used as a camp by the First Battalion of the Worcestershire Regiment who came to Dominica for jungle training. The rainforest crowds around you as you enter the Northern Forest Reserve, with large concentrations of *gommier* attracting riots of feeding jacos at canopy level. The terrain becomes a little trickier and there are a couple of short but steep ascents and descents. Use tree roots to help you. The trail evens out again and arrives a small river. Cross over it and pick up the trail on the other side. Walk through a lovely rainforest environment to a deep river gully. Cross over carefully and continue your rainforest walk.

Negotiate a second small river and at a very clear trail junction go right. The forest continues to be dominated by large *chatanier, gommier* and *karapit*. Notice the different layers of forest growth; primary, secondary and tertiary – all competing for space and light. The trail undulates through this beautiful forest reserve and you will eventually find yourself on a high ridge. Down to your left you may hear a river. The trail now descends steeply to meet it. This is the Melville Hall River (the one that runs alongside the airport). Cross carefully, either by wading or using the large log. Over the other side you pass over a small tributary and then meet the river again. Cross carefully and head back into the forest. Soon you come to another tributary. Though quite wide, it is fairly shallow so wading across is easy. The trail climbs though it gives you a respite with flat stretches. Look out for signs of wild pigs in this area. Cross a small stream.

Continue your uphill journey until you come to a very steep section. This is the beginning of the climb to the top of Mosquito Mountain. At the time of writing there were plans to construct simple wooden shelters around here. Check the time, your water and energy levels. Decide whether you are going to continue or whether you need to rest up and perhaps overnight here. It is at least three hours to the end of the segment from this point. The climb to the top of the mountain takes about an hour. It is a steep and difficult climb. You must use tree roots and ropes to pull you up. Take your time, always be sure of your footing before moving on, and test each root or branch before giving it your full weight. The environment transitions from rainforest to montane thicket; the trees become shorter and branches tend to be covered in dripping wet mosses and lichens. Follow a narrow ridge to the top. Once there you should have great views if the surrounding thicket is not too high. There may also be a simple wooden shelter if you need it.

The descent to Petite Macoucherie takes around two hours, the first of which is a rather tricky hike along the southern ridge of the mountain. There is a series of short but steep descents and ascents though you do not lose much by way of elevation. From time to time the vegetation opens up to give you views. The terrain is difficult and your legs are tired. Be careful not to trip, slide or stumble on tree roots. Eventually you come to a long, steep descent which drops you into a rainforest environment once again. Take your time going down.

At the bottom you will come to a small stream. The water is good for drinking if you need a top-up. Follow a much easier trail out of the forest to some abandoned farmland. The grassy trail may be a little overgrown. Cross a small brook and come to a rough feeder road. Keep going until you come to a junction with a paved road. This is Petite Macoucherie and the end of the segment. To your left is a very long walk down to Mero (at the junction further down, go left), and to your right is Segment 9.

SEGMENT 9: PETITE MACOUCHERIE TO COLIHAUT HEIGHTS

(*Difficulty: T: 3; R: 3; E: 3; D: 4; Rating = 8.1*)
The remoteness of Segment 8 continues into Segment 9. You leave behind the farmlands of Petite Macoucherie and enter an unspoilt environment of primary rainforest and semi deciduous woodland, emerging several hours later at the farmlands of Colihaut Heights. Along the way you should encounter parrots, you will see lots of magnificent species of *gommier*, *karapit* and *chatanier* trees, and you will come across a hidden waterfall.

PRACTICALITIES This trail ought to be dubbed the 'segment of ridges'. Though it starts and ends on farm feeder roads, the middle section of the trail is replete with steep ridge climbing and river crossings. Both technically and physically challenging, this hike needs planning and lots of time. Give yourself at least seven to eight hours.

Both the start and end points of this hike are remote. At the time of writing there is nowhere to stay or to purchase supplies. There are plans to establish either camping pitches or simple lodges, however, and there may even be the possibility of arranging transportation via the National Trail office itself; check updates.bradtguides.com/dominica or the Waï'tukubuli National Trail website for updates. If you are not trekking and camping, you will have to arrange for a drop off and a pick up. An option is to try to get a ride with farmers though you should not rely on this as vehicular traffic in these parts is infrequent to say the least.

TRAIL DESCRIPTION Follow the paved feeder road from the junction where Segment 8 ends (see above) for about an hour. You will pass alongside both working and abandoned farms of bananas, plantains, dasheens, christophenes, passionfruit and citrus crops. The road crosses a pretty little river and begins to climb. Hopefully you are here on a nice day because the scenery is absolutely gorgeous. Stick with the road – it is very broken up and a little overgrown in places – as it climbs a little more steeply and reaches a junction. Take the rough feeder track to the right (the paved feeder road to the left goes all the way to Salisbury – about 20 minutes by car). Stick with this feeder road as it climbs alongside banana fields and then ends rather abruptly at a shed. Before continuing, enjoy the view; without doubt one of the most beautiful on the island. You are looking south across farmland and countless valleys. The large mountain is Morne Trois Pitons. The pointed peak to the right is Morne Anglais; the mountain to the left is Foundland.

The trail passes to the right of the shed. It may well be overgrown so take your time picking out the route which heads downhill and circles back beneath the structure. The terrain is a little tricky so be careful. The trail soon widens and heads rather steeply downhill. You are following the western boundary line of the Northern Forest Reserve. At the bottom of the hill you will arrive at your first river crossing. Negotiate it carefully and then begin a steep uphill climb. Use tree roots and ropes to help you whenever you can but be sure to test everything first. At the top of the ridge, take a breather and then head very steeply down the other side. Once again, cross over the river at the bottom. If you need a refill, the water is good.

The next ascent is yet another steep one. At the top of the ridge you will see a trail junction. Go straight ahead and down the next ridge to a dry river gully. Climb up and out – a little shorter distance this time – and you will hear a river down to your left. You may also hear jaco parrots. Head steeply down to a lovely river and take a well deserved breather.

The next ascent is interrupted for a short distance by a flattish area before heading very sharply uphill. Cross over the peak and negotiate the severe drop down the other side. You are passing through some of Dominica's oldest forest; remote and untouched for centuries. Again the trail is quite even for a while as it passes through a beautiful forest environment. Head down to the next river where you will see a small cascading waterfall.

Ready for the next climb? It is another steep one up to the top and then down the other side of the next sharp ridge where you come to a lovely river. Cross over carefully and almost immediately negotiate two further rivers before climbing again. Be careful on these rivers; the stones are slippery. At the top of the next ridge you come to a more open area with abandoned farmlands. Stick to the right, following the boundary of the forest reserve for a short distance before coming to a junction. Take a sharp left and head uphill. The trail widens; this whole area was once full of thriving banana farms. It is hard to believe. Now abandoned to the forest, this area is yet another reminder of the decline of small island agriculture.

The trail narrows again as you head downhill. It undulates for a distance before dropping steeply to a river. Cross it and after a very short distance on the other side, turn around to your left. You should see a tall, cascading waterfall. Take a seat and enjoy being where you are (which is high above the west coast village of Coulibistrie – this is the Coulibistrie River).

The trail heads upwards again; it is a steep hike this time rather than a climb. From the top head down again and cross over a small river. At the top of the next steep ridge you will come to a junction where you must go right. The trail is a little easier, meandering through the forest and passing through thickets of tall bamboo. Again, listen out for parrots.

Use the ropes to help you down the next steep descent, cross the river at the bottom and follow the trail until it joins up with another one. This is the trail to Kachibona Lake (see page 213). Stick to the left (right goes to the lake) and follow the very clear and wide trail downhill to your final river crossing. Over the other side head uphill and use the ropes to help you. Eventually you will come to a wooden shelter. Take a rest; you have about 20 minutes to go.

Continue the climb through much drier forest until you come to a farm. Follow the trail along its margins until you arrive at a roughly paved feeder road. Go right and walk a short distance downhill. At the next junction go right. Walk for about ten minutes to reach the end of Segment 9 and the beginning of Segment 10. The feeder road continues down to the village of Colihaut (about 20 minutes by car).

SEGMENT 10: COLIHAUT HEIGHTS TO SYNDICATE

(*Difficulty: T: 2; R: 0; E: 1; D: 2; Rating = 3.1*)

Like many trails, this one began as a route that people used to access hillside lots where they grew *ground provisions*, bananas and so on. Many of these trails were developed into feeder roads so that farmers could use vehicles to more easily access their land and bring produce to market. In recent times agriculture has been in a state of decline as it has become more and more difficult for small island farmers to compete (see page 18). Many family farms have been abandoned and young people tend to find the profession unappealing due to the imbalance of effort to reward. To a certain extent this trail tells a little of that story. The route follows one of the very first feeder roads that was constructed on the island and it passes both abandoned and active farmsteads. You will meet farmers who seem to be working land in the middle of nowhere, growing yams or dasheen on steep hillsides, or bananas on the slopes of river valleys. In Syndicate, a traditional farming area, you will see a number of larger farms where citrus is grown in abundance, yet you will also see signs advertising land for sale.

This is an interesting walk with great views of the west coast and the forest-covered peaks of the Morne Diablotin National Park. It ends at Syndicate, a very beautiful area and notable habitat of Dominica's endemic Amazonian parrots. The Syndicate visitor centre offers a chance to rest and enjoy some refreshments after your walk.

PRACTICALITIES This is an easy walk and should take no longer than four hours to complete. For the most part the trail is downhill. The terrain is also easy going.

The trail ends at Syndicate where there are no hotels, but there is a small shop selling snacks and refreshments. Be warned, it is not always open. The nearest accommodation is in Picard, on the road to Portsmouth. If you have not arranged transportation to pick you up, you will have to walk down to the west coast highway (about 30–45 minutes) where you can catch a bus. Your hotel will be able to arrange transportation to bring you back here if you are planning to continue on Segment 11.

TRAIL DESCRIPTION The start of Segment 10 is on a feeder road in the hillside high above the village of Colihaut. Ideally you should arrange transportation to get here – it is a long way. Follow the road that heads inland from the junction where the west coast highway meets the village.

Follow the old feeder road around the heights of the Colihaut River Valley. It winds its way around and down the hillside and is very easy going. You will see heliconias, ginger lilies, bamboo thickets and tree ferns. The track crosses a couple of streams before reaching a small farm of bananas and citrus. Note the crotons and colourful hibiscus. There are also nice views of the Caribbean Sea.

Continue around the slopes of the river valley, sticking to the main track. You will come to another viewpoint before beginning a gentle climb. Tree ferns and bamboo continue to line the trail as you ascend. Once over a crest you begin a gentle descent. Notice the small pond to your left; rather fittingly this area is called L'Etang (lake). The track continues its gentle ascent meandering upwards around the margins of a wide valley and then in a series of switchbacks until it evens out again. Stick to the main track as you round the apex of a bend and begin a gradual descent.

Soon you come to a wonderful viewpoint. Ahead of you is the volcanic summit of Morne Aux Diables. To the left is Prince Rupert Bay, Portsmouth, the twin peaks of the Cabits National Park – you can even see the Fort Shirley garrison – and the patchwork swamps joining the Cabrits to the mainland. If conditions are good you should also be able to see the Saints and Guadeloupe on the horizon. Around the next corner the views continue. This time you can see Morne Diablotin, Dominica's highest mountain.

Listen out for parrots as you get ever closer to Syndicate and the Morne Diablotin National Park. The track is a little steep in places and the terrain uneven and muddy. Towards the bottom of the slope the track crosses a river and arrives at some of the larger farmsteads of Syndicate. You will see bananas and citrus trees on the left, yams and dasheen beyond the tree ferns on your right. At a junction go right and stick to the main feeder road which continues downhill and soon becomes paved. A farm on your left is full of citrus trees and its road boundary is lined with coffee trees. Can you see all the beans?

Eventually you come to a main road. To the left is the west coast highway and to the right is the Syndicate visitor centre. It takes about 20 minutes to walk to the visitor centre and about 40 minutes to reach the west coast highway.

SEGMENT 11: SYNDICATE TO BORNES

(*Difficulty: T: 2; R: 2; E: 3; D: 4; Rating = 6.9*)
This hike takes you from the visitor centre at Syndicate to the village of Bornes which is located on the main road between Portsmouth and Calibishie. The first section of the hike follows an abandoned logging road and then continues through semi-deciduous, rainforest and coastal woodland habitats. You will see a very pretty river cascade with bathing pool and hot spring and there are said to be some areas of forest where it is possible to encounter wild pigs.

PRACTICALITIES Though it starts very gently, this segment is very long (perhaps too long) and it has some very steep ups and downs. There are some river crossings which may eventually be bridged. If not, be careful with your footing. When crossing rivers always avoid dark stones and look for light patches of river bed where there is gravel or sand and less chance of slipping.

At Bornes you can catch a bus to either Portsmouth or Calibishie. There are good accommodation options in both places. Brandy Manor (see page 180) and Indigo (see page 199) are also located both near and at the end of this segment. Brandy Manor also offers good budget accommodation, camping and refreshments.

TRAIL DESCRIPTION The start of Segment 11 is at the Syndicate visitor centre. As you face the centre and car park you will see that the paved road continues to the left and becomes a rough track that passes through citrus orchards. Look out for orange and grapefruit trees, but please do not take anything without permission. At a junction, take the trail to the right and follow it to the rusting skeleton of a Timberjack logging vehicle. Rather like an artificial reef in the ocean, it is slowly being enveloped by nature and rather ironically becoming part of the environment it was once brought here to destroy.

The woodland trail is wide for a long stretch – around an hour until it arrives at a turn-off to the right on the apex of a bend. Saying farewell to the old logging road also marks the end of the easy part of this hike. From now on it becomes much more challenging.

The trail heads rather steeply downhill, winding its way through the trees until the gradient eventually becomes a little shallower. This is a pretty area of semi-deciduous woodland and rainforest. The descent is steep again as you make your way down the side of a ridge. Use trees and roots to help you negotiate the route safely. At the bottom of a gully pass over a small stream and then, after a short climb, enjoy your first real views. You can see Prince Rupert Bay, the twin peaks of the Cabrits National Park, the northern edge of Picard, Glanvillea and Portsmouth.

The trail heads downhill again, through a banana plantation and then to a junction with a feeder road where there are also some banana sheds. It may be possible to get a drink here. At the time of writing there were plans to construct refreshment and washroom facilities. Here you have to cross the Picard River. There are some fabulous pools a little higher up and also a hot spring. It is a great place to relax and freshen up for a while. Ahem, but not for too long. There is still a good way to go.

Climb up out of the river gully and follow the trail through the forest. Climb up the ridge and enjoy another great view of Prince Rupert Bay and Portsmouth. A short but steep descent brings you into a gully of large boulders which is followed by a long and tiring climb to the top of another ridge. Once you are there, the trail widens and levels out for a while, with just a few gentle undulations through what is now a rather dry coastal forest habitat.

Descend steeply again into a dry river gully and follow it to the left. After about 25m, pick up the trail on your right and climb out. Follow the trail down into a second gully but go straight across this one and climb up the other side. It is another long and steep climb to the top of a ridge where the view opens up and you are rewarded with a fabulous panorama of Prince Rupert Bay, Portsmouth, Morne Aux Diables ahead of you, and even the Saints and Guadeloupe across the sea in the distance.

Take a right at the junction and follow the trail along an undulating ridge. Descend steeply into a dry river gully and then climb up and out to the left before descending steeply again into a wet valley. Follow the trail up out of the valley and then along a gradual gradient downwards until the surroundings begin to open up around you and the trail reaches a wide feeder road. You should see Brandy Manor a little to the left in front of you. This is a good place to stop for a drink, bathe in the Brandy River, have some food, rent a room, pitch a tent and sleep.

No? Okay then. Walk left along the feeder road past Brandy Manor to a junction. Segment 11 continues along the left-hand spur. If you have decided this is really enough after all, you can bail out by following the paved road to the right, over the river and up to the main road in just a few minutes. At the main road, left goes to Portsmouth, right to Calibishie. Buses and vehicles pass frequently so you should be able to get a ride without having to wait too long.

For the die-hards who want to make it to the very end of this long segment, follow the spur through a rather swampy habitat which is typical for this area (you are not that far from the Indian River and the Glanvillea Swamp). The trail actually follows the route of Dominica's first and last railway line that once ran from the Brandy Estate to the Indian River. It was part of a short-lived logging endeavour and was used to transport timber from the forest to the Indian River and then the coast. The project was abandoned after just two years and rail sections were plundered and used in building construction in Portsmouth. Brandy Manor has some remnants of the rolling stock for those who are interested.

The trail follows the river and then crosses it. There are some interesting examples of mangrove vegetation here, notably the *Rhizophora*, known as red mangrove or bloodwood, with its unique, contorted roots. The trail eventually meets the main highway. Follow the signs and pick it up again on the other side. The pretty woodland trail runs east towards Bornes, crossing a couple of small rivers *en route*. It eventually reaches a feeder road which emerges near the Indigo Art Gallery (see page 199) and a junction which leads either to the main Portsmouth to Calibishie road (to the right) or the continuation of the National Trail (to the left).

SEGMENT 12: BORNES TO PENNVILLE

(*Difficulty: T: 3; R: 1; E: 3; D: 4; Rating = 6.9*)
This is one of the most scenic segments of the National Trail. It runs from Bornes up to Morne Destinee, through the farmlands of the Moore Park Estate, and up and across the lower elevations of the Morne Aux Diables volcano. It emerges in the pretty village of Vieille Case and continues along a very beautiful stretch of coastline to Pennville before heading up again to the remote and idyllic farmlands of Delaford. The views on this trail are spectacular so pick a day with good weather.

PRACTICALITIES This is quite a long segment with some rather steep ups and downs and occasionally fairly challenging terrain. Towards the end, on the section from Pennville to Delaford (where Segment 12 ends and Segment 13 begins), you have to walk on the main highway for around 3–4km, which is not ideal, though the views along the way are lovely.

At Delaford you may be able to catch a ride or an occasional bus across Morne Aux Diables to Portsmouth or back down to Vieille Case. There is no accommodation to speak of up here though it is worth asking at Eldrich's Tavern. Perhaps the best option if you are planning on completing the National Trail is to stay in Portsmouth, come back here the following day and then take on segments 13 and 14 together. This is eminently possible if you set off early enough as Segment 13 is very short (see overleaf). You can also re-supply in Portsmouth. See page 177 for places to stay.

TRAIL DESCRIPTION Starting near the Indigo Art Gallery in Bornes (see above), follow the trail up a paved feeder road. It is a steep climb up towards Morne Destinee past farmlands of bananas, mangos, avocados, and coconuts, but the views are great. If the weather is clear, you should be able to see Morne Diablotin behind you.

At the top of the hill the paved road comes to an end. A grassy track becomes a narrow trail and heads steeply downhill and then along the sides of a wide valley.

10

There are views to your right of the Atlantic coastline all the way down to the Red Rocks at Pointe Baptiste (see page 194). The undulating trail continues through semi-deciduous woodland and runs down into the Grand Riviere Valley and across a bridge at the bottom.

Up and out the other side the trail widens and joins with a paved feeder road. To the right is the village of Paix Bouches. This area is the Moore Park Estate. Head left and follow the feeder road to its conclusion. Continue along the trail through farmlands and enjoy the mountain views all around. Pass around a beautiful river valley, alongside fields of yam and bananas, and over a pretty brook until you reach the narrow spine of a steep ridge. It is a tough climb, but you can pause for breath and enjoy fabulous views behind you all the way up. The trail up this ridge is grassy so do not be surprised if it is a little overgrown. Follow it up and then take a right when you near the top. Look for the sign.

Now follow the trail downhill. Soon you will see the village of Vieille Case below you. The views are fabulous. Continue all the way down to a paved feeder road which runs to the village. Walk through it until you reach the main highway at the bottom where you must turn left. Follow the highway for about 1km until you see a sign on the right-hand side. It is on a bend near a fenced house and garden.

This section of the trail takes you down into a river valley and then back up and out the other side in a series of switchbacks. It is a lovely area, perhaps because of its simplicity and remoteness, but also because it was an area Amerindians once occupied and, when you reach the large volcanic boulders along the river, you can almost imagine them still here. Notice also the littoral woodland; the way the coastal trees have been shaped by the weather on this windward coast. And look out across the Atlantic. The flat island you may see on the horizon is Marie-Galante. It is a French island that now belongs to Guadeloupe but was also once home to Amerindians. A bridge carries you over a second river crossing and then the trail leads you uphill. You will reach a lovely viewpoint where you should sit and rest for a while. The rugged coves, bays, inlets and beaches of Autou, Wombati Bay, Ans Soldat, Batibou Bay and Hampstead run all the way around the northeast coast to the unmistakable Red Rocks formation at Pointe Baptiste.

From the viewpoint you come to the village of Lower Pennville. Follow the steep paved road all the way up through the village to the main highway. To the left is Vieille Case. Take a right and follow the highway for about 3–4km all the way to the Delaford Estate where this segment ends and the next one begins. *En route* you will pass the Demitrie River cascade which is a nice spot to freshen up.

SEGMENT 13: PENNVILLE TO CAPUCHIN

(*Difficulty: T: 1; R:1; E: 2; D:2; Rating = 3.8*)
This segment takes you along the very north coast of Dominica. It begins at the remote Delaford Estate and ends at Canna, near the village of Capuchin. Before the road across Morne Aux Diables was constructed, this route was used to get across the island as well as to access small farm holdings.

PRACTICALITIES This is an easy hike that follows steady uphill and then downhill gradients. It crosses one very small river that barely registers in terms of difficulty, and it is also a short hike that you should be able to complete in three hours.

Capuchin is remote and there is no accommodation there. Buses run occasionally to and from Portsmouth but you will have to walk from Canna down to the village to stand a chance of catching one. Perhaps the best option is to take on segments

13 and 14 together so that you end up in Portsmouth. Start early. If you get tired or the day closes in, you could stay at Heaven's Best in Savanne Paille (see page 180).

TRAIL DESCRIPTION The start of the trail is by a very small bar in Delaford, just off the main road to Pennville. It passes a few simple buildings and farmland, curving around the Delaford River Valley and beginning a gradual climb. A very easy route to follow, the track hugs the hillside along a series of broad coastal valleys. On a bend, in an area of cultivated plants, head to the left. In some areas the trail is a little narrow and the terrain loose and rocky, but it is not especially challenging. The incline grows a little steeper but reaches its highest point about an hour or so into the hike. The best views of the coastline are also up to this point.

Now follow the clear route downhill through dry coastal woodland and coconut palms in a series of switchbacks until you meet the Taffia River which, once it meets the northern cliffs, tumbles as a waterfall into the sea. An easy river crossing brings you back out towards the coast where the trail becomes wide track. Stick with it all the way to Dominica's most northwesterly point where this segment comes to an end at Canna. This area, settled by Amerindians and later by Capuchin monks, has a small cannon battery at its most westerly point from where there are great views of the Saints and Guadeloupe on a clear day. This is also where Segment 14 begins.

SEGMENT 14: CAPUCHIN TO CABRITS

(*Difficulty: T: 3; R: 1; E: 2; D: 3; Rating = 5.6*)
The final leg of the Wai'tukubuli National Trail is a rather odd one, though not without challenge or interest. From Canna on the northwestern tip of the island, the trail takes you down to the rocky shoreline which you follow all the way to the settlement of Morne Soleil near Cottage. From there a rather long walk along the highway brings you through the pretty seaside village of Toucari, past the equally beautiful Douglas Bay, and through the Cabrits Swamp to the end of your journey. Canna, where the hike begins, was the site of an Amerindian settlement and then a gun battery emplacement. Capuchin monks are also thought to have lived in this region, giving the area its name. A cannon is still in situ, pointing out across the sea towards the Saints where the famous battle of 1782 took place (see page 203).

The shoreline trail, if you can call it that, has been used by local people for many years to access boats, fishing pots, and to bathe in the waters around the sea mounts of Ans Crainte.

PRACTICALITIES The greatest challenge of this hike is the terrain. The beaches are not sand but pebbles and rocks, all very loose, offering lots of opportunities to slip, or worse, turn or twist ankles. Stretches of beach are interrupted by the occasional river or stream, which do not offer too much of a challenge, but rocky bluffs and large boulders are hazardous and must be negotiated with care. The Wai'tukubuli National Trail office, at the time of writing, is suggesting that if sea conditions are rough, or hikers do not fancy this troublesome coastal terrain, they can simply follow the paved main road from Capuchin to the Cabrits. Not ideal.

Once at the Cabrits you are not far from Portsmouth and Picard where you have a good choice of accommodation and places to eat (see pages 177 and 181). Buses can take you south down the west coast or across to the northeast (see page 50). It makes a lot of sense to tackle segments 13 and 14 together by setting off early. Though the beach section of this segment is challenging, you come out on to the main highway two-thirds of the way to the Cabrits where the going is much easier

10

and you can relax. Heaven's Best Guesthouse is also *en route* should you wish to call it a day early (see page 180).

TRAIL DESCRIPTION From the sign at Canna, follow the trail down to the left or go straight to the cannon and viewpoint and pick it up from there. The trail heads downhill through dry coastal woodland. Look out for ruins on your left. Towards the bottom it gets quite steep and you must negotiate the rocky mouth of a ravine before emerging on the shoreline. The cathedral-like sea mount to your right is worth a photo before heading south.

With cliffs to your left and the sea to your right, take it easy along the pebble beach. You may find yourself constantly looking down so remember to stop, take a rest and a look around. After negotiating your first set of boulders you will come to a jetty, a boatshed and a sea wall. This is also where the road passes close to the shore so you may wish to walk here instead before heading back to the beach when the road curves away to the left.

At the time of writing the next section is tough. Clamber over and around some large boulders and then come to a rather weird place where trees grow between rocks in front of a shallow cave. The going is easier for a stretch as you pass a swampy river mouth and a grove of coconut palms. Clamber carefully over the next rocky outcrop and look back along the coast and the views of Guadeloupe and the Saints.

The next set of boulders is also very tricky so take care and try not to get wet. As you round the bluff you will see two rugged sea mounts and beyond them, your destination, the Cabrits headland. There is a nice lagoon at the sea mounts which is very difficult to resist. Getting wet may also be the easier way to get beyond them, too. However you tackle it, take care not to slip or scratch yourself on sharp rocks.

Follow the pebble beach beyond the sea mounts, crossing the mouth of a river. Now look for a sign pointing to the left. It is next to a small ravine where water flows down the beach. You may also see fishing boats and baskets around here. Follow a narrow track through trees. It forks almost immediately. Take the right-hand spur, crossing the gully. Do not drink or bathe in this water – it is a run-off from the village above. The climb is a little steep but not too long. You will emerge by some houses in Morne Soleil. Follow the track to a paved road where you turn left and walk to a road junction. This is Cottage and the start of your road hike.

Take a right and stick with the main road all the way. You will head downhill to the pretty village of Toucari and then have a steep climb out the other side to Morne A Louis and Savanne Paille. From here it is downhill all the way. Pass through Tantane and along the shoreline of the very pretty Douglas Bay. Look for a sign and a trail on your right as you reach the end of Douglas Bay and approach the swamplands. Follow the trail through the Cabrits Swamp, first westwards along the shore and then south along the margin of the Cabrits National Park. Keep going straight until you reach the road and Prince Rupert Bay. To the right is the Cabrits National Park and Fort Shirley (see page 184); to the left Lagoon and Portsmouth (see page 177). A good place to rest up is Purple Turtle Beach, to the left, where there is a bar and restaurant (see page 198).

Congratulations. You have completed the Wai'tukubuli National Trail. It is quite an achievement. Enjoy a cold beer and write me an email telling me all about your adventure (e *paulcrask@gmail.com*).

Appendix 1

ACCOMMODATION AT A GLANCE

Accommodation name	Location	Type	Price Code	Page
Anchorage Hotel	Castle Comfort, Roseau	H	$$$	101
Bay View Lodges	Calibishie	SC	$$	179
Beau Rive	Castle Bruce	H	$$$$	155
Brandy Manor	Bornes	H	$–$$	180
Calibishie Cove	Hodges Bay, Calibishie	SC	$$$	179
Calibishie Lodges	Calibishie	H	$$$	179
Carib Territory Guesthouse	Crayfish River	H	$	156
Caribbean Sea View Apartments	Mero	SC	$$–$$$	206
Casaropa Apartments	Portsmouth	SC	$	180
Castle Comfort Dive Lodge	Castle Comfort, Roseau	H	$$–$$$	101
Chez Fie Dou Dou	Giraudel	SC	$$	135
Chez Ophelia Cottage Apartments	Copthall	H	$$	117
Cocoa Cottages	Shawford	H	$$$	116
Coffee River Cottages	Melville Hall	SC	$$$$	178
Comfort Cottages	Blenheim	H	$$$$	178
Comfortel De Champ	Picard	H	$$$	179
Cozy Inn Motel	Mero	H	$	207
Crescent Moon Cabins	Riviere La Croix	H	$$$	206
Domcan's Guesthouse	Castle Bruce	H/SC	$	156
Dominica's Sea View Apartments	Calibishie	SC	$$	179
Elegant Suites	Check Hall	H	$$	206
Evergreen Hotel	Castle Comfort, Roseau	H	$$$	101
Exotica Cottages	Gommier, Giraudel	H	$$–$$$	135
Fort Young Hotel	Roseau	H	$$$–$$$$	100
Garraway Hotel	Roseau	H	$$$	101
Gingerlily Cottage	Riviere Cyrique	SC	$	156
Grace Apartments	Wotten Waven	SC	$	117
Harmony Villa	Pont Cassé	SC	$$$$$	205
Heaven's Best Guesthouse	Savanne Paille	H/SC	$$	180
Hibiscus Valley Inn	Concord	H	$$	156
Hide-Out Cottage	Geneva, Grand Bay	SC	$	135
Hiker's Retreat	Fayal, Rosalie	H	$$$$$ all incl	157
Hummingbird Inn	Castaways, Roseau	H	$$–$$$	101
Itassi Cottages	Morne Bruce, Roseau	H	$$	102
Jacoway Inn	Calibishie	H/SC	$$	180
Jungle Bay Resort & Spa	Delices	H	$$$$$	155
Kai Woshe Guest House	Delices	H	$–$$	156

La Flamboyant Hotel	Roseau	H	$$	102
Le Petit Paradis	Wotten Waven	H/SC	$	117
Ma Bass Central Guesthouse	Roseau	H	$	102
Manicou River Resort	Tanetane, Portsmouth	SC	$$$	178
Mermaid's Secret	Rosalie	SC	$$	156
Morning Bird Suite Hotel	Mero	SC	$$	206
My Father's Place	Marigot	SC	$-$$	180
Ocean View Apartments	Scotts Head	SC	$	135
Pagua Bay House	Marigot	H	$$$	178
Papillote Wilderness Retreat	Trafalgar	H/SC	$$$	116
Peppers Cottage	Pottersville, Roseau	H	$	102
Picard Beach Cottages	Picard	H	$$$	179
Pointe Baptiste Estate	Pointe Baptiste, Calibishie	SC	$$$$$	178
Portsmouth Beach Hotel	Picard	H	$$	180
Rainforest Retreat Cottages	Shawford	H/SC	$$$	117
Rainforest Shangri-La Resort	Wotten Waven	H	$$$	116
Ramelton Estate	Layou	SC	$$$$$	205
Rasta Yoga Nurture Retreat	Rosalie	H	On request	157
Red Rock Haven	Pointe Baptiste, Calibishie	H/SC	$$$$$	177
River Rush Eco Retreat	Concord	H	$$$	155
Roots Jungle Retreat	Concord	H	$$	156
Rosalie Bay Eco Resort	Rosalie	H	$$$$$	155
Rosalie Forest	Rosalie	H	$-$$	156
Roxy's Mountain Lodge	Laudat	H	$$	117
Sea Cliff Cottages	Calibishie	SC	$$	179
Sea World Guesthouse	Citronierre, Roseau	H	$	102
Secret Bay	Petite Baie, Portsmouth	SC	$$$$$	178
Secret Garden	Wotten Waven	SC	$	117
Silks Hotel	Hatton Garden	H	$$$	155
Sisserou Lodge & Villa	Reigate, Roseau	SC	$$$	101
Sister Sea Lodge	Picard	H	$$	180
St James Guesthouse	Goodwill, Roseau	H	$	102
Suite Pepper	Jimmit	SC	$	206
Sunset Bay Club	Batali, Coulibistrie	H	$$$	206
Sutton Place Hotel	Roseau	H	$$-$$$	101
Symes Zee Guesthouse	Roseau	H	$	102
Symes Zee Villa	Laudat	H	$	117
Tamarind Tree Hotel	Macoucherie	H	$$$	206
Tia's Bamboo Cottages	Wotten Waven	H	$	117
Titiwi Inn	Citronniere, Roseau	SC	$$-$$$	101
Veranda View Inn	Calibishie	H	$$	180
Villa Vista	Calibishie	SC	$$$$$	178
Villa Passiflora	Calibishie	SC	$$$$$	177
Windblow Estate	Calibishie	SC	$$$	179
Zandoli Inn	Stowe	H	$$$	135
Zen Gardens	Gleau Gommier, Bells	H	$$	206

Appendix 2

HIKES AT A GLANCE

TRED RATING

Terrain	Unchallenging	Easy	Moderate	Challenging	Severe	Hazard!
Score	0	1	2	3	4	H
River X	No crossings	Easy	Moderate	Challenging	Severe	Hazard!
Score	0	1	2	3	4	H
Elevation	Flat	Easy	Moderate	Challenging	Severe	Hazard!
Score	0	1	2	3	4	H
Duration	< 1 hour	1–2 hours	2–4 hours	4–6 hours	> 6 hours	
Score	0	1	2	3	4	

For more information about this rating system see page 77.

HIKES

Hike	T	R	E	D	Rating	Page
Boeri Lake	2	1	2	1	3.8	124
Boiling Lake from Ti Tou Gorge	3	2	3	4	7.5	122
Bord La Mer (Secret Beach)	1	0	1	0	1.3	170
Bwa Nef Waterfall	2	1	2	1	3.8	200
Charles Warner Secret Pools	2	2	1	2	4.4	170
Chemin L'Etang	2	0	2	2	3.8	125
Dernier Falls	2	0	3	1	3.8	167
Douglas Bay Battery & Garrison Ruins	2	0	2	1	3.1	202
East Cabrit Trail	2	0	2	1	3.1	202
Freshwater Lake Trail	2	0	3	1	3.8	126
Galion & Morne Crabier	2	0	3	2	4.4	149
Glassy Point	2	0	1	1	2.5	172
Horseback Ridge	1	0	2	1	2.5	172
Jacko Steps	3	3H	3	2	6.9H	224
La Chaudiere	2	2	2	1	4.4	201
Middleham Falls from Cochrane	2	1	2	1	3.8	127
Middleham Falls from Laudat	2	1	2	1	3.8	127
Milton (Syndicate) Falls	2	2	1	1	3.8	223
Morne Anglais	3	0	4	3	6.3	146
Morne Diablotin	4H	0	4	4	7.5H	222
Morne Micotrin	3H	0	4	3	6.3H	128
Morne Prosper to Morne Nicholls	3H	2	3	2	6.3H	129
Morne Trois Pitons	4H	0	4	3	6.9H	131
Perdu Temps	3	3	2	3	6.9	150

Sari Sari Falls	3	2	2	2	5.6	173
Soufriere–Palmiste Loop	3	0	4	2	5.6	147
Spanny Falls	3	0	3	1	4.4	224
Syndicate Nature Trail	1	0	0	1	1.3	221
Victoria Falls	3	3H	1	2	5.6H	174
Wavine Cyrique	4H	0	4	1	5.6H	175
West Cabrit Trail	2	0	2	1	3.1	202
WNT Seg 1: Scotts Head to Soufriere	3	0	4	2	5.6	227
WNT Seg 2: Soufriere to Bellevue Chopin	2	0	3	4	5.6	230
WNT Seg 3: Bellevue Chopin to Wotten Waven	3	1	3	4	6.9	232
WNT Seg 4: Wotten Waven to Pont Cassé	2	1	3	3	5.6	235
WNT Seg 5: Pont Cassé to Castle Bruce	2	2	1	3	5.0	236
WNT Seg 6: Castle Bruce to Hatton Garden	2	2	2	4	6.3	237
WNT Seg 7: Hatton Garden to First Camp	2	2	3	3	6.3	241
WNT Seg 8: First Camp to Petite Macoucherie	4H	2	4	4	8.8H	242
WNT Seg 9: Petite Macoucherie to Colihaut Heights	3	3	3	4	8.1	244
WNT Seg 10: Colihaut Heights to Syndicate	2	0	1	2	3.1	246
WNT Seg 11: Syndicate to Bornes	2	2	3	4	6.9	247
WNT Seg 12: Bornes to Pennville	3	1	3	4	6.9	249
WNT Seg 13: Pennville to Capuchin	1	1	2	2	3.8	250
WNT Seg 14: Capuchin to Cabrits	3	1	2	3	5.6	251

Appendix 3

FURTHER INFORMATION

If you have enjoyed Dominica and wish to pursue your interest, here is a selection of further reading options. The listings below are by no means comprehensive; they are just meant as a starting point for further research.

Dominica has a number of talented writers and poets, many of whom self-publish their work locally and in very small quantities. A good way of seeking them out is to attend the annual Nature Island Literary Festival & Book Fair (see page 63) and also to visit the Roseau Public Library (see page 98).

NON-FICTION
History and culture

Andre, Irving & Christian, Gabriel *Death By Fire* Pont Cassé Press, 2007; ISBN 978 0973734768
Bell, Stewart *Bayou of Pigs* Wiley, 2008; ISBN 978-0470153826
Boyd, Stanley A W *A Brief History of the Cathedral of Roseau* Roseau Public Library archives
Burton, Eileen *National Dress of Dominica* Paramount, 2003. Available from Dominica book stores.
D'jamala Fontaine, Marcel *Dominica's Diksyonne, English Creole Dictionary* ISBN 1 85465074 2
Honychurch, Lennox *The Dominica Story* Macmillan, 1975; ISBN 0 333 62776 8
Jacob, Jeno J *Dominica's Folk Beliefs* 2008. Available from Dominica book stores.

Natural history

Adams, C Dennis *Caribbean Flora* Nelson Caribbean, 1976; ISBN 0 17 566186 3
Bannochie, Iris & Light, Marilyn *Gardening in the Caribbean* Macmillan, 1993; ISBN 0 333 56573 8
Evans, Peter G H & James, Arlington *A Guide to Geology, Climate and Habitats*. Available from Dominica book stores and Forestry, Wildlife & Parks Division.
Evans, Peter *Birds of the Eastern Caribbean* Macmillan Caribbean, 2009; ISBN 978 0333521557
Evans, G H & James, Arlington *Wildlife Checklists*. Available from Dominica book stores and Forestry, Wildlife & Parks Division.
James, Arlington; Durand, Stephen; & Baptiste, Bertrand Jno *Dominica's Birds*. Available from Dominica book stores and Forestry, Wildlife & Parks Division.
James, Arlington *Plants of Dominica's Southeast*. Available from Dominica book stores and Forestry, Wildlife & Parks Division.
James, Arlington *Flora and Fauna of Cabrits National Park*. Available from Dominica book stores and Forestry, Wildlife & Parks Division.
Lennox, G W & Seddon, S A *Flowers of the Caribbean* Macmillan, 1978; ISBN 0 333 26968 3
Lennox, G W & Seddon, S A *Trees of the Caribbean* Macmillan Caribbean, 1980; ISBN 978 0333287934
Malhotra, Anita & Thorpe, Roger S *Reptiles and Amphibians of the Eastern Caribbean* Caribbean, 2007; ISBN 978 0333691410

Guides and travelogues

Bird, Jonathan *Dominica, Land of Water* Jonathan Bird Photography, 2004; ISBN 978 0972863414

Bond, James *Birds of the West Indies* Houghton Mifflin Harcourt, 1993; ISBN 978 0618002108

Bourne, M J; Seddon, S A; & Lennox, G W *Fruits and Vegetables of the Caribbean* Macmillan, 1988; ISBN 978 0333453117

Evans, P C H & Honychurch, Lenox *Dominica, Nature Island of the Caribbean* Hansib Publishing, 2009; ISBN 978 1906190255

Evans, Peter G H & James, Arlington *A Guide to Nature Sites.* Available from Dominica bookstores and Forestry, Wildlife & Parks Division.

Fermor, Patrick Leigh *The Traveller's Tree, A Journey Through the Caribbean Islands* John Murray Publishers Ltd, 2005; ISBN 978 0719566844

Honychurch, Lennox *Dominica, Isle of Adventure* Macmillan Caribbean, 1998; ISBN 978 0333720653

James, Arlington *An Illustrated Guide to Dominica's Botanic Gardens.* Available from Dominica bookstores and Forestry, Wildlife & Parks Division.

Kamyab, A *Dominica, A Tropical Paradise* AuthorHouse, 2009; ISBN 978 1438915678

Lawrence, Michael *Diving & Snorkelling Dominica* Lonely Planet, 1999; ISBN 0 86442764 6

McCanse, Anna *Dominica* Other Places Publishing, 2011; ISBN 978 09822619 72

Pattullo, Polly & Baptiste, Anne Jno *The Gardens of Dominica* Papillote Press, 1998; ISBN 0953222403

Pattullo, Polly *Roseau Valley Guide* Papillote Press, 2007. Available directly from the publisher, Papillotte Wilderness Retreat gift shop and Dominica bookstores.

Sullivan, Lynne M *Adventure Guide, Dominica & St Lucia* Hunter, 2005; ISBN 978 1588433930

Biographical

Higbie, Janet *Eugenia, the Caribbean's Iron Lady* Macmillan Caribbean, 1993; ISBN 978 0333572351

Kalinago People of Dominica *Yet We Survive* Papillote Press, 2007; ISBN 978 09532224 21

Napier, Elma *Black And White Sands, a bohemian life in the colonial Caribbean* Papillote Press, 2009; ISBN 978 09532224 45

Paravisini-Gebert, Lizabeth *Phillis Shand Allfrey, a Caribbean Life* Rutgers University Press, 1996; ISBN 0 813 52265 X

Pattullo, Polly & Sorhaindo, Celia, compiled by *Home Again, stories of migration and return* Papillote Press, 2009; ISBN 978 09532224 52

Pizzichini, Lilian *The Blue Hour, a life of Jean Rhys* W W Norton & Company, 2009; ISBN 978 0393058031

FICTION
Novels and short stories

Aaron, Philbert *Decorated Broomsticks, a novel of political independence* Paramount, 2007; ISBN 978 97682121 84

Allfrey, Phyllis Shand *It Falls Into Place* Papillote Press, 2004; ISBN 978 0 9532224 14. Short stories.

Allfrey, Phyllis Shand *The Orchid House* Rutgers University Press, 1996; ISBN 978 0813523323

Brand, Pete *Harken's Caribbean Sea* Authorhouse, 2006; ISBN 978 1425947514

Children of Atkinson school, Dominica *The Snake King of the Kalinago* Papillotte Press, 2010; ISBN 978 0 9532224 69

Christian, Gabriel *Rain on a Tin Roof* Pont Cassé Press, 1999; ISBN 978 0966845419

John, Marie-Elena *Unburnable* Harper Paperbacks, 2007; ISBN 978 0060837587

Kincaid, Jamaica *The Autobiography of My Mother* Plume, 1997; ISBN 978 0452274662

Lazare, Alick *Pharcel, runaway slave* iUniverse inc, 2006; ISBN 978 0595395781
Rhys, Jean *Wide Sargasso Sea* W W Norton & Company, 1998; ISBN 978 0393960129
Shillingford, Christborne *Most Wanted, street stories from the Caribbean* Papillote Press, 2007;
    ISBN 978 0 9532224 38

Poetry and storytelling
Brumant, Lawrence *Ki Mannyè Donmnik Touvé Non'y (How Dominica Got its name and Four
    Other Konts)*. Available from Dominica book stores.
Dominica Writers' Guild *Words, Sound and Power, a collection of Dominican poetry*. Available
    from Dominica bookstores.
John, Giftus *The Island Man Sings His Song* Writer's Showcase, 2001; ISBN 0595180906
John, Giftus *Mesyé Kwik! Kwak!* Virtualbookworm.com Publishing, 2005; ISBN 1589397649
Sorhaindo, Paula *Pulse Rock* Parnassus Publishing, 1993; ISBN 978 1871800401

INTERNET SITES
www.avirtualdominica.com A general guide to Dominica
www.dexiaexport.com Dominica Export Import Agency (DEXIA)
www.dhta.org Dominica Hotel & Tourism Association
www.dominica.dm Website of the Discover Dominica Authority
www.dominica.gov.dm Government of Dominica
www.dominica-registry.com Dominica Maritime Registry
www.dominicawatersports.com Dominica Watersports Association
www.dominica-weekly.com Informative news and travel features on Dominica
www.investdominica.com Website of the Invest Dominica Authority
www.imagesdominica.com Stock photography and contract services
www.paulcrask.com The author's website
www.thedominican.net Dominica news and comment
www.tropicaltiesdominica.com Stock photography and photographic products
www.visit-dominica.com Dominica business listings and visitor information

Index

Page numbers in *italic* indicate maps

abòlò 8
accommodation 54
accordion 24
ackee 58
ackra 56
adventure park 90, 219
agouti 7
agriculture 18
agrotourism 19
airlines 37
airports 37
ajoupa 160
alcohol 59
Allfrey, Phyllis Shand 28
almond 5
Amerindians 13
amphibians 8
anchorages 38
Anse Du Mai 38, *195*, 196
Anse Soldat *195*, 196, 197
anthurium 6
ants 43
annatto 5
aquatic life injuries 45
Arawak 13, 153
architecture 25
artisans 27
arts 62
artists 25
Atkinson 169, *152*
ATM machines 48

Bagatelle *141*, 143
baggage allowance 38
bakes 56
Balla 14, 166, 210
bananas 18
ban mauvais 214
banks 48
bananaquit 7
barbadine 58
barracoon 95
basketwork 159
Bataca *152*, 160
Batali 214, *215*

Batibou Beach *195*, 197
bats 8
Battle of the Saints 203
bay leaf 143
beer 60
beggars and begging 67, 108
bélé 24
Bell, Hesketh 14
Bellevue Chopin *134*, 136
Bellevue Chopin Organic
  Farmers 139
Bells 209, *220*
Bense *195*, 196
Berekua 140
Bethesda Methodist Church
  92, *96*, 100
Bioche *208*, 210
birds 6
birdwatching 71
Black West India Regiment
  185
Blenheim Estate *195*, 196
boa constrictor 8
boat tours 73
Boeri Lake 11, *114*
  hike 124
Boetica *167*, 168
Boiling Lake 11, *114*
  hike 123, 129, 212
Bois Cotlette *134*, 148
Boli Falls *114*, *167*, 212
Bord La Mer *167*
  hike 170
Bornes 197
Botanical Gardens 99, 109,
  110
bougainvillea 6
boumboum 24
Bout Sable Bay *167*, 168
braf 55
Brandy Falls 197
breadfruit 55–8
Breton, Father Raymond
  190, 210
bromeliad 5

Bruce, James Captain 110,
  163, 184
Brunias, Agostino 25
budgeting 48–9
bus and jeep tours 73
buses 50–1
bush tea 58
business 66
butterflies 9
bwa bandé 4, 59, 115
bwa kwaib 6, 110, 184
Bwa Nef Waterfall 190, *191*
  hike 200

Cabrits National Park 184,
  185
Cachacrou 12, 83, *134*, 138,
  139, 144
Café Dominique 58
calabash 6, 27
calalou soup 56
Calibishie 194, *195*
calypso 24, 25
Campbell *217*
camping 54
Canefield 100, *217*
Canefield Airport 37, *217*
canep 58
canoe 154
canyoning 74
Capuchin *189*
car hire 52
carambola 58
Carib 153
Carib War 239
Carnegie, Andrew 98
Carnival 25, 31
cassava 161
Castle Bruce 163, *165*
Castle Comfort 100, *134*
Cathedral canyon 74, 119
Cenotaph *92*, *96*, 98
Central Forest Reserve 208,
  220
Champagne Reef 83, *134*, 145

260

chante-mas 25
chanteulles 25
charities 69
Charles, Dame Eugenia 15
Charles Warner 171
  hike *152*, 170
chatanier 4
chatou water 56
Chemin L'Etang 119
  hike *114*, 125
chiggers 42
children 47
christophene 58
Citronniere 100, *134*
Clifton *189*
climate 3
Coal Pot 142
cocoa 19, 58, 76
coconut 6, 19, 57, 61
Cold Soufriere *189*, 198
Colihaut *208*, 210
Columbus, Christopher 13
Concord *152*, 159, 169
conservation 4
consulates 36
copra 194
coral reefs 9
Cottage *189*
cottage industries 20
couliana 13
Coulibistrie *208*, 211
coup 15
couriers 66, 183
crabbacks 56
crapaud 8
Crayfish River *152*, 159
Creole 14
  culture 23
  cooking classes 76
  costume 23
  cuisine 55
  festivals 31, 62
  language 21
  music and dance 24
crime 45
cruise ships 19, 31
crustaceans 9
culture 23
currency 48
curried goat 56
custard apple 58
customs 36, 38
cutlass 21
cycling 74

dance 24
dasheen 58

dehydration 43
Delices *167*, 168
Demitrie 190, *191*
dengue fever 41
departure tax 36
Dernier Falls *167*
  hike 171
diarrhoea 43
disabled travellers 46
dive sites 82–6
dolphin fish 56
dolphins 11, 89
Dominica Coconut Products
  218
Dominica Festival of Arts
  (DOMFESTA) 63
Dominica Museum 98
Douglas Bay 188, *189*, 197
Douglas Bay Battery *185*
  hike 202
driving in Dominica 53
drugs 67
Dublanc 164, *208*, 210
Dubuc *141*, 142
DVT 42

East Cabrit 184, *185*
  hike 202
eating and drinking 55
economy 16
ecotourism 19
education 22
Eggleston *134*, 136
electricity 48
elfin woodland 4
embassies 36
Emerald Pool 115, 119, *220*
emergencies 44
English Creole 21
entry requirements 36
ethnicity 20
etiquette 67

Fabre *141*, 143
Fairtrade Foundation 18
ferns 5
ferry, inter island 38
fig 55, 58
fish 19
fishing 19, 75
flora 5
flower show 137
folklore 29
Fond St Jean *141*, 143
food and drink 55
forest reserves 12
Fort Shirley 184, *185*, 186

Fort Young *92*, 98, *96*
fougère 5
Foundland 140, *141*
French Quarter 97
Freshwater Lake *114*
  hike 126
frogfish 10
frogs 8
fruits and vegetables 58
fumarole vegetation 5

Galion *134*
  hike 149
gardens 75
gas stations *see* petrol stations
Gaulette River *152*, 159
gay travellers 47
gecko 8
Geneva 28, *141*, 142
Geneva Heritage Park 144
geography 3
giant leatherback turtle 10
ginger 6
Giraudel *134*, 136
Glassy Point *167*
  hike 172
goat water 56
gommier 4, 13, 154
Good Hope 165
Goodwill *92*, 100
government 15
Grand Bay 140, *141*
Grand Fond *167*, 168
green banana 58
ground lizard 8
guava 58
guides 79

habitats 4
Hampstead Beach *195*, 197
Hampstead Estate 194, *195*
Hatton Garden *152*, 169
health 39, 86
heliconia 6
Hercules beetle 9
heritage 23
hibiscus 6
highlights 32
hikes
  Boeri Lake *114*, 124
  Boiling Lake *114*, 122
  Bord La Mer *167*, 170
  Bwa Nef Waterfall *191*, 200
  Charles Warner 'Secret
    Pool' *152*, 170
  Chemin L'Etang *114*, 125,
    171

hikes *continued*
Dernier Falls *122*, 167
Douglas Bay Battery *185*,
202
East Cabrit Trail *185*, 202
Freshwater Lake *114*, 126
Galion and Morne Crabier
134, 149
Glassy Point *167*, 172
Horseback Ridge *152*, 172
Jacko Steps *220*, 224
La Chaudiere *195*, 201
Middleham Falls *114*, 127
Milton Falls *208*, 223
Morne Anglais *134*, 146
Morne Diablotin *208*, 222
Morne Micotrin *114*, 128
Morne Prosper to Morne
Nicholls *114*, 129
Morne Trois Pitons *114*,
131
Perdu Temps *141*, 150
Sari Sari Falls *167*, 173
Soufriere–Palmiste Loop
147
Spanny Falls *220*, 224
Syndicate Nature Trail
208, 221
Victoria Falls *167*, 174
Wavine Cyrique *167*, 175
West Cabrit Trail *185*, 202
WNT Segment 1 227,
228–9
WNT Segment 2 *228–9*,
230
WNT Segment 3 *228–9*,
232
WNT Segment 4 *228–9*,
235
WNT Segment 5 *228–9*,
236
WNT Segment 6 *228–9*,
237
WNT Segment 7 *228–9*,
241
WNT Segment 8 *228–9*,
242
WNT Segment 9 *228–9*,
244
WNT Segment 10 *228–9*,
246
WNT Segment 11 *228–9*,
247
WNT Segment 12 *228–9*,
249
WNT Segment 13 *228–9*,
250

hikes *continued*
WNT Segment 14 *228–9*,
251
hiking 76
hiking gear 78
hiking guides 79
history 12
hitching 53
Hodges Bay *195*, 198
Honychurch, Lennox 12,
29, 186
hospital 44, *92*
Horseback Ridge *152*, 169
hike 172
horseriding 80, 169, 199
hot pepper sauce 56
hot springs 89
House of Assembly *92, 96*, 100
hummingbirds 7
hurricanes 4

Igbo 24
Igneri 13
iguana 8
independence 15
Indian River *187*, 199
Indigo Art Gallery 199
injiri 24
independence 15
insect bites 41
internet 65
Isulukati Waterfall 219, *220*
ital food 57
Itassi 190
itineraries 33

Jack's Walk 110, *111*
Jacko Steps 220
hike 224
Jacko Waterfall 219, *220*
Jacks Falls 151, *167*
jaco parrot 6
jing ping 24
jombie 29
Jones, Joseph 109
juice 57

kai kwéyòl 25
Kachibona Lake 213, 246
kaklen 4
Kalinago 13, 153
basketwork 159
canoe 154
Chief 159
cultural groups 163
Kalinago Barana Auté 160,
152, 161

Kalinago Territory *152*, 158
Kalinago Touna Auté *152*,
162
pottery 160
kampech 5
kanki 157
karapit 5
karbet 161
kavalyé 24
kayaking 81, 144
King George V Street 97
kockoy 21, 192
kont 29
Kouanari 163
Koulirou 168
kouwès 8
Kubuli 60, 107
Kwéyòl 21

L'Escalier Tete Chien *152*, 162
La Belle Croix 140
La Chaudiere *195*, 196
hike 201
la diablesse 29
La Haut 190, *191*
la peau cabrit 24, 214
La Plaine *167*, 168
La Roche Pagua *see* Pagua
Rock
lakes
Boeri Lake 11, *114*
hike 124
Boiling Lake 11, *114*
hike 123, 129, 212
Freshwater Lake *114*
hike 126
Kachibona Lake 213, 246
Mathieu Lake 219, *220*
Lallay 140
language 21
larouma reed 13, 159
Laudat *113*, *114*, 119
law 16
Layou River 209, *220*
library *see* Public Library
literature 28
literary festival 28, 63
littoral woodland 5
local products 107
local dishes 55
Loubiere *134*, 137
lunch 55

mabouya 8
machete 21
Macoucheri 59, 216, *217*
Madjini *152*, 162

madras 24
Mahaut *217*, 218
Mahaut River *152*, 159
maho cochon 115
mammals 7
mang blanc 5, 115, 208
mang wouj 5, 208
mangosteen 58
manicou 7
manioc 161
Marigot 192, *193*
marine environment 9
marine reserve 12
maroons 14, 210
marriage 35
Mas Domnik 25
Massacre *217*, 218
massage 88
Mathieu Lake 219, *220*
matador 24
mazook 24
Melville Hall Airport 37, *193*
Mero *215*, 216
Middleham Falls *114*
  hike 127
Milton Falls *208*
  hike 200
Miracle Lake *see* Mathieu
  Lake
mobile phones 65
money 48
montane forest 4
Moore Park *191*, 196
Morgan River Falls *167*, 170
Morne Anglais 11, *134*
  hike 146
Morne Bruce 110, *111*
Morne Crabier *134*, 227
  hike 149
Morne Diablotin 3, 11, 207,
  208
  hike 222
Morne Diablotin National
  Park 11, 72, 207, *208*
Morne Espagnol *208*, 209
Morne Jaune *167*, 168
Morne Micotrin 11, *114*
  hike 128
Morne Nicholls *114*, 123
Morne Plat Pays *134*, 137, 140
Morne Prosper *113*, 119
Morne Raquette *208*, 214
Morne Trois Pitons 11, 114
  hike 131
Morne Trois Pitons National
  Park 11, 113, *114*, 115
Morne Watt 11, *114*

mosquitoes 41
mountain biking 74
mountain chicken 8
mountain palm 4
mountain whistler 7
music and musicians 24, 62,
  106
myths and legends 29

Napier, Elma 28, 201
national dress 23
national flower 6
national parks 11
natural history 4
newspapers 63
Newtown *92*, 100, *134*
non-alcoholic drinks 57
noni 58
Northern Forest Reserve 12

obeah 29
off-roading 81
okra 58
Old Mapou Tree Trail 167, *168*
Old Market, Roseau 98
Old Mill Cultural Centre 27,
  63, 100, *217*
opossum 7
orchids 5
organic farming and food 12,
  19, 75, 105, 139, 144
ouicou 160
Ouyuhayo 186

Pagua River *152*, 168
Pagua Rock *152*, 160
painters 26
Paix Bouche *191*
Papillote Gardens *113*, 120
parishes 15
parrot sanctuary *111*
parrots 6
passionfruit 59
Patois 21
pawpaw 59
Peebles Park *92*, *96*, 98
pelau 56
Pennville 190, *191*
people 20
Perdu Temps *141*
  hike 150
performing arts 63
Petite Savanne *141*, 143
Petite Soufriere *165*, 166
petrol stations 52
pharmacies 108
photography 64, 67

photography tours 81
Picard *187*, 188
Pichelin *141*
plantain 59
plants and flowers 5
poets 28, 63
Point Jaco 190, *191*
Pointe Baptiste 194, *195*
Pointe Michel *134*, 136
politics 15
population 20
ports of entry 38
Portsmouth 177, *187*
postal service 64, 109
Pottersville *92*, 100
pottery 160
president 15
prickly heat 43
prime minister 15
Prince Rupert Bay 38, 184,
  185, *187*
provisions 55
public holidays 60
Public Library *92*, 98
public transport 50–1
Purple Turtle beach *187*, 198
pwi pwi 13, 137

quad-biking 81
quadrille 24

radio 63
railway 197
rainforest 4
Rainforest Aerial Tram *114*,
  120
rappelling 74
recompression chamber 44
Red Dog 15, 16
Red Rocks *195*, 200
religion 22
reptiles 8
Rhys, Jean 28
river tubing 82
Riviere Cyrique *167*, 168
Rodney's Rock 84, *217*
Rodney's Wellness Retreat
  and Carrod's Gardens
  134, 146
Rosalie 166, *167*
Roseau *92*, 93, *96*
Roseau Cathedral *92*, *96*, 97
Ross University School of
  Medicine 75, *187*, 188
roti 57
roucou 5
rum 59

safety 45
sailing 38
Saint Sauveur *165*
Sairi 93
Salisbury 214, *215*
Salybia *152*, 159
sancoche 56
Sandy Beach 192, 193
sapodilla 59
Sari Sari Falls *167*
  hike 173
scooter hire 53
Scotts Head *134*, 138
scuba diving 82
sculptors 27
sea grape 5
seamoss 58
sensay 25, 214
shak-shak 24
Shawford *113*
shopping 61, 105
Sineku *152*, 159, 162
Sisserou Falls *152*, 169
sisserou 6
site fees 71
slavery 14
snakes 8
snorkelling 86
Soltoun 213, *220*
sorrel 57, 59
soucouyan 29
Soufriere *134*, 137
Soufriere Scotts Head Marine
  Reserve (SSMR) *134*, 138
Soufriere Sulphur Springs
  134, 146
Spanny Falls *220*, 224
St Cyr *152*, 159
St David's Bay 163, *165*
St George's Anglican Church
  92, *96*, 100
St Joseph *215*, 216, *217*
State House *92*, *96*, 99
storytellers 28
Stowe *141*, 142
sugar apple 59
sulphur spas 89
sweet potato 59
Syndicate Falls *see* Milton
  Falls
Syndicate Nature Trail 72,
  208, 218, 221

Taberi *167*, 168, 212
tamarind 59
tambal 24
tambou 15

Tanetane 188, *189*
tannia 59
taro 59
Tarou 216, *217*
taxis 50
telephone 64
television 63
tête en l'air 24
Tete Morne *134*, 140
Téwé Vaval 164
Thibaud *191*
ti kai 25
titiwi 9, 56
Ti Tou Gorge 74, *114*, 119, 120
toilets 109
Tou Santi 127
Toucari *189*
Touna Village *see* Kalinago
  Touna Auté
tour operators 34, 71
tourism 19
tourist offices 36, 98, 184
traditional costume 23
Trafalgar *113*, 118
Trafalgar Falls *113*, 121
travel clinics 39
travelling positively 69
tree fern 5, 158
tree lizard 8
turtle watching 170
turtles 10
Twa Basens *167*, 169

UNESCO 11
University of the West Indies
  (UWI) 23, 75

Valley of Desolation 11, *114*,
  115, 123
Value Added Tax (VAT)
  54, 56
veti ver 173
Victoria Falls *167*
  hike 174
Vieille Case 190, *191*

Wacky Rollers Adventure
  Park, *see* zip-lining
Wai'tukubuli 13
Wai'tukubuli National Trail
  227, *228*
water 39, 58
waterfalls
  Boli Falls *114*, *167*, 212
  Brandy Falls 197
  Bwa Nef Waterfall 190, *191*
    hike 200

Cathedral canyon 74, 119
Dernier Falls *167*
  hike 171
Emerald Pool 115, 119, *220*
Isulukati Waterfall 219,
  220
Jacko Waterfall 219, *220*
Jacks Falls 151, *167*
La Chaudiere *195*, 196
  hike 201
Middleham Falls *114*
  hike 127
Milton Falls *208*
  hike 200
Morgan River Falls *167*,
  170
Sari Sari Falls *167*
  hike 173
Sisserou Falls *152*, 169
Soltoun 213, *220*
Spanny Falls *220*, 224
Ti Tou Gorge 74, *114*, 119,
  120
Trafalgar Falls *113*, 121
Victoria Falls *167*
  hike 174
Wavine Cyrique *167*
  hike 175
wedding services 35
wellness 86
wellness practitioners 88
Wesley *193*
West Cabrit *185*
  hike 202
whales 11
whale watching 89
what to take 47
wild pigs 7
Windsor Park Sports Stadium
  92, 96
wob dwiyet 23
women travellers 46
wood carving 27
Woodford Hill 193, *195*
World Creole Music Festival
  62
Wotten Waven *113*, 118
writers 28

yachting facilities 39
yam 59
yoga 88

zandoli 8
z'ailes mouches 5
zemi 13
zip-lining 90